ADVANCES IN DIGITAL FORENSICS III

IFIP – The International Federation for Information Processing

IFIP was founded in 1960 under the auspices of UNESCO, following the First World Computer Congress held in Paris the previous year. An umbrella organization for societies working in information processing, IFIP's aim is two-fold: to support information processing within its member countries and to encourage technology transfer to developing nations. As its mission statement clearly states,

> *IFIP's mission is to be the leading, truly international, apolitical organization which encourages and assists in the development, exploitation and application of information technology for the benefit of all people.*

IFIP is a non-profitmaking organization, run almost solely by 2500 volunteers. It operates through a number of technical committees, which organize events and publications. IFIP's events range from an international congress to local seminars, but the most important are:

• The IFIP World Computer Congress, held every second year;
• Open conferences;
• Working conferences.

The flagship event is the IFIP World Computer Congress, at which both invited and contributed papers are presented. Contributed papers are rigorously refereed and the rejection rate is high.

As with the Congress, participation in the open conferences is open to all and papers may be invited or submitted. Again, submitted papers are stringently refereed.

The working conferences are structured differently. They are usually run by a working group and attendance is small and by invitation only. Their purpose is to create an atmosphere conducive to innovation and development. Refereeing is less rigorous and papers are subjected to extensive group discussion.

Publications arising from IFIP events vary. The papers presented at the IFIP World Computer Congress and at open conferences are published as conference proceedings, while the results of the working conferences are often published as collections of selected and edited papers.

Any national society whose primary activity is in information may apply to become a full member of IFIP, although full membership is restricted to one society per country. Full members are entitled to vote at the annual General Assembly, National societies preferring a less committed involvement may apply for associate or corresponding membership. Associate members enjoy the same benefits as full members, but without voting rights. Corresponding members are not represented in IFIP bodies. Affiliated membership is open to non-national societies, and individual and honorary membership schemes are also offered.

ADVANCES IN DIGITAL FORENSICS III

IFIP International Conference on Digital Forensics,
National Center for Forensic Science, Orlando,
Florida, January 28- January 31, 2007

Edited by

Philip Craiger
University of Central Florida, Orlando, Florida, USA

Sujeet Shenoi
University of Tulsa, Tulsa, Oklahoma, USA

 Springer

Advances in Digital Forensics III

Edited by P. Craiger and S. Shenoi

p. cm. (IFIP International Federation for Information Processing, a Springer Series in Computer Science)

ISSN: 1571-5736 / 1861-2288 (Internet)

ISBN 978-1-4419-4473-3   eISBN: 13: 978-0-387-73742-3
Printed on acid-free paper

9 8 7 6 5 4 3 2 1
springer.com

Contents

PART VII   NETWORK FORENSICS

PART VIII   PORTABLE ELECTRONIC DEVICE FORENSICS

PART IX   EVIDENCE ANALYSIS AND MANAGEMENT

PART X   FORMAL METHODS

Contributing Authors

Charles Adams is a Professor of Law at the University of Tulsa, Tulsa, Oklahoma. His research interests include intellectual property law and digital forensics.

Kweku Arthur is an M.Sc. student in Computer Science at the University of Pretoria, Pretoria, South Africa. His research interests include information assurance and digital forensics.

Alexander Barclay is a Ph.D. student in Computer Science at the University of Tulsa, Tulsa, Oklahoma. His current research focuses on adaptive access control, file system forensics and bioinformatics security.

Nicole Beebe is a Ph.D. candidate in Information Systems and Technology Management at the University of Texas at San Antonio, San Antonio, Texas. Her research interests include digital forensics, information security and assurance, and data mining.

Joshua Benson is a Captain in the U.S. Air Force. His research interests include digital forensics, software security and cyber operations.

Phillip Bradford is an Assistant Professor of Computer Science at the University of Alabama, Tuscaloosa, Alabama. His research interests include computer security, digital forensics and high performance computing.

Paul Burke is a Senior Digital Evidence Research Assistant at the National Center for Forensic Science, University of Central Florida, Orlando, Florida. His research interests include network security, digital forensics and open source operating systems.

Carole Chaski is the President of ALIAS Technology, LLC and the Executive Director of the Institute for Linguistic Evidence, Georgetown, Delaware. She is also an Adjunct Professor of Linguistics at the University of Delaware, Newark, Delaware. Her research interests include authorship identification and validation methods in forensic linguistics.

Brian Chee is the Director of the Advanced Network Computing Laboratory at the School of Ocean and Earth Science and Technology, University of Hawaii, Manoa, Hawaii. He is also a Senior Contributing Editor of InfoWorld. His research interests include network performance and testing methodologies.

Ramkumar Chinchani is a Senior Software Engineer with Cisco Systems, San Jose, California. His research interests include information security, programming languages and operating systems.

Philip Craiger is an Assistant Professor of Engineering Technology and Assistant Director for Digital Evidence at the National Center for Forensic Science, University of Central Florida, Orlando, Florida. His research interests include digital forensics and information security.

Alta de Waal is a Senior Researcher at the Council for Scientific and Industrial Research, Pretoria, South Africa. Her research interests include text modeling, Bayesian analysis, computational methods for Bayesian inference and nonparametric Bayesian analysis.

Glenn Dietrich is an Associate Professor and Chair of Information Systems and Technology Management at the University of Texas at San Antonio, San Antonio, Texas. His research interests include digital forensics, information assurance, systems theory and innovation.

Barbara Endicott-Popovsky is the Director of the Center for Information Assurance and Cybersecurity at the University of Washington, Seattle, Washington. She has a joint faculty appointment with the Information School at the University of Washington at Seattle, and the Department of Computer Science at the University of Washington, Tacoma, Washington. Her research interests include network forensics, critical infrastructure protection and secure coding practices.

Eduardo Fernandez is a Professor of Computer Science and Engineering at Florida Atlantic University, Boca Raton, Florida. His research interests include data security, object-oriented design, fault-tolerant systems and security patterns.

Kelli Frakes is a Research Project Manager with the Justice and Safety Center at Eastern Kentucky University, Richmond, Kentucky. Her research interests include intelligence-led policing, cyber crime and digital evidence.

Timothy Franz is a Major in the U.S. Air Force and a graduate student at the Air Force Institute of Technology, Wright-Patterson AFB, Ohio. His research interests are in the area of cyberspace operations.

Deborah Frincke is the Chief Scientist for Cyber Security Research in the Computational Sciences Directorate at Pacific Northwest National Laboratory, Richland, Washington. Her research interests include very large system defense, forensics, infrastructure protection, security visualization, SCADA security and information assurance education.

Ashish Gehani is an I3P Postdoctoral Fellow at SRI's Computer Science Laboratory in Menlo Park, California. His research interests include multimedia protection, sensor and storage network security, intrusion response and DNA computing.

Rajni Goel is an Assistant Professor of Information Systems and Decision Sciences at Howard University, Washington, DC. Her research interests include information assurance, digital forensics, control systems security and data mining.

James Graham is the Henry Vogt Professor of Computer Science and Engineering at the University of Louisville, Louisville, Kentucky. His research interests include information security, digital forensics, critical infrastructure protection, high performance computing and intelligent systems.

David Greer is a Ph.D. student in Computer Science at the University of Tulsa, Tulsa, Oklahoma. His research interests include digital forensics, cyber law, and information security education and training.

Duc Ha is a Ph.D. student in Computer Science and Engineering at the University at Buffalo, Buffalo, New York. His research interests include information assurance, network security, distributed and source-based routing systems.

John Hale is an Associate Professor of Computer Science at the University of Tulsa, Tulsa, Oklahoma. His research interests include enterprise security management, applied formal methods, access control and multi-stage attack analysis.

Mark Hartong is a Senior Electronics Engineer with the Office of Safety, Federal Railroad Administration, U.S. Department of Transportation, Washington, DC, and a Ph.D. student in Information Technology at George Mason University, Fairfax, Virginia. His current research focuses on various aspects of software engineering, software systems safety, information assurance, control systems security and digital forensics.

Patrick Juola is an Associate Professor of Computer Science at Duquesne University, Pittsburgh, Pennsylvania. His research interests include humanities computing, computational psycholinguistics, and digital and linguistic forensics.

Maria Larrondo-Petrie is the Associate Dean of Academic and International Affairs and Professor of Computer Science and Engineering at Florida Atlantic University, Boca Raton, Florida. Her research interests include software engineering, data security, formal methods and parallel processing.

James Lyle is a Computer Scientist at the National Institute of Standards and Technology in Gaithersburg, Maryland. His research interests include digital forensics and forensic tool testing.

Gavin Manes is the President of Oklahoma Digital Forensics Professionals, Inc., Tulsa, Oklahoma. He is also a Research Assistant Professor with the Center for Information Security at the University of Tulsa, Tulsa, Oklahoma. His research interests include digital forensics and critical infrastructure protection.

Christopher Marberry is a Senior Digital Evidence Research Assistant at the National Center for Forensic Science, University of Central Florida, Orlando, Florida. His research interests include digital forensics, computer security and virtualization technologies.

Lodovico Marziale is a Ph.D. student in Computer Science at the University of New Orleans, New Orleans, Louisiana. His research area is digital forensics.

Sunu Mathew is a Ph.D. student in Computer Science and Engineering at the University at Buffalo, Buffalo, New York. His current research interests include various aspects of information assurance and network security.

Robert McGrew is a Ph.D. student in Computer Science at Mississippi State University, Mississippi State, Mississippi. His research interests include honeypots and attack profiling.

Steven Mead is a Computer Scientist at the National Institute of Standards and Technology in Gaithersburg, Maryland. His research interests include digital forensics and forensic tool testing.

Hung Ngo is an Assistant Professor of Computer Science and Engineering at the University at Buffalo, Buffalo, New York. His research interests include computer networks, network security, algorithms and combinatorics.

Martin Olivier is a Professor of Computer Science at the University of Pretoria, Pretoria, South Africa. His research interests include privacy, database security and digital forensics.

Juan Pelaez is a Research Scientist with the U.S. Army Research Laboratory in Adelphi, Maryland. He is also a Ph.D. student in Computer Science and Engineering at Florida Atlantic University, Boca Raton, Florida. His research interests include VoIP networks and network forensics.

Gilbert Peterson is an Assistant Professor of Electrical and Computer Engineering at the Air Force Institute of Technology, Wright-Patterson AFB, Ohio. His research interests include digital forensics, steganography, image processing, robotics and machine learning.

Raquel Phillips is an undergraduate student in Computer Science and Mathematics at the University of Tulsa, Tulsa, Oklahoma. Her research interests include various aspects of digital forensics, file systems and parallel processing.

Nayot Poolsapassit is a Ph.D. student in Computer Science at Colorado State University, Fort Collins, Colorado. His research interests include information security, attack modeling and intrusion detection.

Suranjan Pramanik is a Ph.D. student in Computer Science and Engineering at the University at Buffalo, Buffalo, New York. His research interests include fault-tolerant systems, anomaly detection, insider threats and binary translation.

Richard Raines is an Associate Professor of Electrical Engineering at the Air Force Institute of Technology, Wright-Patterson AFB, Ohio. His research interests include computer and communications network security and vulnerability analysis.

Daniel Ray is a Ph.D. student in Computer Science at the University at Alabama, Tuscaloosa, Alabama. His research interests include various aspects of digital forensics and computer security.

Indrajit Ray, Chair, IFIP Working Group 11.9 on Digital Forensics, is an Assistant Professor of Computer Science at Colorado State University, Fort Collins, Colorado. His research interests are in the areas of information security, security protocols, digital forensics and database systems.

John Reif is the A. Hollis Edens Professor of Computer Science at Duke University, Durham, North Carolina. His research interests span biomolecular computation, nanostructure fabrication, parallel and randomized algorithms, data compression and quantum computing.

Golden Richard III is an Associate Professor of Computer Science at the University of New Orleans, New Orleans, Louisiana, and the co-founder of Digital Forensics Solutions, LLC, New Orleans, Louisiana. His research interests include digital forensics, mobile computing and operating systems internals.

Kelsey Rider is currently on leave from the National Institute of Standards and Technology, Gaithersburg, Maryland, pursuing graduate studies in Mathematics at the University of Nice, Nice, France. His research interests include digital forensics and forensic tool testing.

Benjamin Rodriguez is a Ph.D. student in Electrical and Computer Engineering at the Air Force Institute of Technology, Wright-Patterson AFB, Ohio. His research interests include digital forensics, digital signal processing, digital image and video processing, steganography and steganalysis.

Marcus Rogers is a Professor of Computer and Information Technology at Purdue University, West Lafayette, Indiana. His research interests include psychological digital crime scene analysis, applied behavioral profiling and digital evidence process models.

Vassil Roussev is an Assistant Professor of Computer Science at the University of New Orleans, New Orleans, Louisiana. His research interests include digital forensics, high-performance computing, distributed collaboration and software engineering.

Cristina San Martin received her M.S. degree in Computer and Information Technology from Purdue University, West Lafayette, Indiana. Her research interests include computer forensics, network security and wireless networks.

Kathryn Scarborough is a Professor of Safety, Security and Emergency Management and the Coordinator of the Homeland Security Degree Program at Eastern Kentucky University, Richmond, Kentucky. Her research interests include law enforcement technologies, cyber crime and security, intelligence and police administration.

Sujeet Shenoi is the F.P. Walter Professor of Computer Science at the University of Tulsa, Tulsa, Oklahoma. His research interests include information assurance, digital forensics, critical infrastructure protection and intelligent control.

Michael Stevens is a graduate student in Cyber Operations at the Air Force Institute of Technology, Wright-Patterson AFB, Ohio. His research interests are in the areas of information security and digital forensics.

Christopher Swenson is a Ph.D. student in Computer Science at the University of Tulsa, Tulsa, Oklahoma. His research interests include cryptanalysis, network security and digital forensics.

Adam Todd is an M.S. student at the Air Force Institute of Technology, Wright-Patterson AFB, Ohio. His research interests include digital forensics and intrusion detection.

Shambhu Upadhyaya is an Associate Professor of Computer Science and Engineering at the University at Buffalo, Buffalo, New York. His research interests are in the areas of information assurance, computer security, fault diagnosis, fault tolerant computing and VLSI testing.

Rayford Vaughn is the Billy J. Ball Professor of Computer Science and Engineering and a William L. Giles Distinguished Professor at Mississippi State University, Mississippi State, Mississippi. His research interests include information assurance and high performance computing.

Hein Venter is a Senior Lecturer in the Department of Computer Science, University of Pretoria, Pretoria, South Africa. His research interests include network security, digital forensics and intrusion detection systems.

Jacobus Venter is a Senior Researcher at the Council for Scientific and Industrial Research, Pretoria, South Africa. His research interests include digital forensics training, evidence mining and probabilistic methods.

Doug Wampler is a Ph.D. student in Computer Engineering and Computer Science at the University of Louisville, Louisville, Kentucky. His research interests include digital forensics, information assurance and legacy systems.

Lance Watson is the Vice President of Client Relations at Oklahoma Digital Forensics Professionals, Inc., Tulsa, Oklahoma, and a Ph.D. student in Computer Science at the University of Tulsa, Tulsa, Oklahoma. His research interests include digital forensics and network security.

Anthony Whitledge is an attorney who is retired from the U.S. Department of Justice and the Internal Revenue Service. His research interests include digital forensics, data mining and the application of technology to civil and criminal litigation.

Duminda Wijesekera is an Associate Professor of Information and Software Engineering at George Mason University, Fairfax, Virginia. His research interests include information, network, telecommunications and control systems security.

Cornelius Willers is a Senior Researcher at the Council for Scientific and Industrial Research, Pretoria, South Africa. His research interests include artificial intelligence and intelligent agents.

Preface

In 2006, the Federal Bureau of Investigation (FBI) processed more than two petabytes of digital evidence; in 2007, the volume of digital evidence processed will exceed four petabytes. Electronic devices are becoming smaller and more diverse; memory capacities are increasing according to Moore's Law; distributed networks are growing massively in size and scale. As society embraces new technologies and applications with gusto, digital information will become even more pervasive.

Digital investigations already involve searching for the proverbial needle in the haystack. In five years, possibly sooner, investigators will have to find the one needle in unimaginably large stacks of needles. How will the FBI approach digital investigations of the future? How will state and local law enforcement agents cope?

Digital forensics – the scientific discipline focused on the acquisition, preservation, examination, analysis and presentation of digital evidence – will have to provide solutions. The digital forensics research community must initiate serious efforts to develop the next generation of algorithms, procedures and tools that will be desperately needed.

This book, *Advances in Digital Forensics III*, is the third volume in the annual series produced by the IFIP Working Group 11.9 on Digital Forensics, an international community of scientists, engineers and practitioners dedicated to advancing the state of the art of research and practice in the emerging discipline of digital forensics. The book presents original research results and innovative applications in digital forensics. Also, it highlights some of the major technical and legal issues related to digital evidence and electronic crime investigations.

This volume contains twenty-four edited papers from the Third Annual IFIP WG 11.9 Conference on Digital Forensics, held at the National Center for Forensic Science, Orlando, Florida, January 28–31, 2007. The papers were selected from forty-one submissions, which were refereed by members of IFIP Working Group 11.9 and other internationally-recognized experts in digital forensics.

The chapters are organized into ten sections: legal issues, insider threat detection, rootkit detection, authorship attribution, forensic techniques, file system forensics, network forensics, portable electronic device forensics, evidence analysis and management, and formal methods. The coverage of topics highlights the richness and vitality of the discipline, and offers promising avenues for future research in digital forensics.

This book is the result of the combined efforts of several individuals. In particular, we thank Anita Presley and Christopher Swenson for their tireless work on behalf of IFIP Working Group 11.9. We also acknowledge the support provided by the National Center for Forensic Science, Orlando, Florida, the FBI, the National Security Agency and the U.S. Secret Service.

PHILIP CRAIGER AND SUJEET SHENOI

I

LEGAL ISSUES

Chapter 1

CALIBRATION TESTING OF NETWORK TAP DEVICES

Barbara Endicott-Popovsky, Brian Chee and Deborah Frincke

Abstract   Understanding the behavior of network forensic devices is important to support prosecutions of malicious conduct on computer networks as well as legal remedies for false accusations of network management negligence. Individuals who seek to establish the credibility of network forensic data must speak competently about how the data was gathered and the potential for data loss. Unfortunately, manufacturers rarely provide information about the performance of low-layer network devices at a level that will survive legal challenges. This paper proposes a first step toward an independent calibration standard by establishing a validation testing methodology for evaluating forensic taps against manufacturer specifications. The methodology and the theoretical analysis that led to its development are offered as a conceptual framework for developing a standard and to "operationalize" network forensic readiness. This paper also provides details of an exemplar test, testing environment, procedures and results.

Keywords: Network forensics, aggregating tap, calibration, baseline testing

1.   Introduction

This paper presents an approach – derived from courtroom admissibility standards – for calibrating low-layer network devices employed in collecting data for use in courtroom proceedings. The collected data may be used to prosecute malicious conduct on networks or to seek legal remedy for (or defend against) accusations of network management negligence. While we specifically discuss our approach in the context of aggregator taps, it can be generalized to more complex devices. The model is offered as a first step towards filling a void created by manufacturers who provide general specifications for taps and switches that

Please use the following format when citing this chapter:

Endicott-Popovsky, B., Chee, B., Frincke, D., 2007, in IFIP International Federation for Information Processing, Volume 242, Advances in Digital Forensics III; eds. P. Craiger and S Shenoi; (Boston: Springer), pp. 3-19.

collect forensic data, but offer few guarantees about the actual behavior of these devices.

Several factors are responsible for the lack of calibration regimes for network forensic devices. In an intensely competitive market, vendors often consider the architectural details and precise behavior of their data-gathering network devices as proprietary. Purchasers select and employ these network devices primarily for troubleshooting as opposed to gathering evidence that would withstand courtroom scrutiny [18]. Furthermore, standards and precedents needed to establish the validity of data-gathering devices in legal proceedings are only beginning to emerge. Consequently, even vendors who are interested in meeting the requirements for forensic soundness do not have a set of best practices for device testing and validation.

This paper deals with calibration testing of network devices. In particular, it focuses on the role of calibration in establishing a foundation for expert testimony. While much consideration has been given to recovering forensic data and using it as digital evidence, little attention has been paid to calibrating the hardware devices used to capture network traffic and documenting how they behave "in the field." With information technology and cyber-enabled activities becoming ever more important factors in legal proceedings [17], the consequences of failing to evaluate and validate the behavior of network forensic devices could lead to inadmissible evidence and failed legal action.

2.   Calibration Testing

Lord Kelvin, a giant in the field of measurement science, eloquently described the role of calibration in an 1883 lecture to the Institution of Civil Engineers [3]:

> "I often say that when you can measure what you are speaking about and express it in numbers you know something about it; but when you cannot express it in numbers your knowledge is a meager and unsatisfactory kind; it may be the beginning of knowledge but you have scarcely, in your thoughts, advanced to the stage of science, whatever the matter may be."

Calibration is "the comparison of instrument performance to a standard of known accuracy in order to determine deviation from nominal and/or make adjustments to minimize error" [3]. Calibration is conducted when there is a need for confidence that a piece of equipment performs as intended. Calibration testing can be conducted by professionals performing formal tests at a standards laboratory, by internal experts using an in-house metrology laboratory, or even by users performing verification testing to ensure that the procured equipment meets manufacturing specifications.

A formal calibration test is typically accompanied by documentation that provides traceability to the standard used, the periodicity of the calibration (the interval between tests that provides a continuity of confidence that an instrument is performing within an acceptable band of tolerance), and an expression of imprecision that takes into account the potential for error in the test and/or test equipment [2]. A simple example of calibration is the testing of weights and measures to ensure that a customer purchasing a pound of flour from Merchant A is, in fact, purchasing a full pound.

In the forensic sciences, calibration is employed to ensure that instruments used in the collection and analysis of evidence can be relied upon [13]. For example, radar guns used by police to clock speeders must be calibrated according to state or local laws. These laws also establish the calibration regimes that specify the periodicity of testing, testing documentation requirements, and the duration that records must be maintained [22].

Evidence of radar gun calibration provides the foundation for testimony that an individual was speeding [13]. Absent such evidence, speeding charges may be dismissed [22]. Also, if the testing regime is not followed precisely, a valid defense might be: "*How do you, Mr. State Trooper, know the radar gun was working properly?*"

By analogy, if devices on a network are used to collect electronic evidence, then the performance of the devices must be understood and documented if the collected evidence is to survive similar courtroom challenges. For example, if, at the time of a network incident, the behavior of the forensic device cannot be characterized as adequate for recording relevant network data, a defense could be mounted that it was "someone else" who violated the system. Hypothetically, it could be alleged that significant numbers of packets could have been dropped. A defense attorney might ask: "*Why conclude that my client is responsible when exculpatory evidence may be missing?*"

3.   Frye and Daubert Standards

Certain landmark court cases have established rules for admissibility, which ensure that scientific forensic testimony is "relevant, material and competent" [13]. *Frye v. United States* [23] established the standards under which judges should accept expert testimony. *Daubert v. Merrell Dow Pharmaceuticals, Inc.* [24] established that Rule 702 of the Federal

Table 1. Frye vs. Daubert standards.

Frye Standards	Daubert/Kumho Factors
Is the approach sufficiently established?	Has the technique used to collect evidence been tested? (Or can it be tested?)
Has the technique gained general acceptance in its field?	Has the theory underlying the procedure or the technique itself been subjected to peer review and publication?
Does it require study/experience to gain special knowledge?	Does the scientific technique have a known or potential rate of error?
Does expertise lie in common experience and knowledge?	Do standards exist, along with maintenance standards, for controlling the technique's operation?

Rules of Evidence supercedes Frye. This decision was further enunciated in *Kumho Tire Co. v. Carmichael* [25].

Table 1 summarizes the differences between Frye and Daubert. The main difference is that Frye establishes the general acceptance standard and some rules for the admissibility of evidence, while Daubert relaxes those rules and allows judicial discretion. Frye has tended to support the exclusion of evidence rather than its inclusion, especially when the issue is in doubt. On the other hand, Daubert allows judges more leeway in accepting evidence obtained by the application of new technologies.

Expert testimony is generally used in one of two ways: (i) the expert explains evidence in a way that a jury can understand, or (ii) the issues are so complex that only the expert can understand them; therefore, expert believability is based on trust established with the jury [13]. In the second instance, the opposing counsel may seek to discredit the expert witness and his/her testimony. One strategy is to challenge the testimony's foundation by asking questions such as: *"How do you know this?" "How can you say this?" "How can we believe the validity of what you say?"*

Lack of personal knowledge of the science behind the testimony does not bar a jury's trust. However, the greater the trust expected of the jury, the greater the burden to provide competent foundation that supports both the credibility of the witness and the equipment used to gather evidence [13]. This foundation does not identify the guilty party; instead, it provides the basis for believing the expert's testimony: *"Here is the tool I used." "Here is the data that it describes." "This is why the tool works."* Calibration is part of that description and speaks to the reliability and predictability of the tool.

In a review of several hundred pages of digital forensics testimony involved in cases in the Pacific Northwest from 2000 to present, we discovered that the technical competence of the evidence and the questioning of expert witnesses, ranged from minimally competent to highly professional. In the cases examined, experts represented both the prosecution and the defense. Note that while federal government experts are required to have demonstrated levels of expertise (usually manifested by certifications), the expertise possessed by local law enforcement and defense experts ranged considerably from case to case. In one instance, an uninformed defense "expert" testified there were "100 bits in a byte" and calculated network traffic flow based on this erroneous value [11]! In some cases, a modest, even deficient, understanding of technology was sufficient to introduce "reasonable doubt" in felony trials and persuade juries to acquit the defendants [11].

The Frye and Daubert tests provide some protection against the use of bogus scientific evidence and expert opinion. But in the end, particularly under the Daubert standard, the task of challenging inexact science falls on the attorneys in the courtroom. While the legal bar's understanding of digital forensics is usually very limited, often allowing technically incompetent evidence to go unchallenged, the state of the practice is improving [13]. This makes the establishment of a proper foundation for network evidence gathering even more important. In fact, how other technical devices for gathering evidence (e.g., radar guns, mass spectrometers and gas chromatographs) are maintained and presented in courtroom proceedings provide insight into what will be expected of devices used to collect network evidence.

One option is to suggest that only properly calibrated collection methods be employed, but this is not practical. Organizations are already using switches with span ports and aggregator taps with monitoring ports to capture network forensic data [15, 16]. These devices are rarely, if ever, calibrated to the extent that a proper foundation can be laid for their data-gathering accuracy. To complicate matters, marketing literature for these devices claims "forensic capability" without defining what is meant by "forensic" [5]. Network incident response personnel frequently use the term "forensic" inaccurately to mean troubleshooting (i.e., determining what happened so that the system can be fixed or restored), as opposed to collecting data that meets courtroom admissibility standards.

Sommers [18] calls this forensics with a "little f" in contrast with Forensics with a "capital F," which seeks, in addition, to determine who is responsible. While it is true that span port and aggregator features were designed to support troubleshooting (forensics with a small "f"), there is evidence that some entities are using these devices to collect data for legal proceedings (forensics with a capital "F") [4, 16].

Given the likelihood of increasingly sophisticated examination of expert testimony, courtroom admissibility requirements are expected to become an important consideration for network devices (although at present they do not appear to be quite so important). This provides a window of opportunity for developing standards, tests and regimes for network evidence gathering devices.

4.   Baseline Testing

Absent vendor certification, it is necessary to develop a suite of standard tests for validating manufacturers' specifications for devices used for collecting forensic data. The testing would allow network traffic collected for evidentiary purposes to be described competently during expert witness testimony. A suitable approach is to adapt network baseline testing techniques for this task.

Baselining is defined as "systematically viewing network point-to-point data flow to analyze communication sequencing, extract accurate metrics, develop a technical synopsis of the network and make recommendations" [12]. Quantitative statistical measurements are employed to identify key network issues relevant to supporting the mission of an enterprise [12]. Baseline testing can be used to provide assurances that a network is stable and operating reliably and also to support decision-making, e.g., the need for investment in increased network capacity. The baselined period is usually one week, but some enterprises might experience monthly, quarterly and/or annual peak network loads, requiring the analysis of additional baseline performance data [12].

Baseline testing typically employs devices such as protocol analyzers to reveal network throughput performance. At a minimum, available capacity and utilization are determined; the latter is defined as the amount of capacity used by a certain network segment over a specific time interval that encompasses a typical business cycle [12]. Both average and peak utilization are of interest in determining the appropriate capacity.

While the goal of baselining is to provide a basis for managing network reliability, we believe that the testing approach can confirm the capacity of devices used to collect network forensic data for evidentiary purposes. The test results coupled with an understanding of the baseline performance of the network segment where the device is operating would allow the forensic data gathered by the device to be characterized (e.g., providing a formal statement about data completeness at the time it was collected). For example, if a network typically runs at 20% capacity and if it is known from testing that the device functions at line rate capacity under this condition, then an expert witness might assert that the data collected from the device at that time is complete for all intents and purposes.

To provide additional detail, it is possible to use a suite of typical attacks to determine the likelihood that critical evidence is lost, including under peak loads. For example, in scenarios where there is considerable repetition of forensically-important packets (as in a DDoS attack), the probability that evidence is lost may be quite small. In other cases, such as a subtle attack involving privilege escalation, the probability of evidence loss may be higher. Under specific scenarios, it is important also to consider the perspectives of the prosecution/defense: Is there an advantage for the data gatherer not to gather all of the relevant data? Could a participant have interfered with the gathering of specific evidence to the extent of causing packet loss? Regardless of the scenario, a generalized model underlies the development of each calibration regime.

5. Calibration Test Model

We developed an exemplar case to create a model for calibration tests that could provide an adequate foundation for expert testimony. We identified a preliminary three-step process for devising a calibration test regime to address foundation challenges (Table 2). Subsequently, we applied the process to a case involving the use of a Net Optics 10/100BaseT Dual Port Aggregator Tap to gather forensic data.

5.1 Identifying Potential Challenge Areas

Given that organizations are already using switches and taps to capture forensic data, we limited the consideration of test subjects to switches with span ports and aggregator taps with monitoring ports. In theory, important data could be lost if these devices are oversubscribed. Furthermore, from the perspective of an expert witness, any lack of knowledge about the behavior of these devices could potentially damage his/her credibility with a jury.

Although more switches than taps are used for forensic purposes [16], we examined only taps in our study. Taps function as pass-through de-

Table 2.   Validating foundation through network device calibration.

- **Step 1**: Identify a potential challenge area and perspective.

    - **Identify Challenge Area**: Ask how foundation testimony could be subject to challenge if data is lost.
    - **Perspective**: Expert testifying to completeness of data collection.

    Example Case: An oversubscribed forensic tap could drop packets. Inadequate characterization of the circumstances when this might occur could be used to challenge expert credibility, especially if comprehensive data collection is claimed.

- **Step 2**: Design calibration testing goals to support the challenge area (given the perspective).

    - **Goal**: Verify manufacturer's specification; describe device behavior.
    - **Perspective**: Expert witness determining whether it is reasonable to expect that all relevant data was gathered.

    Example Case: Validate tap capacity; determine when packets begin to be dropped.

- **Step 3**: Devise a test protocol.

    - **Purpose**: Ensure sufficient documentation/assurance that the test and test environment are appropriate for supporting expert testimony.
    - **Process**: Develop a "comprehensive" suite of stress tests that examine the behavior of the device in isolation.

    Example Case: An external laboratory was selected for testing the tap and a suite of tests created for a range of network traffic flows.

---

vices primarily at Layer 1 of the OSI model; switches function at Layer 2 or Layer 3 depending on built-in functionality. Typically, taps neither read/forward at the MAC address layer nor provide confirmation of a link state (both these conditions are necessary in a Layer 2 device). This makes taps simple to test and renders them neutral entities in the forensic data collection process, i.e., they merely pass the data stream without introducing latency. Because switches function at Layer 2 or Layer 3, they may introduce latency in packet forwarding, making the determination of data flow performance much more complex. In addition, manufacturers often treat embedded functionality as proprietary; this may require the switch architecture to be re-engineered to properly test its performance [4]. We selected the Net Optics 10/100BaseT Dual Port Aggregator Tap. This tap operates between Layers 1 and 2 because it incorporates embedded logic that aggregates duplex traffic and forwards it to a monitor port. The tap was one of the first to be marketed as a "forensic" device, when 1 MB buffers were added to provide protection from network traffic spikes.

5.2   Designing Testing Goals

Our study focused on the ability of the Dual Port Aggregator Tap to keep up with data flow at the manufacturer-specified rate. Thus, the goal of the calibration test regime was to verify whether the tap could handle the combined traffic of a single full duplex link when traffic is at, or below, its 100 Mbps capacity [5] and to document any packet-dropping behavior. Any traffic exceeding the capacity was expected to fill the buffers up to 1 MB per side of the full duplex connection before any packets were dropped. We also sought to determine when packets would begin to drop. These goals became the basis for devising a test regime.

5.3   Devising a Test Regime or Protocol

Certain laboratory capabilities were required to ensure that calibration testing would help certify that the equipment and practices met acceptable standards. We began with two objectives for our test environment. The first was to obtain controllable traffic for pushing the tap limits. The second was to isolate tap behavior from other behaviors so that the foundation could be laid for tap performance in any environment, not just the test environment.

Isolating the tap proved challenging. Preliminary tests were unsatisfactory at separating the tap's behavior from NIC cards, the OS and the switch. The first test employed the `iperf` utility (v.1.7.0), part of the Knoppix-STD bootable Linux distribution. The second used the Fluke Optiview Online protocol analyzer. (See [8] for details about both tests.) The next option we considered was the Advanced Network Computing Laboratory (ANCL) facilities at the University of Hawaii, Manoa with multiple test beds set up specifically to eliminate external influences. We selected the Spirent Test Center, a high-speed, local area network test instrument designed to determine failure points in high speed networking equipment [19]. It is capable of generating and analyzing wire-rate traffic up to 10 Gbps, significantly higher than the vendor-specified 100 Mbps limit of the tap.

A series of tests to verify the most basic aspects of the manufacturer's specification was designed and adapted from baseline testing techniques. Since our challenge involved the loss of packets (or buffer overflow), these were the first (and only) tests we included as part of Step 3. The tests are

Spirent Test Center

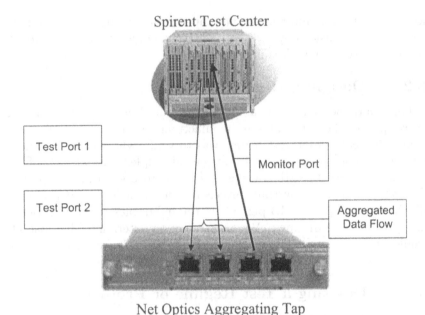

Net Optics Aggregating Tap

Figure 1.   Aggregating tap test configuration.

by no means comprehensive, nor do they indicate anything unexpected about the device (this was not the intent). Rather, the tests demonstrate how a simple pre-courtroom calibration regime could be used to increase the credibility of witnesses who testify about data collected using the tap. In the future, we plan to consider malformed packets and to analyze tap behavior in the presence of common network attacks, with the goal of developing a comprehensive suite of exemplar tests.

The Spirent Test Center was configured as shown in Figure 1 to simultaneously transmit two equivalent data streams of homogeneously-sized UDP packets to Test Ports 1 and 2. The data streams were aggregated inside the tap and sent to the Monitor (forensic) Port where test data was collected. UDP packets were selected to eliminate latency introduced by the three-way TCP session handshake. Packet content was all 0's.

Four tests, each lasting 30 seconds, were conducted with data streams of consistently-sized packets of 64, 512, 1,500 and 9,000 bytes (Table 3). A fifth test involved random-sized packets (Table 3). For each packet size, tests were conducted across a range of data flow rates, expressed as a percent of the tap's 100 Mbps capacity. For example, the 50% and 51% data flow rate tests aggregated the rate of flow to the Monitor Port equal to 100% to 102% of capacity.

Table 3. Spirent Test Center test suite.

Packet Size (Bytes)	64	512	1,500	9,000	Random
Data Flow Rate (%)			30 seconds		
10%		X			
30%	X	X	X	X	
50%	X	X	X	X	X
51%	X	X	X	X	X
60%		X			
100%		X			
Packet Size (Bytes)	64	512	1,500	9,000	Random
Data Flow Rate (%)			300 seconds		
51%		X			
60%		X			

With a testing goal of verifying the tap capacity, we designed a calibration test regime by adapting benchmark test parameters from the Internet Engineering Task Force (IETF) Network Working Group RFC 2544 [6]. A series of duplex data streams from the Spirent Test Center were configured to send 512-byte packets (representative of average traffic) to the tap at varying rates of data flow expressed as a percentage of the tap's 100 Mbps capacity. Several tests were conducted for a duration of 30 seconds (marked "X" in Table 3). In addition, two tests were conducted for a duration of 300 seconds to observe any change in tap behavior. Oversubscription of the tap at a full duplex data flow rate of 51% coming from each side was confirmed with data streams of differently sized packets (64, 1,500 and 9,000 bytes, respectively) and randomly-sized packets [8]. Table 3 displays the series of tests that comprised the test regime.

Table 4 presents the results of the 512-byte packet test. Packets dropped when full duplex traffic was 51% or more of the tap's 100 Mbps capacity. At 10%, 30% and 50%, the Monitor Port received and forwarded the aggregated flow from Test Ports 1 and 2. At or above 51%, the Monitor Port was unable to forward the entire aggregated stream, verifying the 100 Mbps capacity specification at the Monitor Port as implemented by the manufacturer. The expected implementation of a 100 Mbps Monitor Port would forward the entire aggregated stream of 200 Mbps.

Figure 2(a) shows the graph of dropped packets for the 512-byte test series. Note the sharp rise at 51% of tap capacity indicating the data flow rate at which packets begin to drop. Figure 2(b) shows port average

Table 4. Spirent Test Center results (512-byte packets).

Traffic (% Tap Cap.)	Test Port 1 Transmitted	Test Port 2 Transmitted	Monitor Port Received	Dropped Packets
10	70,488	70,488	140,976	0
30	211,461	211,461	422,922	0
50	352,443	352,443	704,886	0
51	359,496	359,496	708,241	10,751
60	422,952	422,952	708,242	137,662
100	704,887	704,887	708,243	701,531

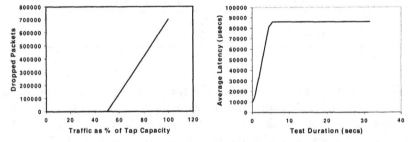

Figure 2. Test results: (a) Dropped packets; (b) Average latency.

latency through the tap. Examining the data, allowing for the one second test ramp up and one-half second period attributed to learning frames and clock variations in the console PC, the tap begins to drop packets four seconds into the test.

5.4 Predicting Packet Loss

Identifying where errors might arise in data collection is important for providing a foundation for evidence. Therefore, we have developed a probability curve for predicting packet loss in aggregating taps. The relationship is given by:

$$T_{sec} = \frac{Bf_{bits}}{BU_{bits/sec} - TC_{bits/sec}} \tag{1}$$

where T_{sec} is the time to buffer overflow (seconds), Bf_{bits} is the buffer size (bits), $BU_{bits/sec}$ is the average bandwidth utilization (bits/sec), and $TC_{bits/sec}$ is the maximum tap bandwidth capacity (bits/sec). Note that Equation 1 specifies a linear relationship; however, in practice (i.e., outside a laboratory environment), variations in network packet sizes and rates are typically represented by Gaussian functions. In fact, the probability of network packet loss in a large network is similar to that in a broadband communications network, for which Gaussian functions have been shown to be very effective [1]. Note that the ability to predict packet loss further supports the task of identifying a potential challenge area that could undermine the foundation testimony (Step 1 in Table 2).

Upon applying Equation 1 to the test case, we confirm the result in Figure 2(b):

$$
\begin{aligned}
Bf_{bits} &= 1\ MB \times 8\ bits \\
BU_{bits/sec} &= 102\ Mbps \\
TC_{bits/sec} &= 100\ Mbps \\
T_{sec} &= \frac{1\ MB \times 8\ bits}{(102 - 100)\ Mbps} = 4\ sec
\end{aligned}
$$

The tap manufacturer did not provide information on how the tap implemented queue management; therefore, we assumed that the FIFO algorithm was used. A more thorough analysis might require consideration of alternate solutions. This would be more important in situations where data was gathered under peak conditions, and even more important if an attack on the queuing system could force the tap to drop pre-determined packets.

6.   Evaluation of Results

In a hypothetical case involving the collection of forensic evidence using a Net Optics 10/100BaseT Dual Port Aggregator Tap that was subjected to the calibration test described above, one might envision the following dialog between the prosecution's expert witness and the defense attorney regarding the soundness of the evidence gathered by the tap.

Defense Attorney:	Are you confident of the data you collected using this tap?
Expert Witness:	Yes, I am.
Defense Attorney:	Why are you confident?
Expert Witness:	I've tested this tap. I rely on it in the course of business. I understand how it performs, that it drops packets at 4 seconds under maximum load test conditions. Our network was functioning well below capacity during the time in question. I am confident that the Monitor Port captured all the data.

Compare this dialog with what might transpire if the expert witness had relied solely on the vendor's marketing description:

Defense Attorney:	Are you confident of the data you collected using this tap?
Expert Witness:	Yes, I am.
Defense Attorney:	Why are you confident?
Expert Witness:	Well, the manufacturer states the tap has a 100 Mbps capacity.
Defense Attorney:	How do you know this to be true? Have you tested this device?
Expert Witness:	Well, no, I haven't.
Defense Attorney:	Then, how do you know that you've captured all the data during the time in question? Isn't it possible that packets were dropped?
Expert Witness:	Well, I'm certain we captured everything.
Defense Attorney:	But you have no basis to be certain, do you?

The question might arise whether or not the test presented is sufficiently precise to be useful in expert testimony. For example, it does not take into account real-world variability of network traffic, buffer delays or packet collisions. After all, probabilities associated with DNA evidence can be as high as 1 billion to one, perhaps setting high expectations for the precision of other scientific evidence. Nevertheless, it should be noted that it has taken two decades to develop DNA as reliable science. Accepted standards exist for DNA laboratories, for collecting and analyzing evidence, and for training personnel, but these have evolved over time as both the science of DNA and legal case history have evolved [13].

In contrast, network forensic evidence is relatively new and the development of standards is in the earliest stages. Moreover, the acceptability of network forensic evidence has developed differently from DNA. Unlike DNA evidence, where practitioners had to convince the legal system of its validity through a series of court cases, network forensic evidence already is considered admissible [13]. What we anticipate are legal challenges to the credibility of this type of testimony as the legal system gains insight into the technology. We expect these challenges to drive the development of standards, especially as cases that rely on network forensic evidence are won or lost [13].

As standards develop, demands for precision of network forensic evidence will evolve as a function of how crucial the evidence is to making the case and whether or not precision would make a difference. Usually criminal cases are based on a collection of facts, network data representing only one piece of the puzzle. Furthermore, it is often the situation that network data is used to justify a search warrant that produces additional evidence, which adds to the weight of the case. Given the current state of legal practice, the demand for precision under these circumstances has been low. We believe this situation will change, especially as the defense and prosecutorial bars gain an understanding of network forensics. Consequently, although the calibration test approach presented in this paper is adequate for now, it is only a starting point for developing standards for network forensic evidence.

7.   Conclusions

Courtroom admissibility is expected to be a critical requirement for network forensic devices in the future, although it is not so important at the present time [4, 13, 16]. The calibration test methodology described in this paper provides sufficient accuracy for establishing a foundation for legal testimony pertaining to network forensic evidence [13]. Nevertheless, as technology advances and legal case history and courtroom challenges grow, it is expected that the standards of accuracy will evolve and that an eventual calibration standard would include additional considerations of precision.

Our calibration testing work is part of a larger research effort examining network forensic readiness [9, 10]. The idea is to maximize the ability of an environment to collect credible digital evidence while minimizing the cost of incident response [20]. Most approaches to network forensic readiness center on tools and techniques, as opposed to a comprehensive framework for enterprise-wide implementation [7, 14, 21]. To properly embed network forensics, it will be important to determine the standards that will be applied to evidence and, thus, to consider the legal challenges for which a foundation must be laid.

References

[1] R. Addie, M. Zukerman and T. Neame, Broadband traffic modeling: Simple solutions to hard problems, *IEEE Communications*, vol. 36, pp. 2–9, 1998.

[2] Agilent Technologies, Metrology Forum: Basics, Terminology (www .agilent.com/metrology/terminology.shtml).

[3] Agilent Technologies, Metrology Forum: Basics, Why calibrate? (www.agilent.com/metrology/why-cal.shtml).

[4] N. Allen, Are you seeing what you expected? presented at *The Agora*, University of Washington, Seattle, Washington, 2006.

[5] R. Bejtlich, *The Tao Of Network Security Monitoring: Beyond Intrusion Detection*, Addison-Wesley, Boston, Massachusetts, 2005.

[6] S. Bradner and J. McQuaid, RFC 2544 – Benchmarking Methodology for Network Interconnect Devices, IETF Network Working Group (www.faqs.org/rfcs/rfc2544.html), 1999.

[7] B. Carrier and E. Spafford, Getting physical with the digital investigation process, *International Journal of Digital Evidence*, vol. 2(2), 2003.

[8] B. Endicott-Popovsky and B. Chee, NetOptics 10/100BaseT Dual Port Aggregator Tap, Spirent Test Center Technical Report, Advanced Network Computing Laboratory, University of Hawaii at Manoa, Honolulu, Hawaii, 2006.

[9] B. Endicott-Popovsky and D. Frincke, Adding the fourth "R" – A systems approach to solving the hacker's arms race, presented at the *Hawaii International Conference on System Sciences Symposium* (www.itl.nist.gov/iaui/vvrg/hicss39), 2006.

[10] B. Endicott-Popovsky and D. Frincke, Embedding forensic capabilities into networks: Addressing inefficiencies in digital forensics investigations, *Proceedings from the Seventh IEEE Systems, Man and Cybernetics Information Assurance Workshop*, pp. 133–139, 2006.

[11] M. Lawson, Expert Witness Testimony (United States vs. Jimmy Myers Brown (Defendant), Case No. 98-14068-CR, Southern District of Florida, Fort Pierce Division, Fort Pierce, Florida, September 13, 2000), Global CompuSearch, Spokane, Washington, 2006.

[12] D. Nassar, *Network Performance Baselining*, Sams, Indianapolis, Indiana, 2000.

[13] I. Orton, King County (Washington) Prosecutor, personal communication, 2006.

[14] M. Pollitt, Unit Chief FBI CART (Retired), personal communication, 2005.

[15] E. Schultz and R. Shumway, *Incident Response: A Strategic Guide to Handling System and Network Security Breaches*, Sams, Indianapolis, Indiana, 2001.

[16] M. Simon, Chief Technology Officer, Conjungi Corporation, Seattle, Washington, personal communication, 2005.

[17] F. Smith and R. Bace, *A Guide to Forensic Testimony: The Art and Practice of Presenting Testimony as an Expert Technical Witness*, Pearson Education, Boston, Massachusetts, 2003.

[18] P. Sommers, Emerging problems in digital evidence, presented at the *Computer Forensics Workshop*, University of Idaho, Moscow, Idaho, 2002.

[19] Spirent Communications, Spirent TestCenter (www.spirent.com /analysis/technology.cfm?media=7&WS=325&SS=117&wt=2).

[20] J. Tan, Forensic readiness, Technical report, @stake, Cambridge, Massachusetts, 2001.

[21] Y. Tang and T. Daniels, A simple framework for distributed forensics, *Proceedings of the Twenty-Fifth IEEE International Conference on Distributed Computing Systems*, pp. 163–169, 2005.

[22] The Tipmra, The genuine Tipmra speeding ticket defense (www .tipmra.com/new_tipmra/washington_state_speeding_ticket.htm).

[23] U.S. Circuit Court of Appeals (DC Circuit), Frye v. United States, *Federal Reporter*, vol. 293, pp. 1013–1014, 1923.

[24] U.S. Supreme Court, Daubert v. Merrell Dow Pharmaceuticals, Inc., *United States Reports*, vol. 509, pp. 579–601, 1993.

[25] U.S. Supreme Court, Kumho Tire Co. v. Carmichael, *United States Reports*, vol. 526, pp. 137–159, 1999.

Chapter 2

ON THE LEGALITY OF ANALYZING TELEPHONE CALL RECORDS

C. Swenson, C. Adams, A. Whitledge and S. Shenoi

Abstract   This paper examines the legal issues related to the access and use of call detail records (CDRs) of telephone subscribers that are maintained by service providers. The scenarios considered involve a federal law enforcement agency obtaining CDRs to identify suspects in a terrorism investigation; a federal, state or local law enforcement agency analyzing CDRs to gain insight into drug trafficking activities by an organized crime family; and a state or local law enforcement agency using CDRs to identify parole violators or motorists who exceed the posted speed limit. In addition, the legality of a service provider analyzing CDRs to support its direct marketing efforts is discussed.

Keywords: Call detail records, collection, analysis, legal issues

1.   Introduction

Telephone conversations are sacrosanct in the United States. Aside from the caller and receiver, it is illegal for a private entity to eavesdrop on or record a conversation. Law enforcement authorities may intercept and record specific conversations, but only with a court order.

However, a wealth of other information about telephone conversations and other communications is routinely collected and preserved by telecommunications service providers. This non-content information includes who communicated with whom, from where, when, for how long, and the type of communication (phone call, text message or page). Other information that is collected may include the name of the subscriber's service provider, service plan, and the type of communications device (traditional telephone, cell phone, PDA or pager).

Typically, non-content information is collected in the form of call detail records (CDRs) that are generated by telephone switches mainly for

Please use the following format when citing this chapter:

Swenson, C., Adams, C., Whitledge, A., Shenoi, S., 2007, in IFIP International Federation for Information Processing, Volume 242, Advances in Digital Forensics III; eds. P. Craiger and S Shenoi; (Boston: Springer), pp. 21-39.

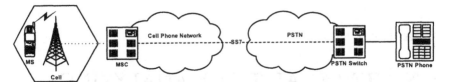

Figure 1. Telecommunications network schematic.

billing purposes [2, 4]. CDRs are created whenever a subscriber makes or receives a call, sends or receives a text message or page, or moves to a new area of coverage. CDRs also identify the cellular towers on which calls were placed and received. Since cellular towers only serve limited geographical regions and all hand-offs between towers are recorded, by analyzing information in CDRs, it is possible to pinpoint a mobile subscriber's location at a specific time and the subscriber's movement over time [10]. Furthermore, location information can be refined using other data maintained by service providers, e.g., directions (azimuths) of mobile subscribers from cellular tower antennae and the power levels of subscriber-to-tower communications.

Because CDRs contain detailed information about subscribers and their communications, including subscriber movements and communication patterns, they can be extremely useful in criminal investigations. But CDRs have other uses. Applying data mining algorithms to large quantities of CDRs could yield valuable intelligence to a government agency attempting to combat terrorism or to a telecommunications service provider hoping to attract new subscribers.

This paper focuses on the legal issues related to the access and use of CDRs of telephone subscribers in a variety of scenarios: terrorism and organized crime investigations as well as more mundane situations such as identifying parole violators or motorists who exceed the posted speed limit. In addition, the legality of service providers applying data mining algorithms on CDRs for use in direct marketing efforts is discussed.

2.   Telecommunications Networks

This section describes the architecture of modern telecommunications networks and provides details about the collection, storage and format of CDRs.

2.1   Network Architecture

Figure 1 presents a schematic diagram of a modern telecommunications network. The core is the public switched telephone network

Table 1. Cellular protocols and providers.

Protocol	Providers
CDMA2000	Verizon, US Cellular
GSM	T-Mobile, Cingular/AT&T
Proprietary	Sprint, Nextel, Cricket

(PSTN), which is controlled by the Signaling System 7 (SS7) protocol [8]. The PSTN incorporates numerous switches that provide service to subscribers using land lines (i.e., traditional telephones).

Cellular networks interface with the PSTN using the SS7 protocol. A cellular network is divided into cells, each served by a cellular tower (base station). The towers enable mobile subscribers (MSs) to make calls. A mobile switching center (MSC) is the heart of a cellular network, permitting subscribers to move seamlessly from cell to cell with automatic reuse of resources.

Three main cellular network technologies are deployed in the United States (Table 1). The newer CDMA2000 networks evolved from (and are usually compatible with) the older CDMA/IS-95, TDMA and AMPS networks [6]. GSM, an international standard built on SS7, is growing in popularity; it will eventually be replaced with UMTS, a more advanced system [3]. Most of the proprietary protocols in use in the United States are based on CDMA2000 technology; they are incompatible with other systems and do not allow roaming with other providers.

2.2 Call Detail Records

Call detail records (CDRs) are logs containing data about communications, not the content of the communications [2]. They are generated during setup (initiation) and teardown (termination) of calls, faxes, SMS messages and pages as well as during certain kinds of hand-offs and roaming events, such as when a subscriber moves from one provider to another or from one region to another. Typically, they are generated by PSTN switches and by MSCs in cellular networks.

CDRs are generated primarily for billing purposes. However, service providers often use CDRs to detect instances of telecommunications fraud, and to support network management and traffic engineering.

The GSM 12.05 Standard specifies 19 different CDR types for GSM networks (Table 2) [4]. Other cellular networks record similar types of information.

Table 2. Standard CDR types (GSM networks).

1. Mobile Originated Call	11. VLR Update
2. Mobile Originated Emergency Call	12. HLR Update
3. Mobile Originated Forwarding	13. Mobile Originated SMS
4. Mobile Terminated Call	14. Mobile Terminated SMS
5. Roaming Call	15. SMS-MO Internetworking
6. Incoming Gateway Call	16. SMS-MT Gateway
7. Outgoing Gateway Call	17. Common Equipment Usage
8. Transit Call	18. Reduced Partial Records
9. Supplementary Services	19. CAMEL Interrogation
10. HLR Interrogation	

Table 3. GSM mobile-originated CDR fields.
(M = mandatory, C = conditional, O = optional)

Field	Type	Description
Record Type	M	Mobile originated
Served IMSI	M	IMSI of calling party
Served IMEI	C	IMEI of calling party (if available)
Served MSISDN	O	Primary MSISDN of calling party
Called Number	M	Number dialed by caller
Translated Number	O	Called number after MSC translation
Connected Number	O	Actual connected number (if different)
Recording Entity	M	Visited MSC producing the record
Location	M	Cell ID of originating call
Change of Location	O	Timestamped changes in location and cell ID
Event Timestamps	C	Incoming traffic channel assignment
	C	Answer
	O	Release
Call Duration	M	Duration of call or holding time
Cause for Termination	M	Reason for connection release
Diagnostics	O	More detailed reason for connection release
Sequence Number	C	Sequence number for partial records
Call Reference	M	Local identifier distinguishing MS transactions
Record Extensions	O	Network/manufacturer-specific extensions

The format of a CDR depends on the configuration of the switch that generates the record. Table 3 presents an example CDR for a GSM 12.05 mobile-originated call record. In GSM, the IMSI is a unique identifier for a subscriber, the IMEI is an identifier for a handset, and the MSISDN is a phone number.

CDRs typically require very little storage. Most events produce CDRs of at most a few hundred bytes. Even though billions of events occur daily, the total volume of CDRs collected and stored is manageable [7]. However, service providers may retain CDRs for limited (and variable) periods of time. In some cases, providers may archive only summarized information from CDRs.

The following sections discuss four scenarios related to the access and use of CDRs by law enforcement authorities and service providers.

3.　Terrorism Investigation

Consider the following terrorism investigation scenario:

> *A reliable informant has indicated that J.S., a resident of Anytown, USA, has been calling individuals in North Waziristan, a tribal region straddling the Afghanistan-Pakistan border. May a U.S. law enforcement agency obtain from J.S.'s telephone service provider all available CDRs related to J.S.'s outgoing and incoming calls so it can identify and investigate members of J.S.'s calling groups?*

Records of telephone calls are treated differently than the contents of telephone conversations. The Supreme Court has ruled that the surreptitious eavesdropping and recording of private conversations constitutes a search under the Fourth Amendment, because there is a reasonable expectation of privacy in the contents of telephone calls [27, 28]. In contrast, the Court has decided that there is no expectation of privacy in information disclosed to a third party [26, 29]. CDRs are analogous to the address information on an envelope, which is used to direct correspondence to its location. Just as there is no reasonable expectation of privacy for address information, there is no reasonable expectation of privacy for CDRs and other customer proprietary network information (CPNI), which belong to the service provider rather than the subscriber.

In Smith v. Maryland [30], the Supreme Court decided that the government's use of a pen register to record the numbers dialed from a suspect's telephone differed significantly from the electronic eavesdropping and recording of telephone calls, because the pen register did not acquire the contents of telephone conversations. Without obtaining either a warrant or a court order, law enforcement agents in the Smith case asked a telephone company to install a pen register at the company's central offices to record the numbers dialed from a telephone at the defendant's home. After the pen register showed a call to a robbery victim, the police obtained a search warrant for the defendant's home. The Supreme Court decided that the defendant had no legitimate expectation of privacy regarding the telephone number that he had called, because when he used his telephone, he voluntarily conveyed the number to the phone company for use in the ordinary course of business. The Court pointed out that subscribers realize that a phone company has facilities for making permanent records of the numbers they call, because their telephone bills include a list of the toll calls they made. The Court also ruled that the defendant assumed the risk that the phone company would disclose the telephone numbers to the government, even though the company used automatic switching equipment instead of a live operator to place the calls. The Court concluded that "[t]he installation and use of a pen register ... was not a search, and no warrant was required."

The Smith decision dealt only with pen registers, which record the telephone numbers for outgoing calls; it did not address trap and trace devices that record the telephone numbers for incoming calls, or the CDRs that are created by service providers. Trap and trace devices and CDRs differ from pen registers in that subscribers may not be aware that a phone company can keep track of incoming calls like it records information about outgoing toll calls for billing purposes. On the other hand, trap and trace devices and CDRs are similar because they do not provide access to the contents of the communications. Therefore, under the Smith decision, installing a trap and trace device or obtaining a suspect's CDRs would not constitute a "search" under the Fourth Amendment. Accordingly, the Fourth Amendment would not require a law enforcement agency to obtain a warrant to install a trap and trace device or to obtain CDRs from a service provider.

While the Fourth Amendment does not require a warrant for obtaining CDRs, law enforcement agencies must satisfy statutory requirements to do so. The particular statutory requirements depend on which of the following three categories of information is sought by law enforcement: (i) contents of electronic communications, (ii) stored records, and (iii) real-time information other than the contents of electronic communications. The contents of telephone communications are governed by the Wiretap Act of 1968, which not only makes electronic eavesdropping and wiretapping crimes punishable by up to five years imprisonment ([19] § 2511(4)), but also prescribes the procedure that law enforcement agencies must follow to obtain authorization for electronic eavesdropping and wiretapping ([19, 23] § 2516). The Electronic Communications Privacy Act (ECPA) of 1986 extended the Wiretap Act to cover the interception of electronic communications in addition to oral and wire communications, which the Wiretap Act had previously covered. The ECPA also added the Stored Communication Act ([19, 23] §§ 2701–2711), which covers stored records and prohibits access to stored electronic communications unless authorized by a court order. Lastly, the ECPA added the Pen Register and Trap and Trace Device Statute ([19, 23] §§ 3121–3127), which covers real-time information other than the contents of electronic communications and prohibits the use of pen registers and trap and trace devices, unless authorized by a court order.

Section 2511 of Title 18 of the United States Code [19] prohibits the unauthorized interception of wire, oral or electronic communications. "Intercept" is defined broadly as the acquisition of the contents of any wire, oral or communication through the use of any device ([19] § 2510(4)). Law enforcement personnel may obtain authorization for the interception of electronic communications by obtaining a court order under Section 2518, but the statute requires a showing of probable cause that the subject of the order is committing, has committed, or is about to commit a crime. Section 2511 would not apply to the scenario under consideration because it is only J.S.'s CDRs, as opposed to the contents of J.S.'s communications, that are being sought.

The means required for a law enforcement agency to obtain J.S.'s CDRs depend on the type of information that the agency is seeking. For land line telephones, the CDRs sought by an agency may include the date, time and duration of each call, the number called and the charges. Since each land line telephone is associated with a specific address, the telephone numbers can identify the physical locations of the calling and called parties. Similar information may be obtained for mobile networks, including the dates, times and durations of calls, and the originating and dialed numbers. In addition, information about the caller's approximate physical location may be revealed by CDRs.

Section 2703(c)(2) of Title 18 [23] requires a service provider to supply the following types of customer information in response to a grand jury subpoena: the customer's name and address, local and long distance connection records, records of session times and durations, telephone or instrument number, and the means and sources of payment for the service. The showing required for issuance of a grand jury subpoena is that the information sought may be relevant to the purpose of the grand jury investigation.

Instead of using a grand jury subpoena, a law enforcement agency may obtain J.S.'s past CDRs by complying with the requirements of the Stored Communications Act, which governs stored records. Section 2703 of Title 18 [23] prohibits a service provider from disclosing subscriber records to any government entity without the subscriber's consent unless the government entity obtains either a warrant or court order for the disclosure. A court order for the disclosure may issue only if the government entity offers specific and articulable facts showing that there are reasonable grounds to believe that the CDRs sought are relevant to an ongoing criminal investigation ([23] § 2703(d)). Penalties for a violation include actual damages of no less than $1,000, punitive damages and reasonable attorney fees ([19] § 2707(c)). In addition, the government entity may be subject to disciplinary action for a willful violation ([23] § 2707(d)).

If the law enforcement agency is seeking prospective CDRs, it would need to satisfy the Pen Register and Trap and Trace Device Statute, which governs real-time information other than the contents of electronic communications. Section 3121(a) of Title 18 [19] provides: "Except as provided in this section, no person may install or use a pen register or a trap and trace device without first obtaining a court order under Section 3123 of this title or under the Foreign Intelligence Surveillance Act of 1978 (Title 50 U.S.C. 1801 *et seq.*)." The terms "pen register" and "trap and trace device" are defined broadly in Section 3127 [23] (as well as in the Foreign Intelligence Surveillance Act (FISA)) to cover CDRs. Section 3122 [19] authorizes federal, state and local law enforcement officers to apply for an order for the installation and use of a pen register or trap and trace device. Section 3123 requires the court to issue the order if it finds that a "law enforcement or investigative officer has certified to the court that the information likely to be obtained by such installation and use is relevant to an ongoing criminal investigation." Thus, in our scenario, law enforcement personnel would be able to obtain J.S.'s CDRs if they can certify to a court that they are relevant to a current criminal investigation.

Alternatively, past CDRs may be obtained under Section 2709 of Title 18 [19, 23] and prospective CDRs may be obtained under FISA if they are relevant to an investigation to protect against international terrorism or clandestine intelligence activities. Section 2709 imposes a duty on a service provider to provide a customer's name, address, length of service, and local and long distance billing records upon the request of a designee of the FBI Director, who certifies in writing that the information is relevant to an investigation to protect against international terrorism or clandestine intelligence activities. This certification is known as a National Security Letter (NSL). In contrast to other means for obtaining CDRs, no court order is required for an NSL.

In addition, Section 1842 of Title 50 of the United States Code [21] provides that designated attorneys for the United States may apply for an order from the FISA court for the installation and use of a pen register or trap and trace device to obtain prospective CDRs. The application must include a certification that the information likely to be obtained is foreign intelligence not concerning a U.S. person or is relevant to an ongoing investigation to protect against international terrorism or clandestine intelligence activities, provided that the investigation of the U.S.

person is not conducted solely upon the basis of activities protected by the First Amendment ([21] § 1842(c)(2)). Therefore, in the scenario under consideration, the law enforcement agency could obtain the CDRs for J.S.'s calls by obtaining an order from the FISA court based on a certification that the CDRs are relevant to an ongoing terrorism investigation.

The requirements for a grand jury subpoena and the certification requirements under the Stored Communications Act, Pen Register and Trap and Trace Device Statute and FISA are significantly less stringent than the probable cause showing required for the issuance of a warrant. A showing of probable cause involves the demonstration of a fair probability that evidence of a crime will be found, and the determination of probable cause has to be made by a neutral judge or magistrate. In contrast, the certification requirements only involve relevance to an ongoing investigation, and the certification is made by law enforcement personnel or an attorney for the United States, rather than a neutral judge or magistrate. Even so, additional information besides the report that J.S. was calling North Waziristan would be required before a certification could be made that the CDRs are related to an ongoing terrorism or criminal investigation.

Once the CDRs are properly obtained, law enforcement officials would be free to investigate the communities of interest and the calling patterns they revealed as long as they do not access the contents of communications. Section 3121(c) of Title 18 [23] requires the government to use technology that restricts the information recorded by a pen register or trap and trace device so as not to include the contents of any wire or electronic communication. This is not an issue as CDRs do not contain any information about the contents of phone calls.

We now discuss a related, but somewhat broader, scenario involving the acquisition of CDRs:

> *U.S. intelligence sources in Pakistan indicate that members of a suspected terrorist cell in Anytown, USA have been communicating surreptitiously with individuals in North Waziristan. May a U.S. law enforcement agency obtain from the telephone companies serving Anytown, USA the CDRs of their subscribers so it can identify and investigate individuals who have made telephone calls to North Waziristan?*

This scenario differs from the previous one in that it involves obtaining the CDRs of all the subscribers in Anytown, USA, rather than just the CDRs for a single individual. As in the previous scenario, a U.S. law enforcement agency could access the CDRs by obtaining a court order based on a certification that the CDRs are related to an ongoing criminal or terrorism investigation. However, while the scope of an investigation would probably extend to all the members of the suspected terrorist cell in Anytown, USA, it is difficult to see why it should extend to subscribers who are not members of the cell. Accordingly, it would be difficult to convince a court of the reasons for obtaining CDRs for all the subscribers in Anytown, USA.

This scenario addresses some of the allegations that have been made in several class action suits that have recently been filed against telecommunications companies for allegedly divulging customer records to the U.S. Government [1, 5]. A class action suit filed in San Francisco, which has been consolidated with seventeen other class actions, alleges that AT&T violated Section 2702(A)(3) of Title 18 of the Stored Communications Act by divulging customer records to the government [13]. The trial judge denied the U.S. Government's motion to dismiss the case on the grounds of the state secrets privilege. However, he stated that he might grant summary judgment later in the case, if he decided that the state secrets privilege would block essential evidence in the case. The judge also emphasized that he was not ruling on whether or not any of the allegations in the case were true [14].

4.　　Organized Crime Investigation

Consider the following scenario:

> *Law enforcement authorities investigating drug trafficking by an organized crime family intend to apply data mining algorithms on CDRs to identify the key players and collaborators, gain insights into command and control techniques, and glean information about drug shipment, distribution and sales patterns. May a law enforcement agency obtain from service providers the CDRs corresponding to phone calls made and received by several members of an organized crime family over a period of one year?*

As discussed in Section 3, a law enforcement agency would not require a warrant to obtain CDRs from a service provider. The Fourth Amendment originally applied only to federal government agencies, but the Supreme Court decided in a series of landmark cases in the 1960s that the Fourth, Fifth, Sixth and Eighth Amendments had been incorporated into the Fourteenth Amendment's guarantee of due process of law, which is applicable to state and local governments. Thus, the Fourth Amendment standards for unreasonable searches and seizures apply to federal, state and local law enforcement agencies [24, 25].

Similarly, the Wiretap Act, the Stored Communications Act, and the Pen Register and Trap and Trace Device Statute are all applicable to federal, state and local law enforcement agencies. Therefore, the agency would need to apply for an order to obtain the CDRs based on a certification that the CDRs are relevant to an investigation. As long as the CDRs are relevant to the investigation, they could be obtained for calls made and received by members of the organized crime family for a period of one year, or even longer. Federal law enforcement authorities would submit their applications to an appropriate federal court, while state and local agencies would submit their applications to an appropriate state or local court ([23] § 3127(2)).

Once the law enforcement agency obtains the CDRs, it may employ data mining algorithms to discover correlations and patterns. These could include identifying the key players and collaborators, obtaining insights into command and control techniques, and gleaning information about drug shipment, distribution and sales patterns.

It might be argued that the use of data mining algorithms to analyze CDRs constitutes an unreasonable search because it indirectly reveals information about the contents of calls made or received by the subjects. This argument might, for example, be based on Kyllo v. United States [33], where the Supreme Court decided that the government's warrantless use of a thermal imaging device directed at the inside of a private home to detect heat lamps for growing marijuana constituted an unlawful search. In reaching its decision, the Court emphasized that the thermal imaging device violated the occupant's reasonable expectation of privacy, because it involved the use of sensor technology that was not in general public use.

Similarly, it might be argued that the application of advanced data mining algorithms to the analysis of CDRs would constitute an unlawful search, because data mining algorithms are not in general public use and the public is not generally aware of data mining algorithms. On the other hand, data mining algorithms merely involve the discovery of correlations between seemingly unrelated events and then drawing inferences based on the correlations. Members of the general public should be quite familiar with the notion of detecting patterns in everyday life and, therefore, it should come as no surprise to them that law enforcement authorities would be able to detect useful patterns by analyzing CDRs.

5. Location-Time Information

Location-time information obtained from CDRs can be used to prove that individuals may be violating certain laws. Since cell towers can only provide service within a small geographical area, it is possible for investigators to use data from CDRs to estimate the whereabouts of subscribers at certain times. The following questions arise:

May a state or local law enforcement agency obtain from service providers the CDRs for convicted felons residing in its jurisdiction to determine whether they have violated certain terms of their parole (e.g., leaving the city, county or state)?

May a state or local law enforcement agency obtain from service providers the CDRs for all calls made and received in the vicinity of a turnpike to identify motorists who have exceeded the posted speed limit?

It appears that a law enforcement agency may be able to obtain historical information about the location of a particular cellular phone upon providing specific and articulable facts that the location is relevant and material to an ongoing criminal investigation. However, it would probably be necessary for law enforcement to obtain a warrant based upon a showing of probable cause to acquire prospective real-time information concerning the location of a cellular phone.

The U.S. Supreme Court considered the application of the Fourth Amendment to the monitoring of electronic tracking devices (beepers) in United States v. Knotts [31] and United States v. Karo [32]. In the Knotts case, the Court decided that law enforcement authorities did not require a warrant to monitor a beeper that was placed in a container of chemicals because the monitoring revealed no more than the authorities would have been able to observe through visual surveillance. In contrast, the Court decided in the Karo case that law enforcement authorities did require a warrant to monitor a beeper that was inside a private residence and not open to visual surveillance. The monitoring in Karo represented a greater threat to privacy because it involved an intrusion into a residence, while the monitoring in Knotts involved a suspect who was traveling in an automobile on public roads where the suspect had no reasonable expectation of privacy.

Under the Knotts and Karo cases, therefore, law enforcement authorities would not require a warrant to track the location of a cellular phone unless the phone was located in a private residence. Nevertheless, a number of U.S. magistrates have decided that a warrant is required for law enforcement authorities to obtain cell site information on account of the Communications Assistance for Law Enforcement Act of 1994 (CALEA).

CALEA was enacted to enable law enforcement agencies to retain their surveillance capabilities despite technological advances in the field of telecommunications. To accomplish this objective, CALEA requires service providers to ensure that their equipment will enable the government to intercept wire and electronic communications and access call-identifying information pursuant to lawful orders ([20] § 1002(a)(2)). During CALEA's Congressional hearings, the proposal was challenged on the grounds that it would authorize the tracking of cellular phone users. However, the then FBI Director Freeh responded to these concerns by proposing the addition of language to the statute that would prevent the use of pen registers and trap and trace devices to track subscribers. Consequently, the following language was added at the end of CALEA's provision dealing with the requirement for telecommunications carriers to provide governmental access to call-identifying information:

> "[E]xcept that, with regard to information acquired solely pursuant to the authority for pen registers and trap and trace devices ([19] § 3127), such call-identifying information shall not include any information that may disclose the physical location of the subscriber (except to the extent that the location may be determined from the telephone number)" ([20] § 1002(a)(2)).

As a result of this provision, law enforcement authorities are barred from acquiring call-identifying information that would disclose the physical location of a subscriber "solely pursuant to the authority for pen registers and trap and trace devices." Nevertheless, government attorneys have sought to get around this provision and acquire cell site information without a warrant by seeking authorization under the Stored Communications Act. This act authorizes the government to obtain a court order for the disclosure of telephone records if it provides "specific and articulable facts" showing that the records are relevant and material to an ongoing criminal investigation ([23] § 2703(c),(d)). The standard for obtaining an order under the Stored Communications Act is similar to the standard under the Pen Register and Trap and Trace Device Statute, and it is less stringent than the standard for obtaining a warrant, which requires probable cause.

Several courts have accepted the government's argument and have granted orders authorizing the government to obtain cell site information [15, 17, 18]. However, the majority of courts have rejected the government's argument primarily because the Stored Communications Act was enacted to allow government access to records in storage, rather than as a means to conduct real-time surveillance through a prospective order for the disclosure of cell site information [11, 12, 16]. For real-time surveillance, the government must rely on the Pen Register and Trap and Trace Device Statute to obtain telephone records or on warrants if it wants to intercept communications or obtain other information. On the other hand, the government may acquire historical CDRs using the Stored Communications Act, and it appears that these could potentially include cell site information [11]. Service providers usually retain CDRs for limited periods of time, and so it is likely that these records might not be available by the time an order for their disclosure can be obtained.

The first question in the scenario is whether a law enforcement agency may obtain cell site information from CDRs for convicted felons to verify whether they have left the area they have been restricted to by the terms of their parole. As a practical matter, the granting of parole would normally be conditioned on consent to track the parolee's location and to the parolee's wearing a tracking device. Naturally, if the parolee's consent had been obtained, no court order would be needed for tracking the parolee. Thus, the remaining discussion presumes the lack of consent.

The majority of courts that have addressed the issue stipulate that the agency must obtain a warrant based on a showing of probable cause to acquire prospective cell site information. To obtain a warrant, the agency would need to show there is a fair probability that evidence of a crime would be found. A showing that an individual is a convicted felon would not be sufficient for issuance of a warrant, because it would not provide any basis for concluding that the person had violated a condition of parole. In addition, even if there were to be a showing that the individual had violated a condition of parole, it would not be sufficient for issuance of a warrant, because a parole violation is not a crime.

The courts that have issued orders for prospective cell site information have required a showing under the Stored Communications Act of specific and articulable facts that the information is relevant to an ongoing criminal investigation. This standard would not be satisfied because parole violations are generally not the subject of ongoing criminal investigations. If the agency sought historical cell site information from a service provider, it would need to rely on the Stored Communications Act, and this would require the same showing of specific and articulable facts that the information was relevant to an ongoing criminal investigation. Consequently, a law enforcement agency could not obtain cell site information from CDRs for convicted felons to check if they have violated conditions of their parole.

The second question is whether a law enforcement agency may obtain cell site information from CDRs for motorists driving on a turnpike to identify speeders. In contrast to a parole violation, speeding is a crime. Nevertheless, to obtain prospective cell site information, the agency would probably need a warrant, and this would require some showing that certain subscribers would be likely to be speeding on the turnpike. It is difficult to imagine how a convincing showing of this sort could be made. Therefore, the agency would not be able to obtain cell site information from CDRs to catch speeders.

6.   Direct Marketing Efforts

"Roamers" are cellular subscribers who have signed up for service with one provider but use the network resources of another provider, for example, when they travel outside their service region. We consider the following question regarding the use of roamers' CDRs for direct marketing efforts by a service provider:

> *Since service providers own their CDRs, may a service provider analyze CDRs in its possession to identify roamers and their calling patterns and target them with customized service plans as part of its direct marketing efforts?*

This scenario differs from the previous scenarios because it involves a private entity rather than a government agency. Section 222 of Title 47 of the United States Code [20] applies across the board to government and private entities, and it would prohibit a service provider's use of CDRs for its own direct marketing efforts. Section 222(c)(1) provides:

> "Except as required by law or with the approval of the customer, a telecommunications carrier that receives or obtains customer proprietary network information by virtue of its provision of a telecommunications service shall only use, disclose, or permit access to individually identifiable customer proprietary network information in its provision of (A) the telecommunications service from which such information is derived, or (B) services necessary to, or used in, the provision of such telecommunications service, including the publishing of directories."

"Customer proprietary network information" (CPNI) is defined to include "information that relates to the quantity, technical configuration, type, destination, location and amount of use of a telecommunications service" ([20] § 222(h)(1)). Therefore, this information would include the identities of roamers and their calling patterns. Each violation is punishable by a fine of not more than $10,000 or imprisonment for a term not exceeding one year, or both ([20] § 501).

However, Section 222 specifies that CPNI may be used or disclosed with the approval of the customer. The regulations authorize service providers to obtain approval for the use or disclosure of CPNI from a customer either expressly or by failure of the customer to object within 30 days after receiving appropriate notification either in writing or by e-mail [22].

The use of CDRs may also be prohibited by state laws. For example, the State of Oklahoma prohibits the procurement of a telephone subscriber's records without the subscriber's authorization [9]. This prohibition is subject to a number of exceptions, including that a telecommunications company may obtain access to telephone records to provide service, to protect its rights, or to protect other subscribers or carriers from unlawful uses of telephone service. The exception would not apply to the use of CDRs for a telecommunications company's direct marketing campaign.

7. Conclusions

CDRs have been traditionally used by service providers for billing purposes, network management, traffic engineering and fraud detection. Because they contain detailed information about subscribers and their communications, including subscriber movements and communication patterns, CDRs are very useful in law enforcement investigations and for gathering intelligence. In particular, the application of data mining algorithms to large quantities of CDRs may yield valuable intelligence to government agencies attempting to combat terrorism or crime, or to a telecommunications service provider hoping to attract new subscribers. However, several legal restrictions are in place to protect the privacy of innocent subscribers. Significant restrictions on the access and use of CDRs by government agencies are imposed by the Pen Register Trap and Trace Device Statute, the Communications Assistance for Law Enforcement Act (CALEA) and the Stored Communications Act. Telephone subscribers are also protected from wanton data mining by service providers by Title 47 of the United States Code and by various state laws. In general, law enforcement agencies may not access and use CDRs without a warrant or court order, which require a showing that the CDRs in question are relevant and material to a criminal or terrorism investigation. Furthermore, service providers may not use CDRs for non-business purposes without obtaining explicit authorizations from their subscribers.

References

[1] L. Cauley, NSA has massive database of Americans' phone calls, *USA Today* (www.usatoday.com/news/washington/2006-05-10-nsa _x.htm), May 11, 2006.

[2] Cisco, Call detail records (www.cisco.com/univercd/cc/td/doc/pro duct/wanbu/das/das_1_4/das14/das14apd.htm).

[3] J. Eberspächer, H. Vögel and C. Bettstetter, *GSM: Switching, Services and Protocols*, Wiley, Chichester, United Kingdom, 2001.

[4] European Telecommunications Standards Institute, ETSI TS 100 616 V7.0.1 (1999-07), Digital Cellular Telecommunications System (Phase 2+), Event and Call Data (GSM 12.05 Version 7.0.1 Release 1998), 1998.

[5] G. Gross, NSA wiretap lawsuits transferred to California court, IDG News Service (www.computerworld.com/action/article.do?comma nd=viewArticleBasic&articleId=9002385), August 11, 2006.

[6] S. Low and R. Schneider, *CDMA Internetworking: Deploying the Open A-Interface*, Prentice Hall, New Jersey, 2000.

[7] T. Moore, A. Meehan, G. Manes and S. Shenoi, Forensic analysis of telecom networks, in *Advances in Digital Forensics*, M. Pollitt and S. Shenoi (Eds.), Springer, New York, pp. 177–188, 2005.

[8] T. Russell, *Signaling System #7*, McGraw-Hill, New York, 2002.

[9] State of Oklahoma, Unauthorized or Fraudulent Procurement, Sale or Receipt of Telephone Records, Title 21, Section 1742.2, *2006 Supplement Oklahoma Statutes (Volume 1)*, Oklahoma City, Oklahoma, p. 1107, 2006.

[10] C. Swenson, T. Moore and S. Shenoi, GSM cell site forensics, in *Advances in Digital Forensics II*, M. Olivier and S. Shenoi (Eds.), Springer, New York, pp. 259–272, 2006.

[11] U.S. District Court (District of Maryland), In the matter of the application of the United States of America for an order authorizing the installation and use of a pen register and caller identification system on telephone numbers and the production of real time cell site information, *Federal Supplement Second Series*, vol. 402, pp. 597–605, 2005.

[12] U.S. District Court (Eastern District of New York), In the matter of the application of the United States of America for an order (i) authorizing the installation and use of a pen register and trap and trace device, and (ii) authorizing release of subscriber information and/or cell site information, *Federal Supplement Second Series*, vol. 396, pp. 294–327, 2005.

[13] U.S. District Court (Northern District of California), Hepting v. AT&T, Amended complaint for damages, declaratory and injunctive relief, No. C-06-0672-JCS, paragraphs 126–132 (www.eff.org /legal/cases/att/att_complaint_amended.pdf), 2006.

[14] U.S. District Court (Northern District of California), Hepting v. AT&T, Order, No. C-06-672-VRW, pp. 35–36 (www.eff.org/legal /cases/att/308_order_on_mtns_to_dismiss.pdf), 2006.

[15] U.S. District Court (Southern District of New York), In re application of the United States of America for an order for disclosure of telecommunications records and authorizing the use of a pen register and trap and trace device, *Federal Supplement Second Series*, vol. 405, pp. 435–450, 2005.

[16] U.S. District Court (Southern District of Texas), In the matter of the application of the United States for an order: (i) authorizing the installation and use of a pen register and trap and trace device, and (ii) authorizing release of subscriber and other information, *Federal Supplement Second Series*, vol. 441, pp. 816–837, 2006.

[17] U.S. District Court (Southern District of Texas), In the matter of the application of the United States for an order: (i) authorizing the installation and use of a pen register and trap and trace device, and (ii) authorizing release of subscriber and other information, *Federal Supplement Second Series*, vol. 433, pp. 804–806, 2006.

[18] U.S. District Court (Western District of Louisiana), In the matter of the application of the United States for an order: (i) authorizing the installation and use of a pen register and trap and trace device, and (ii) authorizing release of subscriber information and/or cell site information, *Federal Supplement Second Series*, vol. 411, pp. 678–683, 2006.

[19] U.S. Government, Title 18: Crimes and Criminal Procedures, *United States Code (Volume 9)*, Washington, DC, pp. 787–1675, 2001.

[20] U.S. Government, Title 47: Telegraphs, Telephones and Radio-Telegraphs, *United States Code (Volume 27)*, Washington, DC, pp. 1–317, 2001.

[21] U.S. Government, Title 50: War and National Defense, *United States Code (Volume 29)*, Washington, DC, pp. 1–724, 2001.

[22] U.S. Government, Customer Proprietary Network Information, Sections 64.2007–2009, Federal Communications Commission, *Title 47, Code of Federal Regulations*, Washington, DC, pp. 323-326, 2006.

[23] U.S. Government, Title 18: Crimes and Criminal Procedures, *United States Code Annotated Supplement*, Washington, DC, pp. 5–146, 2007.

[24] U.S. Supreme Court, Mapp v. Ohio, *United States Reports*, vol. 367, pp. 643–686, 1961.

[25] U.S. Supreme Court, Ker v. State of California, *United States Reports*, vol. 374, pp. 23–64, 1963.

[26] U.S. Supreme Court, Hoffa v. United States, *United States Reports*, vol. 385, pp. 293–322, 1966.

[27] U.S. Supreme Court, Berger v. United States, *United States Reports*, vol. 388, pp. 41–129, 1967.

[28] U.S. Supreme Court, Katz v. United States, *United States Reports*, vol. 389, pp. 347–374, 1967.

[29] U.S. Supreme Court, United States v. Miller, *United States Reports*, vol. 425, pp. 435–456, 1976.

[30] U.S. Supreme Court, Smith v. Maryland, *United States Reports*, vol. 442, pp. 735–752, 1979.

[31] U.S. Supreme Court, United States v. Knotts, *United States Reports*, vol. 460, pp. 276–288, 1983.

[32] U.S. Supreme Court, United States v. Karo, *United States Reports*, vol. 468, pp. 705–736, 1984.

[33] U.S. Supreme Court, Kyllo v. United States, *United States Reports*, vol. 533, pp. 27–52, 2001.

Chapter 3

SURVEY OF LAW ENFORCEMENT PERCEPTIONS REGARDING DIGITAL EVIDENCE

M. Rogers, K. Scarborough, K. Frakes and C. San Martin

Abstract   This paper analyzes state and local law enforcement agents' perceptions about prosecutors' knowledge of digital evidence and their willingness to prosecute cases involving digital evidence, and agents' perceptions about judges' knowledge of digital evidence and their willingness to admit digital evidence in legal proceedings. Statistical analysis indicates that a significant negative correlation exists between the size of the population served by law enforcement agents and their perceptions about judges' knowledge of digital evidence and willingness to admit digital evidence. Also, positive relationships exist between the size of the population served and law enforcement perceptions of prosecutors' knowledge of digital evidence and willingness to prosecute digital evidence cases, and perceptions about judges' willingness to admit digital evidence. The implications of these findings are discussed along with suggestions for future research.

Keywords: State and local law enforcement, digital evidence, prosecutors, judges

1.   Introduction

Digital forensics has recently garnered a considerable amount of attention. Numerous articles have been published on issues ranging from the lack of trained investigators and the use of *ad hoc* procedures to the difficulty of coping with massive amounts of electronic evidence [3–5, 11]. Other issues include the lack of standards in the discipline of digital forensics and the paucity of certifications for practitioners [12, 14]. Most experts agree that systematic educational and research and development initiatives are required if digital forensics is to obtain the scientific and

Please use the following format when citing this chapter:

Rogers, M., Scarborough, K., Frakes, K., San Martin, C., 2007, in IFIP International Federation for Information Processing, Volume 242, Advances in Digital Forensics III; eds. P. Craiger and S Shenoi; (Boston: Springer), pp. 41-52.

legal status of other forensic sciences such as DNA and latent fingerprint analysis [2, 9, 14].

Meanwhile, several studies have focused on the needs of the law enforcement community [1, 8, 14, 15]. The studies have identified that law enforcement needs advanced tools for extracting and analyzing digital evidence, especially evidence residing in large-scale distributed networks. Agencies also require more resources for equipment and personnel, and for education and training of existing personnel.

What is lacking, however, are studies that examine how law enforcement agencies are dealing with the ubiquity of digital evidence in criminal investigations, not just those involving electronic crimes. Certain federal agencies have indicated at least 80% of all cases involve digital evidence, and the volume of evidence per case is increasing (albeit not as rapidly as Moore's law). The quantity and complexity of digital evidence are expected to overwhelm law enforcement capabilities. Moreover, the legal community and the judiciary are unprepared to deal with the digital evidence brought into legal proceedings. According to a preliminary study by Losavio and colleagues [10], judges, in general, are uncomfortable with their knowledge of digital evidence. Furthermore, they are unsure about the weight that should be given to digital evidence and whether or not digital evidence should admitted at trial.

Meanwhile, no studies have been published about how prosecutors and defense lawyers feel about their own abilities regarding digital evidence and their willingness to deal with cases involving digital evidence. Even more important are the perceptions of state and local law enforcement agents (796,518 officers in 17,784 agencies in the United States according to the most recent census [13]), who constitute the first line in the investigative process and who are, therefore, most affected by the quantity and complexity of digital evidence.

This paper attempts to fill a gap in the understanding of the perceptions of state and local law enforcement agents related to digital evidence. In particular, it analyzes state and local law enforcement agents' perceptions about prosecutors' knowledge of digital evidence and their willingness to prosecute cases involving digital evidence. Also, it examines agents' perceptions about judges' knowledge of digital evidence and their willingness to admit digital evidence in legal proceedings.

2.   Law Enforcement Survey

The law enforcement survey described in this paper is part of a larger study sponsored by the National Institute of Justice (NIJ) that examined digital evidence in the context of U.S. state and local law enforcement agencies. This larger study followed up on the work of Appel and Pollitt [1] that investigated how state, local and tribal law enforcement agencies were coping with investigations involving digital evidence.

This paper focuses on two issues regarding state and local law enforcement agents. The first deals their perceptions about prosecutors' knowledge of digital evidence and their willingness to prosecute cases involving digital evidence. The second relates to agents' perceptions about judges' knowledge of digital evidence and their willingness to admit digital evidence at trial. These two issues were chosen because they build on the research conducted by Losavio and co-workers [10], which examined Kentucky circuit court judges' knowledge and attitudes regarding digital evidence.

Given the dearth of research related to digital evidence in general, and state and local law enforcement agencies in particular, the study reported in this paper was strictly exploratory in nature. No hypotheses were tested; rather, the survey was designed to add to the limited knowledge base in the area.

3. Survey Methodology

This section discusses the survey methodology, including the survey participants and the survey instrument.

3.1 Survey Participants

The respondents were drawn from state and local law enforcement agencies in the United States. The agencies were selected from the National Public Safety Information Bureau's database. The sample included the 200 largest agencies, and a stratified sample of municipal and county agencies as well as state bureaus of investigation where appropriate ($N = 279$). The respondents, who were contacted by mail, were asked to answer a series of questions about digital evidence. A total of 667 surveys were mailed; 279 surveys were returned, resulting in a response rate of 41.8%.

Each survey questionnaire was accompanied by a cover letter that presented the objective of the study and the principal investigator's contact information. The cover letter also provided a guarantee of anonymity and discussed the survey's adherence to guidelines related to research involving human subjects. A self-addressed stamped envelope was included for returning the completed questionnaire.

Table 1 shows the numbers of respondents from various law enforcement agencies. The majority of the respondents were from municipal agencies (49.5%).

Table 1.   Respondents by agency type.

Type of Agency	Freq.	Pct.
Municipal	138	49.5
County Sheriff	70	25.1
County Police	19	6.8
State Police	43	15.4
Marshal	3	1.1
Bureau of Investigation	3	1.1
Merged County and Municipal	1	0.4
State Sheriff	1	0.4
City Sheriff	1	0.4
Total	279	100.0

Table 2.   Respondents by state (Total: 279).

State	Freq.	Pct.	State	Freq.	Pct.
Alabama	4	1.4	Montana	0	0.0
Alaska	1	0.4	Nebraska	4	1.4
Arizona	7	2.5	Nevada	2	0.7
Arkansas	3	1.1	New Hampshire	3	1.1
California	19	6.8	New Jersey	7	2.5
Colorado	4	1.4	New Mexico	4	1.4
Connecticut	1	0.4	New York	11	3.9
Delaware	0	0.0	North Carolina	5	1.8
Florida	12	4.3	North Dakota	2	0.7
Georgia	17	6.1	Ohio	12	4.3
Hawaii	2	0.7	Oklahoma	3	1.1
Idaho	2	0.7	Oregon	5	1.8
Illinois	10	3.6	Pennsylvania	5	1.8
Indiana	8	2.9	Rhode Island	2	0.7
Iowa	5	1.8	South Carolina	4	1.4
Kansas	8	2.9	South Dakota	3	1.1
Kentucky	7	2.5	Tennessee	7	2.5
Louisiana	7	2.5	Texas	14	5.0
Maine	0	0.0	Utah	2	0.7
Maryland	6	2.2	Vermont	1	0.4
Massachusetts	5	1.8	Virginia	10	3.6
Michigan	9	3.2	Washington	5	1.8
Minnesota	5	1.8	West Virginia	6	2.2
Mississippi	2	0.7	Wisconsin	8	2.9
Missouri	9	3.2	Wyoming	1	0.4

Table 3. Zero order correlations.

	TA	PS	PK	PW	JK	JW
TA	1.00					
PS	0.49^1	1.00				
PK	0.22^1	-0.04	1.00			
PW	0.22^1	-0.05	0.90^1	1.00		
JK	0.13^2	-0.16^2	0.77^1	0.81^1	1.00	
JW	0.16^2	-0.17^2	0.72^1	0.80^1	0.91^1	1.00

[1] $p < 0.01$; [2] $p < 0.05$

TA: Type of agency; PS: Population served; PK: Prosecutors' knowledge of digital evidence; PW: Prosecutors' willingness to prosecute; JK: Judges' knowledge of digital evidence; JW: Judges' willingness to admit digital evidence.

Table 2 presents the distribution of respondents by state. The state with the largest number of respondents was California (n = 19 agencies, 6.8%).

3.2   Survey Instrument

The survey instrument was developed based on other instruments that have been used to study law enforcement needs related to digital evidence and electronic crime [1, 7, 8, 15]. The questionnaire consisted of 34 items. The first five items collected demographic information about respondents. The remaining questions consisted of Likert scale dichotomous questions (yes/no) and two free-form questions. For heuristic purposes, the Likert scale answers were treated as interval data for the correlational analysis only.

4.   Survey Results

The survey data was analyzed for outliers, missing data and violations of test assumptions using standard SPSS procedures. Given the exploratory nature of the study, a two-tailed test of significance (p = 0.05) was used.

4.1   Correlation Analysis

The results of a zero order correlation analysis are presented in Table 3. The analysis indicates that a positive correlation exists between perceptions of judges' knowledge related to digital evidence and perceptions about their willingness to admit digital evidence at trial (r = 0.91, p = 0.00 < 0.01) (see Table 3). Also, positive correlations exist between perceptions of judges' knowledge and (i) perceptions of pros-

Table 4.   Percentages of criminal investigations involving digital evidence.

Type of Agency	≤25%	26-59%	51-75%	76-100%
Municipal	108 (88.5%)	8 (6.6%)	1 (0.8%)	5 (4.1%)
County Sheriff	44 (66.7%)	9 (13.6%)	9 (13.6%)	4 (6.1%)
County Police	13 (68.4%)	3 (15.8%)	2 (10.5%)	1 (5.3%)
State Police	33 (86.8%)	3 (7.9%)	1 (2.6%)	1 (2.6%)
Marshal	2 (66.7%)	1 (33.3%)	0 (0.0%)	0 (0.0%)
Bureau of Investigation	1 (33.3%)	1 (33.3%)	1 (33.3%)	0 (0.0%)
Merged County and Municipal	1 (100.0%)	0 (0.0%)	0 (0.0%)	0 (0.0%)
Total	202 (80.2%)	25 (9.9%)	14 (5.6%)	11 (4.4%)

ecutors' knowledge about digital evidence ($r = 0.77$, $p = 0.00$), and (ii) perceptions of prosecutors' willingness to prosecute cases involving digital evidence ($r = 0.81$, $p = 0.00$). Moreover, positive correlations exist between perceptions of judges' willingness to admit digital evidence and (i) perceptions of prosecutors' knowledge about digital evidence ($r = 0.72$, $p = 0.00$), and (ii) perceptions of prosecutors' willingness to prosecute cases involving digital evidence ($r = 0.80$, $p = .001$).

The results in Table 3 also show that negative correlations exist between the size of the population served by law enforcement agencies and (i) perceptions of judges' knowledge about digital evidence ($r = -0.17$, $p = 0.01$), and (ii) perceptions of judges' willingness to admit digital evidence ($r = -0.16$, $p = 0.01$). In other words, judges in smaller communities were perceived to be less willing to prosecute cases with digital evidence.

Positive correlations exist between the type of law enforcement agency and (i) perceptions of judges' knowledge of digital evidence ($r = 0.13$, $p = 0.04$), (ii) perceptions about judges' willingness to admit digital evidence ($r = 0.16$, $p = 0.01$), (iii) perceptions about prosecutors' knowledge of digital evidence ($r = 0.22$, $p = 0.00$), and (iv) perceptions about prosecutors' willingness to prosecute cases involving digital evidence ($r = 0.22$, $p = 0.00$).

4.2   Contingency Table Analysis

Table 4 summarizes the survey respondents' assessments of the percentages of criminal investigations that involved digital evidence. Note that 80% ($n = 202$) of the respondents reported that no more than 25% of investigations involved digital evidence, and only 4.4% ($n = 11$) of the respondents reported percentages greater than 76%. Moreover, there is

Table 5. Prosecutors' knowledge of digital evidence.

Population	L	S	ML	K	VK	NA	U	Total
≤50K	32	21	31	10	1	3	4	102
	31.4%	20.6%	30.4%	9.8%	1.0%	2.9%	3.9%	100.0%
50K-100K	3	2	3	1	0	1	1	11
	27.3%	18.2%	27.3%	9.1%	0.0%	9.1%	9.1%	100.0%
100K-250K	9	5	11	2	0	0	1	28
	32.1%	17.9%	39.3%	7.1%	0.0%	0.0%	3.6%	100.0%
250K-1M	9	15	24	10	7	2	0	67
	13.4%	22.4%	35.8%	14.9%	10.4%	3.0%	0.0%	100.0%
>1M	5	9	22	8	5	0	3	52
	9.6%	17.3%	42.3%	15.4%	9.6%	0.0%	5.8%	100.0%
Total	58	52	91	31	13	6	9	260
	22.3%	20.0%	35.0%	11.9%	5.0%	2.3%	3.5%	100.0%

L: Limited knowledge; ML: Moderately limited knowledge; K; Knowledgeable;
VK: Very knowledgeable; NA: Not applicable; U: Unknown.

no significant association between type of law enforcement agency and the percentage of cases involving digital evidence.

As this study was exploratory in nature, the traditional threshold of r = 0.20 for determining the relationships to investigate further was not followed. Each of the significant correlations stated was examined. The contingency table analysis indicates that with regard to the population served variable, only perceptions about (i) prosecutors' knowledge of digital evidence (likelihood ratio = 41.24, df = 20, p = 0.02), (ii) prosecutors' willingness to prosecute cases involving digital evidence (likelihood ratio = 31.5, df = 24, p = 0.02), and (iii) judges' willingness to admit digital evidence in cases (likelihood ratio = 34.32, df = 20, p = 0.02) were significant (see Tables 5, 6 and 7, respectively). Note that the population served variable was collapsed into five categories to reduce the number of cells with expected counts that are less than five.

5. Discussion of Results

The correlation analysis findings are not surprising, although care must be taken when interpreting the results because the dependent and independent variables are ordinal. The positive correlations between law enforcement agents' perceptions of prosecutors' and judges' knowledge of digital evidence and their willingness to prosecute cases/admit digital evidence are to be expected.

In general, law enforcement agencies in urban areas tend to serve larger populations. Therefore, the negative correlation between the pop-

Table 6.　Prosecutors' willingness to prosecute cases involving digital evidence.

Population	NW	SW	MW	EW	NA	U	Total
≤50K	1	39	36	16	2	6	100
	1.0%	39.0%	36.0%	16.0%	2.0%	6.0%	100.0%
50K-100K	0	2	5	3	1	0	11
	0.0%	18.2%	45.5%	27.3%	9.1%	0.0%	100.0%
100K-250K	0	7	13	7	0	1	28
	0.0%	25.0%	46.4%	25.0%	0.0%	3.6%	100.0%
250K-1M	1	10	25	28	2	1	67
	1.5%	14.9%	37.3%	41.8%	3.0%	1.5%	100.0%
>1M	2	12	21	13	0	3	51
	3.9%	23.5%	41.2%	25.5%	0.0%	5.9%	100.0%
Total	4	70	100	67	5	11	257
	1.6%	27.2%	38.9%	26.1%	1.9%	4.3%	100.0%

NW: Not at all willing; Somewhat willing; Moderately willing; Extremely willing;
NA: Not applicable; U: Unknown.

Table 7.　Judges' willingness to admit digital evidence.

Population	NW	SW	MW	EW	NA	U	Total
≤50K	2	28	35	10	4	11	90
	2.2%	31.1%	38.9%	11.1%	4.4%	12.2%	100.0%
50K-100K	0	2	4	1	1	1	9
	0.0%	22.2%	44.4%	11.1%	11.1%	11.1%	100.0%
100K-250K	0	4	15	7	0	1	27
	0.0%	14.8%	55.6%	25.9%	0.0%	3.7%	100.0%
250K-1M	0	9	39	17	1	2	68
	0.0%	13.2%	57.4%	25.0%	1.5%	2.9%	100.0%
>1M	0	7	30	11	0	3	51
	0.0%	13.7%	58.8%	21.6%	0.0%	5.9%	100.0%
Total	2	50	123	46	6	18	245
	0.8%	20.4%	50.2%	18.8%	2.4%	7.3%	100.0%

NW: Not at all willing; Somewhat willing; Moderately willing; Extremely willing;
NA: Not applicable; U: Unknown.

ulation served variable and perceptions of judges' knowledge and willingness to admit digital evidence may be an artifact of urban versus rural attitudes and the ubiquity of technology in urban settings, which would result in greater awareness and comfort in dealing with digital evidence. Note that all the correlations are lower than the usual threshold of r = 0.20 and are relatively weak.

The same observations hold for the positive correlations between the type of law enforcement agency and perceptions about prosecutors' and judges' knowledge of digital evidence and their willingness to prosecute cases/admit digital evidence. The correlations are also relatively weak. Intuitively, prosecutors and judges in urban areas have more exposure and comfort with digital evidence. Also, larger agencies typically have significant personnel and technological resources, enabling them to process digital evidence quickly and efficiently.

The results of contingency table analysis are very interesting. For one, 80% of the respondents reported that no more than 25% of their cases involved digital evidence. This is inconsistent with estimates reported by federal agencies (e.g., approximately 80% of the FBI's cases involve some form of digital evidence).

Even more interesting is the fact that agents from municipal departments reported that most of their cases did not involve digital evidence. One plausible reason is that state and local law enforcement agents mainly focus on traditional physical and/or document-based evidence because they have limited knowledge and resources to deal with digital evidence. This is consistent with the findings of several studies (e.g., [1, 7, 8, 14, 15]) that state and local law enforcement agents have inadequate training and resources for investigating computer crimes and cases involving digital evidence. This finding is troubling as valuable evidence is possibly being overlooked by law enforcement, which may result in dropped or reduced charges as well as wrongful convictions.

Positive relationships exist between the population served variable and perceptions of prosecutors' and judges' knowledge and willingness to prosecute cases/admit digital evidence. Law enforcement agents from larger communities indicated that prosecutors and judges had moderate knowledge and exhibited moderate willingness to prosecute cases/admit digital evidence. However, the Somers' d values for the contingency tables, while positive, were less than 0.20, which indicate weak relationships. These relationships are not surprising as they may be indicative of the rural versus urban effect.

Despite the positive finding using zero order correlation, contingency table analysis did not reveal a significant relationship between the population served variable and perceptions of judges' knowledge about digital evidence. This may be due to the fact that both variables are ordinal, which can affect Pearson correlation analysis. Specifically, problems arise when Likert scale data is treated as interval scale data. In such cases, contingency table analysis using a likelihood ratio is more appropriate. Note also that in the contingency table analysis, several cells had expected counts less than five; this required the use of the likelihood ratio to determine significance.

Since the survey was restricted to U.S. state and local law enforcement agents, caution must be exercised when attempting to generalize these findings to the international community. Future studies should examine the international law enforcement community's perceptions and capabilities related to digital evidence.

6.   Conclusions

The exploratory study of the perceptions of state and local law enforcement agents provides guidance on conducting further investigations on attitudes and requirements related to the use of digital evidence in legal proceedings. The study also provides empirical support for anecdotal reports about law enforcement perceptions regarding digital evidence. The study finds that the current situation regarding digital evidence is similar to how it was with DNA evidence some years ago. Specifically, in the face of limited education, training and awareness, professionals are unwilling to compromise cases by attempting processes (law enforcement agents) and procedures (attorneys and judges) with which they are unfamiliar. The question is: How do we educate and train "teams" of professionals (law enforcement agents, attorneys and judges) who are willing to treat digital evidence with the same familiarity as physical evidence and to use it as evidence in legal proceedings?

Clearly, law enforcement agents from larger organizations with more resources for education, training and awareness, and better facilities for processing digital evidence would be more willing to treat digital evidence in a more routine manner. However, when one considers that the overwhelming majority (approximately 90%) of U.S. law enforcement agencies are relatively small, it is troubling to note that valuable evidence is likely being overlooked by law enforcement, which may result in dropped or reduced charges as well as wrongful convictions. It is, therefore, extremely important to implement broad initiatives that raise the level of expertise of state and local law enforcement agents (as well as attorneys and judges) to ensure that digital evidence is introduced routinely and successfully in legal proceedings.

References

[1] E. Appel and M. Pollitt, Report on the Digital Evidence Needs Survey of State, Local and Tribal Law Enforcement, National Institute of Justice, U.S. Department of Justice, Washington, DC (www.jciac .org/docs/Digital%20Evidence%20Survey%20Report.pdf), 2005.

[2] H. Armstrong and P. Russo, Electronic forensics education needs of law enforcement, *Proceedings of the Eighth Colloquium on Information Systems Security Education*, 2004.

[3] M. Caloyannides, *Computer Forensics and Privacy*, Artech House, Norwood, Massachusetts, 2001.

[4] E. Casey (Ed.), *Handbook of Computer Crime Investigation: Forensic Tools and Technology*, Elsevier, London, United Kingdom, 2002.

[5] R. Clifford, D. Moreau, M. Miquelon-Weismann, D. Lamb, I. Orton, J. Savage and S. Brenner, *Cybercrime: The Investigation, Prosecution and Defense of Computer-Related Crime*, Carolina Academic Press, Durham, North Carolina, 2006.

[6] B. Etter, The challenges of policing cyberspace, *Proceedings of the NetSafe II Conference* (www.netsafe.org.nz/Doc_Library/netsafepapers_barbaraetter_policing.pdf), 2003.

[7] Institute for Security Technology Studies (ISTS), Law Enforcement Tools and Technologies for Investigating Cyber Attacks: A National Needs Assessment, Dartmouth College, Hanover, New Hampshire (www.ists.dartmouth.edu/TAG/lena.htm), 2002.

[8] Institute for Security Technology Studies (ISTS), Law Enforcement Tools and Technologies for Investigating Cyber Attacks: Gap Analysis Report, Dartmouth College, Hanover, New Hampshire (www.ists.dartmouth.edu/TAG/gap_analysis.htm), 2004.

[9] E. Lambert, T. Nerbonne, P. Watson, J. Buss, A. Clarke, N. Hogan, S. Barton and J. Lambert, The forensic science needs of law enforcement applicants and recruits: A survey of Michigan law enforcement agencies, *Journal of Criminal Justice Education*, vol. 14(1), pp. 67–81, 2003.

[10] M. Losavio, J. Adams and M. Rogers, Gap analysis: Judicial experience and perception of electronic evidence, *Journal of Digital Forensic Practice*, vol. 1(1), pp. 13–17, 2006.

[11] A. Marcella and R. Greenfield (Eds.), *Cyber Forensics: A Field Manual for Collecting, Examining and Preserving Evidence of Computer Crimes*, Auerbach/CRC Press, Boca Raton, Florida, 2002.

[12] R. Mercuri, Challenges in forensic computing, *Communications of the ACM*, vol. 48(12), pp. 17–21, 2005.

[13] B. Reaves and M. Hickman, Census of state and local law enforcement agencies, 2000, *Bureau of Justice Statistics Bulletin*, NCJ 194066, U.S. Department of Justice, Washington, DC (www.ojp.usdoj.gov/bjs/pub/pdf/csllea00.pdf), 2002.

[14] M. Rogers and K. Seigfried, The future of computer forensics: A needs analysis survey, *Computers and Security*, vol. 23(1), pp. 12–16, 2004.

[15] H. Stambaugh, D. Beaupre, D. Icove, R. Baker, W. Cassady and W. Wiliams, State and local law enforcement needs to combat electronic crime, National Institute of Justice, U.S. Department of Justice, Washington, DC (www.ncjrs.gov/pdffiles1/nij/183451.pdf), 2000.

II

INSIDER THREAT DETECTION

Chapter 4

INSIDER THREAT ANALYSIS USING INFORMATION-CENTRIC MODELING

D. Ha, S. Upadhyaya, H. Ngo, S. Pramanik, R. Chinchani and
S. Mathew

Abstract   Capability acquisition graphs (CAGs) provide a powerful framework for
modeling insider threats, network attacks and system vulnerabilities.
However, CAG-based security modeling systems have yet to be deployed
in practice. This paper demonstrates the feasibility of applying CAGs
to insider threat analysis. In particular, it describes the design and operation of an information-centric, graphics-oriented tool called ICMAP.
ICMAP enables an analyst without any theoretical background to apply
CAGs to answer security questions about vulnerabilities and likely attack scenarios, as well as to monitor network nodes. This functionality
makes the tool very useful for attack attribution and forensics.

Keywords: Insider threats, capability acquisition graphs, key challenge graphs

1.   Introduction

A comprehensive model is required for understanding, reducing and
preventing enterprise network attacks, and for identifying and combating
system vulnerabilities and insider threats. Attacks on enterprise networks are often complex, involving multiple sites, multiple stages and
the exploitation of various vulnerabilities. As a consequence, security
analysts must consider massive amounts of information about network
topology, system configurations, software vulnerabilities, and even social information. Integrating and analyzing all this information is an
overwhelming task.

A security analyst has to determine how best to represent individual
components and interactions when developing a model of a computing
environment. Depending on the environment and task at hand, the analyst may deal with network traffic data [15], routing data [14], network

Please use the following format when citing this chapter:

Ha, D., Upadhyaya, S., Ngo, H., Pramanik, S., Chinchani, R., Mathew, S., 2007, in IFIP International Federation for
Information Processing, Volume 242, Advances in Digital Forensics III; eds. P. Craiger and S Shenoi; (Boston:
Springer), pp. 55-73.

connections [2], and, in the case of static analysis, network configurations [13]. Visualization is an effective method for integrating and analyzing diverse information, mostly because humans can process large amounts of data through images, maps and graphs.

For this reason, attack graphs have received considerable attention by the research community [6, 8, 10, 11]. Attack graphs provide a powerful visual framework for understanding the effects of the interactions of local vulnerabilities and for identifying global, less visible vulnerabilities that are combinations of local vulnerabilities.

However, attack graphs have several limitations. The manual construction of attack graphs for real network configurations is labor intensive, tedious and error-prone; this means that automating the construction of attack graphs is critical. Several attack graph methods employ model checking, which often produces an internal state explosion. This is because model checking may examine all possible states although only a fraction of states are eventually analyzed. Large state spaces require significant processing time; for example, the NuSMV tool may take two hours to analyze a network with a handful of hosts [12]. Even when they are available, attack graph tools lack automation features and support for interpreting results. For example, initial configuration data is usually required as input, but its format is unnatural for humans, e.g., Boolean tables for network connectivity or binary relations for capturing all relationships [12]. Furthermore, due to their size and notational differences, it can be difficult to relate attack graphs to the original physical context; this is a task often left to the user.

Capability acquisition graphs (CAGs) (formerly known as key challenge graphs (KCGs)) have been proposed as a modeling technique for insider threat analysis [4, 5]. From the user's point of view, CAGs are more intuitive than attack graphs because they closely resemble the input network topology [5]. Although originally developed for insider threat modeling, CAGs are capable of modeling vulnerability-exploited privilege escalation, similar to attack graphs.

This paper describes a novel CAG-based tool, which we call ICMAP (Information-Centric Modeler and Auditor Program). ICMAP has several useful features:

- Users may import information in a convenient, systematic manner. The initial input to ICMAP is a physical graph, which is easy to construct as it is similar to a network configuration.

- ICMAP automatically converts the physical graph to a logical graph (CAG). Users may adjust the CAG and add new relationships before performing further analysis.

- System analysts may use ICMAP to answer questions about the security of network setups, likely attack strategies and vulnerable points. ICMAP helps in identifying locations for positioning monitoring systems. The results are also mapped to the original network context, making the display easy to comprehend.

- Streaming alerts from IDS sensors and network monitoring tools can be correlated to generate attack tracks. These attack tracks can be compared with projected tracks during off-line analysis to narrow probable attack paths and facilitate forensic analysis.

The next section presents an overview of CAGs and their applications to threat assessment. Section 3 describes the architecture of ICMAP, a CAG-based information-centric modeling and analysis tool. Sections 4 and 5 discuss cost assignment techniques, scalability issues, and a scenario involving a corporate network. Section 6 examines the forensic applications of CAGs and CAG-based tools. The final section, Section 7, presents our conclusions and discusses avenues for future research.

2. Capability Acquisition Graphs

This section describes capability acquisition graphs (CAGs), which were formerly known as key challenge graphs (KCGs) [5].

DEFINITION 1 *A capability acquisition graph is a tuple represented by:*

$$CAG = (V, E, K, V_0, V_S, \pi, \delta) \tag{1}$$

V is a set of nodes; each entity in the physical network (hosts, firewalls, user accounts) has a node in the graph. E is a set of edges; two nodes are connected by an edge if it is possible to reach one node from the other. K is a set of tokens; a token can represent system information or individual information (e.g., password, date-of-birth or mother's maiden name). V_0 is the set of start nodes from where an attack can be launched; the skill set of an attacker can be modeled by adjusting the set V_0. V_S is the set of target nodes in the logical graph that an attacker intends to compromise. The function $\pi : V \to K$ assigns tokens to nodes, e.g., a database node may have records as tokens. The function $\delta : E \to K \times N \times N$ represents the edge attributes, consisting of token challenges and transition costs.

A CAG can be viewed as an abstract representation of a user's walk in a network. The user starts from a particular node in the graph with certain tokens (knowledge). From the starting node, the user chooses an edge, $e(u, v) = (token, min, max)$, to move to an adjacent node. If the *token* is already present in his set of knowledge, he incurs a cost of *min* otherwise he incurs a cost of *max*. If V' is the set of visited vertices, then the cost of visiting a new vertex $v \notin V'$ is the minimum cost edge (u, v) for all $u \in V'$. The cost of an attack sequence or attack trail $(v_1, v_2, \ldots, v_n)$ is the sum of the costs of visiting a new vertex from the set of already-visited vertices. An attacker might try to minimize his cost of reaching a target node by choosing edges with simple token challenges. The goal of a systems administrator is to maximize the cost of attacks by assigning proper token challenges to the edges. By enumerating the paths of least resistance it is possible to identify the most likely attack paths and either remove them from the network or place sensors along the path to detect the attacks.

Model specification begins by identifying the scope of the threat; it could be a small portion of the organization or the entire organization. The size of the resulting model is a polynomial function of the input information. However, the problem of determining the cost of least resistance in a CAG is NP-Hard [4]. In fact, the problem is not even approximable to within $2^{(\log n)^{1-\delta}}$ where $\delta = 1 - \frac{1}{\log \log^c n}$ for any $c < 1/2$. Therefore, finding a least cost attack in an efficient manner is not possible unless P = NP.

A greedy heuristic approach involving a one-step lookahead may be used to identify an optimal walk [4, 5]. Note that even if a shorter path to a goal exists, an attacker might avoid it believing that sensors might be placed along the path. Therefore, the greedy heuristic approach has to be run multiple times to identify the k best paths instead of one optimal path. CAGs can also represent social engineering channels (e.g., telephone lines when identifying insider abuse paths). Due to the lack of tools for measuring security weaknesses in organizations, which is a primary concern for assessing insider threats, the majority of the tasks related to modeling and analyzing social engineering links fall on the security analyst.

3.   ICMAP Architecture

This section describes ICMAP (Information-Centric Modeler and Auditor Program), a CAG-based information-centric modeling and analysis tool.

3.1   ICMAP Framework

The ICMAP framework is presented in Figure 1. The ICMAP engine is the core of the CAG generation process. It takes the physical network topology and information about vulnerabilities in network services as external inputs, and combines them with network translation rules (Section 3.3) and cost rules (Section 4.1) to obtain the CAG. Once the

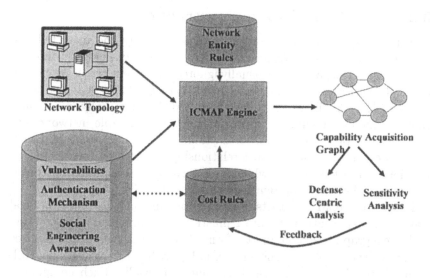

Figure 1. ICMAP framework.

CAG is constructed, various heuristics, e.g., 1-step, k-step (constant k) and n-step lookahead techniques, can be used to find an optimal path from a source to a destination without having to enumerate all possible paths. Also, using combinations of source and destination pairs, it is possible to identify the best locations to position network sensors.

Two separate analyses can be performed on a CAG to refine a threat assessment. The first is sensitivity analysis where different cost assignments are used to identify the optimal cost assignment that results in attack paths that are similar to known attacks. The second is to perform a defense-centric analysis where sensors are placed along the paths of least resistance to help prevent network assets from being compromised. The cost assignment is refined based on these two analyses.

The ICMAP engine is written in Java. It incorporates a GUI that closely models real-world network components. Network topology information such as connectivity and services are imported using drop-down and pop-up menus. ICMAP also engages an underlying database of common entities such as vulnerabilities and services, which users may add to or modify using ICMAP's local menu. To promote interoperability, ICMAP uses the MySQL database management system, and its outputs are in XML format.

3.2   Physical Graph Construction

Entering network configuration data is arguably the most tedious, error-prone and labor intensive work for any security analyst. Unfortunately, this is the part that is usually ignored by current graph generation tools. The data is either not mentioned [1] or implicitly assumed to be provided [12, 13]. Even when data is provided, it is usually in a format that is difficult for humans to comprehend. For example, network connectivity is represented as a Boolean table where the columns and rows are network hosts, and all trust relationships are represented as binary relations. Needless to say, while these formats may simplify computer processing, they are a burden for human analysts.

In contrast, ICMAP assists users in importing data in a most natural way using visualization. Figure 2 illustrates the process of constructing a physical graph based on input information about accounts and services for a host (the topology is shown later in Figure 3). Two types of network entities are depicted: normal hosts and a firewall. Each component serves a different role; therefore, it is associated with a different set of menus for further configuration (e.g., account and service information for hosts and filter rules represented as token/key for firewalls). The component type determines the conversion to a CAG. ICMAP supports several types of components: hosts, firewalls, LANs, database servers, hubs/bridges and switches; additional component types are currently being implemented.

3.3   Logical Graph Construction

ICMAP automates the construction of a logical graph (CAG) from a physical graph. This section describes the process, including the basic rules used to identify the nodes, edges and tokens in a CAG.

As discussed in the context of a physical graph, a network consists of hosts, physical boundary creators such as routers and firewalls, network services such as ssh, ftp, http and nfs, and databases. A host contains the host id, user accounts, network services, vulnerabilities and critical files (henceforth called "jewels"). In order to build the CAG, for each host, it is necessary to draw the user account nodes, service nodes, vulnerability nodes and jewel nodes. A user (or a malicious insider) either connects to a service remotely or logs in from the console. Once the user gains access to a host he uses the network resource and connects to another host, uses the file system resource and edits files, exploits vulnerabilities to escalate his privileges, or uses the cpu resource on the host to execute programs, check mails, browse, etc. To represent the above activities, edges (with their token challenges) are drawn entering

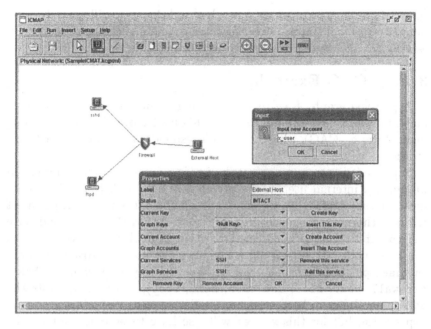

Figure 2. Constructing a physical graph.

the user accounts. The token challenges are marked on the edges. If the token is known, then traversing the edge incurs a cost of *LOW*, otherwise a cost of *HIGH* is incurred. Edges marked "0" do not have a token challenge, so they always incur a cost of *LOW*. From the user accounts there exist zero-cost transitions to the host service, and from the host there exist transitions to other accounts in the network. We also add zero-cost transitions from the root account to other accounts in the same host to express the fact that the root can become any user. Once a user gets to the host, vulnerabilities in the services can be exploited; thus edges are drawn from the services to their vulnerabilities. The tokens in the vulnerability node can be used to escalate privileges (e.g., become root). Finally, edges exist from the user accounts and network services (e.g., ssh and ftp) to the file system (e.g., nfs) of the host and from the file system to the jewels.

It is important to mention that the automatic graph conversion is intended to reduce the work of analysts, not to limit it. After the conversion, an analyst can still perform various adjustments to the logical graph (e.g., add/remove relationships, tokens and change the costs). Adjustments to the physical graph at this step are also automatically updated to the CAG. Because a CAG does not incorporate icons as in a physical graph, it employs various colors and shapes to differentiate component types and status. These features promote visual comprehension, especially when dealing with large networks.

3.4   CAG Example

A physical graph of a subnet consisting of an ssh server, ftp server and a firewall is presented in Figure 3. Figure 4 shows the corresponding logical graph (CAG) whose nodes correspond to the various network entities.

Suppose it is necessary to determine if an external user, x-user, can become an internal user in the presence of a firewall that allows only incoming ssh traffic. To become root on the ssh server, x-user must traverse the node sequence (x-user, host, firewall, root) and have the root_pd token to make the transition from the firewall node to the root node. If x-user does not have the root_pd token but only the user_pd token, then he can traverse the sequence (x-user, host, firewall, user, sshd, ssh-vuln, sshd, root), where he exploits the ssh vulnerability to become root. Similar steps can be followed for the ftp service, but for this x-user will also have to become root on the firewall by changing the firewall rules.

3.5   System Analysis

A major goal of any graph-based security analysis is to identify likely attack scenarios based on system configuration and settings, attacker's knowledge and potential targets. This task can be done quite easily using ICMAP. All the nodes corresponding to the initial states of the attacker are marked as compromised. The nodes corresponding to entities that must be protected (e.g., root account on a host) are marked as targets.

Next, the CAG is analyzed using brute force or a heuristic Dijkstra-like algorithm. In our experience, a brute force approach is not practical for graphs with more than 20 nodes. Readers are referred to [4] for a discussion of the brute force and heuristic algorithms. The final top k attack scenarios (based on minimum total cost), where k is a configurable parameter, are returned in a separate file; only the top scenario is displayed by ICMAP. Note that because the CAG nodes do not represent network states as in attack graphs, each scenario is not necessarily a path, but a walk (or a trail) with some nodes visited multiple times. Presenting a walk using directed edges on top of a logical graph is visually complicated, so ICMAP only shows the induced spanning tree of a walk. However, it is still possible to visualize the complete attack sequence using ICMAP's animation feature.

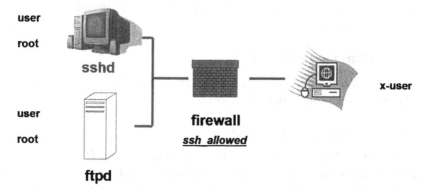

Figure 3. Physical graph of a subnet.

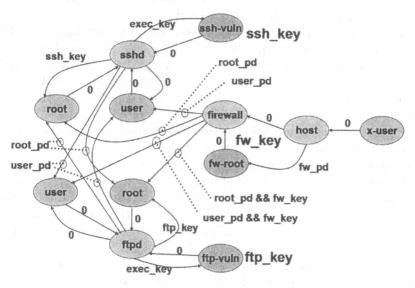

Figure 4. Logical graph of a subnet.

An attacker does not necessarily follow the shortest path when attempting to compromise a computer system or network. Critical points are points in a graph that the attacker has to pass through no matter what attack trail is chosen. These points suggest critical weaknesses in the system such as certain service vulnerabilities. They are also ideal locations for system administrators to deploy IDS sensors or security controls.

ICMAP is able to identify the critical points in a graph. ICMAP recommends these points based on the top k walks returned from the analysis (see Section 5). Note that finding the set of critical points is an NP-Hard problem [9].

4.   Practical Issues

This section discusses practical issues related to CAGs, including cost assignment, scalability and abstraction.

4.1   Cost Assignment

After identifying the nodes, edges and tokens in a CAG, the next step is to assign costs to the edges. The costs are determined based on attack templates, CERT vulnerability reports (www.cert.org), attacker privileges, and the assets that must be protected. They are divided into three categories: LOW, MEDIUM and HIGH; however, the number of cost categories can be adjusted as desired.

The cost of a transaction depends on certain categories, e.g., authentication mechanism, system patching rate, knowledge of vulnerability, etc. We begin by describing the cost values determined by each category and then present a technique for combining the cost values. Note that attack graphs either assign probabilities for transitions based on the transition profile [12] or implicitly consider zero costs for atomic attacks.

Figure 5 presents the two-tier classification hierarchy used for determining costs. The top tier consists of categories such as remote services, level of social engineering and authentication mechanism. The second tier consists of the security level within each category. For example, remote services can be accessed in cleartext, or through the use of an authentication mechanism on top of cleartext, or via an encrypted channel with authentication. The difficulty of compromising such services increases as one moves down security levels (Figure 5); hence, the cost increases. The classification hierarchy is not fixed, and may be extended by adding more categories and security levels. Also note that the actual numeric values of the cost categories, as well as the default costs are stored in the database and can be set at the user's convenience through the ICMAP configuration menu.

The minimum and maximum costs of traversing an edge are computed by querying the cost database. Figure 6 illustrates the queries made for two edges. The first edge represents a connection to the root account through the ftp service. Assuming that the ftp service belongs to categories such as authentication mechanism, remote access method, social engineering, and resources being protected, the cost for each category is determined; these are then combined to compute the overall cost.

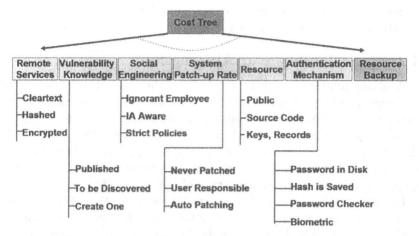

Figure 5. Cost tree.

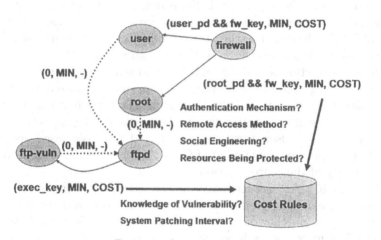

Figure 6. Cost computation.

The second edge is the cost of exploiting a vulnerability in the `ftp` server. Queries are made for the knowledge of vulnerability and the system patching rate to find the cost of this edge. The cost is computed by taking the average of the values returned by the queries and using the average as an exponent so that the cost increases exponentially as the difficulty of making the transition increases. Thus, if $n_1, n_2, \ldots, n_k$ are the responses of the k queries made to the cost database, then the cost of the edge is $2^{\frac{\sum_{i=1}^{k} n_i}{k}}$. For flexibility, the actual numeric value corresponding to each category is also stored in the database and can be adjusted via the configuration menu.

4.2   Scalability and Abstraction

A major limitation of attack graphs is their inability to deal with the large numbers of states involved in real-world applications. This issue becomes critical for visualization-based tools – when the graph is too large, it is extremely difficult for security analysts to assimilate the presentation and manipulate the graph, significantly impeding the analysis. Consequently, it is important to reduce the size of an attack graph without hindering the accuracy of the representation.

In contrast, the size of a CAG is a polynomial function of the number of hosts, services, accounts and vulnerabilities. In fact, the number of CAG vertices equals the total number of these entities. Moreover, the number of edges is quite small because certain connection topologies can be abstracted at the logical level. For example, a physical ring topology of hosts is represented not as full mesh, but as a star topology in the logical CAG. The center of this star is an abstract node representing the connections of individual hosts in the original topology.

Other abstraction techniques may also be used to reduce the complexity of the final graph. One approach is to consider generalized, role-based accounts. This is due to the fact that administrators often manage multiple user accounts as groups sharing the same privileges, rather than dealing with each user account separately. Using role-based accounts significantly reduces the number of CAG vertices without compromising the accuracy of the representation.

However, ICMAP has certain scalability issues that remain to be addressed. For example, even when the number of CAG vertices is a linear function of the number of vulnerabilities, dealing with a database of a thousand or more entries is overwhelming. Fortunately, it is not necessary to represent each vulnerability in the CAG; instead, a representative abstract node can be created for each service. We intend to implement this capability in a future version of ICMAP.

5.   Enterprise Network Example

This section illustrates the use of a CAG for modeling an enterprise network. In particular, the example elicits the relationships between hosts, services, users and vulnerabilities. The network has subnets corresponding to four departments. Each domain has several network services, hosts, resources and user accounts. One or more network services are associated with a host and every host has at least one user account and one root account. Moreover, every service has at least one vulnerability, which can be exploited to obtain root access.

Figure 7 presents the network topology. The Civil Affairs, Logistics and Procurement network domains each have five machines while the Security network domain has seven machines. Each machine runs a service and has at least two accounts (one root and one normal account). Figure 8 presents the corresponding physical graph constructed by ICMAP. Note that all the information (services, user accounts and tokens) is not shown in the figure, but these are imported into the CAG.

Figure 9 presents the CAG generated by ICMAP from the physical graph. Hosts are represented by square boxes, accounts by circles, and vulnerabilities by ellipses. The source is selected to be the account rd_ooty on Ooty, while the target is a jewel file on Taos. In the current setup, only the root account on Taos has access to the jewel. However, ICMAP's analysis discovered that an insider could access the file by logging into Ooty as rd_ooty, then logging into Taos as rd_taos, exploiting a sshd vulnerability to become root_taos, and finally accessing the jewel file. Figure 9 also shows a superimposed attack trail, which may be displayed as an animation.

ICMAP recommended that network sensors be positioned at the LAN, switch, source and target. These recommendations are expected; however, the real benefits of ICMAP are realized when the network being analyzed is large and a limited number of sensors can be placed.

6. Forensic Applications

Forensic tools such as EnCase Enterprise Automated Incident Response Suite provide sophisticated data gathering and analysis capabilities, but are not as useful at assisting with investigations of insider attacks. Due to the complexity of insider attacks, special guidance schemes are necessary to perform attack attribution. The digital forensics research community has only recently started to address this issue. One strategy is to use a layered genetic algorithm-based technique to generate an optimized rule set that identifies unauthorized processes and performs role-based process verification [3]. However, this work is only at a preliminary stage and is admittedly fraught with false alarms. This section describes two strategies through which the attack semantics embedded in ICMAP can be used to facilitate post-attack analysis.

As seen in the previous sections, ICMAP's off-line analysis produces a list of top k probable attack trails. These trails are constructed based on the knowledge of network topology, service vulnerabilities, authentication mechanisms used for the various services and social engineering

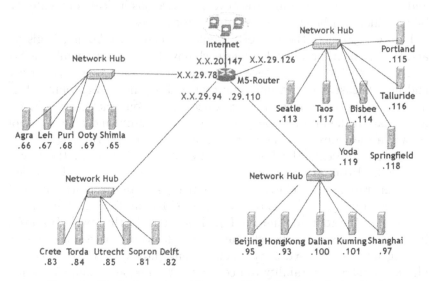

Figure 7.   Testbed topology (Courtesy Telcordia Technologies, Inc.).

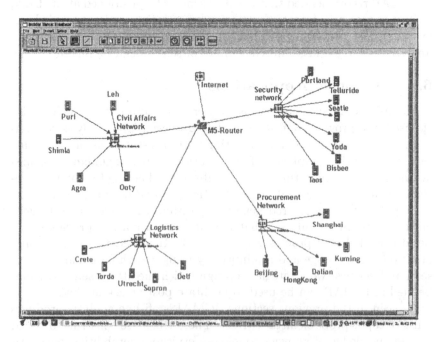

Figure 8.   Physical topology.

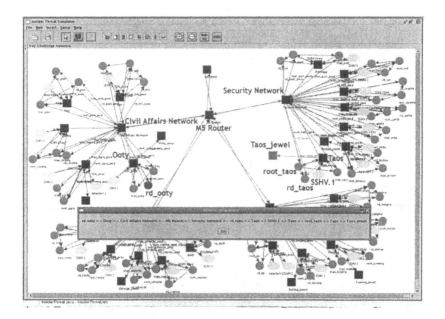

Figure 9. Security analysis results along with a superimposed attack trail.

possibilities. In a system where alerts from intrusion detection sensors and audit logs (Apache, Windows IIS log files, etc.) are monitored, such real-time data can be used to narrow down the list of probable attack trails. Since the ICMAP-generated attack trails already have the attack semantics embedded in them (attack origination nodes and possible attack sequences), the real-time data can be utilized in a variety of ways to understand the details of the attacks.

The first strategy requires no changes to the CAG model and the ICMAP engine. The top k attack trails that are generated *a priori* by ICMAP constitute the most likely attacks on the system. The set of likely attacks can be further refined using forensic data such as IDS alerts and audit logs (Figure 10). The refinement can be run periodically at the discretion of the system analyst or forensic investigator.

The refinement module can make use of well-known techniques for correlating alerts in the case of multi-stage attacks. These techniques would label involved nodes (hosts) either as stepping stones or as victims of full-fledged attacks. Bayesian causality graphs [7] could then be used to construct evidence graphs from the evidence stream obtained from the log events. Having created the evidence graphs, a sequence of nodes may be extracted from these graphs and matched (fully or partially) with the

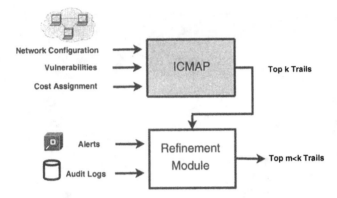

Figure 10.   Combining monitored data sequentially for forensic analysis.

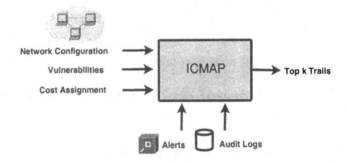

Figure 11.   Combining monitored data with static knowledge for forensic analysis.

k attack trails generated by ICMAP to determine $m < k$ most probable attack trails. In a sense, the refinement module works as a likelihood function in statistics. Indeed, some likelihood estimators could play a major role in implementing the module.

The second strategy is to use a notion of "distance" to indicate how close an attack is to the observed data stream. For instance, depending on how real-life events are captured and modeled, an investigator may be able to reconstruct the CAG edges that most likely caused the security compromise. This way the set of events would correlate strongly to a set of CAG edges. A suitable distance function in this case is the number of "real-life" edges contained in an attack trail.

The first strategy is highly modular, allowing for increased design flexibility. The main limitation is inaccuracy due to the fact that the top k attack scenarios are generated *a priori* without considering the events that actually occurred.

Implementing the second strategy requires the CAG model and the ICMAP engine to be modified to accommodate incremental updates of the physical network graphs (Figure 11). For example, logged events may change tokens at vertices, edge costs and token challenges. Each incremental update to the parameters and/or topology of the CAG requires an adjustment to the top k attack trails. Ensuring that the current heuristic technique works with on-line updates is an important topic for future research. This feature is useful not only for forensic purposes, but also for speeding up the heuristic technique when there are actual (good) changes made by system administrators. The advantage of this strategy is more accurate input, which leads to more accurate top k trails.

7. Conclusions

According to the annual CSI/FBI surveys, internal attacks and insider abuse constitute a significant portion of security incidents in enterprise networks. Insider attacks are extremely damaging and can be launched with a short or non-existent reconnaissance phase. Security controls such as firewalls and intrusion detection systems developed to protect against external attacks are inadequate because insider attacks may be launched from any server and from a position of privilege in terms of resource access and knowledge of targets and vulnerabilities. Consequently, insider threat detection and attack attribution have become major issues, which are just beginning to be addressed by the research community.

The ICMAP tool presented in this paper is very effective at modeling insider threats, analyzing vulnerabilities and evaluating sensor deployment locations. Red teams can also use the tool to determine attack trails when evaluating network security.

ICMAP has several features that make it very useful for conducting post-incident (forensic) analyses. In particular, it captures the semantics of possible insider attacks via the generation of top k attack trails. Moreover, the CAG representation retains the topological structure of the enterprise network; this facilitates the mapping and displaying of the results of forensic analysis in the original network context.

Our future research will refine the cost estimation process of ICMAP based on larger real-world experiments. Also, we will investigate summarization methods to address scalability while retaining the visualization features. Another important topic is to enhance automation capabilities, e.g., automatic configuration, file input and output format conversion (to promote interoperability with other tools). Finally, we will work on refining ICMAP to support large-scale network forensic investigations, which require comprehensive analysis and visualization facilities.

References

[1] P. Ammann, D. Wijesekera and S. Kaushik, Scalable, graph-based network vulnerability analysis, *Proceedings of the Ninth ACM Conference on Computer and Communications Security*, pp. 217–224, 2002.

[2] R. Ball, G. Fink and C. North, Home-centric visualization of network traffic for security administration, *Proceedings of the ACM Workshop on Visualization and Data Mining for Computer Security*, pp. 55–64, 2004.

[3] P. Bradford and N. Hu, A layered approach to insider threat detection and proactive forensics, *Proceedings of the Twenty-First Annual Computer Security Applications Conference (Technology Blitz)*, 2005.

[4] R. Chinchani, D. Ha, A. Iyer, H. Ngo and S. Upadhyaya, On the hardness of approximating the Min-Hack problem, *Journal of Combinatorial Optimization*, vol. 9(3), pp. 295–311, 2005.

[5] R. Chinchani, A. Iyer, H. Ngo and S. Upadhyaya, Towards a theory of insider threat assessment, *Proceedings of the International Conference on Dependable Systems and Networks*, pp. 108–117, 2005.

[6] M. Dacier and Y. Deswarte, Privilege graph: An extension to the typed access matrix model, *Proceedings of the European Symposium on Research in Computer Security*, pp. 319–334, 1994.

[7] M. Jordan (Ed.), *Learning in Graphical Models*, MIT Press, Cambridge, Massachusetts, 1998.

[8] S. Mauw and M. Oostdijk, Foundations of attack trees, in *Information Security and Cryptography (LNCS 3935)*, D. Won and S. Kim (Eds.), Springer, Berlin-Heidelberg, Germany, pp. 186–198, 2005.

[9] C. Phillips, The network inhibition problem, *Proceedings of the Twenty-Fifth Annual ACM Symposium on the Theory of Computing*, pp. 776–785, 1993.

[10] C. Phillips and L. Swiler, A graph-based system for network vulnerability analysis, *Proceedings of the New Security Paradigms Workshop*, pp. 71–79, 1998.

[11] B. Schneier, Attack trees: Modeling security threats, *Dr. Dobb's Journal*, December 1999.

[12] O. Sheyner, J. Haines, S. Jha, R. Lippmann and J. Wing, Automated generation and analysis of attack graphs, *Proceedings of the IEEE Symposium on Security and Privacy*, pp. 273–284, 2002.

[13] L. Swiler, C. Phillips, D. Ellis and S. Chakerian, Computer-attack graph generation tool, *Proceedings of the DARPA Information Survivability Conference and Exposition*, vol. 2, pp. 307–321, 2001.

[14] S. Teoh, K. Ma and S. Wu, A visual exploration process for the analysis of Internet routing data, *Proceedings of the Fourteenth IEEE Visualization Conference*, pp. 523–530, 2003.

[15] X. Yin, W. Yurcik, M. Treaster, Y. Li and K. Lakkaraju, Visflow-connect: Netflow visualizations of link relationships for security situational awareness, *Proceedings of the ACM Workshop on Visualization and Data Mining for Computer Security*, pp. 26–34, 2004.

Chapter 5

AN INTEGRATED SYSTEM FOR INSIDER THREAT DETECTION

Daniel Ray and Phillip Bradford

Abstract   This paper describes a proof-of-concept system for detecting insider threats. The system measures insider behavior by observing a user's processes and threads, information about user mode and kernel mode time, network interface statistics, etc. The system is built using Microsoft's Windows Management Instrumentation (WMI) implementation of the Web Based Enterprise Management (WBEM) standards. It facilitates the selection and storage of potential digital evidence based on anomalous user behavior with minimal administrative input.

Keywords: Insider threats, anomaly detection, proactive forensics

1.   Introduction

Insider threats are "menaces to computer security as a result of unauthorized system misuses by stakeholders of an organization" [3]. A substantial percentage of reported computer crime incidents are perpetrated by insiders [6]. Insider attacks are problematic because they are difficult to detect, and because insiders are likely to have intimate knowledge about potential targets as well as physical and logical access to the targets. Insider threat detection systems seek to discover attacks perpetrated by organization insiders.

Our insider threat model [2] analyzes computer use from a behavioral perspective such as data about the programs that employees use on a daily basis and the programs' underlying processes. Our research suggests that illicit activities are indicated by variations from a statistical norm (anomaly detection). Moreover, to be effective, an insider threat detection system must remotely and unobtrusively gather aggregate information about user workstation activity for analysis.

Please use the following format when citing this chapter:

Ray, D., Bradford, P., 2007, in IFIP International Federation for Information Processing, Volume 242, Advances in Digital Forensics III; eds. P. Craiger and S Shenoi; (Boston: Springer), pp. 75-86.

The generalized statistical approach to detecting intrusions was first outlined by Denning [5]. Research on statistical intrusion detection is described in [7] and in several survey articles [1, 10, 13, 14]. Significant efforts include SRI's EMERALD [19], a distributed system for intrusion detection in large-scale networks, and the use of data mining for dynamic intrusion detection by Lee, *et al.* [12]. More recently, Kahai and colleagues [11] proposed a system for profiling external attacks while proactively storing forensic information in the event of compromise. Our insider threat detection approach draws from research in intrusion detection and the sequential hypothesis testing approach to proactive forensics [2, 3].

Our proof-of-concept insider threat system makes use of the Web Based Enterprise Management (WBEM) standards. The WBEM initiative was created to address the difficulty of dynamically managing distributed IT environments; its goal was to develop a set of standards that unified the management of diverse systems [4]. The idea was that companies would embrace the WBEM initiative and develop systems conforming with WBEM standards, making it possible for a single application to manage all the components of an IT infrastructure. Microsoft adopted the WBEM standards in its Windows Management Instrumentation (WMI) architecture. WMI inherits classes defined according to the WBEM standards, which makes management data available in structured form.

This paper discusses how development tools targeted for system administration (based on WBEM/WMI) can serve as the foundation for a real-time insider threat detection system. Our approach is fundamentally different from traditional anomaly-based intrusion detection systems. First, our system only requires that additional resources be focused on anomalous users; this is different from systems that require immediate action upon receiving threshold-based alerts (of course, our system can act on threshold-based alerts, if necessary). Second, our system requires security administrators to be trusted; these administrators are hard to monitor as they may be aware of the details that are being measured. Finally, our system is built using standard embedded functionalities.

2.   Common Information Model

The WBEM initiative led to the creation of the Common Information Model (CIM) standard, which models management data in an object-oriented fashion [4]. The CIM standard provides a method for expressing useful management data for computer systems. It does not enforce a scheme for naming classes or specific properties, methods, etc., that are to be included in classes. Rather, it is "a well-defined collection of class definitions that all (participating) companies agree to follow" [4].

The CIM schema provides a logical hierarchical structure of class definitions. For instance, the base class CIM_LogicalElement is a management class from which CIM_Process instances are derived. Each CIM_Process instance contains information about a particular process such as minimum and maximum working set size, process ID, execution path, etc. The class CIM_LogicalFile derives CIM_Directory, whose instances contain information about directories, and CIM_DataFile, whose instances contain information about operating system metadata files. CIM has hundreds of classes [15], which make it attractive for modeling information involved in managing computer systems.

The key to leveraging management information for insider threat detection is to dynamically select, aggregate and store all data that could be useful during an investigation (all of this is supported by WBEM). CIM and its implementations (e.g., WMI) also provide aggregated statistics such as detailed performance information about active processes [15] for responding to certain system events.

3. Windows Management Instrumentation

Windows Management Instrumentation (WMI) is a "technology built into Windows that enables organizations to manage servers and user PCs connected to their networks" [20]. The WMI architecture has three layers.

- Layer 1: Managed Objects and Providers
- Layer 2: WMI Infrastructure
- Layer 3: Management Applications

In the WMI nomenclature, "producers" provide information that is used by "consumers" [17]. The information produced is stored in a set of data structures called the WMI repository. The managed objects and providers of Layer 1 represent the WMI producers. Managed objects are physical or logical components in the environment that are being managed. Providers are responsible for monitoring the managed objects and passing real-time information about the objects to the WMI infrastructure. Each managed object is represented by a WMI class. New classes may be derived to manage additional objects that are not managed by default.

Layer 2 represents the WMI infrastructure provided by Windows. The WMI infrastructure, which serves as a bridge between WMI producers and consumers, has two main components, the WMI repository for storing information and the WMI service, which is responsible for providing data to management applications.

Layer 3 constitutes applications that consume WMI information from the WMI repository (e.g., our insider threat detection system). The System.Management namespace of the .NET framework provides the classes needed to interface with WMI in order to build such applications.

Our insider threat detection application employs WMI components called PerformanceCounter classes along with WMI event handlers. In the following, we briefly discuss the design and use of these components via the .NET framework.

WMI allows remote access to instrumentation on another computer via its namespace scheme. Code provided in [8] demonstrates the instantiation of a ConnectionOptions class, which is used to store the username and password of an administrator of a networked machine.

Class properties define the characteristics of the real-world object that the class represents. For example, consider the Win32_Process class derived from CIM_Process mentioned above. Each instance of the class represents a different process and each instance has 45 properties that describe the corresponding process. WMI properties may be queried using the WMI Query Language (WQL), a subset of SQL92 [9]. WQL provides a syntax for Select statements but not for updating or deleting WMI information [17].

Figure 1 (adapted from [8]) presents a sample WQL query that accesses class properties. First, the ManagementScope class is instantiated, the scope is set to the CIMV2 namespace on the local machine, and the ManagementObjectSearcher class is instantiated with the appropriate arguments. Next, the Get method of class ManagementObjectSearcher is invoked; this returns the collection of objects that satisfies the WQL query. The collection of objects is stored in an instantiation of the ManagementObjectCollection class. The objects stored in the collection are searched serially, the Description and ProcessId properties of the returned objects are referenced by name, and their values are converted to strings.

4.   WMI Techniques and Threat Detection

This section introduces advanced WMI techniques used to implement insider threat detection. We first focus on accessing performance counter classes, which provide statistical information about the state of computer systems (e.g., average processor load, average network traffic, etc.). Such statistics offer clues to uncovering insider attacks.

```
      string queryString
         = ''SELECT Description, ProcessId FROM Win32_Process'';
      string scopeStr = @''\\.\root\CIMV2'';
      SelectQuery query = new SelectQuery(queryString);
      ManagementScope scope
         = new System.Management.ManagementScope(scopeStr);
      ManagementObjectSearcher searcher
         = new ManagementObjectSearcher(scope, query);
      ManagementObjectCollection processes = searcher.Get();
      foreach(ManagementObject mo in processes)
      {
         // Handle getting data from management object here
         string teststring1 = mo[''Description''].ToString();
         string teststring2 = mo[''ProcessId''].ToString();
      }
```

Figure 1. C# example of a WQL query.

Next, we discuss the management of WMI events. These events can be set to automatically alert a listening application (e.g., an insider threat detection system) when certain criteria are met. We also introduce methods for creating custom performance counters and event triggers.

4.1 Accessing Performance Counters

WMI's "Performance Counter Classes" reveal real-time, Windows native statistics about the state of computer systems. For example, Win32_PerfFormattedData_PerfOS_System provides statistical and aggregated information about the operating system, including file read and write operations per second, number of processes or threads, and number of system calls per second.

```
      PerformanceCounter cpuCounter = new PerformanceCounter
         (''Processor'', ''% Processor Time'', ''_Total'');
      int value = cpuCounter.NextValue();
```

Figure 2. Obtaining performance counter data.

System.Diagnostics is the principal .NET namespace for handling WMI performance counters. Figure 2 (from [16]) shows how an object of the PerformanceCounter class (member of the System.Diagnostics namespace) is used to obtain WMI performance counter information.

In Figure 2, the `PerformanceCounter` class takes as parameters the category of performance data, the particular performance category class, and the handle of a particular instance of this class (in this example, the keyword _Total) to aggregate all processes. A `PerformanceCounter` object is returned. The `NextValue` method can be called on this object to retrieve the current statistic represented by the object.

```
bool pleaseContinue = true
public void doit()
{
    int processID =
        System.Diagnostics.Process.GetCurrentProcess().Id;
    int workingSet = 30000000;
    string wqlQuery = String.Format(
        @''Select * FROM __InstanceModificationEvent WITHIN 1
        WHERE TargetInstance ISA 'Win32_Process' AND
        TargetInstance.ProcessId = {0} AND
        TargetInstance.WorkingSetSize >= {1} AND
        PreviousInstance.WorkingSetSize < {2} '',
    processId, workingSet, workingSet);
    WqlEventQuery query = new WqlEventQuery(wqlQuery);
    ManagementEventWatcher watcher =
        new ManagementEventWatcher(query);'
    watcher.EventArrived +=
        new EventArrivedEventHandler(onEvent);
    watcher.Start();
    ArrayList array = new ArrayList();
    while(pleaseContinue){
        array.Add(1);
        if(i%1000 == 0) System.Threading.Thread.Sleep(1);
}

public void onEvent(object sender, EventArrivedEventArgs e)
{
    pleaseContinue = false;
    Console.WriteLine(''Found a misbehaving process'');
}
```

Figure 3. Dealing with WMI events.

4.2   Event Handlers

WMI event handlers define and consume events related to data handled by WMI. The code in Figure 3 (from [16]) shows how a .NET application can specify the events it is interested in capturing. The internal WMI event __InstanceModificationEvent fires whenever a value in the namespace is updated. The WQL statement selects instances from the set of stored WMI events where a value in the namespace Win32_Process changes, the ProcessId is 1367, and the working set size is more than 30,000,000. The code then creates an event watcher object whose EventArrived method is invoked when such an event occurs. The code dictates that a .NET event handler should be initiated so that the specific code for handling an event can be managed in a different onEvent function according to .NET conventions. In this case, the event is handled by printing ''Found a misbehaving process'' and exiting the loop.

This technology is powerful and has "out of the box" functionality that provides useful statistics about system operations to any application interfacing with WMI. Numerous possibilities exist for leveraging these statistics to detect insider threats.

4.3   Custom Performance Counters and Events

WMI enables programmers to create custom performance counters and to expose custom events to WMI. Thus, WMI can generate and store highly specialized data at individual workstations rather than relying on complicated WQL statements and statistical calculations at a centralized server.

Creating custom performance counters involves defining the metadata about the new performance counter, giving it proper types, etc. The System.Diagnostics.PerfomanceCounter class that was used to read in performance counter information [16] may be used to create custom performance counters for WMI. To prevent naming collisions, the Exists method must be invoked to check if a performance counter with the same name already exists. If not, a new performance counter is created using the Create method.

The code in Figure 4 (from [16]) implements this functionality. It creates a CounterCreationDataCollection object and populates it with CounterCreationData instances. The performance counter merely indicates the number of 7's in an integer parameter to a web service. A PerformanceCounterType is assigned to each performance counter that is created in order to determine how the NextValue method works. Several statistics are supported (average, difference, instantaneous, percentage and rate), but the type chosen (NumberOfItems32) simply returns the number of items [16]. PerformanceCounterCategory.Create then adds the counter to the WMI CIM repository.

```
// Check if the category already exists or not.
if (!PerformanceCounterCategory.Exists(categoryName))
{
  CounterCreationDataCollection creationData =
    new CounterCreationDataCollection();

  // Create two custom counter objects
  creationData.Add(new CounterCreationData(''Number of 7s - Last'',
    ''Number of occurences of the number 7 in the last WS call'',
    PerformanceCounterType.NumberOfItems32));

  // Bind the counters to a PerformanceCounterCategory
  PerformanceCounterCategory myCategory =
    PerformanceCounterCategory.Create(''TestWS Monitor'',
    helpInfo, creationData);
}
```

Figure 4. Creating custom performance counters.

The code in Figure 5 (from [16]) may be used to read from a custom performance counter.

```
PerformanceCounter counter = new PerformanceCounter
  (''TestWS Monitor'', ''String Length - Last'', false);
counter.RawValue = count;
```

Figure 5. Reading from a custom performance counter.

The code in Figure 6 (from [16]) shows how to make extensions to WMI CIM events that can be consumed by event consumer applications. It uses several .NET namespaces described in [16].

The `CustomEvent` class, which is created in Figure 6, extends the `System.Management.Instrumentation.BaseEvent` class. Such an extended class could contain any properties and methods deemed appropriate to its task [16]. Calling the event is as easy as creating a `CustomEvent` instance and invoking the `Fire` method inherited from `BaseEvent`.

5.　　Insider Threat Detection System

Our insider threat detection system is designed to be an asset to systems administrators. It leverages system management tools to obtain system information; it archives the information and compiles it into useful information about expected versus actual user behavior. It alerts administrators to take action when anomalous user activity is indicated.

```
// Specify which namespace the Management Event class is created
// in [assembly:Instrumented(''Root/Default'')]

// Let the system know you will run installUtil.exe against this
// assembly -- add reference to System.Configuration.Install.dll
// [System.ComponentModel.RunInstaller(true)]

public class CustomEventInstaller:DefaultManagementProjectInstaller{}

namespace WorkingSetMonitor
{
    // Event class: Renamed in the CIM using ManagedNameAttribute
    // [ManagedName(''SuperEvent'')]
    public class CustomEvent : BaseEvent
    {
        string data; // Not exposed to the CIM -- its primitive
        int state;   // Exposed via public property
        public CustomEvent(string data)
        {
            this.data = data
        }

        public int State
        {
            get { return state; }
            set { state = value; }
        }
    }
}
```

Figure 6. Creating custom events.

Moreover, it provides this functionality without placing any demands on systems administrators.

The insider threat detection system has a three-tier architecture. The first tier is the functionality provided by WMI. The second is the server-side insider threat detection application, which uses C# code to interface remotely with WMI. This application also performs statistical analyses on raw WMI data; the computations are performed on a central server to determine if aberrant user behavior is occurring. The third tier is a database that stores raw WMI data and the results of statistical analysis.

The database is required to store historical user behavior and to demonstrate that a threat actually exists. This is because insider threat detection relies on statistics that compare current user behavior with past behaviors.

6. WMI Service Expectations

The WMI repository must have up-to-date data; therefore, the time interval at which data is updated is an important issue. The more frequent the updates, the more likely the recorded data will accurately portray the current system state. An equally important issue is the speed at with WQL queries are fielded. This section discusses whether or not WMI can offer service guarantees on providing accurate, up-to-date information.

Because WQL is a subset of SQL92, optimizing the execution of the WQL Select statement falls in line with research for optimizing SQL statements in general [18]. More importantly, it is necessary to arrive at reasonable expectations of the speed of execution of queries and updates to the WMI repository.

Tunstall and Cole [20] suggest that it is possible to provide certain service guarantees. They discuss the notion of "high performance classes" that provide real-time information about current activity. Special registry keys are used to provide fast access to information on remote computers. The high performance classes built into Windows are exposed by WMI's performance counter classes. As explained in [20], a refresher object can be called to quickly make real-time data available to a WMI application. But "quickly" and "real-time" are relative terms that depend on the functioning of Windows internals, which is not public knowledge.

However, experiments can be conducted to obtain assessments of WMI service guarantees. Our insider threat detection system was interfaced with the WMI repository and a local SQL database; Microsoft SQL Server 2005 was attached to a local network. In our experiment, a simple remote WQL query was issued 1,000 times in succession to another machine on the same laboratory subnet, and the results were stored in a database housed on a server located elsewhere in the building. The query requested the remote machine for its local time (this type of query is consistent with querying for information about processes).

Our analysis showed that each operation set consisting of querying the remote machine, receiving a reply and writing to the database took 35.01 milliseconds on the average. We believe this meets moderate service expectations. Our future research will investigate the handling of forensic evidence that is more ephemeral in nature.

7. Conclusions

The insider threat detection system described in this paper is intended to operate as a watchdog within an enterprise environment, remotely and covertly gathering data from user workstations. The design leverages several technologies that were originally designed to expose important enterprise management information to IT administration personnel. These include system-independent Web Based Enterprise Management (WBEM) schemas and a system-dependent implementation of Microsoft Windows Management Instrumentation (WMI).

It is important to note that the data exposed by WMI (and WBEM implementations for other operating systems) conveys user activity on individual workstations. Moreover, these implementations are ubiquitous and their activities are abstracted from the normal user by the operating system.

Our insider threat detection system facilitates the selection and storage of potential digital evidence based on anomalous user behavior with minimal administrative input. In particular, it leverages WMI to support remote access, expose current information about user activity, provide basic aggregated statistical information and event handling, and support custom event handling and statistical aggregation for applications that access WMI via the .NET framework.

References

[1] S. Axelsson, Intrusion Detection Systems: A Survey and Taxonomy, Technical Report 99-15, Department of Computer Engineering, Chalmers University of Technology, Goteborg, Sweden, 2000.

[2] P. Bradford, M. Brown, J. Perdue and B. Self, Towards proactive computer-system forensics, *Proceedings of the International Conference on Information Technology: Coding and Computing*, vol. 2, pp. 648–652, 2004.

[3] P. Bradford and N. Hu, A layered approach to insider threat detection and proactive forensics, *Proceedings of the Twenty-First Annual Computer Security Applications Conference (Technology Blitz)*, 2005.

[4] J. Cooperstein, Windows management instrumentation: Administering Windows and applications across your enterprise, *MSDN Magazine* (msdn.microsoft.com/msdnmag/issues/0500/wmiover), May 2000.

[5] D. Denning, An intrusion-detection model, *IEEE Transactions on Software Engineering*, vol. 13(2), pp. 222–232, 1987.

[6] J. Evers, Computer crime costs $67 billion FBI says, CNET News .com, January 19, 2006.

[7] M. Gerken, Statistical-based intrusion detection, Software Engineering Institute, Carnegie Mellon University, Pittsburgh, Pennsylvania (www.sei.cmu.edu/str/descriptions/sbid.htm).

[8] K. Goss, WMI made easy for C#, C# Help (www.csharphelp.com /archives2/archive334.html).

[9] C. Hobbs, *A Practical Approach to WBEM/CIM Management*, Auerbach/CRC Press, Boca Raton, Florida, 2004.

[10] A. Jones and R. Sielken, Computer System Intrusion Detection: A Survey, Technical Report, Department of Computer Science, University of Virginia, Charlottesville, Virginia, 2000.

[11] P. Kahai, M. Srinivasan, K. Namuduri and R. Pendse, Forensic profiling system, in *Advances in Digital Forensics*, M. Pollitt and S. Shenoi (Eds.), Springer, New York, pp. 153–164, 2005.

[12] W. Lee, S. Stolfo and K. Mok, A data mining framework for building intrusion detection models, *Proceedings of the IEEE Symposium on Security and Privacy*, pp. 120–132, 1999.

[13] T. Lunt, Automated audit trail analysis and intrustion detection: A survey, *Proceedings of the Eleventh National Computer Security Conference*, 1988.

[14] T. Lunt, A survey of intrusion detection techniques, *Computers and Security*, vol. 12(4), pp. 405–418, 1993.

[15] Microsoft Corporation, WMI classes (msdn2.microsoft.com/en-us /library/aa394554.aspx), 2006.

[16] J. Murphy, A quick introduction to WMI from .NET, O'Reilly Network (www.ondotnet.com/pub/a/dotnet/2003/04/07/wmi.html), 2003.

[17] K. Salchner, An in-depth look at WMI and instrumentation, DeveloperLand (www.developerland.com/DotNet/Enterprise/145.aspx), 2004.

[18] L. Snow, Optimizing management queries, *.NET Developer's Journal* (dotnet.sys-con.com/read/38914.htm), July 21, 2003.

[19] SRI International, Event Monitoring Enabling Responses to Anomalous Live Disturbances (EMERALD) (www.csl.sri.com/proj ects/emerald).

[20] C. Tunstall and G. Cole, *Developing WMI Solutions*, Pearson Education, Boston, Massachusetts, 2002.

III

ROOTKIT DETECTION

Chapter 6

ANALYSIS OF TOOLS FOR DETECTING ROOTKITS AND HIDDEN PROCESSES

A. Todd, J. Benson, G. Peterson, T. Franz, M. Stevens and R. Raines

Abstract   Rootkits pose a dilemma in forensic investigations because hackers use them surreptitiously to mislead investigators. This paper analyzes the effectiveness of online and offline information analysis techniques in detecting rootkits and determining the processes and/or files hidden by rootkits. Five common rootkits were investigated using a live analysis tool, five rootkit detection tools (RDTs) and four offline analysis tools. The experimental results indicate that, while live analysis techniques provide a surprising amount of information and offline analysis provides accurate information, RDTs are the best approach for detecting rootkits and hidden processes.

Keywords: Rootkits, rootkit detection, live analysis, offline analysis

1.   Introduction

A rootkit is a program that provides the means to create an undetectable presence on a computer [14]. It is an executable that hides processes, files and registry values from users and other programs. The presence of a rootkit can have an adverse effect on the outcome of an investigation. In legal proceedings, several individuals have claimed ignorance of their crimes, instead laying the blame on an unknown hacker who left a rootkit on their machines [1].

Forensic investigators may detect rootkits using live analysis techniques, rootkit detection tools (RDTs) or by forensically imaging the drive and performing an offline analysis. Live analysis provides valuable, volatile information that may not be available during an offline analysis of a hard drive, e.g., dynamic data such as running processes and open ports, which are only available during system operation. However, when one of the processes on a machine includes a rootkit, the

Please use the following format when citing this chapter:

Todd, A., Benson, J., Peterson, G., Franz, T., Stevens, M., Raines, R., 2007, in IFIP International Federation for Information Processing, Volume 242, Advances in Digital Forensics III; eds. P. Craiger and S Shenoi;(Boston: Springer), pp. 89-105.

investigator must question if the results of a live analysis are tainted. When rootkits are running, the data and processes they have modified are still in use by the operating system, but this fact is not visible to the user. In fact, our experiments demonstrate that even if a live response cannot detect what is hidden, it can still provide an investigator with details about what was available to the user. This information can also help the investigator determine what the rootkit was hiding.

RDTs, which detect rootkits and/or files hidden by rootkits, may be employed as part of a live analysis. However, there are limitations associated with any program that attempts to detect rootkits while a rootkit is running. The fundamental problem is the lack of trust in the operating system (and system files and functions). Most RDTs cross-compare information provided by corrupted system calls with system information gathered by the RDT, identifying anomalies as possible rootkits.

A rootkit hides information by manipulating operating system function calls. This information cannot be hidden from an offline scan that does not use the corrupted system calls and searches the entire hard drive for rootkit signatures. However, using offline analysis to determine what a rootkit was attempting to hide is much more difficult.

This paper examines the efficacy of live response, RDTs and offline analysis in detecting rootkits and determining what they conceal. Experiments were conducted on five rootkits: AFXRootkit [22], Vanquish [22], Hacker Defender [15], FU [22] and FUTo [22], which use both user-level and kernel-level hiding techniques [9, 14]. The experimental results demonstrate that live analysis techniques perform better than expected in rootkit-tainted environments, but rootkits obscure the data enough to make investigation difficult. Offline analysis can identify all the data from a hard drive, but finding a rootkit and what it is hiding is nearly impossible. Finally, rootkit detectors provide the most information about a system when a rootkit is running, but the investigator must be willing to accept some loss of forensic integrity of the hard drive.

2.   Related Work

Relatively few experiments have been conducted to measure the effectiveness of rootkit detection tools (RDTs). Two exceptions are the studies conducted by Claycomb [6] and CMS Consulting [7].

Claycomb [6] analyzed five publicly-available RDTs (IceSword, Ghost-Buster, BlackLight, RootkitRevealer, Vice) and one custom RDT (Bluestone). These RDTs were tested against three user-level rootkits (Hacker Defender, AFXRootkit2005, Vanquish) and three kernel-level rootkits (SonyBMG, FU, FUTo) running on Windows XP and Windows Server

2003 machines. The study determined that IceSword (v1.12) and Ghost-Buster had the best detection capabilities; BlackLight and RootkitRe-vealer had above average but lesser reliability; and Vice and Bluestone were the least reliable of the RDTs investigated.

The CMS Consulting study [7] analyzed the effectiveness of eight publicly-available RDTs (IceSword, GhostBuster, BlackLight, Rootk-itRevealer, Flister, Keensense, Process Guard, GMER) against three user-level rootkits (Hacker Defender, AFXRootkit2005, Vanquish) and one kernel-level rootkit (FU). IceSword (v1.18), BlackLight, Keensense, ProcessGuard and GMER were determined to be 100% effective in de-tecting the rootkits. Flister, RootkitRevealer and Ghostbuster demon-strated above average but lesser reliability.

2.1 Rootkits

With the exception of the Claycomb and CMS Consulting studies, information about rootkit detection is mainly gleaned from chat rooms and online forums rather than from published articles. Most of the claims are largely unproven or anecdotal in nature, but the discussions about rootkit detection and evasion techniques are very valuable. Some of the prominent contributors are Hoglund [14], Butler [3, 4], BPSparks [3, 4, 28], Rutkowska [23], Rutkowski [24, 25], Levine [17, 18], and individuals from Microsoft [29] and Symantec [10].

2.1.1 Traditional Rootkit Techniques. Rootkits are cat-egorized by the techniques they use to hide themselves and their pro-tected files and applications. Traditional (user-level) rootkits operate at the same privilege level as user programs; they intercept API calls and change the outputs of functions by removing references to the files and processes hidden by the rootkit. This is done by either hooking the API call, which redirects the function call to a compromised ver-sion of the function, or by patching the correct function with malicious code that modifies the correct output before returning the output to the calling process. Kernel-level rootkits operate in kernel memory space and are, therefore, protected from user-level programs such as certain anti-virus scanners and rootkit detectors. Kernel-level rootkits can also hook API calls, but at the higher privilege level of the kernel. Addition-ally, a kernel-level rootkit may utilize direct kernel object manipulation (DKOM) and affect the data structures that track system processes [14].

2.1.2 Modern Rootkit Techniques. Kernel data manipu-lation, which originated in 2003, is generally considered to be the first "modern" rootkit technique. Instead of changing kernel code, a modern rootkit unlinks its process from the *PsActiveProcessLinkHead* list. This list is not used by the scheduler, so the hidden process still gets CPU time. The technique can be detected by comparing the *PsActive-ProcessLinkHead* list to a scheduler list (e.g., *KiDispatcherReadyList-Head*) [24]. A more sophisticated technique called "Innocent Threads" evades detection by unlinking from the *PsActiveProcessLinkHead* list and having the malicious thread masquerade as one belonging to a legitimate system process (e.g., `winlogon.exe`) [23].

2.1.3   Advanced Rootkit Techniques.   Some of the newest rootkit techniques have been implemented during the past year. These include using polymorphic code, using covert channels and subverting virtual memory. Rootkits with polymorphic code generators allow the creation of a different binary image for every system on which they are installed [23]. Covert channel communications permit rootkits to communicate with their hidden applications without being detected [27]. Finally, although rootkits are becoming more proficient at controlling their execution, they still find it difficult to conceal their code and memory-based modifications within operating system components. This leaves them vulnerable to detection by even the most primitive in-memory signature scans. Virtual memory subversion enables rootkits to control memory reads by the operating system and other processes, allowing them to see only what the rootkit wants them to see [3].

2.2   Rootkit Detection

Rootkit detectors are typically categorized into five classes [4]:

- **Signature-Based Detectors:** These detectors scan system files for byte sequences representing rootkit "fingerprints."

- **Heuristic/Behavior-Based Detectors:** These detectors identify deviations from "normal" system patterns or behavior.

- **Cross-View-Based Detectors:** These detectors enumerate system parameters in at least two different ways and compare the results. Typically, this means invoking APIs for information and using an algorithm specific to the RDT to obtain the same information without going through the APIs.

- **Integrity-Based Detectors:** These detectors compare a current snapshot of the filesystem or memory with a trusted baseline.

- **Hardware-Based Detectors:** These detectors are independent of the potentially subverted operating system. They typically have their own CPU and use Direct Memory Access (DMA) to scan physical memory for rootkit signatures such as hooks in the System Service Descriptor Table (SSDT), alterations to kernel functions, and modifications to key data structures.

3. Experimental Methodology

To determine which of the three analysis techniques (live analysis, RDTs or offline analysis) provides the most information about rootkit behavior, three sets of experiments were conducted against six target hosts. The first set of experiments (live response) involved one system under test (SUT), the second set (RDTs) involved five SUTs, and the third (offline analysis) involved four SUTs. A full-factorial design consisting of sixty total experiments was conducted. Five different metrics were employed. The metrics were designed to capture forensic information about rootkits, i.e., what they were concealing from the user in terms of processes, services, drivers, ports and files.

Table 1. Target host configurations.

Configuration	Operating System	Rootkit Installed	Hiding Technique
A	Windows XP SP2	None	n/a
B	Windows XP SP2	AFXRootkit (2005)	User-level
C	Windows XP SP2	Vanquish (0.2.1)	User-level
D	Windows XP SP2	Hacker Defender (1.0.0r)	User-level
E	Windows XP SP2	FU (2004)	Kernel-level
F	Windows XP SP2	FUTo (2006)	Kernel-level

3.1 Target Host Configurations

The baseline target host (Configuration A in Table 1) was a clean installation of Microsoft Windows XP Professional with Service Pack 2 running on a virtual machine using VMWare 5.5. Five publicly available rootkits were used as the workload to the SUTs, consisting of three user-level rootkits (AFXRootkit, Vanquish, Hacker Defender) and two kernel-level rootkits (FU, FUTo). AFXRootkit uses API patching to hide the resident directory of the executable, as well as files in the directory, registry keys with the same name as the directory, and processes owned by programs running from the directory [2]. Hacker Defender uses API hooking to hide files, processes, registry settings and ports, as long as they are in the hxdef.ini file. Additionally, it creates a password-protected backdoor on the host and redirects packets to help mask the source of traffic for an attack against a third machine [15]. Vanquish uses DLL injection for API hooking to hide all files, services and registry settings containing the magic string "vanquish." It also has a password logging function bundled into the executable [31]. Both FU and FUTo use DKOM to manipulate the handle table to hide processes; they may also raise the privileges of processes by manipulating the table. FUTo, the successor to FU, was created to address certain weaknesses in IceSword and BlackLight. It evades detection by manipulating the process handle table without using function calls [26].

Table 2.   Experiment Set I.

Experiment Set	Live Response SUTs
I-1	Windows Forensic Toolchest [19]

3.2   Experiment Set I (Live Response)

Experiment Set I involved performing a live response on each workload configuration using one SUT in order to determine the SUT's effectiveness in detecting the workload rootkits (Table 2). The SUT used was the Windows Forensic Toolchest (WFT) [19]. WFT is specifically designed for detecting processes, services, drivers, ports and files. WFT functions that may be used for rootkit detection are listed in Table 3.

3.3   Experiment Set II (Rootkit Detectors)

Experiment Set II involved the execution of five rootkit detectors (Table 4) on each workload configuration (Table 1) to determine the effectiveness of each SUT in detecting the workload rootkits. Rootkit-Revealer provides user-level and kernel-level detection by comparing information returned by the Windows API and raw FAT/NTFS structures [8]. RKDetector [20] uses its own NTFS/FAT32 filesystem driver to provide a filesystem browser, rootkit detector, ADS scanner, registry browser and hidden registry key scanner [21]. BlackLight loops through all possible process IDs attempting to open each process, and compares the information it gathers with that returned by the Windows API [12]. IceSword [30] detects hidden process, services, drivers, files, ports and registry settings, and identifies hooked system calls and open TCP/UDP ports [26].

Table 3. Functions packaged in WFT.

WFT Function	Target
PSLIST	Processes
PS	Processes
LISTDLLS	Processes
PSTAT	Processes
TLIST	Processes
CMDLINE	Processes
HANDLE	Processes
PSSERVICE	Services
SC	Services
NET START	Services
SERVICELIST	Services
DRIVERS	Drivers
NET STAT	Ports
FPORT	Ports
OPENPORTS	Ports
TREE	Files

Table 4. Experiment Set II.

Experiment Set	Rootkit Detector SUTs
II-1	RootkitRevealer (1.7) [8]
II-2	RKDetector (Beta 2.0) [20]
II-3	BlackLight (Beta 2.2.1046) [12]
II-4	IceSword (1.12) [30]
II-5	IceSword (1.18) [30]

Table 5. Experiment Set III.

Experiment Set	Offline Analysis SUTs	Tool Type
III-1	Clam-AV [16]	Signature-Based AV
III-2	F-Prot [11]	Signature-Based AV
III-3	EnCase [13]	Forensic Investigation
III-4	Autopsy [5]	Forensic Investigation

3.4   Experiment Set III (Offline Analysis)

Experiment Set III involved performing an offline analysis on each of the workload configurations using four different SUTs (Table 5) to determine the effectiveness of each SUT in detecting the workload rootkits. Two SUTs are signature-based anti-virus tools and the other two are forensic tools that were used to visually inspect the target workloads. Rootkit information cannot be hidden from an offline analysis. Therefore, the study focused on determining what was hidden and when it was hidden (if the rootkit was operating when the machine was seized).

4.   Experimental Results and Observations

This section presents the results and observations from the three sets of experiments that covered ten SUTs and six target configurations.

4.1   Workload Capabilities and Limitations

Each of the five rootkit workloads hides different processes, services, drivers, ports and/or files.

- **AFXRootkit:** This user-level rootkit hides two running processes (rootkit `root.exe` and backdoor `bo2k.exe`), one running service (`treasure`), one port (54320), and several files including its current directory (`c:\treasure`). No drivers are used to root the system.

- **Vanquish:** This user-level rootkit is not a constantly running process. It starts, hides its payload using patching, and then stops. Vanquish hides the rootkit service (`vanquish`), port (54320), and all files and directories with "vanquish" in their names.

- **Hacker Defender:** This user-level rootkit hides two running processes (rootkit `hxdef100.exe` and backdoor `bo2k.exe`), one running service (`Hacker Defender100`), one port (54320), and the files specified in the rootkit's initialization file (`hxdef100.ini`). Hacker Defender also hides a driver (`hxdefdrv.sys`), which it uses to gain system access.

- **FU:** This kernel-level rootkit only hides processes. FU is not a constantly running process, so it only hides the one process it is directed to hide (backdoor `bo2k.exe`). FU does not hide ports or files, and it does not create a system service. FU uses a driver (`msdirectx.sys`) to gain system access, but it does not hide this driver.

- **FUTo:** This kernel-level rootkit only hides processes. Like its predecessor FU, FUTo is not a constantly running process, so it only hides one running process (backdoor `bo2k.exe` in our tests). FUTo does not hide ports or files, and it does not create a system service. FUTo uses a driver (`msdirectx.sys`) to gain system access, but it does not hide it.

Table 6. Experiment Set I results.

Rootkit	Processes	Services	Drivers	Ports	Files
AFXRootkit	Y	Y	n/a	N	N
Vanquish	Y^2	N	n/a	Y^2	N
Hacker Defender	Y^1	N	Y	N	N
FU	Y^1	n/a	Y^1	Y^2	Y^2
FUTo	N	n/a	Y^1	Y^2	Y^2

[1] WFT detected the rootkit, but provided limited information.
[2] Rootkit did not attempt to hide this information.

4.2 Experiment Set I Results

The first set of experiments performed a live analysis using WFT on each of the five rootkits. The results are summarized in Table 6.

Since rootkits subvert the system functions that list active process, open ports and other files, it was surprising that WFT's incident response tools were able to detect so much information hidden by the rootkits. WFT provided considerable information associated with running processes and system drivers. FUTo was the only rootkit that could completely hide information about the backdoor's process. However, although the results indicate a high rootkit detection rate, WFT was unable to provide reliable information about system files, open ports and system services. Nevertheless, WFT provided useful information and, when it could not detect a rootkit, still gave an accurate depiction of what the user would normally see.

Note that an investigator must look closely at the PSTAT and PRO-CESS HANDLES utilities when using WFT to detect rootkit processes. PSTAT provides generic process information, which helps detect simple rootkits, e.g., AFXRootkit. PROCESS HANDLES provides more detailed system information that was scrubbed clean only by FUTo. The information listed here may only identify a "<Non-existent Process>," but this indicates to the investigator that a covert process is running.

When using WFT to detect items (e.g., drivers, ports and files) that a rootkit may be hiding, the investigator should use the NET START utility to identify services and DRIVERS to identify drivers. NET START only works against basic rootkits (e.g., AFXRootkit). DRIVERS lists system drivers, but it was able to detect all the rootkit drivers in our experiment. Rootkits also hide ports and files; however, WFT did not reveal any information about ports and files that were actively hidden.

Table 7.   Experiment Set II results.

RDTs	AFXRootkit	Vanquish	Hacker Defender	FU	FUTo
RootkitRevealer	Y	N	Y	N^1	N^1
RKDetector	Y	Y	Y	N^1	N^1
BlackLight	Y	Y	Y	Y^3	Y^{23}
IceSword 1.12	Y	Y	Y	Y^3	N
IceSword 1.18	Y	Y	Y	Y^3	Y^{23}

[1] RDT did not look for hidden processes, services, drivers and ports.
[2] RDT detected a discrepancy, but could not provide all the process information.
[3] RDT did not detect the actual rootkit, just the hidden processes.

4.3   Experiment Set II Results

Table 7 summarizes the results of using rootkit detection tools (RDTs) in a live analysis and their success in detecting rootkits.

The results show that the four RDTs fall into two groups: one group (RootkitRevealer and RKDetector) only detects hidden files and is not effective against all rootkits, while the second group (BlackLight and IceSword) is highly effective against all rootkits. BlackLight detects the same rootkits as IceSword. However, IceSword is a more robust tool that identifies hooked system calls, hidden drivers and open TCP/UDP ports. This information enables an investigator to classify the anomalous behavior identified by the detector as an actual rootkit. The following subsections summarize the four RDTs used in our study.

4.3.1   RootkitRevealer.   RootkitRevealer primarily identifies hidden files and registry settings; it does not look for hidden processes, ports, services and drivers. It can detect rootkits that hide executables, images and other illegal content, but not those that can hide running processes. Specifically, RootkitRevealer detected all the hidden files in the current directory of AFXRootkit and all the files and registry settings listed in the Hacker Defender initialization file (hxdef100.ini), but it was unable to detect the files hidden by Vanquish. RootkitRevealer listed no discrepancies when executed against FU and FUTo because they only hide processes, but this is misleading because the rootkits were hiding information from the user. RootkitRevealer had mixed results for

the five rootkits that were tested, and it provided the least amount of information.

4.3.2 RKDetector.

RKDetector primarily identifies hidden files; it does not look for hidden processes, ports, services and drivers. Like RootkitRevealer, it can detect rootkits that hide executables, images and other illegal content, but not those that can hide running processes. It had good results when executed against the five rootkits, detecting the three that hide files. RKDetector detected all the hidden files in the same directory as AFXRootkit, all the hidden files containing the keyword "vanquish," and all the hidden files and registry settings listed in the Hacker Defender initialization file (hxdef100.ini). However, it was ineffective against FU and FUTo because they do not hide files. RKDetector presents its findings in an easy-to-understand file tree that marks directories containing hidden files and directories, and highlights the actual hidden files and directories. In addition to standard rootkit detection, it allows the investigator to explore the registry and alternate data streams on the hard drive.

4.3.3 BlackLight.

BlackLight scans a system for hidden items, providing a list of hidden items and options to remove or clean them. However, the list of hidden items does not include services, drivers, ports and registry settings. BlackLight identified all the files hidden by AFX-Rootkit, Vanquish and Hacker Defender, but it did not list the folder containing these files which was, in fact, hidden. It detected FU's hidden process (bo2k.exe). However, when executed against FUTo, Black-Light detected the hidden process, but was unable to provide its name. Against both FU and FUTo, BlackLight detected the process hidden by the rootkit, but was unable to identify the rootkit. Nevertheless, BlackLight performed extremely well in our experiments, detecting all five rootkits.

4.3.4 IceSword.

IceSword identifies hidden processes and services, and attempts to provide a clean list of all files, registry settings, ports, items set to start up automatically, browser helper objects and message hooks. IceSword detected all the files, directories, services, ports and processes hidden by AFXRootkit, Vanquish and Hacker Defender. IceSword v1.12 and v1.18 both detected FU's hidden process (bo2k.exe). IceSword v1.12 could not detect FUTo's hidden process; on the other hand, IceSword v1.18 detected the process and provided its name. However, when executed against both FU and FUTo, IceSword could not identify the rootkit that was responsible for hiding the process.

Nevertheless, IceSword performed extremely well in our experiments, detecting all five rootkits (v1.18).

Table 8.   Anti-virus scan results.

AV Scanner	AFXRootkit	Vanquish	Hacker Defender	FU	FUTo
Clam-AV	N	N	Y	Y	N
F-Prot	Y	N	Y	Y	N

4.4   Experiment Set III Results

Table 8 presents the results produced by anti-virus scans during the offline analysis. The results are surprising, since the tools are specifically designed for UNIX and Linux environments, not Windows. Visual analysis of the images using EnCase [13] and Autopsy [5] could not determine when the rootkit was running and what it was hiding. However, some information was obtained during offline analysis. In particular, identifying the rootkit can help determine what is hidden, e.g., knowing that the Vanquish rootkit was present could lead an investigator to search for items using the keyword "vanquish." AFXRootkit and Vanquish also provide some relative time information. They update the last access date and time stamp of their DLL files (`hook.dll` and `vanquish.dll`, respectively) upon startup. These findings indicate that it may be difficult to detect when a rootkit was running via offline analysis; this is discernable from DLL time stamps only in some instances. This is a concern with the FU and FUTo rootkits, as they must be started by a user on the machine and there is no mechanism to determine if they were running.

5.   Case Study

The investigative techniques and tools identified in this paper were used in the 2006 Cyber Defense Exercise (CDX), an annual network defense competition between student teams from the five U.S. service academies and the Air Force Institute of Technology. The competition teams designed, implemented and defended a realistic network that provided services based on an overall architectural concept of operations. As part of the initial network setup, each team received preconfigured systems of unknown security state. This required each system to be analyzed to determine vulnerabilities.

Table 9. Preconfigured systems.

Configuration	Operating System	System Role	Installed Rootkit
A	Windows Server 2003 SP1	Exchange Server	Hacker Defender
B	Windows Server 2003 SP1	Domain Controller	Hacker Defender
C	Fedora Core 2	Web Server	F-ck'it Rootkit
D	Fedora Core 2	SMB Server	F-ck'it Rootkit
E	Windows XP SP2	Workstation 1	Vanquish
F	Windows XP SP2	Workstation 2	None
G	Windows XP SP2	Workstation 3	AFXRootkit
H	Windows XP SP2	Workstation 4	None

5.1   Preconfigured Systems

Each competition team was given eight preconfigured systems (Table 9). The systems were virtual machines operating on a Windows XP Service Pack 2 host system using VMWare 5.5. Most of the preconfigured systems contained malicious software, e.g., rootkits, backdoors, keyloggers, as shown in Table 9.

Table 10. Investigation tools.

Investigation Tool	Tool Type
Clam-AV	Signature-Based AV
F-Prot	Signature-Based AV
IceSword v1.12	RDT (Windows)
RootkitRevealer v1.7	RDT (Windows)
BlackLight (Beta 2.2.1046)	RDT (Windows)
Rootkit Hunter v1.2.8	RDT (Linux)
Chkrootkit	RDT (Linux)

5.2   Investigation Methodology

Each preconfigured system was analyzed for malicious software including rootkits. A combination of offline and live response tools, including RDTs, was used (Table 10).

Table 11.   Investigation results.

Tool	Exchange Server	Domain Controller	Web Server	SMB Server	Client	Client
Clam-AV	Y	Y	N	N	N	N
F-Prot	Y	N	N	N	N	Y
IceSword v1.12	Y	Y	n/a	n/a	N^2	Y
RootkitRevealer v1.7	Y	Y	n/a	n/a	N	Y
BlackLight (Beta 2.2.1046)	Y	Y	n/a	n/a	N	Y
Rootkit Hunter v1.2.8	n/a	n/a	Y	Y	n/a	n/a
Chkrootkit	n/a	n/a	Y^1	Y^1	n/a	n/a

[1] Information was discovered, but the rootkit was not identified.
[2] The presence of the rootkit was not revealed, but the hidden files could be viewed.

5.3   Analysis Results

The results of using the various tools for offline and live analysis and their success at detecting hidden process and rootkits on the six pre-configured systems are shown in Table 11. Note that all the systems contained a rootkit, but the specific rootkit varied between machines.

The results indicate that RDTs are effective even in unconstrained environments and without prior knowledge of the rootkits involved. All three Windows RDTs appeared to be equally effective. However, in practice, IceSword is preferred as it provides additional information that permits the viewing of all hidden files. Rootkit Hunter was the most effective and robust tool of the two Linux RDTs tested. Clearly, RDTs are the best tools for conducting forensic investigations of rootkits.

6.   Conclusions

Rootkits hide processes, files and other system information from users and often obscure malicious activity in digital forensic investigations. However, forensic investigators may apply three techniques to detect rootkits and hidden processes: live response, rootkit detection tools (RDTs) and offline analysis.

Our experiments indicate that using a rootkit detection tool during a live response generates the largest amount of data and the most useful information. It is still possible to detect rootkits using a non-invasive live response, but live response procedures are subject to the effects of the rootkits and it can very time consuming to sift through the resulting data. Offline analysis has the advantage of being able to examine all the data from the hard drive, but finding a rootkit, what it was hiding, and when it was hiding are nearly impossible. RDTs are very effective at determining the presence of rootkits and identifying their targets, but the investigator should be willing to pay the penalty of lower forensic integrity of the evidentiary hard drive.

Our future research will attempt to determine the exact effects of RDTs and how they might compromise the overall forensic integrity of digital evidence. This may make it possible to create an offline RDT, with the benefit that the rootkit would not be able to run and, therefore, not be able to hide any information. An alternative would be to perform anomaly detection on the generated live response data to identify data items associated with the rootkit, thereby speeding up live response analysis.

Acknowledgements

This research was sponsored by the Anti-Tamper Software Protection Initiative Technology Office, Sensors Directorate, U.S. Air Force Research Laboratory. The views expressed in this paper are those of the authors and do not reflect the official policy or position of the U.S. Air Force, U.S. Department of Defense or the U.S. Government.

References

[1] E. Abreu, Hackers get novel defense; the computer did it (www.fo rbes.com/markets/newswire/2003/10/27/rtr1124430.html), 2003.

[2] Aphex, `ReadMe.txt` (www.iamaphex.net), 2006.

[3] J. Butler and S. Sparks, Windows rootkits of 2005: Part two (www .securityfocus.com/infocus/1851), 2005.

[4] J. Butler and S. Sparks, Windows rootkits of 2005: Part three (www .securityfocus.com/infocus/1854), 2006.

[5] B. Carrier, *File System Forensic Analysis*, Addison-Wesley, Boston, Massachusetts, 2005.

[6] C. Claycomb, Analysis of Windows Rootkits, M.S. Thesis, Department of Electrical and Computer Engineering, Air Force Institute of Technology, Wright-Patterson Air Force Base, Ohio, 2006.

[7] CMS Consulting, Hidden rootkits in Windows (www.task.to/events /presentations/TASK_Hidden_Rootkits_in_Windows.pdf), 2005.

[8] B. Cogswell and M. Russinovich, RootkitRevealer v1.71 (www.sys internals.com/Utilities/RootkitRevealer.html).

[9] K. Dillard, What are user-mode vs. kernel-mode rootkits? (search windowssecurity.techtarget.com/originalContent/0,289142,sid45_gc i1086469,00.html), 2005.

[10] E. Florio, When malware meets rootkits, *Virus Bulletin*, 2005.

[11] Frisk Software International, F-Prot Antivirus Scanner (www.f-prot .com/products/home_use/linux).

[12] F-Secure Corporation, Blacklight (www.f-secure.com/blacklight/bl acklight.html).

[13] Guidance Software, EnCase (v.4) (www.guidancesoftware.com).

[14] G. Hoglund and J. Butler, *Rootkits: Subverting the Windows Kernel*, Addison-Wesley, Boston, Massachusetts, 2005.

[15] Holy_Father, Hacker Defender (hxdef.org/download.php).

[16] T. Kojm, Clam AntiVirus (www.clamav.net).

[17] J. Levine, B. Culver and H. Owen, A methodology for detecting new binary rootkit exploits, *Proceedings of the IEEE SouthEastCon*, 2003.

[18] J. Levine, J. Grizzard, P. Hutto and H. Owen, A methodology to characterize kernel level rootkit exploits that overwrite the system call table, *Proceedings of the IEEE SoutheastCon*, pp. 25–31, 2004.

[19] M. McDougal, Windows Forensic Toolchest (WFT) (www.foolmoon .net/security/wft), 2005.

[20] RKDetector.com, RKDetector v2.0 (www.rkdetector.com).

[21] RKDetector.com, RKDetector v2.0 Engine (www.rkdetector.com).

[22] Rootkit.com (www.rootkit.com/download.php).

[23] J. Rutkowska, Concepts for the Stealth Windows Rootkit (The Chameleon Project) (invisiblethings.org/papers/chameleon_concep ts.pdf), 2003.

[24] J. Rutkowski, Advanced Windows 2000 rootkit detection (hxdef.org /knowhow/rutkowski.pdf), 2003.

[25] J. Rutkowski, Execution path analysis: Finding kernel rootkits (doc .bughunter.net/rootkit-backdoor/execution-path.html), 2004.

[26] P. Silberman, FUTo (uninformed.org/?v=3&a=7), 2006.

[27] Simple Nomad, Covering your tracks: Ncrypt and Ncovert, presented at *Black Hat USA 2003* (www.blackhat.com/html/bh-media-archives/bh-archives-2003.html), 2003.

[28] S. Sparks, Shadow Walker: Raising the bar for rootkit detection, presented at *Black Hat USA 2005* (www.blackhat.com/pre sentations/bh-jp-05/bh-jp-05-sparks-butler.pdf), 2005.

[29] Y. Wang, B. Vo, R. Roussev, C. Verbowski and A. Johnson, Strider Ghostbuster: Why it's a bad idea for stealth software to hide files, Microsoft Research Technical Report, MSR-TR-2004-71, Microsoft Corporation, Redmond, Washington, 2004.

[30] XFocus.net, IceSword (v1.12 and v1.18) (www.xfocus.net).

[31] XShadow, Vanquish v0.2.1 (www.rootkit.com/vault/xshadoe/read me.txt), 2005.

Chapter 7

A METHOD FOR DETECTING LINUX KERNEL MODULE ROOTKITS

Doug Wampler and James Graham

Abstract   Several methods exist for detecting Linux kernel module (LKM) rootkits, most of which rely on *a priori* system-specific knowledge. We propose an alternative detection technique that only requires knowledge of the distribution of system call addresses in an uninfected system. Our technique relies on outlier analysis, a statistical technique that compares the distribution of system call addresses in a suspect system to that in a known uninfected system. Experimental results indicate that it is possible to detect LKM rootkits with a high degree of confidence.

Keywords: Linux forensics, rootkit detection, outlier analysis

1.   Introduction

The primary goals of an intruder are to gain privileged access and to maintain access to a target system. A rootkit is essentially a set of software tools employed by an intruder after gaining unauthorized access to a system. It has three primary functions: (i) to maintain access to the compromised system; (ii) to attack other systems; and (iii) to conceal or modify evidence of the intruder's activities [5].

Detecting rootkits is a specialized form of intrusion detection. Effective intrusion detection requires the collection and use of information about intrusion techniques [21]. Likewise, certain *a priori* knowledge about a system is required for effective Linux rootkit detection. Specifically, an application capable of detecting unauthorized changes must be installed when the system is deployed (as is typical with host-based intrusion detection), or system metrics must be collected upon system deployment, or both. But the time, effort and expertise required for these activities is significant. It should be noted that some Linux rootkit detection methodologies are not very effective when installed on an infected

Please use the following format when citing this chapter:

Wampler, D., Graham, J., 2007, in IFIP International Federation for Information Processing, Volume 242, Advances in Digital Forensics III; eds. P. Craiger and S Shenoi;(Boston: Springer), pp. 107-116.

system. On the other hand, rootkit detection applications for Microsoft Windows are typically based on heuristics; these applications may be installed to detect kernel rootkits even after infection has occurred.

This paper focuses on the detection of Linux kernel rootkits. The methodology engages a statistical technique based on knowledge about the operating system and architecture instead of *a priori* system-specific knowledge required by most current rootkit detection techniques.

2.   Background

This section presents an overview of rootkits, an analysis of rootkit attack techniques, and a summary of existing rootkit detection techniques.

2.1   Rootkits

The earliest rootkits date back to the early 1990s [20]. Some components (e.g., log file cleaners) of known rootkits were found on compromised systems as early as 1989. SunOS rootkits (for SunOS 4.x) were detected in 1994, and the first Linux rootkits appeared in 1996 [5]. Linux kernel module (LKM) rootkits were first proposed in 1997 by Halflife [5]. Tools for attacking other systems, both locally and remotely, began appearing in rootkits during the late 1990s.

In 1998, Cesare [4] proposed the notion of non-LKM kernel patching. He discussed the possibility of intruding into kernel memory without loadable kernel modules by directly modifying the kernel image (usually in /dev/mem) [5]. The first Adore LKM rootkit, which was released in 1999, altered kernel memory via loadable kernel modules. The KIS Trojan and SucKit rootkits were released in 2001; these rootkits directly modified the kernel image. In 2002, rootkits began to incorporate sniffer backdoors for maintaining access to compromised systems [5].

2.2   Rootkit Classification

Rootkits are generally classified into three categories. The first and simplest are binary rootkits, which are composed of Trojaned system binaries. A second, more complex, category includes library rootkits – Trojaned system libraries that are placed on systems. These two categories of rootkits are relatively easy to detect: either by manually inspecting the /proc file system or by using statically-linked binaries.

The third, and most insidious, category of rootkits constitutes kernel rootkits. There are two subcategories of kernel rootkits: (i) loadable kernel module rootkits (LKM rootkits), and (ii) kernel patched rootkits that directly modify the memory image in /dev/mem [22]. Kernel rootkits attack system call tables by three known mechanisms [12]:

- **System Call Table Modification:** The attack modifies certain addresses in the system call table to point to the new, malicious system calls [8].

- **System Call Target Modification:** The attack overwrites the legitimate targets of the addresses in the system call table with malicious code, without changing the system call table. The first few instructions of the system call function are overwritten with a jump instruction to the malicious code.

- **System Call Table Redirection:** The attack redirects all references to the system call table to a new, malicious system call table in a new kernel address location. This attack evades detection by many currently used tools [12]. System call table redirection is a special case of system call target modification [1] because the attack modifies the system_call function that handles individual system calls by changing the address of the system call table in the function.

2.3 Rootkit Detection

The first kernel rootkits appeared as malicious loadable kernel modules (LKMs). UNIX processes run either in user space or kernel space. Application programs typically run in user space and hardware access is typically handled in kernel space. If an application needs to read from a disk, it uses the open() system call to request the kernel to open a file. Loadable kernel modules run in kernel space and have the ability to modify these system calls. If a malicious loadable kernel module is present in kernel space, the open() system call will open the requested file unless the filename is "rootkit" [5, 20]. Many systems administrators counter this threat by simply disabling the loading of kernel modules [20].

Host-based intrusion detection systems, e.g., Tripwire and Samhain, are very effective at detecting rootkits [20]. Samhain also includes functionality to monitor the system call table, the interrupt description table, and the first few instructions of every system call [5]. This is an example of using *a priori* knowledge about a specific system in rootkit detection.

The Linux Intrusion Detection System (LIDS) is a kernel patch that requires a rebuild (recompile) of the kernel. LIDS can offer protection against kernel rootkits through several mechanisms, including sealing the kernel from modification; preventing the loading/unloading of kernel modules; using immutable and read-only file attributes; locking shared memory segments; preventing process ID manipulation; protecting sensitive /dev/ files; and detecting port scans [6].

Another detection method is to monitor and log program execution when `execve()` calls are made [6]. Remote logging is used to maintain a record of program execution on a system, and a Perl script implemented to monitor the log and perform actions such as sending alarms or killing processes in order to defeat the intruder [6].

Several applications are available for detecting rootkits (including kernel rootkits). These include `chkrootkit` [13], `kstat` [2], `rkstat` [23], St. Michael [23], `scprint` [19], and `kern_check` [17]. `chkrootkit` is a user-space signature-based rootkit detector while others, e.g., `kstat`, `rkstat` and St. Michael, are kernel-space signature-based detectors. These tools typically print the addresses of system calls directly from `/dev/kmem` and/or compare them with the entries in the `System.map` file [18]. This approach relies on a trusted source for *a priori* knowledge about the system in question in that the systems administrator must install these tools before the system is infected by a rootkit. Since `chkrootkit`, `kstat`, `rkstat` and St. Michael are signature-based rootkit detectors, they suffer from the usual shortcomings of signature-based detection. The remaining two tools, `scprint` and `kern_check`, are utilities for printing and/or checking the addresses of entries in system call tables.

Some rootkit detection techniques count the numbers of instructions used in system calls and compare them with those computed for a "clean" system [16]. Other detection techniques involve static analysis of loadable kernel module binaries [11]. This approach leverages the fact that the kernel exports a well-defined interface for use by kernel modules; LKM rootkits typically violate this interface. By carefully analyzing the interface, it is possible to extract an allowed set of kernel modifications.

Until recently, rootkit detection involved software-based techniques. Komoku Inc. now offers a low-cost PCI card ("CoPilot") that monitors a system's memory and file system [10, 14]. However, CoPilot uses "known good" MD5 hashes of kernel memory and must be installed and configured on a "clean" system to detect future deployments of rootkits [15].

Spafford and Carrier [3] have presented a technique for detecting binary rootkits using outlier analysis on file systems in an offline manner. Our technique is unique in that it permits the real-time detection of kernel rootkits via memory analysis.

3.   LKM Rootkit Detection Technique

Our technique for detecting LKM rootkits does not require the prior installation of detection tools or other software. Trojaned system call addresses (modified addresses) are identified without using any *a priori* knowledge about a system. In particular, rootkits are detected by comparing the distribution of system call addresses from a "suspect" system with the distribution of system call addresses from a known "good" (uninfected) system. Outlier analysis is used to identify infected systems. This method not only identifies the presence of a rootkit, but also the number of individual attacks on a kernel and their locations.

In the following, we demonstrate that the distribution of system call table addresses fits a well-known distribution for more than one architecture. Also, we show how to detect Trojaned system call addresses (the result of rootkit activity) using outlier analysis on the underlying distribution of table addresses from an uninfected system.

3.1 Model Stability

A fundamental assumption of our statistical approach to rootkit detection is that the distribution of system call addresses for a specific kernel version is similar across architectures. This is a necessary condition if analysis is to occur without *a priori* knowledge of the system. We tested this hypothesis by conducting preliminary experiments on a 32-bit Intel machine and a 64-bit SPARC machine with different kernel compilation options. The experimental results are presented in Tables 1 and 2. The two tables show the Anderson-Darling (AD) goodness of fit scores for various distributions. The better the goodness of fit of a distribution, the lower its AD score.

The results show that, while the *Largest Extreme Value* distribution best fits the system call addresses for the 32-bit Intel machine (Table 1), it is not the best fit for the 64-bit SPARC machine (Table 2). However, the *Largest Extreme Value* is still a good fit (and a close second) for the SPARC machine. Although more observations are required to make claims about the goodness of fit of system call addresses for different computer systems, our preliminary results suggest that the claims may be justified, especially for architectures that use the same kernel version.

3.2 Experimental Results

When an LKM rootkit is installed, several entries in the system call table are changed to unusually large values (indicative of the system call table modification attack discussed previously). This changes the goodness of fit score for the *Largest Extreme Value* distribution – the data no longer has such a good fit. Because of the Linux memory model and the method of attack, the outliers are on the extreme right side of the distribution [1]. If these outliers are eliminated one by one, the

Table 1. Distribution fits for a 32-bit Intel machine (kernel 2.4.27).

Distribution	AD Score
Largest Extreme Value	5.038
3-Parameter Gamma	6.617
3-Parameter Loglogistic	7.022
Logistic	7.026
Loglogistic	7.027
3-Parameter Lognormal	10.275
Lognormal	10.348
Normal	10.350
3-Parameter Weibull	49.346
Weibull	49.465
Smallest Extreme Value	49.471
2-Parameter Exponential	81.265
Exponential	116.956

Table 2. Distribution fits for a 64-bit SPARC machine (kernel 2.4.27).

Distribution	AD Score
Loglogistic	10.599
Largest Extreme Value	11.699
Logistic	11.745
Lognormal	19.147
Gamma	20.460
Normal	23.344
3-Parameter Gamma	26.456
3-Parameter Weibull	32.558
3-Parameter Loglogistic	34.591
Weibull	36.178
3-Parameter Lognormal	37.468
Smallest Extreme Value	41.015
2-Parameter Exponential	52.604
Exponential	102.787

distribution slowly moves from an AD score near 100 to very close to the original AD score of approximately five for the 32-bit Intel machine (Table 1).

This idea is the basis of our technique for detecting LKM rootkits. The rootkits modify memory addresses in the system call table, which originally fit the *Largest Extreme Value* distribution very well (AD score of approximately five). The results appears to hold for multiple architectures. In fact, our experiments on the Intel 32-bit and SPARC 64-bit architectures yield similar results.

In the first experiment, we installed the Rkit LKM rootkit version 1.01 on a 32-bit Intel machine with Linux kernel version 2.4.27. We chose Rkit 1.01 because it attacks only *one* system call table entry (sys_setuid). If only one outlier can be detected using this method, rootkits that attack several system call table entries may be detected more easily.

The 32-bit Intel computer running Linux kernel 2.4.27 has a 255-entry system call table that fits the *Largest Extreme Value* distribution with an AD goodness of fit score of 5.038 (Table 1). When Rkit 1.01 is installed, the AD score changes to 99.210 (Table 3). Clearly, an outlier is present in the form of the sys_setuid system call table entry with a much higher memory address. In fact, the rootkit changes the sys_setuid system call table entry address from 0xC01201F0 (good value) to 0xD0878060. The decimal equivalents are 3,222,405,616 (good value) and 3,498,541,152 (approximately 8.5% higher than the good value).

Table 3. Rkit 1.01 results.

System	AD Score
Clean	5.038
Trojaned	99.210
Trojans Removed	4.968

As shown in Table 3, when one system call table address is Trojaned, the AD goodness of fit score for the *Largest Extreme Value* distribution changes from 5.038 to 99.210, an increase of approximately 1,970%. When the Trojaned sys_setuid memory address is removed, the AD score improves to 4.968, within 1.4% of the original score of 5.038.

Table 4. Knark 2.4.3 results.

System	AD Score
Clean	5.038
Trojaned	109.729
Trojans Removed	5.070

In the second experiment, we installed the Knark LKM rootkit version 2.4.3 on the same test system (32-bit Intel computer running Linux kernel version 2.4.27). The Knark 2.4.3 rootkit attacks nine different memory addresses in the system call table. As shown in Table 4, the

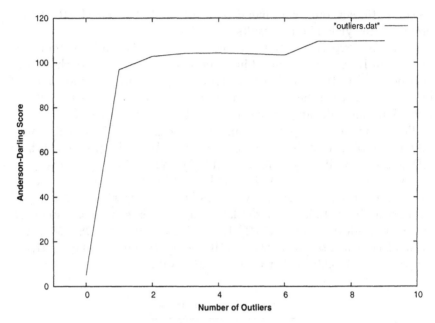

Figure 1. AD score improvement as outliers are removed (Knark 2.4.3).

results are similar to those obtained in the case of Rkit 1.01: a 2,178% decrease in the AD goodness of fit, followed by a return to within 0.7% of the original AD score when the outlying Trojaned addresses are removed.

Also in the second experiment, as the Trojaned system addresses are removed one by one, the AD score improves, but the improvements are not dramatic until the final outlier is removed (Figure 1). This is an example of the concept of "complete detection." Thus, a rootkit that Trojans only *one* system call table address can be successfully detected. Moreover, it is possible to detect not just some or most Trojaned system call addresses, but *all* Trojaned system call addresses.

4.   Conclusions

This research was limited in that only LKM rootkits were investigated and only one operating system (Linux kernel version 2.4.27) was considered for two architectures (Intel 32-bit and SPARC 64-bit machines). Nevertheless, our experiments demonstrate that it is possible to detect these rootkits with a high degree of confidence using outlier analysis.

Our future work will evaluate the generality of the rootkit detection technique by testing it on other operating systems, architectures and

LKM rootkits. Also, we will attempt to verify the principal assumption that system call addresses in a system call table have (or closely fit) the same distribution for all architectures and kernel versions.

Other avenues for future research involve testing systems with security patches that could modify the kernel (and system call table entries), and developing techniques for detecting new kernel rootkits that modify system call table targets instead of addresses.

Acknowledgements

This research was supported in part by a grant from the U.S. Department of Homeland Security through the Kentucky Critical Infrastructure Protection Institute. The authors would also like to thank Drs. Adel El-maghraby, Mehmed Kantardzic and Gail DePuy for their suggestions.

References

[1] M. Burdach, Detecting rootkits and kernel-level compromises in Linux (www.securityfocus.com/infocus/1811), 2004.

[2] A. Busleiman, Detecting and understanding rootkits (www.net-security.org/dl/articles/Detecting_and_Understanding_rootkits.txt) 2003.

[3] B. Carrier and E. Spafford, Automated digital evidence target definition using outlier analysis and existing evidence, *Proceedings of the Fifth Annual Digital Forensics Research Workshop* (www.dfrws.org/2005/proceedings/index.html), 2005.

[4] S. Cesare, Runtime kernel patching (reactor-core.org/runtime-kernel-patching.html).

[5] A. Chuvakin, An overview of Unix rootkits, iALERT White Paper, iDefense Labs (www.megasecurity.org/papers/Rootkits.pdf), 2003.

[6] D. Dittrich, Root kits and hiding files/directories/processes after a break-in (staff.washington.edu/dittrich/misc/faqs/rootkits.faq), 2002.

[7] Honeynet Project, Know your enemy: The motives and psychology of the black hat community (www.linuxvoodoo.org/resources/security/motives), 2000.

[8] P. Hutto, Adding a syscall (www-static.cc.gatech.edu/classes/AY 2001/cs3210_fall/labs/syscalls.html), 2000.

[9] Integrity Computing, Network security: A primer on vulnerability, prevention, detection and recovery (www.integritycomputing.com/security1.html).

[10] Komoku Inc. (www.komoku.com/technology.shtml).

[11] C. Kruegel, W. Robertson and G. Vigna, Detecting kernel-level rootkits through binary analysis (www.cs.ucsb.edu/~wkr/publica tions/acsac2004lkrmpresentation.pdf), 2004.

[12] J. Levine, B. Grizzard and H. Owen, Detecting and categorizing kernel-level rootkits to aid future detection, *IEEE Security & Privacy*, pp. 24–32, January/February 2006.

[13] M. Murilo and K. Steding-Jessen, chkrootkit (www.chkrootkit .org), 2006.

[14] R. Naraine, Government-funded startup blasts rootkits (www.eweek .com/article2/0,1759,1951941,00.asp), April 24, 2006.

[15] N. Petroni, T. Fraser, J. Molina and W. Arbaugh, Copilot – A co-processor-based kernel runtime integrity monitor, *Proceedings of the Thirteenth USENIX Security Symposium*, pp. 179-194, 2004.

[16] J. Rutkowski, Execution path analysis: Finding kernel based rootkits (doc.bughunter.net/rootkit-backdoor/execution-path.html).

[17] Samhain Labs, kern_check.c (la-samhna.de/library/kern_check.c).

[18] J. Scambray, S. McClure and G. Kurtz, *Hacking Exposed: Network Security Secrets and Solutions*, McGraw-Hill/Osborne, Berkeley, California, 2001.

[19] SecurityFocus, scprint.c (downloads.securityfocus.com).

[20] E. Skoudis, *Counter Hack: A Step-by-Step Guide to Computer Attacks and Effective Defenses*, Prentice-Hall, Upper Saddle River, New Jersey, 2001.

[21] W. Stallings, *Network Security Essentials*, Prentice-Hall, Upper Saddle River, New Jersey, 2003.

[22] R. Wichmann, Linux kernel rootkits (coewww.rutgers.edu/www1 /linuxclass2006//documents/kernel_rootkits/index.html), 2002.

[23] D. Zovi, Kernel rootkits (www.sans.org/reading_room/whitepapers /threats/449.php), SANS Institute, 2001.

IV

AUTHORSHIP ATTRIBUTION

Chapter 8

FUTURE TRENDS IN AUTHORSHIP ATTRIBUTION

Patrick Juola

Abstract   Authorship attribution, the science of inferring characteristics of an author from the characteristics of documents written by that author, is a problem with a long history and a wide range of application. This paper surveys the history and present state of the discipline – essentially a collection of *ad hoc* methods with little formal data available to select among them. It also makes some predictions about the needs of the discipline and discusses how these needs might be met.

Keywords: Authorship attribution, stylometrics, text forensics

1.   Introduction

Judges 12:5–6 describes a harsh, but linguistically insightful, solution to the problem of identifying potential security threats:

> 5 And the Gileadites took the passages of Jordan before the Ephraimites: and it was so, that when those Ephraimites which were escaped said, Let me go over; that the men of Gilead said unto him, Art thou an Ephraimite? If he said, Nay;
> 6 Then said they unto him, Say now Shibboleth: and he said Sibboleth: for he could not frame to pronounce it right. Then they took him, and slew him at the passages of Jordan: and there fell at that time of the Ephraimites forty and two thousand.

This barbaric method would not stand up to modern standards regarding rules of evidence – or for that matter, civil rights such as fair trials, appeals or access to counsel. But it illustrates a problem that modern society also has to grapple with. In a world full of bad guys, how can one sort the bad guys from the good ones? If you are looking for a specific bad guy, how can you tell when you have found him?

Please use the following format when citing this chapter:

Juola, P., 2007, in IFIP International Federation for Information Processing, Volume 242, Advances in Digital Forensics III; eds. P. Craiger and S Shenoi;(Boston: Springer), pp. 119-132.

Much of the field of forensics addresses this problem. If you know something about who you are looking for, you look for identifying features specific to that person. These features might be his fingerprints, his DNA, his shoeprints – or his language.

2.   Problem Definition

"Authorship attribution," is broadly defined as the task of inferring characteristics of a document's author, including but not limited to identity, from the textual characteristics of the document itself. This task, of course, has been the bread-and-butter of handwriting examiners, who are recognized as experts at spotting the idiosyncratic loop of an 'e' or slant of an 'l' that reliably characterize the writer. Similar experts can testify to the off-line character that identifies a particular typewriter. But software-only documents – this paper qualifies – do not have these quirks; one flat-ASCII 'A' looks identical to any other. Traditional network forensics may be able to trace a piece of email to a specific computer at a specific time. But who was actually sitting at that computer (perhaps at a public-access terminal in a public library) and typing the document?

Chaski [10, 11] has published several case studies where the authorship of specific digital documents has been a crucial factor in the case. In one case, for example, an employee was dismissed on the basis of emails admittedly written at her desk and on her computer. But in an open-plan office, anyone can wander into any cubicle and use any computer. Did she really write the relevant emails, or was she wrongfully dismissed? In another case, a software "diary" provided crucial exculpatory evidence against the claims of its author. But were the entries genuine, or had they been planted? In a third case, an investigation of a death turned up a suicide note "written" on a computer. Was this note genuinely written by the decedent, or had it been written by the murderer to cover his tracks?

In each of these cases, the computer that created the document was not in question, but the authorship of the document was. And in each case, traditional handwriting analysis was out of the question because the documents were purely electronic. As electronic documents continue to flourish (and possibly displace paper), one can expect that questions and cases like these will only become more common, more divisive and more important.

Of course, the problem of inferring authorship is not limited to the present nor to issues of litigation and criminal prosecution. Generations of scholars have discussed at length the question of whether or not

William Shakespeare was the actual author of the works commonly attributed to him [14, 30]. The 17th-century tradition of anonymous political pamphlets (e.g., *Common Sense*, attributed by scholars to Thomas Paine) has provided work for thousands of historians. This tradition, of course, continues to the present day, for example, in the anonymous publication of *Primary Colors*, attributed to Joe Klein, and *Imperial Hubris*, attributed to Michael Scheuer.

Traditional approaches to this kind of analysis involve close reading by scholarly experts. The potential problems with this are apparent. Although Shakespeare experts may be readily available, how many experts are there on the writing style of Michael Scheuer? And how can the accuracy of such experts be measured, especially to the demanding standards of a Daubert hearing? For this reason, there has been increasing attention paid in recent decades to the development of testable, objective, "non-traditional" methods of authorship attribution, methods that rely not simply on expert judgment, but on the automated detection and statistical analysis of linguistic features. This emerging discipline has been variously called "stylometry," "non-traditional authorship analysis," or simply "authorship attribution."

Within this general framework, we can also identify several different categories of problems. For example, the Judges quotation above is not about identifying individual persons, but identifying members of a specific class (the Ephraimites). This is analogous to the difference between analyzing handwriting using "document analysis" and "graphoanalysis" – where a document analyst may feel comfortable identifying a specific person as the author of a document, she may be quite out of her depth at describing characteristics of that person, such as age, sex, race and personality profile. The discipline of "graphoanalysis" claims roughly the opposite, to be able to analyze handwriting "to provide insight into personality traits and evaluation of a writer's personality" [20], but not to identify individuals. In contrast, stylometrists have been exploring a wide variety of related questions and research topics:

- **Did this person write that document?** This, of course, is probably the oldest, clearest and best-defined version of the authorship attribution question. It has garnered considerable research attention. Holmes [15] provides a good history of the research in this field dating back to the late 1800s.

- **Which of these people wrote that document?** This slightly harder problem describes a typical authorship investigation [35, 43]. The Mosteller-Wallace investigation [35] described later is almost a prototypical example, in that the set of candidate authors was well-defined by previous investigation, and the analysts were merely called upon to referee among them. One can, of course, distinguish two sub-categories of this problem, depending upon whether or not "none of the above" is an acceptable answer.

- **Were all these documents written by the same person?** In many cases, this could serve as a starting point for further investigation [5, 7], but this question may be evidence in and of itself. For example, if a purportedly single-author "diary" or "journal" could be shown to have multiple authors, that in and of itself could show tampering, without needing to find and name alternate authors.

- **When was this document written?** This type of analysis could apply either to the development of a person's writing style [9, 24] or to the general *Zeitgeist* typical of a certain period [23]. In either case, the evidence provided by document dating could prove to be crucial in settling issues of timing.

- **What was the sex of the author?** This question could obviously be generalized from sex [32] to many other aspects of group identity, such as education level [4, 28].

- **What was the mental capacity of the author?** To the extent that language capacity can be used as a diagnostic instrument [6], it can also be used as evidence of someone's mental capacity or to identify the severity and type of insanity.

Given the wide variety of questions that can be posed within this framework, it is not surprising that an equally wide variety of people may be interested in the answers. Beyond the obvious forensic applications for law enforcement and the legal profession, and the equally obvious applications for literature scholars, interested groups might include historians, sociologists and other humanities scholars, educators in general (especially those concerned about plagiarism and academic integrity), psychologists, intelligence analysts and journalists. The ability to infer past the words to the author is a key aspect of many types of humanistic inquiry.

3.   Theory of Stylometry

Although the problem of stylometry has been around since antiquity, the specific application of statistics to this problem is about 150 years old. Holmes [15] cites Mendenhall's 1887 study [34] as the first modern example of statistical stylometry, and traces a flurry of research during the 20th century. A key historical development was the detailed

Mosteller-Wallace [35] study of *The Federalist Papers*, as described below.

3.1   Theoretical Background

From a theoretical perspective, stylometry is no different from many other accepted forensic techniques. Traditional handwriting analysis, for example, assumes that people have specific, individual, persistent and uncontrollable habits of penmanship that can be reliably identified by skilled practitioners. A similar theory underlies DNA analysis, fingerprints, toolmarks, and ballistic markings – one cannot consciously or through an effort of will change the patterns of ridges on one's fingers or the genetic markers in one's blood. Authorship attribution assumes similarly that people have specific, individual, persistent and uncontrollable habits of thought and/or phrasing; some researchers [41] call this a "stylome" in deliberate analogy to the DNA "genome." Although the strict implications of this analogy may be incorrect – in particular, if the "stylome," like the "genome," is fixed and unchangeable, how is it possible to do document dating via stylometry? – it is nevertheless fruitful to explore.

Language, like genetics, can be characterized by a very large set of potential features that may or may not show up in any specific sample, and that may or may not have obvious large-scale impact. The Judges passage above is one example; each language (or dialect subgroup) has a characteristic inventory of sounds. Other accessible examples would include lexical items characteristic of a particular dialect, cultural or social group (such as "chesterfield" among Canadians [12] or "mosquito hawk" among southeastern Americans [21]), or individual quirks (such as an idiosyncratic misspelling of "toutch" [42]). By identifying the features characteristic of the group or individual of interest, and then finding those features in the studied document, one can support a finding that the document was written by that person or a member of that group. The question, then, becomes what features are "characteristic" and how reliable those features are.

Unfortunately, the current state of affairs is something of an *ad hoc* mess. A 1998 paper [37] stated that more than 1,000 different features have been proposed at various times for authorship attribution. At least several dozen analytic methods have been proposed, and even the methods of document treatment vary widely. As a result, space precludes a detailed or even a cursory examination of all the research over the past century and a half.

3.2   Examining the Proposals

Instead, we will try to analyze the structure of the proposals themselves. The first obvious area of variance is the type of feature to be
analyzed. An analysis of "average word length," for example, is not influenced by an author's grammar and syntax, but only her vocabulary.
An analysis of the distribution of sentence lengths is, by contrast, only
influenced by her grammar/syntax and not at all by her vocabulary. We
can divide the types of features analyzed into several broad categories:

- **Lexicographic:** Analysis of the letters and sub-lexical units (such
  as morphemes) in the document [22, 26].

- **Lexical:** Analysis of specific words or their properties such as
  length and distribution, or an analysis of the general content [3,
  18, 19, 43].

- **Syntactic:** Analysis of syntactic patterns, including aspects such
  as word n-grams, distribution of parts of speech, and punctuation.
  We can also include function word analysis into this category, since
  function words tend to illustrate syntactic rather than lexical or
  semantic aspects of the text [4, 7, 31, 35, 40].

- **Layout:** Use of formatting, spacing, color, fonts and size changes,
  and similar non-linguistic aspects of information presentation [1,
  2].

- **"Unusual:"** Finally, of course, there are examples that fail to fit
  neatly into any of these categories or that span multiple levels of
  language [10, 42].

We could make a similar categorization of the proposed analysis methods used – principal components analysis [5, 7, 16], "delta" (t-tests) [8,
18, 19], linear discriminant analysis [4, 41], similarity judgments and k-
nearest neighbors [23, 28], neural networks [40], support vector machines
[3], etc. – but would simply end up cataloging the fields of machine
learning, classification and pattern recognition.

What has unfortunately not been performed, but is badly needed, is a
systematic cross-comparison of these methods. The Daubert criteria for
evidence demand as a principle of law that any proposed forensic analysis
method be subject to rather stringent study, including published error
analysis. Legal requirements aside, any ethical analyst, of course, wishes
to use the most appropriate and most accurate methods available, and
should be able to make informed and objective choices about what those
"best practices" should be. Furthermore, it is possible, perhaps even

likely, that the most effective practices may be a combination of features and techniques from several different proposed methods. What is needed is a stable, objective, and representative test bed to compare proposed methods head-to-head.

As an example of the current muddle, we look in more detail at the Mosteller-Wallace study [35] and its aftermath. *The Federalist Papers* are a set of newspaper essays published between 1787 and 1788 by an anonymous author named "Publius," in favor of the ratification of the newly-proposed Constitution of the United States. It has since become known that "Publius" was a pseudonym for a group of three authors: John Jay, Alexander Hamilton and James Madison. It has also become known that of the eighty-odd essays, Jay wrote five, Madison wrote fourteen, and Hamilton wrote 51, with three more essays written jointly by Madison and Hamilton. The other twelve essays, the famous "disputed essays," are attributed to both Madison and Hamilton.

Modern scholarship is almost unanimous in assigning authorship of the disputed essays to Madison on the basis of traditional historical methods. Mosteller and Wallace were able to make this determination purely on the basis of statistically-inferred probabilities and Bayesian analysis.

In particular, we note that an author has almost complete freedom to choose between the words "big" and "large" or similar synonym pairs; neither the structure of English grammar nor the meanings of the words place any constraints. By observing that one author consistently makes one choice and another the opposite, one has a noticeable, topic-free, and consistent way to differentiate between the authors.

Mosteller and Wallace [35] attempted to apply this technique to *The Federalist Papers*, but found that there were not enough synonym pairs to make this practical. Instead, they focused on so-called "function words," words like conjunctions, prepositions and articles that carry little meaning by themselves (think about what "of" means), but that define relationships of syntactic or semantic functions between other ("content") words in the sentence. These words are, therefore, largely topic-independent and may serve as useful indicators of an author's preferred way to express broad concepts such as "ownership." Mosteller and Wallace, therefore, analyzed the distribution of 30 function words extracted from the text of *The Federalist Papers*.

Because of the circumstances of this problem, *The Federalist Papers* are almost a perfect test bed for new methods of authorship attribution. First, the documents themselves are widely available (albeit with many potential corruptions), including over the Internet through sources such as Project Gutenberg. Second, the candidate set for authorship is well-defined; the author of the disputed papers is known to be either Hamilton or Madison. Third, the undisputed papers provide excellent samples of undisputed text written by the same authors, at the same time, on the same topic, in the same genre, for publication via the same media. A more representative training set would be hard to imagine. For this reason, it has become almost traditional to test a new method on this problem, see, e.g., [17, 22, 33, 36, 38, 40] However, even in this limited situation, it is not possible to compare results directly between analyses, since the corpus itself is not consistently defined. As Rudman [37, 38] has pointed out, different versions of the corpus contain numerous textual flaws, including differences in source versions, wrong letters and misspelling, inconsistency in decisions about what to include or to exclude (such as titles), inclusions of foreign language phrases and quotations, and so on. Even when two researchers ostensibly analyze the same documents, they may not be analyzing the same data!

Some attempts have been made to standardize test corpora for such purposes; examples include the Forsyth corpus [13], the Baayen corpus [4] and the Juola corpus [25]. For the most part, however, papers report on an analysis of samples of convenience that are not necessarily representative or even widely available. The accuracy rates reported usually hover in the 90% range, but that means little when one considers that 90% of ten documents between three authors is a far cry from 90% of a thousand documents between 250 authors.

The generalization question is also unaddressed. Do we have reason to believe that a method that performs brilliantly on Dutch will perform equally well on English? (Or vice versa?) Do successful methods generalize across genres? How much data is needed for a given method to work? Current studies [27] suggest that there is a strong correlation of method performance across different environments, but that may amount to little more than the observation that a method with only mediocre performance in one environment is not likely to miraculously improve in a new and untested one.

4.   The Future

The field of authorship attribution is, therefore, in need of clearly-defined and well-documented standards of practice. Juola has defined a theoretical framework [26] to help establish these standards through the development of modular software [29] specifically to encourage this sort of validation, testing and possible cross-development. The details of this have been described elsewhere [27], and so will be summarized here. In short, the proposed system uses a three-phase structure abstraction of canonization, event determination and inferential statistics, any of which can be defined in several different technical implementations.

Projects like this are, one hopes, only the tip of the iceberg in terms of what the future of authorship attribution will bring. There are a number of crucial issues that need to be addressed to make stylometry a fully-fledged and standard forensic discipline. Fortunately, the seeds of most of the issues and developments have already been planted.

Better test data, for example, is something of a *sine qua non.* Some test corpora have already been developed, and others are on the way. A key aspect to be addressed is the development of specific corpora representing the specific needs of specific communities. For example, researchers such as NYU's David Hoover have been collecting large sets of literary text such as novels, to better aid in the literary analysis of major authors. Such corpora can easily be deployed to answer questions of literary style, such as whether or not a given (anonymous) political pamphlet was actually written by an author of recognized merit, and as such reflects his/her political and social views, to the enrichment of scholars. Such a corpus, however, would not be of much use to law enforcement; not only is 18th or 19th century text unrepresentative of the 21st century, but the idea of a 100,000 word ransom note being analyzed with an eye towards criminal prosecution borders on the ludicrous. The needs of law enforcement are much better served by developing corpora of web log (blog) entries, email, etc. – document styles that are used routinely in investigations. So while we can expect to see much greater development of corpora to serve community needs, we can also expect a certain degree of fragmentation as different subcommunities express (and fund) different needs.

We can expect to see the current *ad hoc* mess of methods and algorithms to be straightened out, as testing on the newly developed corpora becomes more commonplace. Programs such as JGAAP [29] will help support the idea of standardized testing of new algorithms on standardized problems, and the software programs themselves can and will be made available in standard (tested) configurations for use by non-experts. Just as digital forensic tools like EnCase and FTK make file carving and undeletion practical, so will the next generation of authorship attribution tools.

At the same time, concerns such as Rudman's about the handling of questioned documents can be expected to crystallize into standardized procedures about treatment of "dubitanda," aspects of documents of questionable relevance to the authorship question. Further testing will formalize issues such as what kind of documents are "comparable" (it is highly unlikely that there will be ransom notes of known authorship to compare with the ransom note found at the crime scene; are business letters sufficiently "comparable"?) or how much data is "enough" for a confident analysis (it is unlikely that anything useful can be learned from a single-expletive email, but equally unlikely that the suspect will provide investigators with millions of words of text). TREC-style competitions will more than likely provide a source of continuous improvement as well as establish a continuing stream of new "standard" test beds tuned to specific problems.

The new level of computer support will trigger new levels of understanding of the algorithms. Although some efforts (most notably Stein and Argamon [39]) have been made to explain not only that certain methods work, but also why they work, most research to date has been content with finding accurate methods rather than explaining them. The need to explain one's conclusions to a judge, jury and opposing counsel will no doubt spur research into the fundamental linguistic, psychological, and cognitive underpinnings, possibly shedding more light on the purely mental aspects of authorship.

Finally, as scholarship in these areas improves and provides new resources, the acceptance of non-traditional authorship attribution can be expected to improve. Just as handwriting analysis and ballistics are accepted specialist fields, so will "authorship attribution," with the corresponding professional tools, credentials and societies.

5.   Conclusions

This paper has presented a survey, not only of the present state of non-traditional authorship attribution, but of what may be expected in the near-term future. It should be apparent that authorship attribution at present is at a crossroads or, perhaps, at a threshold. The current state of affairs is that of a professional adhocracy, where many different researchers have proposed many different methods, all of which tend to work. However, in the current muddle, there is no clear direction about which methods work better under what circumstances, about what the expected rates of reliability should be under field conditions, and about why particular methods work as well as they do.

These issues will need to be addressed if authorship attribution is to become an accepted a forensic discipline like footprint, toolmark and fingerprint analysis. Fortunately, these issues are being addressed by researchers at the same time as non-specialists in the larger community – whether they be forensic scientists, law enforcement agents or even English professors – are becoming more aware and more accepting of the possibilities, pitfalls and potentials of authorship attribution.

References

[1] A. Abbasi and H. Chen, Identification and comparison of extremist-group web forum messages using authorship analysis, *IEEE Intelligent Systems*, vol. 20(5), pp. 67–75, 2005.

[2] A. Abbasi and H. Chen, Visualizing authorship for identification, in *Proceedings of the IEEE International Conference on Intelligence and Security Informatics (LNCS 3975)*, S. Mehrotra, *et al.* (Eds.), Springer-Verlag, Berlin Heidelberg, Germany, pp. 60–71, 2006.

[3] S. Argamon and S. Levitan, Measuring the usefulness of function words for authorship attribution, *Proceedings of the Joint International Conference of the Association for Literary and Linguistic Computing and the Association for Computers and the Humanities*, 2005.

[4] R. Baayen, H. van Halteren, A. Neijt and F. Tweedie, An experiment in authorship attribution, *Proceedings of JADT 2002: Sixth International Conference on Textual Data Statistical Analysis*, pp. 29–37, 2002.

[5] J. Binongo, Who wrote the 15th Book of Oz? An application of multivariate analysis to authorship attribution, *Chance*, vol. 16(2), pp. 9–17, 2003.

[6] C. Brown, M. Covington, J. Semple and J.Brown, Reduced idea density in speech as an indicator of schizophrenia and ketamine intoxication, presented at the *International Congress on Schizophrenia Research*, 2005.

[7] J. Burrows, "an ocean where each kind...:" Statistical analysis and some major determinants of literary style, *Computers and the Humanities*, vol. 23(4-5), pp. 309–321, 1989.

[8] J. Burrows, Questions of authorships: Attribution and beyond, *Computers and the Humanities*, vol. 37(1), pp. 5-32, 2003.

[9] F. Can and J. Patton, Change of writing style with time, *Computers and the Humanities*, vol. 38(1), pp. 61–82, 2004.

[10] C. Chaski, Who's at the keyboard: Authorship attribution in digital evidence investigations, *International Journal of Digital Evidence*, vol. 4(1), 2005.

[11] C. Chaski, The keyboard dilemma and forensic authorship attribution, in *Advances in Digital Forensics III*, P. Craiger and S. Shenoi (Eds.), Springer, New York, pp. 133–146, 2007.

[12] G. Easson, The linguistic implications of Shibboleths, presented at the *Annual Meeting of the Canadian Linguistics Association*, 2002.

[13] R. Forsyth, Towards a text benchmark suite, *Proceedings of the Joint International Conference of the Association for Literary and Linguistic Computing and the Association for Computers and the Humanities*, 1997.

[14] W. Friedman and E. Friedman., *The Shakespearean Ciphers Examined*, Cambridge University Press, Cambridge, United Kingdom, 1957.

[15] D. Holmes, Authorship attribution, *Computers and the Humanities*, vol. 28(2), pp. 87–106, 1994.

[16] D. Holmes, Stylometry and the Civil War: The case of the Pickett Letters, *Chance*, vol. 16(2), pp. 18–26, 2003.

[17] D. Holmes and R. Forsyth, The Federalist revisited: New directions in authorship attribution, *Literary and Linguistic Computing*, vol. 10(2), pp. 111–127, 1995.

[18] D. Hoover, Delta prime? *Literary and Linguistic Computing*, vol. 19(4), pp. 477–495, 2004.

[19] D. Hoover, Testing Burrows' delta, *Literary and Linguistic Computing*, vol. 19(4), pp. 453–475, 2004.

[20] International Graphoanalysis Society (IGAS), (www.igas.com).

[21] E. Johnson, *Lexical Change and Variation in the Southeastern United States 1930–1990*, University of Alabama Press, Tuscaloosa, Alabama, 1996.

[22] P. Juola, What can we do with small corpora? Document categorization via cross-entropy, *Proceedings of the Interdisciplinary Workshop on Similarity and Categorization*, 1997.

[23] P. Juola, The rate of language change, *Proceedings of the Fourth International Conference on Quantitative Linguistics*, 2000.

[24] P. Juola, Becoming Jack London, *Proceedings of the Fifth International Conference on Quantitative Linguistics*, 2003.

[25] P. Juola, Ad-hoc authorship attribution competition, *Proceedings of the Joint International Conference of the Association for Literary and Linguistic Computing and the Association for Computers and the Humanities*, 2004.

[26] P. Juola, On composership attribution, *Proceedings of the Joint International Conference of the Association for Literary and Linguistic Computing and the Association for Computers and the Humanities*, 2004.

[27] P. Juola, Authorship attribution for electronic documents, in *Advances in Digital Forensics II*, M. Olivier and S. Shenoi (Eds.), Springer, New York, pp. 119–130, 2006.

[28] P. Juola and H. Baayen, A controlled-corpus experiment in authorship attribution by cross-entropy, *Literary and Linguistic Computing*, vol. 20, pp. 59–67, 2005.

[29] P. Juola, J. Sofko and P. Brennan, A prototype for authorship attribution studies, *Literary and Linguistic Computing*, vol. 21(2), pp. 169–178, 2006.

[30] D. Kahn, *The Codebreakers*, Scribner, New York, 1996.

[31] V. Kešelj and N. Cercone, CNG method with weighted voting, presented at the *Joint International Conference of the Association for Literary and Linguistic Computing and the Association for Computers and the Humanities*, 2004.

[32] M. Koppel, S. Argamon and A. Shimoni, Automatically categorizing written texts by author gender, *Literary and Linguistic Computing*, vol. 17(4), pp. 401–412, 2002.

[33] C. Martindale and D. McKenzie, On the utility of content analysis in authorship attribution: The Federalist Papers, *Computers and the Humanities*, vol. 29(4), pp. 259–270, 1995.

[34] T. Mendenhall, The characteristic curves of composition, *Science*, vol. IX, pp. 237–249, 1887.

[35] F. Mosteller and D. Wallace, *Inference and Disputed Authorship: The Federalist*, Addison-Wesley, Reading, Massachusetts, 1964.

[36] M. Rockeach, R. Homant and L. Penner, A value analysis of the disputed Federalist Papers, *Journal of Personality and Social Psychology*, vol. 16, pp. 245–250, 1970.

[37] J. Rudman, The state of authorship attribution studies: Some problems and solutions, *Computers and the Humanities*, vol. 31, pp. 351–365, 1998.

[38] J. Rudman, The non-traditional case for the authorship of the twelve disputed Federalist Papers: A monument built on sand, *Proceedings of the Joint International Conference of the Association for Literary and Linguistic Computing and the Association for Computers and the Humanities*, 2005.

[39] S. Stein and S. Argamon, A mathematical explanation of Burrows' delta, *Proceedings of the Digital Humanities Conference*, 2006.

[40] F. Tweedie, S. Singh and D. Holmes, Neural network applications in stylometry: The Federalist Papers, *Computers and the Humanities*, vol. 30(1), pp. 1–10, 1996.

[41] H. van Halteren, R. Baayen, F. Tweedie, M. Haverkort and A. Neijt, New machine learning methods demonstrate the existence of a human stylome, *Journal of Quantitative Linguistics*, vol. 12(1), pp. 65–77, 2005.

[42] F. Wellman, *The Art of Cross-Examination*, MacMillan, New York, 1936.

[43] G. Yule, *The Statistical Study of Literary Vocabulary*, Cambridge University Press, Cambridge, United Kingdom, 1944.

Chapter 9

THE KEYBOARD DILEMMA AND AUTHORSHIP IDENTIFICATION

Carole Chaski

Abstract   The keyboard dilemma is the problem of identifying the authorship of a document that was produced by a computer to which multiple users had access. This paper describes a systematic methodology for authorship identification. Validation testing of the methodology demonstrated 95% cross validated accuracy in identifying documents from ten authors and 85% cross validated accuracy in identifying five-sentence chunks from ten authors.

Keywords: Forensic linguistics, authorship identification

1. Introduction

The "keyboard dilemma" is a fundamental problem in forensic linguistic and digital forensic investigations. The keyboard dilemma is posed as follows: Even if a document can be traced to a particular computer and/or IP address, how can we identify who was actually at the keyboard composing the document? It is a particular problem in environments where multiple users may have access to the same computer or when users do not have to authenticate themselves to access a particular account. The keyboard dilemma enables defense lawyers to use the "keyboard defense," suggesting that an unknown person obtained access to the suspect's computer. This is a very possible scenario in corporate cubicles where machines are left running and unattended, or in an open access area such as a public library.

This paper focuses on authorship identification as a means for resolving the keyboard dilemma. It discusses the main issues underlying authorship identification, and proposes a syntactic analysis methodology for authorship identification. This systematic methodology for author-

Please use the following format when citing this chapter:

Chaski, C., 2007, in IFIP International Federation for Information Processing, Volume 242, Advances in Digital Forensics III; eds. P. Craiger and S Shenoi;(Boston: Springer), pp. 133-146.

ship identification is implemented in the Automated Linguistic Identification and Assessment System (ALIAS) [1, 3].

2.   Authorship Identification

Several cases involving the successful collaboration of digital investigations and authorship identification have been documented [1, 3]. The cases include a suicide note left on a home computer, racially-targeted e-mails to a supervisor sent from an open access machine at a government agency, and an electronic diary maintained in a military research laboratory that was accessible by military and civilian personnel [3]. Other recent cases have involved common access environments such as classrooms, public libraries, Internet chat rooms, news groups and blogs. The discussion of authorship identification begins with a case that involved the author of this paper as a defense expert.

The author was contacted by the defense attorney of a thirty-year-old female high school teacher who was accused of having sexual relations with a seventeen-year-old male student. The prosecution's evidence was based on several love notes found on a classroom computer. The unsigned love notes were purported to have been written by the teacher and the student. The authorship of some of the love notes was fairly obvious based on their content (e.g., if a note mentioned having to take a test, it was assumed to have originated from the student). For a few notes, it was difficult to tell whether the author was the teacher or the student. Based on their content, sixteen notes, comprising 1,749 words, were first classed as the teacher's love notes; seven notes, comprising 470 words, were classed as the student's love notes.

The defendant maintained that she had not authored any of the attributed love notes. She claimed that the computer had belonged to a former teacher who was involved with students, and who had subsequently left the state. Another possible scenario was that the student authored all the love notes, fabricating the entire correspondence.

The defense attorney supplied the author of this paper with copies of all the love notes as well as several e-mail messages that were known to be from the defendant. The defendant's seventeen known writing samples (1,988 words in total) included e-mail correspondence to parents regarding students' progress reports, and e-mail messages to friends and family members. The author of this paper also requested writing samples from the teacher whom the defendant claimed had written the notes, but the defense attorney could not supply the samples due to jurisdictional and constitutional obstacles.

The issues for this case were: Did the defendant write the teacher's love notes? In other words, were the teacher's purported love notes identifiable with or different from the teacher's known e-mails? Alternatively, did the student write the teacher's and student's love notes? Specifically, were the teacher's purported love notes identifiable with or different from the student's purported love notes?

To answer these questions, the author of this paper applied an authorship identification methodology (described later) called ALIAS [1, 3]. The ALIAS methodology showed that the writing samples from the student and the defendant were clearly different, with the two sets of documents being separated with 100% cross validated accuracy. All the defendant's texts were classified correctly, as were the student's purported love notes. Since the student claimed that he had written love notes to the teacher, and the defendant acknowledged her own writing samples, the 100% separation of the student and defendant demonstrated that the ALIAS methodology could be accurately applied to the data at hand. If the ALIAS methodology had separated the two known authors with lower (say 70%) accuracy, further testing would not have been conducted because the authorship prediction model would not have been sufficiently accurate.

Next, the author of this paper used a discriminant function to predict the authorship of the sixteen love notes purported to have been written by the teacher. Of the sixteen notes, only three were classified as the student's writing while the remaining thirteen were classified as the defendant's writing. At that point it became clear that the teacher's claims were not entirely true.

Even though the analysis pointed to the defendant's authorship of the love notes, the notes themselves revealed that the relationship might not have been consummated. The defense attorney was advised that the authorship analysis was not helpful to his client, but that the content of the notes could provide a defense against the charge of having sexual relations with a minor. Even though the defendant continued to insist that she did not author any love notes, she was found guilty of taking indecent liberties with a minor. She was found not guilty of the more serous crime of having sexual relations with a minor.

3. Forensic Authorship Identification

This section describes factors relevant to real-world authorship identification, namely scarcity, mixed text type and brevity. In addition, it discusses a cross validation approach for verifying the accuracy of authorship attribution methodologies.

3.1   Scarcity, Mixed Text Type and Brevity

Authorship attribution is a pattern recognition problem whose goal is to estimate how similar two sets of patterns are from each other, based on patterns of linguistic behavior in documents of known and unknown authorship. The primary challenges to authorship attribution are text scarcity, mixed text type and brevity of questioned and known texts.

Forensically-relevant texts are typically scarce for several reasons. First, investigators are often expected to act as soon as possible to protect victims. If a person has received threatening communications, the police certainly would not tell the victim to wait until thirty more threats are received. Second, it may not be in the best interest of an investigation to make the suspect aware that authenticated (known) samples of his/her writing are being collected. Third, in some scenarios, e.g., suicide investigations, investigators cannot obtain additional writing samples and so the only available comparison documents are what is at hand. Fourth, from the operational security perspective, minimal communication should be used to gather intelligence so that plots can be foiled before they are set into motion.

Related to the scarcity of texts is another aspect of forensic author identification – text type – which non-forensic author identification methods typically never consider. Text type or register of the comparative known documents is often not the same as the register of the questioned document. For instance, if the suspect document is a suicide note, it is rare that the alleged author would have written other suicide notes that could be compared with the questioned document. If the suspect document is a threat and the known documents are also threats, there is no need to determine the suspect document since the known threats already settle the fact that the author sent threats. If the document is a business e-mail, it might have to be compared to blog posts or love letters or corporate reports. Thus, forensic authorship identification usually has to deal with cross-register or mixed text type data.

Many of the newer authorship identification methods derived from machine learning focus on e-mail or blog text. E-mail and blogs are attractive because of their availability and cultural pervasiveness, but their use in validating authorship identification methods should take into account certain caveats. One problem with this kind of data is that e-mails and blog posts cannot be independently authenticated: the researcher trusts that the screen name was used by one person (again, the keyboard dilemma). Since the very issue to be tested is how accurately a method discriminates authors' writings, it is unwise to test the method on data for which authorship is unknown. For instance, in one recent test [4], it was argued that two writers must have used the same screen name because the test results split the documents from one screen name into two separate classes. But the other obvious interpretation is that the authorship identification method simply erred in the classification. Because the data was not independently authenticated, there really is no way to assess the accuracy of the method.

E-mail and blog data are not ideal testbeds for authorship identification because the documents typically only include one text type on one topic. Ideally, forensic authorship identification methods should accurately discriminate between authors even when the known and comparative texts are different text types on different topics. A forensic authorship identification method is called upon to compare, for instance, a threat letter to business e-mails, listserv posts, love letters, perhaps even a blog narrative, so the method must be able to work across registers and should not be confined to test data of only one text type.

Forensically-relevant texts are typically brief. Threat letters, suicide notes, ransom demands and phony letters of recommendation are text types that, in general, do not lend themselves to verbosity. The Unabomber's Manifesto is obviously an exception.

Given these characteristics of forensic data, forensic authorship identification methods must be able to cope with a minimal amount of brief documents ranging across different text types. If a method cannot function under these conditions, it may neither be feasible nor reliable enough to be used in a forensic investigation.

3.2 Cross Validation

The accuracy of a classification algorithm is tested using a cross validation technique. This involves withholding a portion of the original data from model building and then classifying it using the model. "Leave-one-out cross validation" involves withholding each text from model building and subsequently using the model to predict its class. In contrast, in "n-fold cross validation," a certain fraction, e.g., one-tenth (n = 10), of the data is withheld from model building and later classified by the model. If ten documents are available and the leave-one-out cross validation methodology is employed, then ten models are built using nine documents each and each document is classified using a model it did not help build. The numbers of hits and misses for each model are averaged to obtain the final cross validated accuracy score.

Suppose Authors A and B have provided the same number of text samples, then any text has an equal (50%) chance of being classified correctly as having been written by A or B. If a classification algorithm based on certain linguistic features returns a cross validated accuracy score of 100%, then it is clear that A and B can be classified correctly much higher than the base rate of 50%. However, if the algorithm returns an accuracy score of 50%, then A and B can only be classified at the base rate or chance level of 50%.

Cross validation accuracy scores answer two questions. First, whether the selected linguistic features can distinguish two authors using the particular classification algorithm. Second, whether the classification algorithm can distinguish the two authors with the particular set of linguistic features.

Note that an accuracy score does not provide data on the likelihood that Author A wrote a particular text. Rather, the accuracy score is a record of hits and misses for the classification algorithm.

4. ALIAS Methodology

ALIAS (Automated Linguistic Identification and Assessment System) is a syntactic forensic authorship identification methodology that was developed specifically to cope with scarcity, brevity and mixed types [1, 3]. ALIAS has been validated using the Writer Sample Database [1, 3], a forensically-realistic and linguistically-controlled testbed. This section describes the ALIAS implementation, the Writer Sample Database and the validation testing results.

4.1 ALIAS Implementation

ALIAS was developed by Chaski [1, 3] for the purpose of storing, accessing and analyzing texts in a forensically-relevant manner. ALIAS combines data management and computational linguistics tools. Searching and sorting are automatically optimized by building the system within a database platform; natural language analysis is implemented via scripts. ALIAS is built on the Filemaker Pro platform, which provides rapid development and testing on Windows and Macintosh platforms as well as a robust scripting language and plug-ins.

ALIAS includes routines for analyzing natural language and for calculating results based on these analyses. ALIAS implements numerous standard methods and algorithms, including tokenizing, lemmatizing, stemming, n-graphing, n-gramming, sentence-splitting, text-splitting, punctuation tagging, part-of-speech tagging, abbreviation-tagging and phrasal parsing. While ALIAS implements all of these routines for the English language, it can handle multilingual data and non-Roman orthographies for many of these routines.

Tokenizing breaks each text into its words or tokens. Lemmatizing or typing produces the base or dictionary form of a word, from which all other variants of the word can be derived. Stemming, which often overlaps with lemmatizing, produces the main stem by stripping away prefixes and suffixes, e.g., stemming produces "book" from "rebooked" by stripping the prefix "re" and suffix "ed." The n-graphing routine breaks text into a substring of characters or graphs of a length specified by n; n-gramming analyzes the text into a substring of words (or tokens or lemmata or stems or part-of-speech tags) of a length specified by n. Sentence-splitting breaks text into its component sentences so that sentences and structures within the sentences can be analyzed. Text-splitting breaks text into a specified number of sentences. Punctuation-tagging identifies each punctuation mark in the text, while part-of-speech tagging identifies for each word its specific grammatical function (such as noun, adjective, modal verb, finite verb, etc.). Abbreviation-tagging identifies common abbreviations. Phrasal parsing gathers part-of-speech tags into phrases which the words form.

Given the outputs of these routines, ALIAS performs many important computational linguistic calculations. These include calculating type-token ratios for words, lemmata and stems; frequency counts for words, lemmata, stems, punctuation marks, POS tags, n-graphs, n-grams, POS n-grams, sentences, abbreviations, paragraphs within texts, and user-specified patterns; and the lengths and average lengths of words, lemmata, stems, sentences, paragraphs and texts. Additionally, ALIAS produces frequency counts of proprietary patterns related to the distribution of punctuation and syntactic phrase types.

ALIAS offers several functions that are very useful to investigators: authorship identification, intertextuality, threat assessment, interrogation probing and dialectal profiling. Each function implements linguistic methods that have been validated independent of any litigation. ALIAS enables investigators to answer important questions such as: Who authored a text? How similar are two texts? Is this text more like a real threat or a simulated threat? Are there indications of deception in this text? What demographics are associated with this text?

Each function uses specific combinations of the routines described above to produce linguistic variables that are analyzed statistically. The analysis uses simple statistical procedures within ALIAS, but ALIAS also interfaces with SPSS and DTREG [5] statistical software. Other statistical programs such as SAS or Weka [6] may also be used.

Within the authorship identification component, ALIAS includes routines for lemmatizing, lexical frequency ranking, calculating lexical, sentential and text lengths, punctuation-edge counting, POS-tagging, n-graph and n-gram sorting, and markedness subcategorizing, all based on standard linguistic theory and computational linguistic algorithms. ALIAS is thus able to incorporate a large number of linguistic variables.

Authorship identification in ALIAS uses only three types of variables: punctuation related to syntactic edges, syntactic structures sorted by internal structures and word length. ALIAS produces numerical outputs for these variables that are analyzed statistically. SPSS is used for discriminant function analysis, and DTREG is used for support vector machines and tree model computations.

4.2   Writer Sample Database

The Writer Sample Database [1, 3] was created for the purpose of empirically validating forensic linguistic methods. The database incorporates a collection of texts from 166 subjects of both genders and several races. For inclusion in the study, subjects had to: (i) be willing to write between three to ten texts at their leisure for a small payment; (ii) be students or be employed in positions for which writing was a part of their normal lifestyle; (iii) be similar to each other in dialectal backgrounds so that the methods could be tested to discern sub-dialectal level differences as well as dialectal similarities; and (iv) have at least a senior-year high school educational level and be at least seventeen years of age.

Several factors affected the selection of topics for writing samples. Research has shown that the social context and communicative goal of a message affects its form. It is also known that intra-writer performance varies when the writer is writing for home or personal consumption as opposed to business or professional purposes. Yet, as discussed earlier, forensic methods must accommodate comparisons between two disparate types of text. The tasks also have to be similar to the kinds of text that are actually forensically relevant. To evoke both home and professional varieties, and emotionally-charged and formal language across several text types, subjects were asked to write about the following topics.

- Describe a traumatic or terrifying event in your life and how you overcame it.

- Describe one or more persons who have influenced you.

- What are your career goals and why?

- Write a letter of complaint about a product or service.

- Write a letter to your insurance company.

- Write a letter of apology to your best friend.

Table 1. Demographics of subjects in validation testing data.

Subject	Race	Sex	Age	Education
16	White	Female	40	College (1)
23	White	Female	20	College (2)
80	White	Female	48	College (3)
96	White	Female	39	College (3)
98	White	Female	25	College (2)
90	White	Male	26	College (1)
91	White	Male	42	College (3)
97	White	Male	31	College (3)
99	White	Male	22	College (4)
166	White	Male	17	High School (4)

- Write a letter to your sweetheart expressing your feelings.

- What makes you really angry?

- Write an angry or threatening letter to someone you know who has hurt you.

- Write an angry or threatening letter to a public official or celebrity.

4.3 Validation Testing Data

Ten subjects were selected for the validation tests. Table 1 presents demographic data pertaining to these subjects.

Each subject was set a target of at least 100 sentences and/or approximately 2,000 words, sufficient data to produce reliable statistical indicators. One author (Subject 98) needed only four documents to hit both targets because she produced numerous long sentences. Two authors (Subjects 80 and 96) needed ten documents to produce at least 100 sentences and/or 2,000 words. Three authors (Subjects 16, 91 and 97) needed six documents to hit the sentence target, but only one of the three exceeded the word target. Subject 16 wrote very long sentences that produced the largest number of words, although she produced only 107 sentences in six documents. Details about each author's data are shown in Tables 2 (Females) and 3 (Males).

4.4 Document Level Testing

In many forensic situations, the issue is whether or not a particular document has been authored by a particular person. Therefore, the first validation test was run at the document level.

Table 2. Female authors and texts in the validation testing data.

Subject	Task ID	Texts	Sentences	Words	Av. Test Size (min, max)
16	1-4, 7, 8	6	107	2,706	430 (344, 557)
23	1-5	5	134	2,175	435 (367, 500)
80	1-10	10	118	1,959	195 (90, 323)
96	1-10	10	108	1,928	192 (99, 258)
98	1-3, 10	4	103	2,176	543 (450, 608)
Total		35	570	10,944	

Table 3. Male authors and texts in the validation testing data.

Subject	Task ID	Texts	Sentences	Words	Av. Test Size (min, max)
90	1-8	8	106	1,690	211 (168, 331)
91	1-6	6	108	1,798	299 (196, 331)
97	1-7	6	114	1,487	248 (219, 341)
99	1-7	7	105	2,079	297 (151, 433)
166	1-7	7	108	1,958	278 (248, 320)
Total		34	541	9,012	

ALIAS extracted linguistic patterns (punctuation related to syntactic edges, syntactic structures sorted by internal structures and word length) for each sentence of each document. Next, the sentence output for each document was totaled to obtain the document level data. For each document, the document level counts were divided by the total number of words in the document. This normalization procedure regulated the differences in document lengths.

The document level data was then analyzed using SPSS's linear discriminant function analysis (LDFA) procedure. The procedure was set to use leave-one-out cross validation. Every author was tested against every other author, resulting in a total of 45 tests.

Table 4 presents the results for pairwise testing. For example, the first column of Table 4 shows that Subject 16's documents were discriminated with 100% cross validated accuracy from Subject 23's documents, Subject 80's documents, etc., but were discriminated with only 80% cross validated accuracy from Subject 98's documents. The author average shows the average of the cross validated accuracy scores for an author against all other authors in the testbed. Subject 16's documents on av-

Table 4. Cross validation accuracy scores for document level testing.

Subject	16	23	80	90	91	96	97	98	99	166
16	X	100	100	100	100	100	100	80	100	100
23	100	X	100	100	100	100	100	89	92	100
80	100	100	X	94	100	70	100	100	82	100
90	100	100	94	X	71	94	100	100	87	80
91	100	100	100	71	X	100	92	100	nvq	100
96	100	100	70	94	100	X	88	100	88	100
97	100	100	100	100	92	88	X	100	100	100
98	80	89	100	100	100	100	100	X	91	100
99	100	92	82	87	nvq	88	100	91	X	93
166	100	100	100	80	100	100	100	100	93	X
Average	97	98	94	92	95	93	98	94	92	97

erage are accurately distinguished 97% of the time from the documents of the other nine subjects. Subjects were not tested against themselves, so the corresponding test cells are marked with an "X." Test cells are marked with an "nvq" when no variables qualified for the linear discriminant function.

Table 4 shows that the ALIAS methodology provides an overall accuracy of 95% for the validation testbed.

4.5   Five-Sentence-Chunk Level Testing

In some cases no more than 100 sentences may be available for analysis. The sentences could come from one document or from several short texts. The investigator might have only been able to obtain a sentence or two from one place and a few sentences from somewhere else. The primary issue is the level of reliability that the ALIAS methodology can provide for extremely short documents. This issue is addressed by running a validation test with sentence level data bundled into five-sentence chunks.

As explained earlier, ALIAS outputs sentence level data. Therefore, the first 100 sentences from each of the subjects were used in the test so that every author was represented by 100 sentences. The 100 sentences came from different documents, and a five-sentence chunk might come from two different documents.

SPSS's linear discriminant function analysis (LDFA) procedure and machine learning classification algorithms from DTREG were used in the experiment, along with the leave-one-out cross validation strategy. Ten-fold cross validation was used for the support vector machines with

Table 5.   Results for five-sentence chunk level testing.

Subject	Documents	SVM	RBF	Polynomial	DT Forest
16	97	95.28	95.28	95.83	92.50
23	98	88.33	85.28	80.56	82.78
80	94	85.56	80.56	77.78	81.39
90	92	76.67	81.94	80.28	76.11
91	95	74.17	81.94	78.89	75.28
96	93	83.61	78.61	76.11	76.11
97	98	85.83	83.61	79.44	82.22
98	94	84.17	79.44	76.11	82.50
99	92	82.50	78.06	74.17	80.83
168	97	88.89	76.39	79.72	86.39
Average	95	84.50	82.11	79.89	81.61

radial basis function (RBF) and polynomial kernels. The default out-of-bag validation provided by DTREG was used for the decision tree forest (DT Forest) predictive model.

The intent is to show how the different algorithms perform on the data. Therefore, Table 5 does not report the pairwise results for each author; instead, it presents the average for each author and the author average from Table 4 to contrast the document level data and the sentence-chunk level data.

Table 5 shows that Subject 16's five-sentence chunks are highly distinguishable from the nine other authors for an overall average hit rate of 95.28% for discriminant function analysis and support vector machine with radial basis function kernel, 95.83% for the support vector machine with polynomial kernel, and 92.50% for the decision tree forest. Subject 91 shows the lowest average hit rate for discriminant function analysis at 74.17%, with an improved rate of 81.94% for the support vector machine with radial basis function. For the ten subjects, the highest overall accuracy rate of 84.50% was achieved using discriminant function analysis, but the support vector machine and decision tree forest algorithms achieved only slightly lower total hit rates of approximately 80%.

The results for the five-sentence chunk data are lower than the rates for the document level data. But these results are surprisingly good when one considers that the "documents" contained only five sentences. The results suggest that there is at least an investigative function for authorship attribution in the forensic setting, even when the textual data available to investigators is in small five-sentence chunks or in even smaller chunks that are put together to create five-sentence chunks. The methodology thus appears to hold promise for analyzing blog posts, e-mail messages, pornographic requests and, perhaps, chat room conversations.

5. Conclusions

The ALIAS methodology is a powerful syntactic analysis technique for authorship identification. The validation testing results indicate that the methodology is effective even when the textual data available for analysis is in small chunks, including chunks that are put together from even smaller chunks.

To effectively address the keyboard dilemma, it is important that investigators use a forensic linguistic method that has been validated on forensically-feasible data independently of any litigation. The forensic linguistic method should also have a track record of admissibility. Known writing samples should be authenticated independently and reliably. If samples cannot be authenticated or if there is a possibility that a suspect or attorney may not be telling the truth about the authorship of a known writing sample, it is important to seek out other known samples that can be authenticated.

As in any science, precautions must be taken to avoid confirmation bias. Therefore, the forensic linguist should not be exposed to any details of the case prior to conducting authorship analysis. A digital forensics investigation should be conducted to complement the analysis if the case and the evidence warrant such an investigation. But it is important that the forensic linguist not see the results of the digital forensic analysis and the digital forensics analyst not be privy to any results from the linguistic analysis. The independent convergence of results would serve to strengthen both analyses.

References

[1] C. Chaski, Who wrote it? Steps toward a science of authorship identification, *National Institute of Justice Journal*, vol. 233, pp. 15–22, 1997.

[2] C. Chaski, A Daubert-inspired assessment of language-based author identification, Technical Report NCJ 172234, National Institute of Justice, Washington, DC, 1998.

[3] C. Chaski, Who's at the keyboard? Recent results in authorship attribution, *International Journal of Digital Evidence*, vol. 4(1), 2005.

[4] J. Li, R. Zheng and H. Chen, From fingerprint to writeprint, *Communications of the ACM*, vol. 49(4), pp. 76–82, 2006.

[5] P. Sherrod, DTREG: Software for predictive modeling and forecasting (www.dtreg.com).

[6] I. Witten and E. Frank, *Data Mining: Practical Machine Learning Tools and Techniques*, Morgan Kaufmann, San Francisco, California, 2005.

V

FORENSIC TECHNIQUES

Chapter 10

FACTORS AFFECTING ONE-WAY HASHING OF CD-R MEDIA

Christopher Marberry and Philip Craiger

Abstract   While conducting a validation study of proficiency test media we found that applying the same hash algorithm against a single CD using different forensic applications resulted in different hash values. We formulated a series of experiments to determine the cause of the anomalous hash values. Our results suggest that certain write options cause forensic applications to report different hash values. We examine the possible consequences of these anomalies in legal proceedings and provide best practices for the use of hashing procedures.

Keywords: Cryptographic hash functions, one-way hashing, CD-R media

1.   Introduction

Digital forensics professionals frequently use hash algorithms such as MD5 [7] and SHA-1 [4] in their work. For example, they may identify notable files (e.g., malware or child pornography) on media by comparing their known hash values with the hash values of files that exist on the media. Examiners also use hash values to identify and exclude common files, e.g., system files and utilities, thereby reducing the search space in investigations of digital media. But the most important use of hashing is the verification of the integrity of evidentiary media: verifying that a forensic duplicate is a bit-for-bit copy of the original file, and, in particular, verifying that a forensic duplicate has not been altered during the chain of custody. This use of cryptographic hashing is critical in judicial proceedings as it helps preserve a defendant's right to a fair trial.

While conducting a validation study of digital forensics proficiency test media we were surprised to find that several commonly used forensic applications reported different hash values for the same CD. Since a hash value is computed based on the contents of a file, a different hash value

Please use the following format when citing this chapter:

Marberry, C., Craiger, P., 2007, in IFIP International Federation for Information Processing, Volume 242, Advances in Digital Forensics III; eds. P. Craiger and S Shenoi; (Boston: Springer), pp. 149-161.

should be obtained only if the file's contents were modified. Changes in a file's metadata, e.g,. date and time stamps, location and name, should not affect the computed hash value.

To determine the cause of the anomalous results, we formulated a series of experiments using several variables: CD write options, system hardware, operating system and CD drive. The experiments involved the use of four popular forensic applications to calculate MD5 hash values of several test CDs. Our results suggest that certain write options cause forensic applications to report different hash values. We examine the possible consequences of these anomalies in legal proceedings and provide best practices for the use of hashing procedures.

2.   Experimental Method

To reduce the number of factors in our experimental design, we chose variables that were most likely to affect the hash values. These variables were: (i) CD write options, (ii) system hardware, (iii) operating system, and (iv) CD drive.

2.1   CD Write Options

Several dozen write attributes are available for writing a CD. The CD used in our original validation study was created using the k3b application in Linux. We used default writing methods to write the CD, which included track-at-once, ISO-9660 + Joliet, and non multi-session.

We employed three common write attributes in our experiments. Each attribute had two options, resulting in eight distinct experimental cells. The three attributes, which are described in more detail below, were: (i) disk-at-once (DAO) versus track-at-once (TAO), (ii) multi-session versus non multi-session, and (iii) ISO 9660 versus ISO 9660 + Joliet.

2.1.1   Disk Write Method.   The track-at-once (TAO) disk write method, by default, inserts a two-second pause between tracks during the writing process. It is commonly used to write disks with multiple tracks or disks with audio and data tracks [12]. The disk-at-once (DAO) option writes all the tracks on a CD in one pass, allowing a variable-length pause or no pause between tracks. Unlike TAO, DAO, by default, does not insert gaps between tracks [12]. DAO is commonly used when there is no need to insert gaps between tracks or when a gap that is not two seconds long is needed [12].

2.1.2   Session.   The multi-session write option allows multiple sessions to be written on a disk. A session is a container for the individual components that make up the structure of a CD. The session components comprise a lead-in area, the track(s) containing data, and a lead-out area [11]. The lead-in area contains the table of contents for the session, which gives the location of each track in the session (similar to a partition table) [11]. Tracks are the sequential sectors on the disk itself. The lead-out area closes the session on the disk [11]. The non multi-session write option only allows for one session to be opened and closed on a disk. As with a multi-session disk, the session on a non multi-session disk contains a lead-in area, data tracks, and a lead-out area.

2.1.3   File System.   The ISO 9660 file system, which was developed for CDs, allows data to be written so that it is accessible by any operating system [3]. The Joliet extension to the ISO 9660 standard allows filenames up to 64 characters [10]. (The ISO 9660 standard restricted filenames to eight characters.)

Table 1.   Test systems.

Hardware and Operating System	Optimal Drive and Firmware
System 1: Dell Optiplex 260 w/ Windows 2000 SP4	Samsung SC-148C w/ Firmware B104
System 2: Dell Optiplex 620 w/ Windows Server 2003 SP1	NEC ND-3550A w/ Firmware 1.05
System 3: Dell Poweredge 2800 Dual Booting Windows XP SP2/Linux	Samsung SN-324S w/ Firmware U304

2.2   Test Systems

We used three computer systems in our tests, each with a different optical drive in order to determine if different hardware configurations might produce different hash values. We also used different operating systems – Windows 2000, Windows XP, Windows 2003 Server and Redhat Linux Enterprise Workstation 4 – to establish if they had an effect on the hash results. The hardware, operating system and optical drive configurations are presented in Table 1. Since this is not a fully crossed experimental design, it is not possible to separate the hardware configuration and operating system effects.

2.3   Hashing Applications

We selected commonly used forensic applications to hash the test media. For the Windows systems, the applications included Guidance

Software's EnCase 4 and EnCase 5 [5], AccessData's Forensic Toolkit (FTK) [1] and X-Ways Forensics [13]. Specifically, EnCase 4.22a, En-Case 5.05a, FTK Imager 2.2 and X-Ways Forensics 13.0 were installed on each system (see Table 1). For the Redhat Enterprise Linux 4 applications, we used the command line utility md5sum 5.2.1, readcd 2.01 and isoinfo 2.01. We used md5sum to produce the MD5 hash for each disk, readcd [2] to report the TOC and the last sector used for each disk, and isoinfo [2] to report and verify that certain write options were in fact used to create the disk [8].

2.4   CD Test Media

The CD test media used were Imation brand 700MB 52x rated CD-Recordable disks. The test CD disks were created using Nero Burning ROM version 6.6.1.4 [6] on an IBM ThinkPad T43 laptop with a Mat-shita UJDA765 drive, firmware revision 1.02. We selected Nero because it is a popular CD writing application that is often bundled with OEM computers and retail optical drives [6].

Each disk had the three test components enabled within the tabs of the new compilation menu in Nero. Each disk was set to Data Mode 1, ISO Level 1 for filename length, and ISO 9660 for the character set. Data Mode 1 is a part of the Yellow Book Standard for CD-ROMs; this mode is traditionally used for disks containing non-audio/video data [9]. Data Mode 2 is traditionally used for disks containing audio or video data. Mode 1 utilizes EDC and ECC error correction techniques to ensure data integrity whereas Mode 2 does not [3]. ISO 9660 Level 1 only allows file names with a maximum length of eight characters with a three character extension and a directory depth of eight levels to be written to the disk [10]. The ISO 9660 character set is a subset of the ASCII standard that allows for alpha characters a-z, numbers 0-9 and the underscore "_" [10].

The relaxation options, "Allow path depth of more than 8 directories," "Allow more than 255 characters in path," and "Do not add the ';1' ISO file version extension" were unchecked except for the "Allow more than 64 characters for Joliet names" if an ISO 9660 + Joliet disk was used [6]. The label was the default automatic with a label of "new" and the date's information was also the default [6].

We copied the same executable file to each CD. We expected the forensic applications to report the same hash value for the same CD. Because of the different write options, timestamps, etc., for each of the eight test CDs, it made no sense to compare hash values across CD test conditions as the hash values would be expected to be different.

Table 2. Hash values for Test 1.

Application	Hash Value	Sectors
EnCase 4	48D3F3AAA43A3AFF516902F0278F849B	1,207
EnCase 5	70E4FA9880726AA8B5BA1E752576CAA9	1,208
FTK	70E4FA9880726AA8B5BA1E752576CAA9	1,208
X-Ways	70E4FA9880726AA8B5BA1E752576CAA9	1,208
md5sum/readcd	70E4FA9880726AA8B5BA1E752576CAA9	1,208
	(System 3 Only)	

3. Experimental Results

This section presents the results of the eight tests. Note that the only valid comparison of hash values is within a particular test. This is because each write option creates different information on a disk, resulting in different hash values for the eight test CDs. Only one table (Table 2) is provided for Tests 1–4 because no variations were observed across tests and systems.

Tests 1–4 (DAO, Multi-Session, ISO 9660)

Systems 1, 2 and 3 reported the same results for the first test disk (Test 1), with the exception of EnCase 4. The EnCase 4 result is anomalous in that it detected and scanned one less sector than the other forensic applications (1,207 sectors instead of 1,208 sectors reported by the other programs). For System 3, md5sum reported the same hash value as the Windows applications. isoinfo correctly verified the presence of an ISO 9660 disk with no Joliet support. readcd reported that the last sector used was 1,208, which correlated with the results for all the Windows applications except EnCase 4.

Results of Tests 1–4

Due to space constraints and consistent results for Tests 1–4, specific results for Tests 2–4 are omitted. The results of Tests 2–4 have the same pattern as those of Test 1, for which EnCase 5, FTK, X-Ways and md5sum reported the same hash results (within each test). EnCase 4 exhibited the same behavior for Tests 1–4 in that it reported one less sector than the other applications and, therefore, produced different hash values. The results indicate that no combination of write options, hardware or operating systems had an effect on the hash values produced. The only anomaly was observed for EnCase 4, which undercounted the number of sectors $(n-1)$ and always produced a different hash value. Further study indicated this behavior to be consistent for all CDs using the DAO condition, which always resulted in a different hash value (corresponding to $n-1$ sectors hashed).

Table 3. Hash values for Test 5 (Systems 1 and 2).

Application	Hash Value	Sectors
EnCase 4	A296A352F2C8060B180FFE6F32DE6392	1,207
EnCase 5	A296A352F2C8060B180FFE6F32DE6392	1,207
FTK	44133FEB352D37BC365EC210DF81D7FD	1,208
X-Ways	050EA9954ADA1977CE58E894E73E0221 (1 Read Error)	1,208

Table 4. Hash values for Test 5 (System 3).

Application	Hash Value	Sectors
EnCase 4	A296A352F2C8060B180FFE6F32DE6392 (1 Read Error)	1,207
EnCase 5	7A1366AE9CC3A96FD9BF56B9B91A633B	1,206
FTK	44133FEB352D37BC365EC210DF81D7FD	1,208
X-Ways	2211A026EC7F309517050D55CEEE2954 (2 Read Errors)	1,208
md5sum/readcd	(I/O Errors; System 3 Only)	1,208

Test 5 (TAO, Multi-Session, ISO 9660)

Test 5 resulted in discrepancies in reported hash values between systems and applications. Consequently, the results are presented in two tables (Table 3 for Systems 1 and 2, and Table 4 for System 3). EnCase 4 and 5 produce the same results for Systems 1 and 2. The results for EnCase 4 were the same for all three systems, even though a read error was reported for System 3. Note that EnCase 5 reported a different hash and sector count $(n-1)$ for System 3. X-Ways encountered a read error and reported the same hash value for Systems 1 and 2, but a different value for System 3. X-Ways also reported two read errors for System 3. Note that md5sum reported an I/O error and would not hash the CD. FTK reported the same hash value for all three systems; however, this value was different from the hash values reported by the other applications. isoinfo correctly verified the presence of an ISO 9660 disk with no Joliet extensions enabled. readcd reported that the last used sector was 1,208, which correlated with the results obtained with FTK and

X-Ways. On the other hand, both versions of EnCase reported 1,207 sectors.

Interestingly, EnCase 4 and 5 reported the same hash value for the test CD with Systems 1 and 2, which is inconsistent with the different results obtained for Tests 1–4. It is not clear why the Test 5 results are consistent for Systems 1 and 2, but inconsistent for System 3. EnCase 5 reported $n - 1$ sectors, while FTK, X-Ways and readcd reported n (1,208) sectors on the same disk. It is not clear why EnCase 5 exhibits this behavior.

Of special concern to examiners is the fact that not a single consistent hash value was reported for System 3. In all, five different hash values were reported for the test disk (Test 5). Given the inconsistent results for System 3, it would not be possible to determine which hash value is correct if System 3 was the only one used to validate a CD.

Table 5. Hash values for Test 6 (Systems 1 and 2).

Application	Hash Value	Sectors
EnCase 4	A0B7E6A28FB17DB7AB1F5C0E1ED414C5	1,211
EnCase 5	A0B7E6A28FB17DB7AB1F5C0E1ED414C5	1,211
FTK	2109A7DBCF1B83D357EA0764100672B1	1,212
X-Ways	0006AEA93E620C864530ADF7FC287A61 (1 Read Error; System 2 Only)	1,212

Table 6. Hash values for Test 6 (System 3).

Application	Hash Value	Sectors
EnCase 4	A0B7E6A28FB17DB7AB1F5C0E1ED414C5 (1 Read Error)	1,211
EnCase 5	CE37E507FCCFFF857B2BB79F3E57483B	1,210
FTK	2109A7DBCF1B83D357EA0764100672B1	1,212
X-Ways	B703C2E0D42E301ECA71F1C3C1BF6C71 (2 Read Errors)	1,212
md5sum/readcd	I/O Error; System 3 Only)	1,212

Test 6 (TAO, Multi-Session, ISO 9660 + Joliet)

The Test 6 results (Tables 5 and 6) had similar discrepancies as those for Test 5. EnCase 4 and 5 reported the same hash values for Systems 1 and 2. EnCase 4 provided consistent hash values for all three systems, but produced a read error for System 1 (similar to Test 5 above). X-

Ways reported read errors for Systems 1 and 2. For System 3, as in the case of Test 5, the forensic applications produced five different hash values. Note that FTK reported the same hash value for all three systems; however, this value was different from the hash values reported by the other applications. Once again, md5sum reported an I/O error and did not produce a hash value. isoinfo verified an ISO 9660 disk with Joliet extensions enabled. readcd reported that the last sector used was sector 1,212, which correlated with the results for FTK and X-Ways as in Test 5.

Table 7.   Hash values for Test 7 (Systems 1 and 2).

Application	Hash Value	Sectors
EnCase 4	897BA35435EE6183B03B7745E4FFCDC0	1,206
EnCase 5	897BA35435EE6183B03B7745E4FFCDC0	1,206
FTK	978F6D133EE22C7C8B692C1A43EFE795	1,207
X-Ways	BAFF87CEF354BF880D4AD8919A25CB6E	1,207

Table 8.   Hash values for Test 7 (System 3).

Application	Hash Value	Sectors
EnCase 4	897BA35435EE6183B03B7745E4FFCDC0 (1 Read Error)	1,206
EnCase 5	986F1E56D89476ABC8F69958C551A42D	1,205
FTK	978F6D133EE22C7C8B692C1A43EFE795	1,207
X-Ways	664C56F4A3F450A8FD1B1D37C526F47A (2 Read Errors)	1,207
md5sum/readcd	(I/O Error; System 3 Only)	1,207

Test 7 (TAO, Non Multi-Session, ISO 9660)

The pattern of results for Test 7 (Tables 7 and 8) is similar to those for Tests 5 and 6. EnCase 4 and 5 reported the same hash value for Systems 1 and 2. EnCase 4 reported consistent hash values for all three systems, although it again reported a read error for System 3. X-Ways reported read errors for System 3 only. FTK reported consistent hashes for all three systems, as did EnCase 4. Five different hash values were reported for System 3. Once again, md5sum reported an I/O error and did not produce a hash value. readcd reported a sector count of 1,207, which correlated with the results for FTK and X-Ways. isoinfo verified the presence of an ISO 9660 disk with no Joliet extensions enabled.

Table 9. Hash values for Test 8 (Systems 1 and 2).

Application	Hash Value	Sectors
EnCase 4	284EF959A864DACF83206C1AA1A0B4CB	1,210
EnCase 5	284EF959A864DACF83206C1AA1A0B4CB	1,210
FTK	7F49A83724130E46974CD24097C01F3A	1,211
X-Ways	41BD02ED23DF42190F06CACC97275D30	1,211

Table 10. Hash values for Test 8 (System 3).

Application	Hash Value	Sectors
EnCase 4	284EF959A864DACF83206C1AA1A0B4CB (1 Read Error)	1,210
EnCase 5	378D6B62CCB8A81CC5001569AEF1A3D4	1,209
FTK	7F49A83724130E46974CD24097C01F3A	1,211
X-Ways	910962B3A2561FCDB8382B14B9FDDA8B (2 Read Errors)	1,211
md5sum/readcd	(I/O Error; System 3 Only)	1,211

Test 8 (TAO, Non Multi-Session, ISO 9660 + Joliet)

The Test 8 results (Tables 9 and 10) are similar to those for Tests 5–7. For Systems 1 and 2, EnCase 4 and 5 produced matching hash values, albeit with one read error for EnCase 4 with System 3. FTK reported consistent hash values for all three systems, but this value was inconsistent with the hash values reported by the other forensic applications. X-Ways produced matching hash values for Systems 1 and 2, but not for System 3. None of the X-Ways hash values matched the values obtained with the other applications. Once again, md5sum reported an I/O error and did not produce a hash value. readcd reported a sector count of 1,211 that again correlated with the results obtained with FTK and X-Ways. isoinfo verified the presence of an ISO 9660 disk with Joliet extensions enabled.

Results of Tests 5–8

The results for Test 5–8 are inconsistent with those obtained for Tests 1–4. The following anomalous patterns are consistently observed for Tests 5–8.

1. EnCase 4 and 5 produced the same hash value for Systems 1 and 2. However, the number of sectors read was one less than reported by the other Windows applications.

2. EnCase 4 reported the same hash value for Systems 1, 2 and 3, and produced a read error for all tests on System 3.

3. EnCase 4 and 5 reported different hash values for System 3.

4. EnCase 5 reported the same hash value for Systems 1 and 2, and a different hash value for System 3.

5. FTK reported the same hash value for Systems 1, 2 and 3. However, the hash value was different from the values reported by the other applications.

6. X-Ways reported the same hash value for Systems 1 and 2.

7. X-Ways produced read errors for all tests on Systems 1, 2 and 3.

8. md5sum failed to produce a hash value, always reporting an I/O error.

9. For Systems 1 and 2, the sector count pattern was always $n-1$ for both EnCase 4 and 5, and n sectors for FTK and X-Ways.

10. For System 3, the sector count pattern was always $n-1$ for EnCase 4, $n-2$ sectors for EnCase 5, and n sectors for FTK and X-Ways.

In light of these results it is clear that at least some write options and hardware/operating system combinations affected the hash values (especially when the TAO write option was used). In Tests 5–8 for System 3, there were never less than five distinct hash values although two applications (FTK and X-Ways) always reported the same sector count. This is more than likely related to the read errors that X-Ways encountered with most TAO disks used in our experiments. The results should also be cause for concern for examiners who use the forensic applications to hash evidentiary CDs with the aforementioned write options.

It appears that that the write method used (TAO versus DAO) is the primary factor in producing the anomalous results. The results of Tests 1–4, which used DAO, produced the same hash value regardless of session type or file system used. The anomalous results obtained in Tests 5–8 suggest that the TAO write method affects the computed hash values.

4.   Results for a Bad Drive

During our initial testing we found that System 2 configured with a HL-DT-ST GWA4164B drive (firmware version D108) was "bad." The drive was very erratic at reading disks during Tests 1–7; by Test 8, the drive would not read the disk at all. We confirmed that the drive was bad by comparing the hash values obtained in the eight tests with the results obtained when a new drive was installed in System 2; also, we examined the hash values obtained in the eight tests for Systems 1 and 3. We addressed the issue by replacing the bad drive with an NEC ND-3550A drive (firmware version 1.05) to create a new System 2, which was used for Tests 1–8 described above.

Table 11. Test 1 with Bad Drive (System 2).

Application	Hash Value
EnCase4	25E52C25C5841A7415F65301121DF986
EnCase5	A00EF2AD9822461DAC328C743D45638C
FTK	70E4FA9880726AA8B5BA1E752576CAA9
X-Ways	A00EF2AD9822461DAC328C743D45638C

Table 12. Test 1 with Good Drive (System 2).

Application	Hash Value
EnCase4	48D3F3AAA43A3AFF516902F0278F849B
EnCase5	70E4FA9880726AA8B5BA1E752576CAA9
FTK	70E4FA9880726AA8B5BA1E752576CAA9
X-Ways	70E4FA9880726AA8B5BA1E752576CAA9

Table 11 helps illustrate the effects of a bad drive on the reported hash values (Test 1 with System 2). There are some interesting consistencies in the reported hash values for the bad drive (Table 11). For example, EnCase 5 and X-Ways reported the same hash value; however, this value is inconsistent with the other hash values. Another interesting observation is that the hash value reported by FTK was the same for the bad drive (Table 11) and the good drive (Table 12).

The sector counts reported by the bad drive for all the disks in the experiment had the same patterns. EnCase 4 reported n-3 sectors, EnCase 5 n-2 sectors, FTK n sectors, and X-Ways n-2 sectors. The sector count reported by FTK correlates with FTK's results for all three good drives, which might explain why they all produce the same hash values.

5.   Discussion

Our experimental results demonstrate clear trends in the factors affecting the values computed for CDs, especially between the DAO and TAO writing methods. CDs written with the DAO option produced consistent hash values. On the other hand, CDs written under the TAO option produced anomalous results, including inconsistent hash values and sector counts across forensic applications, read errors for certain forensic applications, and inconsistent hash values across hardware configurations and operating systems.

The results obtained in the case of the "bad drive" underscore the importance of verifying that an optical drive or media reader – especially one used in a digital forensics investigation – reports accurate data. This is challenging because there is usually no means of calibrating such a device after it leaves the manufacturing facility. Consequently, we recommend that examiners triangulate hash results across other drives and/or systems. If the time and/or systems are unavailable to triangulate the results, then a comparison of the hash value computed by the untested system with the hash value of a known verified and "triangulated" disk could be used to show that the results reported by a particular drive are accurate.

6.   Conclusions

Cryptographic hashing is crucial to verifying the integrity of digital evidence. Given the results obtained for the TAO disk writing option, the potential exists that the integrity of digital evidence could be challenged on the grounds that the hash value calculated by a defense expert does not match the value presented by the prosecution. Such a challenge, if successful, would almost certainly affect the outcome of the case. However, the fact that different hardware/software combinations produce different hash values for an item of digital evidence does not mean that cryptographic hashing cannot be relied on to verify the integrity of evidence. As long the entire hashing process can be duplicated and the results shown to match, there should be no problems in using hash values to verify the integrity of the evidence. Therefore, it is crucial that examiners maintain detailed documentation about the specific hardware and operating system configurations, optical drives and firmware revisions, and the forensic applications used to produce hash values of evidentiary items.

References

[1] AccessData, Forensic Toolkit (www.accessdata.com).

[2] CD Record (cdrecord.berlios.de/old/private/cdrecord.html).

[3] G. D'Haese, The ISO 9660 file system (users.pandora.be/it3.consult ants.bvba/handouts/ISO9960.html), 1995.

[4] D. Eastlake and P. Jones, US Secure Hash Algorithm 1 (SHA1) (www.ietf.org/rfc/rfc3174.txt), 2001.

[5] Guidance Software, EnCase (www.guidancesoftware.com).

[6] Nero AG, Nero (www.nero.com).

[7] R. Rivest, The MD5 message-digest algorithm (www.ietf.org/rfc/rfc 1321.txt), 1992.

[8] M. Shannon, Linux forensics (www.agilerm.net/linux1.html), 2004.

[9] Sony Electronics, What are CD-ROM Mode-1, Mode-2 and XA? (sony.storagesupport.com/cgi-bin/sonysupport.cgi/M1QyNUjPDA 4dzatpCN5uJ=xjZSMlgW60/faq/view/413).

[10] Wikipedia, ISO 9660 (en.wikipedia.org/wiki/ISO_9660).

[11] Wikipedia, Optical disc authoring (en.wikipedia.org/wiki/Optical _disc_authoring).

[12] Wikipedia, Optical disc recording modes (en.wikipedia.org/wiki /Disc_At_Once).

[13] X-Ways Software Technology AG, X-Ways Forensics (www.x-ways .net).

Chapter 11

DISK DRIVE I/O COMMANDS AND WRITE BLOCKING

James Lyle, Steven Mead and Kelsey Rider

Abstract   A write blocker allows read-only access to digital data on a secondary storage device by placing a hardware or software filter between the host computer and the storage device. The filter monitors I/O commands sent from the application on the host computer, only allowing commands to the device that make no changes to its data. This paper examines the I/O commands used to access secondary storage devices and discusses their implications for BIOS-based and hardware-based write blockers.

Keywords: Data acquisition, forensic tool testing, write blockers

1.   Introduction

A write blocker allows access to digital data on a secondary storage device while not allowing any changes to be made to the data on the device. This is implemented by placing a hardware or software filter between the software executing on a host computer and the secondary storage device that is to be protected. The filter monitors all the I/O commands sent from the application on the host machine and only allows commands to the device that make no changes to its data. This paper examines the I/O commands used to access secondary storage devices and discusses their implications for write blockers.

This research is part of the Computer Forensics Tool Testing (CFTT) Project at the National Institute of Standards and Technology (NIST), which is developing methodologies for testing forensic tools and devices. CFTT is a joint project of the Department of Justice's National Institute of Justice (NIJ) and NIST's Office of Law Enforcement Standards and the Information Technology Laboratory. CFTT is supported by other organizations, including the Federal Bureau of Investigation, Department of Defense Cyber Crime Center, Internal Revenue Service

Please use the following format when citing this chapter:

Lyle, J., Mead, S., Rider, K., 2007, in IFIP International Federation for Information Processing, Volume 242, Advances in Digital Forensics III; eds. P. Craiger and S Shenoi; (Boston: Springer), pp. 163-177.

Criminal Investigation Division, Bureau of Immigration and Customs Enforcement and U.S. Secret Service. CFTT's objective is to provide measurable assurance to practitioners, researchers and other users that digital forensic tools provide accurate results. Accomplishing this requires the development of specifications and test methods for forensic tools, and the subsequent testing of tools against the specifications.

Test results provide the information necessary for developers to improve forensic tools, for users to make informed choices, and for the legal community and others to understand the tools' capabilities. Our approach to testing forensic tools is based on well-recognized methodologies for conformance and quality testing. The specifications and test methods are posted on the CFTT website [4] for review and comment by the digital forensics community.

The next section presents a simplified description of command interfaces to hard drives. Section 3 discusses BIOS access to hard drives, BIOS commands used for hard drive access, and the behavior of several BIOS-based write blockers. Section 4 focuses on hardware-based write blockers and the commands used to access hard drives via the ATA interface. The final section, Section 5, summarizes our observations.

2. Background

A hard drive is usually attached to a computer by a cable to an interface controller located either on the system motherboard or on a separate adapter card. The most common physical interfaces are the ATA (AT Attachment) and IDE (Integrated Drive Electronics) interfaces, including variants such as ATA-2, ATA-3 and EIDE (Enhanced IDE). Other physical interfaces include SATA (Serial ATA), SCSI (Small Computer System Interface), IEEE 1394 (also known as FireWire or i-Link) and USB (Universal Serial Bus).

All access to a drive is accomplished by commands sent from the computer to the drive via the interface controller. However, since the low-level programming required for direct access through the interface controller is difficult and tedious, each operating system usually provides other access interfaces. For example, programs running in a DOS environment can use two additional interfaces: the DOS service interface (interrupt 0x21) and the BIOS service interface (interrupt 0x13). The DOS service operates at the logical level of files and records while the BIOS service operates at the physical drive sector level. More complex operating systems such as Windows XP and UNIX variants (e.g., Linux and FreeBSD) may disallow any low level interface (through the BIOS or the controller) and only permit user programs to access a hard drive via a device driver that manages all access to a device.

There are five basic strategies for ensuring that digital data on a secondary storage device is not modified during a forensic acquisition:

- **No Protection:** If it is not desirable to disrupt an active system, relevant data could be acquired without any explicit protection of the source. For example, if a web server cannot be shut down for business reasons, digital data of interest could be copied to removable media.

- **Trusted OS with Trusted Tools:** These include operating systems designed to meet forensic requirements that are used in conjunction with tools that do not modify secondary storage.

- **Trusted OS with Trusted Tools (Variation):** These include BIOS-based software write blockers running on DOS. Examples are HDL from the Royal Canadian Mounted Police (RCMP) and PDBLOCK (Physical Drive BLOCKer) from Digital Intelligence.

- **Driver-Based Software Write Blockers:** These blockers are designed for operating systems such as Microsoft Windows that use a driver stack model (a stack of driver filters). A write block filter inserted into the driver stack examines all the commands sent to a device through the stack. A command that could modify a protected drive is blocked, i.e., it is not passed on to lower layers of the stack.

- **Hardware-Based Write Blockers:** These devices break the usual one-segment bus between the host and the storage device into two segments with the blocker acting as a bridge between the two bus segments. The blocker intercepts all traffic from the host to the storage device and only issues safe commands to the storage device.

This paper focuses on BIOS-based write blockers and hardware-based write blockers that use the ATA interface.

3. BIOS-Based Write Blockers

A BIOS-based write blocker is intended for use only with a trusted operating system such as DOS. Such a write blocker is usually designed as a Terminate and Stay Resident (TSR) program that, once initiated, intercepts all attempts to access a hard drive through the interrupt 0x13 interface. Only a command that is considered to be "safe" is passed to the hard drive; otherwise the blocker returns to the calling program without passing the command to the hard drive.

While write commands to a device should always be blocked, it is not clear how a write blocker should treat other commands. The 0x13 BIOS interface uses an eight-bit function code (with 256 possible commands). Beyond a core set of commands, most function codes are not used. However, as technology changes, new core commands are often introduced and other commands are no longer implemented. BIOS vendors may implement additional commands as desired. Vendors often introduce system components that implement new commands; also, vendors may enhance the functionality of existing commands. The most significant change to the core command set was the introduction of extended commands (0x41--0x49) for accessing hard drives larger than 8 GB.

Table 1.   Phoenix BIOS 4.0 interrupt 0x13 command set.

Command	Code	Category
Reset	00	Control
Get Last Status	01	Information
Read Sectors	02	Read
Write Sectors	03	Write
Verify Sectors	04	Information
Format Cylinder	05	Configuration
Read Drive Parameters	08	Information
Initialize Drive Parameters	09	Configuration
Read Long Sector	0A	Read
Write Long Sector	0B	Write
Seek Drive	0C	Control
Alternate Drive Reset	0D	Control
Test Drive Ready	10	Information
Recalibrate Drive	11	Configuration
Controller Diagnostic	14	Configuration
Read Drive Type	15	Information
Check Extensions Present	41	Information
Extended Read	42	Read
Extended Write	43	Write
Verify Sectors	44	Information
Extended Seek	47	Control
Get Drive Parameters	48	Information

The command set for a typical BIOS [7] is presented in Table 1. Note that only 22 of the possible 256 command codes are defined. Each command belongs to one of the following six categories:

- **Read:** These commands read from a drive, and should never be blocked.

- **Write:** These commands write to a drive, and should always be blocked.

- **Information:** These commands help obtain information about a drive. They should be allowed or be accurately simulated by the write blocker so that applications can obtain information about the drive (e.g., size and drive capabilities).

- **Control:** These commands request a drive to execute an operation that does not change the drive configuration or contents. It should be safe to allow these commands, but a tool may block some of these commands with no ill effects.

- **Configuration:** These commands change the way a drive appears to the host. They include format and diagnostic commands. Format commands should always be blocked. Diagnostic commands are questionable: it is safer to block them as they are often vendor-specific and undocumented, but in practice they may not make any changes to the drive.

- **Miscellaneous:** These commands, e.g., undefined and discontinued commands, are not included in the other five categories, Since undefined and discontinued commands should not be issued, it usually does not matter if the commands are allowed or blocked as long the write blocker does not encounter these commands. However, if the BIOS command set were to be extended with a new write command, this command should, of course, be blocked.

An experiment was conducted to determine the commands that a write blocker might encounter during a forensic examination (drive preview and acquisition). A monitor was installed to track the interrupt 0x13 commands issued by several common programs doing the routine tasks specified in Table 2. Several different hosts were used to obtain a satisfactory coverage of BIOS implementations, including a host with a legacy BIOS (without the extended read and write commands). The results of the experiment are presented in Table 3.

The experimental results give rise to the following observations:

- Only a few (10) of the 22 possible Phoenix BIOS commands were observed.

- All the defined read commands were observed.

Table 2.   Experimental tasks.

Task
Copy/Edit Tools:Copy *.* to image disk, DOS
Copy/Edit Tools:Edit High Sector, Norton Disk Editor
Copy/Edit Tools:Edit Low Sector, Norton Disk Editor
Imaging Tools:Drive(Entire), EnCase 3.22
Imaging Tools:Drive(Entire), EnCase 4.14
Imaging Tools:Drive(Entire), SafeBack 3.0
Imaging Tools:Partition-High, EnCase 3.22
Imaging Tools:Partition-High, EnCase 4.14
Imaging Tools:Partition-High, SafeBack 3.0
Imaging Tools:Partition-Low, EnCase 3.22
Imaging Tools:Partition-Low, EnCase 4.14
Imaging Tools:Partition-Low, SafeBack 3.0
Induced Drive Read Error:Drive(Entire), SafeBack 3.0

- One command (Read Long) only appeared when a read command failed. This was accomplished by simulating a single bad sector on the drive. A TSR program intercepted each disk read command and, when the designated sector was requested, returned a read error to the application. The application encountering the bad sector then tried the Read Long command to read the simulated bad sector.

- Both the regular write commands were observed, but the Write Long command was not observed. It is unlikely that the Write Long command would be issued by a forensic tool as it should only be used on rare occasions.

- Other commands, e.g., Format Cylinder, that could write to a hard drive should not be issued by forensic tools and were not observed.

- The fact that certain commands were not seen in the experiment does not mean that are never encountered. The missing commands likely manifest themselves with other programs and/or hardware.

Six software write blockers were tested against the NIST CFTT software write blocker specifications [1, 6]. The observation from testing interrupt 0x13 write blockers is that, although there is agreement on the treatment of common commands used by write blockers, there are minor differences in the treatment of the less frequently used commands. The results are presented in Table 4. The "Spec" column has an "A" for commands that should be allowed and a "B" for commands that should

Table 3. Observed Interrupt 0x13 commands observed.

Code	Command	Program	Sum
42	Ext Read	DOS Copy	36
43	Ext Write	DOS Copy	223
41	Check for Extensions	EnCase 3.22	14
42	Ext Read	EnCase 3.22	657722
43	Ext Write	EnCase 3.22	1280151
48	Get Drive Parms	EnCase 3.22	14
08	Read Drive Parms	EnCase 3.22	23
02	Read Sectors	EnCase 3.22	2148
00	Reset	EnCase 3.22	6
41	Check for Extensions	EnCase 4.14	14
42	Ext Read	EnCase 4.14	654989
43	Ext Write	EnCase 4.14	1274995
48	Get Drive Parms	EnCase 4.14	14
08	Read Drive Parms	EnCase 4.14	23
02	Read Sectors	EnCase 4.14	2020
00	Reset	EnCase 4.14	6
42	Ext Read	Norton Disk Editor	2
08	Read Drive Parms	Norton Disk Editor	5
02	Read Sectors	Norton Disk Editor	6
03	Write Sectors	Norton Disk Editor	6
41	Check for Extensions	SafeBack 3.0	16
42	Ext Read	SafeBack 3.0	939146
43	Ext Write	SafeBack 3.0	812666
48	Get Drive Parms	SafeBack 3.0	14
08	Read Drive Parms	SafeBack 3.0	34
0A	Read Long	SafeBack 3.0	1
02	Read Sectors	SafeBack 3.0	85368
00	Reset	SafeBack 3.0	21
04	Verify Sectors	SafeBack 3.0	14
03	Write Sectors	SafeBack 3.0	62416

be blocked according to the NIST specifications. The columns labeled "0.4" through "0.8" present the results obtained for different versions of the RCMP's HDL write blocker; the columns labeled PDB and PDL present the results for PDBLOCK and PDLITE. An "A" in a column indicates that the corresponding tool allowed the command, while a "B" indicates that it blocked the command. For the miscellaneous commands in the last row of Table 4: "A" means all commands were allowed, "A3" that all but three commands were allowed, and "A4" that all but four were allowed.

For the critical commands, all the tools (except for HDL 0.4) are in agreement with the NIST specifications. This is because the HDL

Table 4. HDL and PDBLOCK commands (blocked and allowed).

Command	Code	Category	Spec	0.4	0.5	0.7	0.8	PDB	PDL
Format Track	05	Config.	B	B	B	B	B	B	B
Format Track (with Bad Sectors)	06	Config.	B	B	B	B	B	B	B
Format Cylinder	07	Config.	B	B	B	B	B	B	B
Init. Drive Parms.	09	Config.	B	A	A	A	B	A	A
ESDI Diag. (PS/2)	0E	Config.	B	A	A	A	B	A	A
ESDI Diag. (PS/2)	0F	Config.	B	B	B	B	B	B	B
Cntrlr. RAM Diag.	12	Config.	B	A	A	B	B	A	A
Drive Diag.	13	Config.	B	B	B	B	B	A	A
Cntrlr. Diag.	14	Config.	B	A	A	B	B	A	A
Reset	00	Control	A	A	A	A	A	A	A
Seek Drive	0C	Control	A	A	A	A	A	A	A
Alt. Drive Reset	0D	Control	A	A	A	A	A	A	A
Recalib. Drive	11	Control	A	A	A	A	B	A	A
Extended Seek	47	Control	A	A	A	B	B	A	A
Get Last Status	01	Info.	A	A	A	A	A	A	A
Verify Sectors	04	Info.	A	A	A	A	A	A	A
Read Drive Parms.	08	Info.	A	A	A	A	A	A	A
Test Drive Ready	10	Info.	A	A	A	A	A	A	A
Read Drive Type	15	Info.	A	A	A	B	A	A	A
Chck. Extns. Prsnt.	41	Info.	A	A	A	A	A	A	A
Verify Sectors	44	Info.	A	A	A	A	A	A	A
Get Drive Parms.	48	Info.	A	A	A	A	A	A	A
Read Sectors	02	Read	A	A	A	A	A	A	A
Read Long Sector	0A	Read	A	A	A	A	A	A	A
Extended Read	42	Read	A	A	A	A	A	A	A
Write Sectors	03	Write	B	B	B	B	B	B	B
Write Long Sector	0B	Write	B	B	B	B	B	B	B
Extended Write	43	Write	B	A	B	B	B	B	B
Undefined	Other	Misc.	B	A	A4	B	B	A3	A3

0.4 tool was created before the extended BIOS commands were introduced. Table 4 also documents a change in the design criteria used by the RCMP. Versions 0.4 and 0.5 were designed to block known write commands and allow everything else. However, starting with version 0.7, the criteria changed to allow known safe commands and block everything else; this change occurred because of the uncertainty surrounding the actions of some of the more esoteric commands. As shown in Table 3, several commands were never issued by programs that would be commonly used during an acquisition or initial examination of a hard drive. Although the unused commands may not change data on the hard drive, without adequate documentation about the behavior of these commands, it is safer to simply block them.

4.   Hardware-Based Write Blockers

Hardware-based write blockers use a two-segment bus to connect a host computer and a hard drive, one segment between the host and the write blocker and the other between the blocker and the drive. The two bus segments do not necessarily use the same protocol; one of the first hardware blockers used a SCSI connection to the host computer and an ATA connection to the hard drive. A hardware-based write blocker intercepts each command from the host and selects a desired course of action. The most common actions are:

- The blocker forwards the command to the hard drive.

- The blocker substitutes a different command, which is sent to the hard drive. This is the case when the blocker uses different bus protocols to communicate with the host and the hard drive.

- The blocker simulates the command without actually forwarding the command to the hard drive. For example, the device may already know the size of the drive; upon receiving a request from the host, instead of re-querying the drive, it may return the answer directly to the host.

- If a command is blocked, the blocker may return either success or failure for the blocked operation. However, returning failure for certain commands may cause the host computer to lock up.

The remainder of this section focuses on write blockers that use the ATA protocol for communicating with the host and the hard drive. Table 5 lists the seven releases of the ATA standard [8]; an eighth standard is currently under development.

The ATA protocol has 256 possible command codes. In the ATA-7 standard, approximately 70 codes are defined as general use commands (commands that are not reserved, retired, obsolete or vendor-specific). In addition, there are more than 30 retired or obsolete codes that were defined in the earlier standards.

Table 6 lists the write commands specified in the seven ATA standards. An "S" indicates that the listed command (row) is supported for the given ATA standard (column). Note that only four commands are defined in all seven standards. Also note that three standards introduced new write commands beyond the original commands and three standards

Table 5. ATA standards.

Last Draft Standard	Publication Date
ATA-1 X3T10/791D Revision 4c	1994
ATA-2 X3T10/0948D Revision 4c	March 18, 1996
ATA-3 X3T13 2008D Revision 7b	January 27, 1997
ATA/ATAPI-4 T13/1153D Revision 18	August 19, 1998
ATA/ATAPI-5 T13/1321D Revision 3	February 29, 2000
ATA/ATAPI-6 T13/1410D Revision 3	October 30, 2001
ATA/ATAPI-7 V1 T13/1532D Revision 4b	April 21, 2004

Table 6. History of ATA write commands.

1	2	3	4	5	6	7	Code	Name
N	N	N	N	N	N	S	3A	Write Stream DMA Ext
N	N	N	N	N	N	S	CE	Write Multiple FUA Ext
N	N	N	N	N	N	S	3E	Write DMA Queued FUA Ext
N	N	N	N	N	N	S	3D	Write DMA FUA Ext
N	N	N	N	N	N	S	3B	Write Stream Ext
N	N	N	N	N	S	S	34	Write Sector(s) Ext
N	N	N	N	N	S	S	3F	Write Log Ext
N	N	N	N	N	S	S	39	Write Multiple Ext
N	N	N	N	N	S	S	36	Write DMA Queued Ext
N	N	N	N	N	S	S	35	Write DMA Ext
N	N	N	S	S	S	S	CC	Write DMA Queued
S	S	N	N	N	N	N	E9	Write Same
S	S	S	N	N	N	N	33	Write Long (w/o Retry)
S	S	S	N	N	N	N	32	Write Long (w/ Retry)
S	S	S	N	N	N	N	3C	Write Verify
S	S	S	S	N	N	N	31	Write Sector(s)
S	S	S	S	N	N	N	CB	Write DMA (w/o Retry)
S	S	S	S	S	S	S	E8	Write Buffer
S	S	S	S	S	S	S	30	Write Sector(s)
S	S	S	S	S	S	S	C5	Write Multiple
S	S	S	S	S	S	S	CA	Write DMA (w/ Retry)

discontinued six other write commands. The critical observation is that the command set changes quite significantly every few years.

We conducted an experiment to observe the commands issued during startup by three different computers. A protocol analyzer (Data Transit Corporation Bus Doctor Protocol Analyzer) was used to capture ATA bus activity during the startup and shutdown of various computer-BIOS combinations. The commands listed in Table 7 were issued from the

Table 7. Commands issued from BIOS during startup.

Host and BIOS	Command
Dell Phoenix 4.0 Rel 6.0	10=Recalibrate
Dell Phoenix 4.0 Rel 6.0	90=Exec Drive Diag
Micron Phoenix 4.0 Rel 6.0	90=Exec Drive Diag
Nexar Award V4.51PG	90=Exec Drive Diag
Dell Phoenix 4.0 Rel 6.0	91=Init Drv Params
Micron Phoenix 4.0 Rel 6.0	91=Init Drv Params
Nexar Award V4.51PG	91=Init Drv Params
Dell Phoenix 4.0 Rel 6.0	C6=Set Multiple Mod
Micron Phoenix 4.0 Rel 6.0	C6=Set Multiple Mod
Nexar Award V4.51PG	C6=Set Multiple Mod
Dell Phoenix 4.0 Rel 6.0	E3=Idle
Micron Phoenix 4.0 Rel 6.0	E3=Idle
Nexar Award V4.51PG	E3=Idle
Dell Phoenix 4.0 Rel 6.0	EC=Identify Drive
Micron Phoenix 4.0 Rel 6.0	EC=Identify Drive
Nexar Award V4.51PG	EC=Identify Drive
Dell Phoenix 4.0 Rel 6.0	EF=Set Features 03=Set Transfer Mode
Micron Phoenix 4.0 Rel 6.0	EF=Set Features 03=Set Transfer Mode
Nexar Award V4.51PG	EF=Set Features 03=Set Transfer Mode

BIOS to drive 0 of the primary ATA channel. Note that the BIOS did not issue any write commands to the hard drive for all the systems examined.

We also used the protocol analyzer to observe commands issued by several operating systems (DOS 6.22, PCDOS 6.3, FreeBSD 5.21, Red-Hat Linux 7.1, Red Hat Personal Desktop Linux 9.1, Windows 98, Windows NT 4.0, Windows 2000 and Windows XP Pro) during boot and shutdown. The results of our investigation are presented in Table 8. Neither PCDOS 6.3 nor DOS 6.22 issued any write commands during startup and shutdown. Also, note that the newer operating systems use the faster Write DMA (0xCA) command instead of the slower Write (0x30) command.

Several test reports for hardware-based write block devices have been published by NIJ [1]. These blockers were tested against a specification [5] developed by the CFTT Project. Some interesting results are:

- One write blocker substitutes the Read DMA (0xC8) command for the Read Multiple (0xC4) command [3].

- One write blocker disallows certain read commands [3] (see Table 9).

Table 8. Write commands issued during startup and shutdown

Host/OS	Source	Count	Command
FreeBSD5.2.1	Boot	196	CA=Write DMA
FreeBSD5.2.1	Boot	1	30=Write (w/ Retry)
FreeBSD5.2.1	Shutdown	104	CA=Write DMA
RH7.1	Boot	759	CA=Write DMA
RH7.1	Login	166	CA=Write DMA
RH7.1	Shutdown	297	CA=Write DMA
RH9PD.1	Boot	763	CA=Write DMA
RH9PD.1	Login	186	CA=Write DMA
RH9PD.1	Shutdown	402	CA=Write DMA
W98DS3	Boot	55	CA=Write DMA
W98DS3	Boot	58	30=Write (w/ Retry)
W98DS3	Login	22	30=Write (w/ Retry)
W98DS3	Shutdown	76	30=Write (w/ Retry)
W98dsbd	Boot	10	30=Write (w/ Retry)
W98dsbd	Boot	48	CA=Write DMA
Win2KPro	Boot	424	CA=Write DMA
Win2KPro	Login	277	CA=Write DMA
Win2KPro	Shutdown	269	CA=Write DMA
Win98SE	Boot	65	30=Write (w/ Retry)
Win98SE	Shutdown	90	30=Write (w/ Retry)
WinNT4.0	Boot	452	C5=Write Multiple
WinNT4.0	Login	520	C5=Write Multiple
WinNT4.0	Shutdown	102	C5=Write Multiple
WinXPPro	Boot	967	CA=Write DMA
WinXPPro	Shutdown	272	CA=Write DMA

- Another blocker allowed some commands that could modify a hard drive. However, these commands are not typically used without special software [2]:

  - Download Microcode (0x92): This command enables hard drive firmware to be reprogrammed. While the command could change drive behavior, information about the command is drive-model-specific and is generally not available.

  - Format Track (0x50): This command is not defined in the current ATA specifications; however, it was defined in the older specifications (ATA-1 through ATA-3). The command can be used to erase information on an older drive that supports the instruction, but it cannot be used to change any user or operating system data stored on the drive.

Table 9. Blocker commands.

Commands Sent to Blocker	Commands Allowed by Blocker
20=Read (w/ Retry)	20=Read (w/ Retry)
21=Read (w/o Retry)	24=Read Sector Ext
22=Read/L (w/ Retry)	25=Read DMA Ext
23=Read/L (w/o Retry)	27=Read Max Addr Ext
24=Read Sector Ext	25=Read DMA Ext
25=Read DMA Ext	C8=Read DMA
26=Read DMA Queue Ext	C8=Read DMA
27=Read Max Addr Ext	F8=Read Natv Max Addr
29=Read Multiple Ext	
2A=Read Stream DMA	
2B=Read Stream PIO	
2F=Read Log Ext	
40=Read/V (w/ Retry)	
41=Read/V (w/o Retry)	
42=Read/V (w/ Ext)	
B0=Smart D0=Smart Read Data	
B0=Smart D5=Smart Read Log	
C4=Read Multiple	
C7=Read DMA Queued	
C8=Read DMA	
C9=Read DMA (w/o Retry)	
E4=Read Buffer	
F8=Read Natv Max Addr	

- Smart Write (0xB0, 0xD6): This command records information in a device maintenance log, which is stored in a different data area from the data files and operating system data.

- Vendor-Specific Commands: These commands, which are often undocumented, are specific to hard drive models.

- CFA Erase (0xC0): This command applies to compact flash devices, not hard drives.

- SATA Write FPDMA (0x61): This command was noted by the protocol analyzer in a parallel ATA test, but the command is only valid for Serial ATA (SATA) devices.

5. Conclusions

Our work has focused on BIOS-based and hardware-based write blockers. We have used monitoring software to record BIOS command usage by BIOS-based write blockers in a DOS environment, and a protocol analyzer to record direct ATA command usage by hardware-based write blockers in a variety of environments.

Our experiments indicate that, in the DOS environment, only a small subset of possible BIOS commands are used for system startup, shutdown and routine forensic tool operations.

A similar situation is encountered in the case of ATA commands. While some I/O commands are present in all versions of the ATA specifications, the changes made to the specifications on a fairly regular basis lead to new commands being implemented and several old commands being dropped. For direct access to ATA drives during system startup and shutdown, only a small subset of possible commands are used for a given operating system and the command sets vary for different operating systems. For example, Windows 98 uses the Write (0x30) command, Windows NT uses the Write Multiple (0xC5) command, and Windows XP and Linux versions use the Write DMA (0xCA) command.

Other interesting observations are that write blockers also block certain read commands; some (software and hardware) write blockers disallow known write commands and allow everything else; others allow only known safe commands and block everything else. Furthermore, some write blockers filter commands that may write arbitrary user or operating system data, but they allow some unsupported or atypical commands that have the potential to hide or destroy data (e.g., Download Microcode and Format Track).

Future work related to write blockers will focus on other interfaces, including SATA, SCSI, USB and IEEE 1394.

Finally, although certain company names and products are mentioned in this work, in no case does the identification of these companies and/or products imply any recommendation or endorsement by NIST or the U.S. Government.

References

[1] National Institute of Justice (NIJ), Computer Forensic Tool Testing Project (www.ojp.usdoj.gov/nij/topics/ecrime/cftt.htm).

[2] National Institute of Justice (NIJ), *Test Results for Hardware Write Block Device: FastBloc IDE (Firmware Version 16)*, NIJ Report NCJ 212956, Washington, DC (www.ncjrs.gov/pdffiles1/nij/212956.pdf), 2006.

[3] National Institute of Justice (NIJ), *Test Results for Hardware Write Block Device: MyKey NoWrite (Firmware Version 1.05)*, NIJ Report NCJ 212958, Washington, DC (www.ncjrs.gov/pdffiles1/nij/212958.pdf), 2006.

[4] National Institute of Standards and Technology (NIST), Computer Forensic Tool Testing Project (www.cftt.nist.gov).

[5] National Institute of Standards and Technology (NIST), Hardware Write Block, (www.cftt.nist.gov/hardware_write_block.htm).

[6] National Institute of Standards and Technology (NIST), Software Write Block (www.cftt.nist.gov/software_write_block.htm).

[7] Phoenix Technologies, *PhoenixBIOS 4.0 Revision 6 User's Manual*, Phoenix Technologies, San Jose, California, 2000.

[8] Technical Committee T13 – International Committee on Information Technology Standards (T13–INCITS), AT Attachment (ATA) Storage (www.t13.org).

Chapter 12

A NEW PROCESS MODEL FOR TEXT STRING SEARCHING

Nicole Beebe and Glenn Dietrich

Abstract   Investigations involving digital media (e.g., hard disks and USB thumb drives) rely heavily on text string searches. Traditional search approaches utilizing matching algorithms or database technology and tree-based indexing algorithms result in an overwhelming number of "hits" – a large percentage of which are irrelevant to investigative objectives. Furthermore, current approaches predominantly employ literal search techniques, which lead to poor recall with respect to investigative objectives. A better approach is needed that reduces information retrieval overhead and improves investigative recall. This paper proposes a new, high-level text string search process model that addresses some of the shortfalls in current text string search paradigms. We hope that this model will stimulate efforts on extending information retrieval and text mining research to digital forensic text string searching.

Keywords: Text string search, information retrieval, text mining, process model

1.   Introduction

The digital forensics discipline is experiencing renewed attention at a time when data storage requirements and capabilities are increasing steeply. Hinshaw [10] reports that corporate data storage is doubling every nine months – twice as fast as Moore's Law. Because of this growth, it is not uncommon for larger corporations and law enforcement agencies to face digital investigations involving data sets of a terabyte or more in size [18, 23].

Current digital forensic tools are incapable of handling large data sets in an efficient manner [20]. Their overall efficiency is constrained by their reliance on relatively simple hashing and indexing algorithms. Most forensic tools and processes are not scalable to large data sets [4, 8, 21]. Even with moderately large (200 GB) data sets, data extraction

Please use the following format when citing this chapter:

Beebe, N., Dietrich, G., 2007, in IFIP International Federation for Information Processing, Volume 242, Advances in Digital Forensics III; eds. P. Craiger and S Shenoi; (Boston: Springer), pp. 179-191.

and analysis become inordinately slow and inefficient. Processing times for limited keyword searches (10-20 keywords) can take a day or more, and human analysts are overwhelmed by the number of hits to review.

Digital investigations are also hindered by the limited cognitive processing capability of human analysts. As data sets increase in size, the amount of data required for examination and analysis also increases. This obviates the investigator's ability to meticulously review all keyword search hits, all files by file type, or all applicable system logs. It is, therefore, imperative that the digital investigation process be improved.

Digital investigation processes and tools under-utilize computer processing power through continued reliance on simplistic data reduction and mining algorithms. The analytical burden was shifted to human analysts at a time when human labor was cheap and computers were expensive. For quite some time, however, conditions have been reversed, but the digital forensics field has continued to levy the preponderance of the analytical burden on human analysts.

Digital forensics is not the only discipline faced with the task of sifting through and drawing conclusions from massive volumes of data. Other disciplines have employed data mining and information retrieval techniques to solve this problem. However, little research has focused on applying these techniques to criminal forensics, and even less to digital forensics. This paper explores digital forensics from a systems perspective in order to identify the major constraints and propose solutions. Specifically, the text string search process applied during digital forensic investigations is explored, and a new, high-level, multi-algorithmic approach is proposed in the form of a high-level, theoretical process model.

2.   Background

Digital investigations are categorized as network forensic investigations or media forensic investigations. Mukkamala and Sung [16] define network forensics as "analyzing network activity in order to discover the source of security policy violations or information assurance breaches." Media forensics, on the other hand, involves the analysis of digital media in order to confirm or refute allegations and/or obtain information. Such allegations may be civil or criminal in nature; and the subsequent investigation may be forensic or non-forensic – the difference being whether investigative goals involve judicial action.

Media forensics largely involves four primary investigatory digital search tactics: text string search, file signature search and analysis, hash analysis, and logical data review. Text string search (string matching, pattern matching or index-based searching) is designed to scan the digital media at the physical level (independent of logical data structures, file allocation status, partitioning, etc.) to locate and analyze data wherein a specific text string or pattern is located. File signature search/analysis is designed to search the digital media at the physical level to locate files by file type, without relying on potentially falsified file extensions at the logical level or the absence of them at the physical level (e.g., the file is no longer stored logically). Hash analysis is designed to find files identical to a known exemplar or to eliminate files that are "known goods" – that is to say, they are standard system and/or application files known to be irrelevant to the investigation. Finally, logical data review is designed to examine known repositories of logically stored data with potentially probative value (e.g., temporary Internet files, Internet history, registry and "My Recent Documents").

These tactics are employed for different reasons. While the tactics may produce redundant information, each tends to contribute unique information to the investigation. As a result, all four tactics are often employed during an investigation to obtain all relevant information.

This paper focuses on text string search. Text string searches are relied upon heavily by digital forensic investigators, as readable text and text-based documents are important artifacts in most investigations (e.g., email, web browsing history, word processing documents and spreadsheets). However, digital forensic text string searching is prone to high false positive and false negative rates. Note that false positive and false negative rates are considered in the context of investigative objectives. In other words, false positive means retrieved data that match the query, but that are irrelevant to the investigation. Similarly, false negative means that data relevant to the investigation are not retrieved, because they did not match the query.

Investigators experience extremely high information retrieval overhead with text string searches due to the large number of hits that are irrelevant to the investigation. The average keyword search involving ten keywords or search expressions specified by an experienced investigator (one who knows which words and search expressions are more prone to high false positive rates) on the average hard drive can easily result in tens of thousands or hundreds of thousands of hits.

Investigators also experience poor investigative recall due to the use of literal search techniques. Relevant information is simply not retrieved by text string searches if the investigator's query does not cover all necessary words and/or strings. Given the tendency to limit "keyword list" length, and the effects of synonymy and vocabulary differences between individuals, there is a high likelihood that relevant evidence will not be located by text string searches in many investigations.

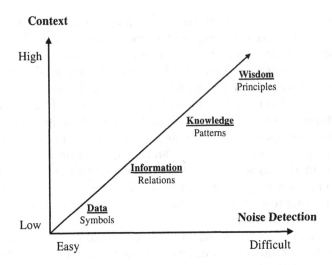

Figure 1. Knowledge Management System (KMS) Understanding Hierarchy [17].

In addition to high false positive rates and poor investigative recall, state-of-the-art digital forensic search tools do not prioritize the hits for the analyst or investigator. The hits are often ordered for presentation based on where they were found on the digital media. At most, the hits are grouped by search string and/or "file item." None of these approaches, however, appreciably reduce the information retrieval overhead. The human analyst or investigator is forced to exhaustively review all the hits to find information pertinent to the investigation, because relevant information could be listed anywhere in the output.

Some analysts and investigators use heuristics to efficiently scan the list of hits and prioritize their analytical efforts. However, such approaches are still performed manually and are relatively inefficient when compared with potential computer information processing techniques.

Indeed, if we consider digital investigations from a system theory point of view, it becomes clear that the current text string search process unnecessarily constrains the overall digital forensic investigation "system."

3. System Analysis

The purpose or mission of the digital forensic system, in the context of a single investigation, is to convert data to knowledge in accordance with the Understanding Hierarchy proposed by Nunamaker, *et al.* [17], which is presented in Figure 1.

The following terms are defined by adapting the definitions of Nunamaker, *et al.* [17] to the digital forensics context:

- **Data:** "...raw symbols that merely exist and have no significance beyond that existence...raw data lacks context and therefore does not have meaning in and of itself nor does it have any meaningful relations to anything else." In the digital forensic system, data refers to the raw data stored on digital media before meaning is extracted from it (i.e., the binary data stream).

- **Information:** "...data organized into meaningful relationships and structures...Information is factual in nature and conveys description..." In the digital forensic system, information refers to data at a higher level of abstraction [2], wherein the data is represented in a form more meaningful to human investigators and analysts, but from which knowledge has yet to be extracted (i.e., representing binary data as a human-readable word).

- **Knowledge:** "...information organized into meaningful patterns and repeatable processes...The patterns develop into knowledge when someone has an awareness and understanding of the pattern and its implications." Knowledge is synthesized information and information in context. It enables the user of information to apply it or to make use of it. In digital forensics, knowledge refers to the synthesis of information by human analysts to attain the investigative goals; it is the set of answers to investigative questions posed.

- **Wisdom:** "...tends to be self-contextualizing...[it] is knowledge organized into principles we use to reason, discern or judge." Wisdom refers to the highest level of understanding. In digital forensics, wisdom is most appropriately defined as the knowledge an investigator takes away from a specific investigation that can enable better (i.e., more effective and/or more efficient) digital forensic investigations in the future.

Given these definitions and the fact that the purpose of a digital forensic investigation is to confirm or refute allegations and/or obtain intelligence information, it becomes clear why the purpose of the digital forensic "system" is to convert data to information and information to knowledge.

The conversion from data to information in the digital forensic system is a two-step process. First, as previously described, a text string search produces a list of hits. Second, the human analyst or investigator reviews the list and creates a prioritized list of hits to guide subsequent analytical efforts. Both the original list of hits and the manually prioritized list of hits represent information. The former is created by computer information processing (CIP) and the latter by human information processing (HIP). The conversion from information to knowledge is facilitated by HIP, as the basic definition of knowledge necessitates. Specifically, the human analyst or investigator reviews the hits, interrogates the raw data and/or information as needed, and draws conclusions related to the investigation. These conclusions represent knowledge.

The information to knowledge conversion process, which uses standard digital forensic analysis tactics, techniques, tools and procedures, is laborious and inefficient. This is because of the high information retrieval overhead and the voluminous output produced by the data to information conversion process. The inefficiency is so stark that investigators often limit the scope of their text string searches to a single search, comprising a keyword or search expression list that is shorter than desired (ten search expressions or less). This action severely constrains the data to information conversion process – some information (in the form of search hits) is not retrieved because of the limited search query. Fundamentally, this constraint runs contrary to the purpose of the digital forensic system.

To illustrate the point that the data to information conversion process is overly constrained (arguably, even artificially constrained), consider a search query issued in a murder investigation. If it is alleged that the suspect sent a web-based email to the victim, wherein she threatened to kill the deceased, the investigator or analyst might wish to search the hard drive for the word "kill." An experienced digital forensics investigator, however, would caution against the inclusion of the word "kill," because of the extremely high number of false positive hits that would result (with respect to investigative objectives). The high false positive rate occurs because the word "kill" is present in various system commands, processes and documentation. Omission of the word "kill" from the search query then becomes a constraint on the data to information conversion process, as certain web-based email evidence may be missed unless it is found by another keyword search or by some other search technique.

The data to information conversion process is also unnecessarily constrained by vocabulary differences – there is only a 20% probability that two people will use the same search terms given the same search objective [7]. For example, a literal search that includes "Saddam Hussein" but not "Iraq" will only retrieve hits containing "Saddam Hussein." It will not retrieve relevant hits that contain the word "Iraq" but do not contain the expression "Saddam Hussein." Non-literal search techniques would retrieve both sets of hits. Thus, literal search techniques overly constrain the data to information conversion process.

A closer examination of the data to information conversion process reveals that it becomes overly constrained to counteract insufficient regulation of the information to knowledge conversion process. In this instance, regulation serves to control the display of information, enhancing knowledge acquisition. A regulator that prioritizes and/or groups search hits according to the probability of each hit being relevant would greatly improve the information to knowledge conversion process. Such regulators have been used by Internet search engines for more than ten years. Surprisingly, they have not yet been employed in digital forensic text string searching.

If we accept the argument that the text string search process (or subsystem) is performing sub-optimally, thereby causing the overall digital forensic investigation system to perform sub-optimally, then the natural question is: How do we improve the system's performance?

4. Process Model

The optimized text string search process (subsystem) can be achieved by *appropriately* constraining the data to information conversion process and by increasing the regulation of the information to knowledge conversion process. Currently, the amount and variety of information produced from the text string search process is overwhelming. This problem exists even in the face of an overly constrained data to information conversion process, wherein only a subset of relevant information is obtained. A regulator is needed to reduce the information retrieval overhead, thereby improving the information to knowledge conversion process.

At the same time, however, problems caused by synonymy and vocabulary differences require that the data to information conversion process be constrained appropriately. In other words, instead of simply reducing the number of permissible search strings (which exacerbates the synonymy and vocabulary differences problems), it is important to handle search strings more intelligently and, possibly, even expand the scope (quantity) of permissible strings.

The proposed text string search process model introduces additional system state transitions and operators to address the problems posed by high information retrieval overhead and poor investigative recall. The two primary types of operators in the text string search process are computer information processing (CIP) operators and human information processing (HIP) operators. As discussed above, the current data to information to knowledge conversion process is a three-step process involving only one CIP approach. The proposed process model involves

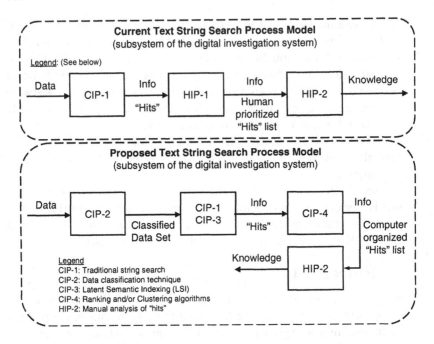

Figure 2. Current and proposed text string search process models.

a four-step process with four advanced CIP approaches and only one HIP approach (Figure 2).

The first step in the proposed text string search process model involves data classification. The goal of this step is to enable filtering so that successive CIP processes may be executed against smaller data subsets. This is important given the increased computational expense that will likely accompany the introduction of additional CIP processes. For example, data may be categorized as text or non-text by a CIP data classification technique such as Shannon's Forensic Relative Strength Scoring System (FRSS) [22], which uses two measures (ASCII proportionality and entropy) to categorize data as text or non-text.

The second step of the text string search process model involves the application of two CIP approaches in concert with each other. The goal of this step is to generate a set of search hits that is more exhaustive (for investigative purposes) than that produced by traditional search techniques. The step also reduces the effects of the synonymy and vocabulary differences problems. The first CIP process is traditional text string searching, which is augmented with a latent semantic indexing (LSI) technique to facilitate the extraction of semantic meaning from text [24]. Latent semantic indexing (LSI) was pioneered in 1990 by

Deerwester, *et al.* [6]. Several variants and improvements have since been developed. Among the most notable is probabilistic latent semantic analysis (PLSA or pLSI), which was introduced by Hofmann [11]. PLSA improves the quality of the semantic dimensions by including and excluding terms from the semantic subspace based on statistical significance rather than quantitative thresholds alone.

In this application, LSI serves to reduce false negatives by allowing hits that are relevant to the investigation to be retrieved; these hits would not otherwise be retrieved via traditional literal search techniques. Using LSI to reduce false negatives also improves the quality of information generated during the data to information conversion process. Such computer information processing techniques have been applied successfully in other areas, including web content mining [5] and semantic extraction from on-line postings [19].

The third step of the text string search process model involves another (new) CIP approach – the application of relevancy ranking and/or clustering algorithms. The goal is to reduce the effects of polysemy. A relevancy ranking algorithm serves to prioritize the hits (i.e., order the hits according to investigative relevance), thereby reducing information retrieval overhead and helping investigators get to the relevant hits faster. As stated previously, this approach is widely employed by Internet search engines, but it has not been used in the digital forensics arena to improve text string searching. This is largely due to the fact the algorithms are not directly applicable to digital forensic text string searching given the variables used by the algorithms and the nature of the data sets. Internet search engine prioritization ranking algorithms rely heavily on web-oriented variables such as PageRank, anchor text and visual properties of the text [1], which are not relevant to digital forensic data sets. Other ranking variables, e.g., proximity measures and query term order, are probably extensible, but research has shown that these variables alone are insufficient to achieve good results.

The basic premise of post-retrieval clustering is that information retrieval overhead can be significantly reduced by thematically grouping query results, thereby enabling the user to find relevant hits more efficiently. This is due to the "cluster hypothesis," which states that computationally similar documents tend to be relevant to the same query [25]. Empirical research has shown that clustered query results improve information retrieval effectiveness over traditional ranked lists using static relevance ranking models. Such results hold true for both traditional text-based information retrieval (i.e., clustering retrieved documents from a digital library) [9, 12–15] and web-based information retrieval [26–28].

The final step of the process model is unchanged from the current process model: HIP-2, the manual analysis of search results. It is postulated that HIP-1, manual prioritization heuristics, will no longer be necessary, and that HIP-2 will be more effective and more efficient. The introduction of additional computer information processing steps will improve investigative recall and decrease information retrieval overhead. We expect that the increased CIP time associated with the additional CIP steps will be greatly overshadowed by the gains in effectiveness and efficiency due to decreased HIP demands.

5.   Conclusions

The proposed process model represents a paradigmatic change in digital forensic text string searching. It is admittedly theoretical and high-level in nature, but it should stimulate new ways of thinking about digital forensic text string searching. Candidate classification, LSI, ranking and clustering algorithms must be identified and empirically tested to assess query precision, query recall and computational expense. Similar algorithms have already been developed for information retrieval, artificial intelligence, data mining and text mining applications. The challenge is to redesign these algorithms to improve text string searching in the area of digital forensics.

The process model has two principal benefits. First, the effectiveness and efficiency of text string searching in digital investigations will be greatly improved. The data to information conversion process will no longer be artificially constrained, and the information to knowledge conversion process will be enhanced. In short, less evidence will be missed, and the human analysis portion of the search process will become much less laborious.

The second benefit is the potential scalability to large data sets. Traditional string matching approaches are impractical for terabyte data sets – the overall process time is inordinately large given the number of false positives and the resulting information retrieval overhead. Most database and tree-indexing algorithms are also impractical when conducting a small number of searches against a terabyte data set. Again, the problem is inordinately high information retrieval overhead. In this instance, however, the problem is not just HIP time, but also excessive CIP time, given the amount of indexing time required before an investigation can begin (and the limited return on investment as the index creation time is not spread across multiple searches).

The proposed approach has certain limitations, including (possibly) high error rates, computational expense and the difficulty of extending data mining algorithms to digital investigations. Error rates have been largely ignored in digital forensics research [3]. An understanding of error rates becomes even more important with the proposed model because of the use of advanced CIP approaches. The data classification step inherently filters the data set leading to concerns that not everything is being searched. The use of ranking and/or clustering algorithms might dissuade investigators from exhaustively reviewing the search results. Moreover, investigators might even cease their reviews when "enough" evidence is obtained.

Clearly, additional and more computationally expensive CIP algorithms will increase computer processing time. The fundamental question, however, is whether or not the processing time is dwarfed by the HIP time that is required when false positives and false negatives are not controlled, and when results are not prioritized and/or summarized.

Finally, the extensibility of data mining algorithms to digital investigations is a major concern. On the one hand, much of the research in text mining and web content mining has been driven by the demand for eliciting "business intelligence" from massive data sets. On the other hand, raw binary data on digital media is unlike the data sources for which data mining algorithms were developed. Indeed, in digital forensic applications, data sources are likely to be very heterogeneous and unstructured.

The issues related to error rates, computational expense and data mining algorithm extensibility must be carefully considered when candidate algorithms are selected and tested. Nonetheless, it is expected that the proposed process model will drastically decrease false positive and false negative error rates, improve query recall and precision, and reduce the human analytical burden – all while allowing the investigator to increase the number of search terms used on terabyte or larger data sets.

References

[1] S. Brin and L. Page, The anatomy of a large-scale hypertextual web search engine, *Computer Networks and ISDN Systems*, vol. 30(1-7), pp. 107–117, 1998.

[2] B. Carrier, Defining digital forensic examination and analysis tools using abstraction layers, *International Journal of Digital Evidence*, vol. 1(4), pp. 1–12, 2003.

[3] E. Casey, Error, uncertainty and loss in digital evidence, *International Journal of Digital Evidence*, vol. 1(2), pp. 1–45, 2002.

[4] E. Casey, Network traffic as a source of evidence: Tool strengths, weaknesses and future needs, *Digital Investigation*, vol. 1, pp. 28–43, 2004.

[5] S. Das and M. Chen, Yahoo! for Amazon: Opinion extraction from small talk on the web, *Proceedings of the Eighth Asia-Pacific Finance Association Annual Conference*, pp. 1–45, 2001.

[6] S. Deerwester, S. Dumais, G. Furnas, T. Landauer and R. Harshman, Indexing by latent semantic analysis, *Journal of the American Society for Information Science*, vol. 41(6), pp. 391–407, 1990.

[7] G. Furnas, L. Gomez, T. Landauer and S. Dumais, The vocabulary problem in human-system communication, *Communications of the ACM*, vol. 30, pp. 964–971, 1987.

[8] J. Giordano and C. Maciag, Cyber forensics: A military operations perspective, *International Journal of Digital Evidence*, vol. 1(2), pp. 1–13, 2002.

[9] M. Hearst and J. Pedersen, Reexamining the cluster hypothesis: Scatter/gather on retrieval results, *Proceedings of the Nineteenth ACM International Conference on Research and Development in Information Retrieval*, pp. 76–84, 1996.

[10] F. Hinshaw, Data warehouse appliances: Driving the business intelligence revolution, *DM Review Magazine*, September 2004.

[11] T. Hofmann, Probabilistic latent semantic indexing, *Proceedings of the Twenty-Second ACM International Conference on Research and Development in Information Retrieval*, pp. 50–57, 1999.

[12] A. Leuski, Evaluating document clustering for interactive information retrieval, *Proceedings of the Tenth International Conference on Information and Knowledge Management*, pp. 33–40, 2001.

[13] A. Leuski and J. Allan, Improving interactive retrieval by combining ranked lists and clustering, *Proceedings of the Sixth RIAO Conference*, pp. 665–681, 2000.

[14] A. Leuski and J. Allan, Interactive information retrieval using clustering and spatial proximity, *User Modeling and User-Adapted Interaction*, vol. 14(2-3), pp. 259–288, 2004.

[15] A. Leuski and W. Croft, An evaluation of techniques for clustering search results, Technical Report IR-76, Computer Science Department, University of Massachusetts at Amherst, Amherst, Massachusetts, pp. 1–19, 1996.

[16] S. Mukkamala and A. Sung, Identifying significant features for network forensic analysis using artificial intelligence techniques, *International Journal of Digital Evidence*, vol. 1(4), pp. 1–17, 2003.

[17] J. Nunamaker, N. Romano and R. Briggs, A framework for collaboration and knowledge management, Proceedings of the Thirty-Fourth Hawaii International Conference on System Sciences, 2001.

[18] D. Radcliff, Inside the DoD's Crime Lab, *NetworkWorldFusion*, pp. 1–5, March 8, 2004.

[19] B. Rajagopalan, P. Konana, M. Wimble and C. Lee, Classification of virtual investing-related community postings, *Proceedings of the Tenth Americas Conference on Information Systems*, pp. 1–6, 2004.

[20] V. Roussev and G. Richard, Breaking the performance wall: The case for distributed digital forensics, *Proceedings of the Fourth Annual Digital Forensics Research Workshop*, pp. 1–16, 2004.

[21] M. Schwartz, Cybercops need better tools, *Computerworld*, p. 1, July 31, 2000.

[22] M. Shannon, Forensics relative strength scoring: ASCII and entropy scoring, *International Journal of Digital Evidence*, vol. 2(4), pp. 1–19, 2004.

[23] P. Sommer, The challenges of large computer evidence cases, *Digital Investigation*, vol. 1, pp. 16–17, 2004.

[24] D. Sullivan, *Document Warehousing and Text Mining: Techniques for Improving Business Operations, Marketing and Sales*, Wiley, New York, p. 542, 2001.

[25] C. van Rijsbergen, *Information Retrieval*, Butterworths, London, 1979.

[26] O. Zamir and O. Etzioni, Web document clustering: A feasibility demonstration, *Proceedings of the Twenty-First ACM International Conference on Research and Development of Information Retrieval*, pp. 46–54, 1998.

[27] O. Zamir and O. Etzioni, Grouper: A dynamic clustering interface to web search results, *Computer Networks*, vol. 31(11-16), pp. 1361–1374, 1999.

[28] H. Zeng, Q. He, Z. Chen, W. Ma and J. Ma, Learning to cluster web search results, *Proceedings of the Twenty-Seventh ACM International Conference on Research and Development in Information Retrieval*, pp. 210–217, 2004.

Chapter 13

DETECTING STEGANOGRAPHY USING MULTI-CLASS CLASSIFICATION

Benjamin Rodriguez and Gilbert Peterson

Abstract   When a digital forensics investigator suspects that steganography has been used to hide data in an image, he must not only determine that the image contains embedded information but also identify the method used for embedding. The determination of the embedding method – or stego fingerprint – is critical to extracting the hidden information. This paper focuses on identifying stego fingerprints in JPEG images. The steganography tools targeted are F5, JSteg, Model-Based Embedding, OutGuess and StegHide. Each of these tools embeds data in a dramatically different way and, therefore, presents a different challenge to extracting the hidden information. The embedding methods are distinguished using features developed from sets of stego images that are used to train a multi-class support vector machine (SVM) classifier. For new images, the image features are calculated and evaluated based on their associated label to the most similar class, i.e., clean or embedding method feature space. The SVM results demonstrate that, in the worst case, embedding methods can be distinguished with 87% reliability.

Keywords: Steganalysis, multi-class classification, support vector machine

1.   Introduction

Steganography is a data hiding and transmission technique that attempts to conceal and prevent the detection of the true content of a message. The steganographic process uses a cover object – often an image – to conceal the message ("stego data"). An embedding algorithm combines a cover image and the stego data to produce a stego image, which is an image that contains the hidden message. Steganalysis, the process of breaking steganography, involves examining a set of cover objects to determine if steganography was used, identifying the fingerprint of the embedding algorithm, and then extracting the embedded content.

Please use the following format when citing this chapter:

Rodriguez, B., Peterson, G., 2007, in IFIP International Federation for Information Processing, Volume 242, Advances in Digital Forensics III; eds. P. Craiger and S Shenoi; (Boston: Springer), pp. 193-204.

Several methods are available for detecting hidden information in images, but the embedding algorithm must be known for any of these methods to be effective. Unfortunately, such steganography fingerprinting is a major challenge as there are more than 250 steganography programs available [16]. To address this issue, it is necessary to develop detection methods that use a combination of features to identify the class or type of embedding method.

This paper presents a multi-class classification method that focuses on classifying unseen instances to their specific embedding method (class). The method categorizes JPEG stego images based on feature classification in which instances are associated with exactly one element of the label set. The multilevel energy band features presented in this paper are used with the multi-class support vector machine (SVM) classification technique. The features are generated from higher order statistics of the multilevel energy bands of the discrete cosine transform (DCT).

The test results are based on an image database of 1,000 high-quality JPEG images taken with a Nikon Coolpix 5. The stego images were created using five steganography tools (F5, JSteg, Model-Based Embedding, OutGuess and StegHide). Each of these tools embeds data using a different technique, with the exception of OutGuess and StegHide that embed similarly but use different randomization techniques. The results demonstrate that, in the worst case, embedding methods can be distinguished with 87% reliability.

The next section discusses embedding methods and multi-class classifiers. Section 3 describes the multilevel energy feature generation technique. This is followed by a description of the multi-class SVM classification method in Section 4. Section 5 presents the results of the SVM classifier using multilevel energy features. This paper ends with concluding remarks and a discussion of future work.

2.   Related Work

Each embedding method leaves a fingerprint on the stego image representative of the algorithm used to create the image. Our approach is to use multi-class classifiers to detect specific classes of embedding methods using stego fingerprints. This section discusses the main JPEG image data embedding methods used by steganography tools and the primary multi-class classification methods.

2.1   Embedding Methods

Digital images are often used to hide stego data because numerous redundant portions within the images can be altered without affecting the quality as observed by the human eye [16]. This paper examines five prominent tools for embedding data in JPEG images: F5, JSteg, Model-Based Embedding, OutGuess and StegHide.

The JPEG image format is currently the most prevalent image storage format [16]. The vast number of JPEG images available on the Internet makes them ideal cover images for hiding secret data. A JPEG embedding process embeds the data in discrete cosine transform (DCT) coefficients. First, the DCT coefficients of an image are computed; the coefficients of an 8×8 block of image pixels $f(x, y)$ are denoted by $F(u, v)$. The coefficients are divided by the quantization matrix, which quantizes the coefficients for compression. After this process, most JPEG embedding methods use the least significant bits (LSBs) of the quantized DCT coefficients. Redundant bits are used to embed the hidden message so that the embedding has no effect on the binary encoder. While the embedding does not affect the compression process, modifying a single DCT coefficient affects all 64 pixels in the 8×8 image block.

F5 [18] was developed as a challenge to the steganalysis community. This method exploits the JPEG compression algorithm by decrementing the absolute values of the DCT coefficients in a process known as matrix encoding. An estimated embedding capacity is computed based on the total number of DCT coefficients. A recursive algorithm is then used to match the bits of the message in a hash function to determine the encoding, stopping when one of the coefficients is reduced to zero. An F5 embedding is identifiable by the unnatural coefficient histograms produced by the embedding technique.

Model-Based Embedding [14] fits the coefficient histogram into an exponential model using maximum likelihood. This method addresses the limitations of other embedding methods; it can successfully hide large messages so that they are undetectable by certain statistical analyses and it can achieve maximum capacity. Model-Based Embedding is accomplished by identifying the ideal embedding structure based on the statistical model of the DCT coefficients of the original cover image, and ensuring that the statistical model is retained after the embedding. Although the embedding technique is similar to that used by F5, it does not produce unnatural histogram frequencies for adjacent DCT coefficients. This embedding technique is identified by combining several higher-order statistics.

The JSteg tool encodes messages in JPEG images by manipulating the LSBs of the quantified DCT coefficients. The message is formatted so that the first five bits of the frequency band coefficient indicate the length of the band (size of the embedded message), which is also referred to as the capacity of the block. The next set of bits indicates the bit length of the actual message. This message length indication scheme avoids generating large numbers of zeros that occur when short messages are embedded using a fixed bit length to indicate message size [10]. This type of embedding does not spread the encoded bits among the 14 coefficients; therefore, it can be identified using a first-order statistic (e.g., mean).

OutGuess [13] was designed to evade detection by statistical steganalysis techniques such as the chi-square statistical attack. The embedding technique modifies the LSBs of the DCT coefficients by statistically checking the original image DCT heuristics against the embedded image; it then manipulates nearby DCT blocks to maintain the original DCT histogram. The coefficients $(F(u, v) \notin [0, 1])$ are selected using a pseudo-random number generator. The statistical correction method embeds hidden data within the coefficient LSBs while offsetting nearby LSB coefficients with minor bit changes to preserve the chi-square statistic.

StegHide [8] hides data in multiple types of image and audio files. In the case of JPEG images, the color representation sample frequencies are not changed, which makes this method robust to first-order statistical attacks. This robustness is the direct result of embedding stego data within the LSBs of DCT coefficients that have large variations with adjacent coefficients. However, this embedding technique can be detected using a higher-order statistic (e.g., energy).

Proper identification of the embedding technique is crucial to any attempt at extracting the hidden information. The five tools considered in this paper embed data into the quantized DCT coefficients of a JPEG image. Each DCT encoding introduces certain statistical irregularities that constitute a signature. The fundamental problem is to classify the signatures left by the tools.

2.2   Multi-Class Classification Methods

More than 250 tools are available for performing steganography on digital images [16]. Because of this, multi-class classification is an attractive technique for identifying the potential signatures of steganography embedding algorithms. This section describes two promising multi-class classification techniques.

In many multi-class classification methods, two-class classifiers are combined using the posterior probabilities of their outputs. The multi-class learning algorithm must create hyperplane boundaries in kernel space where each hyperplane depends on the margin of separation obtained at the support vector nodes. This is achieved by combining the two-class classification methods using voting and combinations of approximate posterior probabilities, where the use of posterior probabilities enhances the solution by eliminating ties [12]. Another approach is to use combinations of binary classification methods with a naive Bayes classifier, which generalizes to multiple classes [17].

Several multi-class SVM classifiers employ a winner-take-all approach, assigning the class labeling based on a majority vote for the class [7]. The winner-take-all approach uses multiple two-class SVM prototypes per class, separating one class identity from the others. The method combines multiple sets of support vectors to create a large decision boundary separating the desired classes. This is achieved using a constrained quadratic search to find locally-optimal solutions for non-convex objective functions. In this way, the winner-take-all strategy creates a set of linear functions, each of which provides an ordering of the classes for a sample, where the "winner" is the first class in the ordering.

Our approach uses a majority-vote-wins strategy. However, in order to perform classification, a suitable set of features is required. The following section describes the features used to perform steganalysis via multi-class classification.

3. Features

This section describes the DCT multilevel energy bands method for calculating the transform domain features from a JPEG image. The features are obtained by computing the DCT energy bands for each block of 8×8 coefficients.

The transform domain features presented in Figure 1 focus on the energy bands of the DCT coefficients. Figure 1(b) shows the representation of the energy bands after the DCT. The DCT used in JPEG compression does not generate the multilevel energy bands produced by wavelet decomposition. Moreover, the multilevel energy band representation in Figure 1(b) does not allow for the energy levels to be extracted based on the edges of the original image as shown in Figure 1(c). Instead, the DCT output is rearranged in a wavelet decomposition structure to show the energy bands. This structure is created using 8×8 pixel blocks, which are the same as those used during JPEG compression. For each 8×8 block, the DCT energy band decomposition of vertical, diagonal and horizontal edges are formed via zigzag (Figure 1(d)) and Peano scans (Figure 1(e)). Rearranging the coefficients of the DCT splits the frequency spectrum into uniformly spaced bands containing vertical, horizontal and diagonal edges. The ideal representation of the energy bands is shown in Figure 1(f).

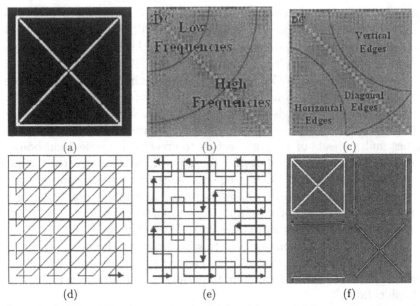

Figure 1. DCT multilevel energy bands: (a) Input image; (b) Energy band representation; (c) Extracted edges; (d) Vector with zigzag; (e) Peano scan matrix; (f) Level1 representation.

The structure presented captures the energy better than the normal DCT, and at least as well as wavelet decompositions used in image processing. The transformed coefficients are matched to higher level linear predicted neighboring coefficients, which result in an unstructured (non-Gaussian) distribution. Higher-order statistics are appropriate for measuring the coefficients for non-Gaussian processes.

The features are calculated using a mask, which, for a coefficient c, calculates the difference between c and its neighbors q, as shown in Figure 2. Similar methods have been used in pattern recognition [2] and steganography detection [1, 11] with wavelets. Higher-order statistics and predicted log errors are calculated across all of the mask values in order to create additional features.

Our classification methodology uses the features calculated from the DCT multilevel energy bands of JPEG images to separate the various embedding algorithms. This approach differs from other feature generation schemes (e.g., [1, 11]) that use different coefficients or wavelets. The most similar work to ours is that of Fridrich [6], which uses features that are specifically designed to distinguish classes of embedding algorithms, e.g., features that can distinguish an F5 embedding from an OutGuess embedding. Our features are developed for JPEG images, which makes

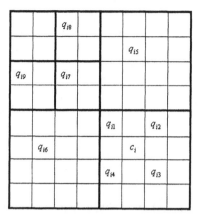

Figure 2.   Target coefficients.

them applicable to the more general problem of anomaly detection as well.

4.   SVM Multi-Class Classification

Multi-class classifiers are built on a winner-take-all set of class labels, each label representing one of the available classes. We employ a multi-class support vector machine (SVM) classifier, which separates classes by creating a hypersurface that maximizes the margins between all the classes.

SVMs have traditionally been applied to two-class or binary classification problems [15]. However, SVMs can be applied to multi-class classification. The techniques include: (i) the one-versus-all approach, which uses binary classifiers to encode and train the output labels; (ii) the one-versus-one approach, which uses a multi-class rule based on the majority-vote-wins approach; and (iii) training two-class classifiers and using voting and combinations of approximate posterior probabilities. Another approach to multi-class SVM classification is to train multi-class kernel-based predictors that use a compact quadratic optimization solution [5]. Our approach to SVM multi-class classification uses a one-versus-one majority-vote-wins strategy.

Figure 3 shows a multi-class SVM with support vectors (encapsulated in circles) and inter-class decision boundaries. SVM classification is performed by placing the classifying hyperplane, which separates the classes, in the center of the margin of separation. The margin of separation is calculated by locating the training points, x_i, that are closest to the opposing class and result in the largest margins of separation. Under this

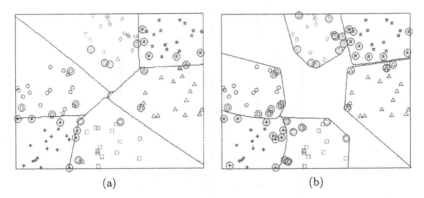

Figure 3.   Multi-class SVM: (a) SVM without hyperplane; (b) SVM with hyperplane.

condition, the decision surface is referred to as the maximally separating hyperplane [3] (Figure 3(a)). The result shown in Figure 3(b), which is used to perform multi-class steganalysis, was obtained using the maximization of the margins of separation as the classification mechanism. This produces fewer false positives for each of the classes, but increases the number of anomalies when the data is unknown.

Our classification problem involves several aspects such as the amount of stego, the embedding method and the compression scaling factor. This leads to a complex multi-class classifier. In order to generate a multi-class classifier, a set of binary classifiers $g^1, ..., g^M$ is first constructed; next, each binary classifier is trained to separate one class from the rest; then, the classifiers are combined using a majority-vote-wins policy [3]. In the case of SVM, multi-class generalization involves a set of discriminant functions designed according to the maximal output. The majority voting strategy is used to implement the multi-class classifier [4]:

$$f(x) = \arg \max_{j=1,...,M} g^j(x) \qquad (1)$$

where $g^j(x) = \sum y_i \alpha_i^j K(x, x_i) + b^j$. The classification y_i provides the sign of the coefficients of x_i. The weight values α_i^j are proportional to the number of times the misclassification of x_i causes the weights to be updated. $K(x, x_i)$ is a radial basis kernel (RBF), and b^j is the bias vector. Each $g^j(x)$ value is a classifier's assignment for a sample, which may also be used to decide when a classification is too close to call and should be rejected.

The kernel function is used to transform input data sets in the feature space (which are not linearly separable) to the kernel feature space where the classification is performed. In general, the kernel function is explicitly specified (it implicitly defines the feature space). By defining the kernel function, the complexity of non-linear class separation is avoided not only when computing the inner product, but also when designing the learning machine. In this work, the training vectors x_i are mapped into a higher-dimensional space by the mapping function ϕ. The kernel function used is a Gaussian radial basis kernel function $< \phi(x)\dot{\phi}(x_i) >= K(x, x_i) = e^{|x-x_i|^2/\sigma^2}$ [9].

To understand our approach, assume that the difference between the two largest $g^j(x)$ values is used as the measure of confidence in the classification of x. If the measure falls short of a threshold, the classifier rejects the pattern and does not assign it to a class (which produces an anomaly). The consequence is that a lower error rate is produced for the remaining patterns.

5. Results

This section presents the results based on testing data sets from the five tools (F5, JSteg, Model-Based Embedding, OutGuess, StegHide), and a clean data set. The experiments used a mixture of 1,000 (512×512 color JPEG) files comprising clean images and images created using the six embedding techniques described in Section 2.1. A total of 4,000 characters – equivalent to about one page of text – was embedded within each image file. The percentage of altered coefficients varied with the embedding method. The numbers of features used to represent the images were reduced from 120 to 40 features by eliminating features with similar correlations. The results in Table 1 were generated using five-fold cross validation where 80% of the data was used for training and 20% for testing; the test was conducted five times.

Table 1 shows the confusion matrix for the classification of the clean image set and five embedding method sets (F5, JSteg (JS), Model-Based Embedding (MB), OutGuess (OG) and StegHide (SH)). The matrix shows that the clean set is clearly separable from the remaining feature sets (Clean column and Clean row). In this multi-class classification, OutGuess and StegHide have the largest number of exemplars that are misclassified as each other. While these two methods are immune to statistical methods such as the chi-square test, they are vulnerable to higher-order statistics and transforms. These statistics, e.g., inertia, "compress" the energy bands of the DCT when the coefficients have not been modified and "expand" the energy bands when coefficients have been modified.

F5 and Model-Based Embedding also have mixed classification results. Therefore, we combined OutGuess and StegHide along with F5

Table 1. Confusion matrix for a six-class SVM classification.

	Actual					
Pred	Clean	F5	MB	OG	JS	SH
Clean	90.2 ± 4.5	3.4 ± 2.0	4.9 ± 2.2	1.4 ± 1.6	0.1 ± 0.0	0.0 ± 0.0
F5	4.2 ± 1.5	83.0 ± 5.4	6.7 ± 3.2	4.8 ± 1.1	0.2 ± 0.0	1.1 ± 0.9
MB	3.6 ± 2.3	16.8 ± 5.2	75.1 ± 9.1	2.4 ± 1.2	0.1 ± 0.0	2.0 ± 1.3
OG	0.4 ± 0.01	1.4 ± 1.6	0.4 ± 0.2	52.3 ± 12.2	6.6 ± 2.9	38.9 ± 7.6
JS	1.0 ± 0.5	3.4 ± 1.6	2.2 ± 2.0	6.8 ± 3.8	82.2 ± 5.8	4.4 ± 3.0
SH	0.6 ± 0.0	1.2 ± 0.7	1.7 ± 1.8	40.0 ± 7.0	7.1 ± 2.8	49.4 ± 10.9

and Model-Based Embedding to create a four-class classification (Table 2). Unlike OutGuess and StegHide, F5 and Model-Based Embedding produce DCT coefficients that are undetectable using sophisticated statistical measures. The features for F5 and OutGuess are not affected by the re-compression of the embedding. The statistical measures of inertia, energy and entropy show prominent features in the diagonal, vertical and horizontal energy bands, respectively. These findings stress the importance of separating the energy bands into the edge components and measuring each energy band with various statistics.

Table 2. Confusion matrix for a four-class SVM classification.

	Actual			
Pred	Clean	F5 & MB	OG & SH	JS
Clean	94.8 ± 3.3	2.4 ± 1.7	1.5 ± 0.4	1.3 ± 0.8
F5 & MB	4.5 ± 2.9	87.0 ± 7.6	6.5 ± 2.6	2.0 ± 1.8
OG & SH	3.2 ± 0.9	3.6 ± 2.0	90.7 ± 3.8	2.5 ± 2.2
JS	0.0 ± 0.0	4.0 ± 1.7	6.4 ± 2.4	89.6 ± 6.7

Because of similarities in the embedding techniques, the multi-class classifier was unable to identify the embedding methods in the six-class classification (Table 1). However, better classification results were obtained by recognizing similarities in the embedding techniques and performing a four-class classification (Table 2). The results in Table 2 show that combining OutGuess and StegHide produces a classification accuracy of 90.7% (up from roughly 50%). This allows the identification of the two embedding techniques. While the results for F5 and Model-Based Embedding are not as dramatic as those for OutGuess and StegHide, an increase in classification accuracy is achieved, which enables the two techniques to be distinguished from the other embedding techniques.

6.   Conclusions

It is practically impossible to extract hidden data from a steganographic image without first identifying the embedding technique. The multi-class SVM-based technique presented in this paper can reliably determine if a JPEG image contains a hidden message and, if so, the type of lossy steganography that embedded the hidden data. The novel classification approach uses features constructed from DCT energy bands and engages a winner-take-all hierarchical classification structure.

Our future research will focus on two problems that must be solved after the embedding technique is identified. The first is to identify the algorithm that performed the embedding; this will require an additional multi-class classifier that is trained to recognize specific embedding algorithms. The second problem is to predict the amount of data embedded in an image and identify the image regions that contain the most embedded data; solving this problem would, of course, be crucial to developing techniques for extracting hidden messages.

Acknowledgements

This research was partially funded by the U.S. Air Force Research Laboratory, Information Directorate/Multi-Sensor Exploitation Branch, Rome, New York. The views expressed in this paper are those of the authors and do not reflect the official policy or position of the U.S. Air Force, U.S. Department of Defense or the U.S. Government.

References

[1] S. Agaian and H. Cai, Color wavelet based universal blind steganalysis, presented at the *International Workshop on Spectral Methods and Multirate Signal Processing*, 2004.

[2] R . Buccigrossi and E. Simoncelli, Image compression via joint statistical characterization in the wavelet domain, *IEEE Transactions on Image Processing*, vol. 8(12), pp. 1688–1701, 1999.

[3] C. Burges, A tutorial on support vector machines for pattern recognition, *Data Mining and Knowledge Discovery*, vol. 2(2), pp. 121–167, 1998.

[4] N. Cristianini and J. Shawe-Taylor, *An Introduction to Support Vector Machines and Other Kernel-Based Learning Methods*, Cambridge University Press, Cambridge, United Kingdom, 2000.

[5] J. Fridrich, G. Miroslav and H. Dorin, New methodology for breaking steganographic techniques for JPEGs, *Proceedings of the SPIE Symposium on Electronic Imaging*, pp. 143–155, 2003.

[6] J. Fridrich and T. Pevny, Determining the stego algorithm for JPEG images, *IEE Proceedings*, vol. 153(3), pp. 75–139, 2006.

[7] S. Har-Peled, D. Roth and D. Zimak, Constraint classification for multiclass classification and ranking, in *Advances in Neural Information Systems 15*, S. Becker, S. Thrun and K. Obermayer (Eds.), MIT Press, Cambridge, Massachusetts, pp. 785–792, 2003.

[8] S. Hetzl, StegHide (steghide.sourceforge.net).

[9] C. Hsu, C. Chang and C. Lin, A practical guide to support vector classification (www.csie.ntu.edu.tw/~cjlin/papers/guide/guide.pdf), 2005.

[10] T. Lane, P. Gladstone, L. Ortiz, L. Crocker, G. Weijers and other members of the Independent JPEG Group, JSteg (www.stegoarchive.com).

[11] S. Lyu and H. Farid, Steganalysis using color wavelet statistics and one-class support vector machines, *Proceedings of the SPIE Symposium on Electronic Imaging*, 2004.

[12] J. Platt, N. Cristianini and J. Shawe-Taylor, Large margin DAGs for multiclass classification, in *Advances in Neural Information Systems 12*, S. Solla, T. Leen and K. Muller (Eds.), MIT Press, Cambridge, Massachusetts, pp. 547–553, 2000.

[13] N. Provos, OutGuess (www.outguess.org).

[14] P. Sallee, Model-based steganography, *Proceedings of the Second International Workshop on Digital Watermarking*, pp. 154–167, 2003.

[15] B. Scholkopf and A. Smola, *Learning with Kernels: Support Vector Machines, Regularization, Optimization and Beyond*, MIT Press, Cambridge, Massachusetts, 2002.

[16] StegoArchive.com (www.stegoarchive.com).

[17] A. Tewari and P. Bartlett, On the consistency of multiclass classification methods, *Proceedings of the Eighteenth Annual Conference on Learning Theory*, pp. 143–157, 2005.

[18] A. Westfeld, F5 – A steganographic algorithm, *Proceedings of the Fourth International Workshop on Information Hiding*, pp. 289–302, 2001.

Chapter 14

REDACTING DIGITAL INFORMATION FROM ELECTRONIC DEVICES

A. Barclay, L. Watson, D. Greer, J. Hale and G. Manes

Abstract   Redaction is the process of removing privileged information from a document before it is presented to other parties. This paper discusses the major issues associated with the redaction of digital information from electronic devices. A novel technique involving a tokenized representation is presented as a solution to digital redaction in legal proceedings.

Keywords: Electronic discovery, digital information, redaction, tokens

1.   Introduction

With the introduction of digital evidence into the court system [8–12], the private sector and federal government must address a growing number of best practice issues in the field [1–4, 6]. This is especially true for digital redaction. Redaction is the process of removing privileged information from a document before it is presented to other parties. This paper focuses on digital redaction as it applies to the legal community.

During the discovery phase of court proceedings, it is necessary to provide information that is requested by opposing counsel. In general, an attorney's work on a case is protected by the work-product privilege, communications are protected between an attorney and their client, and other parties have no right to this information. The work-product privilege means that any documents prepared in anticipation of litigation or for trial by a party's representative enjoy qualified immunity from discovery. Similar privileges are involved in doctor-patient, priest-penitent and husband-wife relationships. To prove to the court that information is privileged, the party claiming privilege must show that the communication: (i) was made with an expectation of confidentiality, (ii) is essential

Please use the following format when citing this chapter:

Barclay, A., Watson, L., Greer, D., Hale, J., Manes, G., 2007, in IFIP International Federation for Information Processing, Volume 242, Advances in Digital Forensics III; eds. P. Craiger and S Shenoi; (Boston: Springer), pp. 205-214.

to a socially-approved relationship or purpose, and (iii) has not been waived by disclosure of the contents of the communications to persons outside the relationship.

The redaction process produces three items: an In Camera Copy of the privileged information, a Privilege Log and a Redacted Production Copy of the information. The In Camera Copy, which is presented to the judge in the case, contains all the items regarded as privileged. The Privilege Log and Redacted Production Copy are presented to opposing counsel. If a question arises as to whether a particular item in the Privilege Log meets the burden of privilege, the judge can review the material in the In Camera Copy and provide judgment.

Traditionally, the requested information has been presented in paper form. Currently, two methods are used to redact paper documents: "blackout" and physical removal. The blackout method involves using a black marker to conceal the portions of a document that are considered privileged. The physical removal method involves removing certain pages from a set of documents. Depending on the court's requirements, this may necessitate marking the exact locations from which the pages were removed.

The same concerns exist for privileged information residing on electronic storage devices, but no standard method of digital redaction has been adopted by the legal community [7]. Computerized methods that mimic the blackout process exist [5], as do those for mimicking the physical removal method. The former approach may engage a number of techniques to conceal text in a digital document. The latter typically involves collecting all the readable documents from a computer, placing them in a set, and selecting the items to redact. Yet, while electronic blackout and removal methods can sanitize a document found on an electronic device, they do not redact logical copies or copied fragments of the document that may remain.

This paper discusses the process of digital redaction and highlights the major issues associated with redacting digital information from electronic devices. A novel technique involving a tokenized representation is presented as a solution to digital redaction.

2.   Data Redaction

With respect to redaction, it is increasingly necessary to produce the entire contents of computer disks and other electronic storage devices as evidence. This goes beyond simply selecting all readable documents on a drive. It involves producing information that exists in free or slack space, deleted items, document fragments and even data that may not be in a readily identifiable format. The collection process produces what is referred to as a "forensics copy." This encumbers a data image redaction process to remove privileged information from the storage device.

2.1 Challenges and Considerations

The growing variety of electronic devices that integrate digital data storage components complicates the issue of data image redaction. Devices such as cell phones, digital cameras and digital music players, along with laptops and desktop computers store information using various file systems, media technologies and data formats. The sheer diversity of these storage options differentiates digital redaction from its physical pen-and-paper counterpart.

Aside from the variety of storage formats, other challenges to data image redaction in electronic devices include:

- The potential for encrypted data

- Deleted files that are recoverable in slack space or unoccupied regions of file systems

- Data fragmentation and replication

- Isolation of privilege by context for integrated data

A faithful digital redaction process must account for these subtleties in a systematic and comprehensive manner.

To completely redact digital information from an electronic device, it is imperative to determine the logical and physical locations of all pertinent documents and related data fragments that reside on the digital media. This is an issue because data is routinely stored in multiple locations on file systems in electronic devices. For example, Microsoft Word files are normally saved in a user-selected directory, but may also be automatically backed-up in a temporary folder as a part of normal operation; therefore, a Word document may logically exist in at least two separate locations on a computer system.

Deleting privileged information from digital media does not protect it from a thorough forensic examination. The only versions of a document that can be directly deleted are listed in file mapping tables. Other copies of the item are unaffected by the deletion of the original document and, therefore, could be recovered by a forensic examination.

Determining all the physical locations where digital information resides is also important due to the partitioning methods used in electronic media and devices. For example, suppose a user creates a file on a Linux system and subsequently saves it to a FAT partition of a hard drive. If the drive is subsequently repartitioned, the file may fall out of the new logical partition size and be moved into the space on the hard drive reserved for the resized FAT partition. Thus, the file exists in the new location and in its original location.

To determine whether information is privileged, it is necessary to interpret the information rationally; if the information is unreadable, privilege cannot be determined. This presents a problem when the information stored on electronic devices is encoded, protected or encrypted. During the redaction process, digital data without rational interpretation may be produced because it contains no apparent privilege. In fact, the data may contain privileged information that is concealed by the encoding. Consequently, if a rational interpretation is discovered later, the data can be decoded. Thus, the possibility exists that privileged information could be revealed to opposing counsel.

The accuracy of the data image redaction process is also important. When producing a redacted copy, care should be taken to demonstrate that the integrity of the redacted copy is preserved as it relates to the source media. The redaction process should only remove the data segments marked for redaction and leave all other segments untouched. Thus, digital redaction methods should incorporate validation schemes that offer assurance regarding the integrity of the redaction process.

2.2   Foundational Methodology

There are requisite procedural elements for any system that aspires to meet the challenges of data image redaction. The first is to characterize privileged information. Subsequently, an investigation must be conducted on the Work Copy of the electronic device. This investigation should identify privileged information, complex and indeterminate data objects, and produce an index of redactable items. Finally, the data must be redacted to produce both a Redacted Production Copy with an associated Privilege Log, and an In Camera Copy.

Characterizing Privileged Information   Redaction allows for the selective exclusion of information protected under privilege as defined by federal, state and local laws. These protections, e.g., based on attorney-client or doctor-patient relationships, provide different classes of privileged information.

The selection of privileged content is based on the current legal standards for such material. These standards involve communications between accepted members of an accepted privilege class acting in an accepted capacity. Additionally, the court may indicate that certain topics are off-limits and that related material is to be redacted as well.

Forensic investigations of digital media typically employ keyword or pattern-based searches to find relevant information. Such searches can also be used to identify redactable information belonging to a privilege class. By associating search criteria based on metadata and content with specific redaction classes, all the information on a source disk can be classified as privileged or non-privileged, with privileged information being additionally associated with a specific class.

Electronic Device Investigation The redaction process operates on a Work Copy of an electronic device, which is typically a forensic copy of the original media (it could be the original media if it is impractical or impossible to create a copy).

The investigation identifies known and unknown files by data carving the entire source media, finding deleted files in free space, hidden files, slack space, etc., via header and footer analysis. These files and hidden files are then keyword/pattern searched and each file object is labeled as being privileged/non-privileged, complex or indeterminate.

Data Objects A forensic investigation can reveal data that is not immediately interpretable; thus, the keyword/pattern identification will not be able to determine privilege status. Such data may be structured, compressed or otherwise encoded for interpretation by a special application or method (e.g., an Outlook PST file for an e-mail application). Encryption, data scrambling or fragmentation may also prevent immediate interpretation of data. Any data that is encoded or structured (and recognized as interpretable by a special filter or application) is treated as a "complex data object."

A metaphorical example of a complex data object is a sheet of used carbon paper containing interwoven, overlapping documents that are not easily interpreted. Initially, it is unclear if the carbon paper contains privileged information. However, further analysis could yield the individual documents that contain privileged information. Clearly, it would be irresponsible to release the carbon paper sheet to opposing counsel without performing an analysis and redacting privileged information.

Complex data objects are subject to an additional investigative process using appropriate tools and techniques that interpret the data and make it readable. The interpreted data can then be subjected to digital redaction. When no interpretation method is available, they can be regarded as "indeterminate data objects" and may be redacted until a method for interpretation presents itself (at which time the objects transition to complex data objects).

Original Media:	Data	Privileged Data	Data

Token Sequence	Data	Token	Data

Zero/Random:	Data	Zero/Random	Data

Compress:	Data	Data

Figure 1. Data removal methods.

An example of an indeterminate data object is again a sheet of carbon paper, but one that had been used very extensively. Even if it is not possible to extract individual documents based on current process, it would be irresponsible to release the carbon paper sheet because a new process could be created to extract the privilege-bearing documents. Note also that complex data objects may themselves contain complex data objects, which would require redaction to be a recursive process.

Redaction A Redacted Production Copy of a data image is created by copying the Work Copy to sterile media after removing the redacted objects. This copy must contain no privileged information and, depending on the legal mandate, no complex/indeterminate information. Both the Redacted Production Copy and the Privilege Log are provided to the opposing counsel.

The privileged data and metadata are combined to create the In Camera Copy, which is passed to the judge. The judge uses the In Camera Copy to mediate disputes on the appropriateness of a redaction when there is a challenge to reveal redacted information.

Three approaches are available for removing redacted data from an image (Figure 1). The first approach, which is discussed in the next section, is to replace the redacted data with a bit sequence or token. This provides a replacement for the removed data, emulating current physical redaction processes and adding Privilege Log metadata to the Production Copy.

The second approach is to keep the Privilege Log separate, filling the space formerly occupied by the redacted object with zeroed or random data. However, this may not be appropriate in a legal setting due to the potential for inference analysis based on file size and location. It should also be noted that even when fill data is randomized, "pseudo" artifacts such as false file headers in the redacted copy are possible. However, the benefit of this approach is that it closely emulates the original media and is compatible with current investigative strategies.

The third approach is to remove the privileged data and compress the non-privileged data together. This Redacted Production Copy format is a bit sequence with no describing information intact. Inference analysis of the original data would not be readily apparent; however, some reconstruction is possible using allocation tables, etc. if they are not deemed privileged. Like the randomized method above, this technique may introduce "pseudo" artifacts. Many of the implementation constraints identified – such as minimizing inference analysis, mimicking physical redaction, adding value to software examination methods by exposing redaction points, and encoding non-privileged meta-information – are best addressed by implementing a token-based redaction system.

3. Redaction Tokens

Redaction tokens are bit sequences that replace or stand for private data, complex data objects or indeterminate data objects in the Redacted Forensic Copy. As such, they provide a method to describe the redaction process to the court and other examiners. Tokens help confirm the integrity of the redaction process and provide an accessible layer of abstraction for juries. Implementation requirements would, of course, depend on legal statutes and precedence. Nevertheless, redaction tokens have several inherent advantages:

- Tokens can create identifiers that bind redacted data objects to the Privilege Log.

- Tokens can act as markers for interoperability with other programs, making redacted data segments recognizable to external tools. Forensics suites could recognize markers and skip data carving or sliding window analysis on token data/metadata.

- Tokens can provide a basic audit log, with the token encoding information about the examiner, case, etc.

- Tokens can contain a digital signature of the examiner, supporting non-repudiation and chain of custody.

- Tokens can include a one-way hash of the redacted object to verify the integrity of the original object and the In Camera Copy.

- Tokens can emulate the pre-redaction environment; all non-redacted information will appear intact.

- Tokens mimic the paper redaction system familiar to courts, providing a conceptual understanding of digital redaction.

Bit sequences for redaction tokens may be generated in a variety of ways depending on the purpose of the tokens. A token can serve as a method to represent redacted data, bind meta-information and provide accountability, or any combination thereof. The size of the smallest redacted object could also dictate the potential contents of a token, especially if a court requires that the original file sizes be maintained. For the UTF8 encoding format, a name that might be considered privileged could be as small as 6 bytes (thus, this becomes the maximum token size). On the other hand, redaction of large image files increases the prospective size of the token, potentially adding to its abilities.

Several issues must be considered when generating tokens. Tokens for each production must be consistent in format and agreed upon by all parties. Tokens should also be amenable to parsing. This issue is more complex than it might initially appear because tokens must avoid magic numbers and other bit sequences used in file headers and file system constructs. Additionally, tokens should be easily identifiable and generated in a reasonable amount of time. Finally, tokens must never reveal information about the contents of data objects represented in the Redacted Production Copy.

| Start sequence | Random ID | Optional Metadata | Stop sequence |

Figure 2. Basic redaction token schema.

3.1   Token Schema

The basic redaction token schema consists of a common start sequence, unique randomly-generated id, any number of optional enhancements, followed by a common closing sequence. A representative schema is presented in Figure 2, where the required elements are shown with solid lines and optional elements with dotted lines.

3.2   Token Methods

Redaction methods based on overwriting privileged data with tokens vary according to parsing speed, space needs, legal requirements and token schema/size. Token-based redaction methods include (Figure 3):

- Placing a single token in a data segment and compressing the redacted image to eliminate the remaining bytes of the segment.

- Replacing all the bytes in a data segment with a repeated token sequence.

- Placing a copy of the token in a data segment and replacing the rest of the segment with zeroed or random data.

Original Media:	Data	Privileged Data	Data

Single Token	Data	Token	Data	
Repeated Token:	Data	Token	Token	Data
Single Token/Zero:	Data	Token	Zero	Data

Figure 3. Token redaction methods.

The first method substitutes a single copy of the redaction token for the redacted data object, shrinking the image written to the Redacted Production Copy to eliminate the byte-level data storage occupied by the remainder of the object. This confutes inference analysis of the original size and location of the redacted object.

The second method creates a redacted forensic copy in which all the bytes that are selected as redactable are replaced with repeated copies of a token. Consecutive copies of the token are written until the redacted data segment is filled. The last copy of the token is a special case where it can either be written completely or compressed to include the closing stop sequence. This method preserves an accurate forensic copy with only the redacted information removed. It is analogous to blacking out entire documents and leaving them in place in a file box. However, this method permits inferences based on the size and spatial relationships of the redacted data.

The third method replaces all redactable bytes in a data segment with a single token followed by overwriting the remaining privileged bytes with zeroed or random data. This method is analogous to putting a placeholder and the same amount of blank pages as the original document into a file box. It closely models current paper-based redaction, but permits size and spatial inference analysis.

4. Conclusions

The growing volume of digital evidence introduced in legal proceedings makes digital redaction a major issue. Unfortunately, current redaction techniques do not address the complex issues related to evidence residing in electronic devices. Incomplete redaction may enable opposing counsel to access privileged information using digital forensic techniques and tools. Furthermore, criminal entities may be able to prevent electronic discovery based on the claim that privileged information is present and that no methods exist to guarantee privilege removal. The redaction technique presented in this paper addresses these issues by using tokens to systematically and comprehensively remove redactable information.

References

[1] M. Arkfeld, *Electronic Discovery and Evidence*, Law Partner Publishing, Phoenix, Arizona, 2005.

[2] B. Carrier, *File System Forensic Analysis*, Addison-Wesley, Crawfordsville, Indiana, 2005.

[3] A. Choudhri, L. Kagal, A. Joshi, T. Finin and Y. Yesha, PatientService: Electronic patient record redaction and delivery in pervasive environments, *Proceedings of the Fifth International Workshop on Enterprise Networking and Computing in the Healthcare Industry*, pp. 41–47, 2003.

[4] National Institute of Standards and Technology, Computer Forensics Tool Testing (www.cftt.nist.gov).

[5] National Security Agency, Redacting with Confidence: How to Safely Publish Sanitized Reports Converted from Word to PDF, Technical Report I333-TR-015R-2005, Fort Meade, Maryland, 2005.

[6] R. Nichols, D. Ryan and J. Ryan, *Defending Your Digital Assets Against Hackers, Crackers, Spies and Thieves*, McGraw-Hill, New York, 2000.

[7] G. Palmer, A Road Map for Digital Forensics Research, Technical Report DTR-T001-01, Digital Forensic Research Workshop (isis .poly.edu/kulesh/forensics/docs/DFRWS_RM_Final.pdf), 2001.

[8] U.S. District Court (District of Minnesota), Northwest Airlines v. IBT Local 2000, *Labor Relations Reference Manual*, vol. 163, pp. 2460–2461, 2000.

[9] U.S. District Court (Eastern District of Michigan), United States v. Alexander, *Westlaw* 2095701, 2004.

[10] U.S. District Court (Southern District of California), Playboy Enterprises, Inc. v. Welles, *Federal Supplement, Second Series*, vol. 7, pp. 1098–1105, 1998.

[11] U.S. District Court (Southern District of Indiana), Simon Property Group, L.P. v. mySimon, Inc., *Federal Rules Decisions*, vol. 194, pp. 639–644, 2000.

[12] U.S. District Court (Southern District of New York), Anti-Monopoly, Inc. v. Hasbro, Inc., *Westlaw* 649934, 1995.

VI

FILE SYSTEM FORENSICS

Chapter 15

IN-PLACE FILE CARVING

Golden Richard III, Vassil Roussev and Lodovico Marziale

Abstract   File carving is the process of recovering files from an investigative target, potentially without knowledge of the filesystem structure. Current generation file carvers make complete copies of recovered files. Unfortunately, they often produce a large number of false positives – "junk" files with invalid formats that frequently consume large amounts of disk space.

This paper describes an "in-place" approach to file carving, which allows the inspection of recovered files without copying file contents. The approach results in a significant reduction in storage requirements, shorter turnaround times, and opens new opportunities for on-the-spot screening of evidence. Moreover, it can be used to perform in-place carving on local and remote drives.

Keywords: File carving, in-place carving

1.   Introduction

File carving is a useful digital forensic technique for recovering files from an investigative target, potentially without knowledge of the filesystem structure. The process is based on information about the format of the files of interest and on assumptions about how the file data is laid out on the block-level device. Filesystem metadata is typically used – if at all – only to establish cluster sizes and to avoid carving undeleted files (which can be extracted without file carving).

Unfortunately, the current practice of carving recovered data into new files carries a huge performance penalty that is inherent and cannot be solved by optimizing the carving application. The only justification for this approach is that virtually all the tools used to view or process the recovered data require a file-based interface to the data. A new strategy is needed that provides a filesystem interface to the output of the carver without actually creating carved files. In other words,

Please use the following format when citing this chapter:

Richard, G., III, Roussev, V., Marziale, L., 2007, in IFIP International Federation for Information Processing, Volume 242, Advances in Digital Forensics III; eds. P. Craiger and S Shenoi; (Boston: Springer), pp. 217-230.

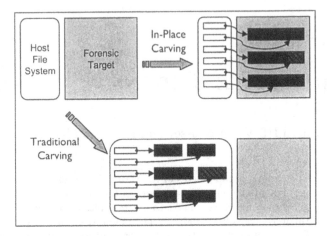

Figure 1. Conceptual differences between traditional and in-place carving.

if a filesystem interface is provided to candidate files without physically recreating them, existing forensic tools can still be used without creating new files, many of which will likely be invalid. We call this approach "in-place" file carving. The approach is similar to that used by current filesystems, except that filesystem metadata is stored outside the target.

Figure 1 illustrates the differences between traditional and in-place carving. The host filesystem and forensic target can be thought of as "input" to both traditional and in-place carving. In traditional carving, both the metadata and the data for carved files are dumped into the host filesystem and the target has no significant role after the carving operation completes. In the case of in-place carving, a database of metadata is inserted into the host filesystem, indicating where potentially interesting files are located in the target.

To understand our motivation, consider a recent case, in which carving a wide range of file types in a modest 8 GB target yielded more than 1.1 million files that exceeded the capacity of the 250 GB drive being used. This represents an "over-carving" factor of more than 32. Clearly, this is a pathological case and an expert user might be able to substantially reduce the number of carved files and the required storage by tinkering with the carving rules. However, with drives in the 200-300 GB range being fairly typical for desktop systems, even an over-carving factor of two or three puts a significant burden on an investigator's resources. First, he must purchase and dedicate a significant amount of temporary storage for file carving. Then, he must pay a substantial price in performance that could easily add days to the investigation.

It is not difficult to pinpoint the reasons for the huge performance penalty. The Scalpel file carving tool we use in our experiments [6] allows us to separate the time taken to identify the candidate files from the time taken to recreate them in the host filesystem. Scalpel performs these two tasks in separate passes. In the first pass, the entire target is processed sequentially to identify the locations of candidates for carving. The result is a list of carving jobs indicating which sequences of blocks constitute candidate files. Given a non-trivial number of rules, the process is CPU-bound because a large number of binary string searches must be performed. During the second pass, the carving jobs are carried out by placing copies of the identified data blocks into newly created files. This is a completely I/O-bound process with write access to the host filesystem being the limiting factor. In general, if there are a large number of candidates to carve, the second pass will require much more time than the first pass.

Although the root of the problem is the false positives generated by the carving rules, the performance penalty is the result of recreating the carved files. Specifically, the main culprit is the randomized set of write accesses generated during the carving process, which causes worst-case performance for mechanical hard drives because writing disk blocks and updating filesystem metadata generate non-sequential disk accesses. Obviously, any over-carving will guarantee randomized disk accesses as the same data block is copied to more than one new location on the host filesystem and the corresponding file metadata is updated. It is worth observing that any optimizations based on interleaving/pipelining Scalpel's two passes (as some other tools attempt to do) has limited potential and will not solve the problem. This is because the creation of carved files clearly dominates total execution time.

Arguably, the penalty for recreating the candidates goes beyond the carving itself and is carried into the subsequent processing steps. Consider our 8 GB target and a "reasonable" over-carving factor of two, and assume that the goal is to carve out all JPEG images. On a modern workstation with 4 GB RAM, 40-45% of the target could conceivably be cached. With proper clustering of file accesses based on information generated by the carving application, it is possible to take advantage of the caching effects most of the time. In contrast, reading 16 GB of recreated files yields no tangible caching benefits due to non-overlapping file operations.

The following subsections explore two baseline scenarios where in-place carving can make a significant difference.

1.1   Large-Scale Carving

It is increasingly common to encounter terabyte-scale targets in digital forensic investigations. We consider such targets as "large-scale" and note that performance problems in dealing with them are compounded by the fact that high-capacity drives tend to be noticeably slower than the fastest drives available. However, we use the term "large-scale" in a relative sense – any target that stretches or exceeds the available resources would be viewed as being large-scale by the examiner, so even a 100 GB target could prove to be a challenge. Economy is also an important factor. The original design of Scalpel was motivated by the fact that file carvers required "elite" hardware to perform acceptably. We now address a different, but related question: Should an investigator who wants to recover data from a 200 GB drive using file carving be expected to have 1 TB or more of available disk space?

The answer is no because in-place carving is much more scalable than traditional carving in terms of storage requirements. The contents of a target are dominated by file data with metadata usually taking up well under 5% of storage. By choosing not to copy file content (often more than once), the overhead is limited to a small fraction of the target size. In our 8 GB example, the new metadata for 1.1 million candidate files would take up less than 128 MB if we allow 128 bytes of metadata per file, or about 1.6% of the target size. Extrapolating to a 1 TB target, the metadata is still small enough to fit on a miniature USB drive.

A second aspect of scalability is turnaround time. How long after initiating file carving operations can the examiner begin to work in earnest on the results? Scalpel v1.60's preview mode performs only the first carving pass and then outputs a database of locations for candidate files. This information is sufficient for the in-place carving architecture described later in the paper to recreate metadata for candidate files on the fly. This means that any of the candidate files from the 8 GB drive mentioned earlier can be delivered after only about 70 minutes of work.

A third aspect to providing a scalable solution is the flexibility to react to the specifics of the target by adjusting the carving settings to minimize false positives or refocus the investigation. Traditionally, investigators make several carving attempts to adjust maximum file sizes and the set of file types to carve. These adjustments are mostly motivated by performance concerns as carving a large number of file types can be expensive. With in-place carving, a large number of file types with large maximum carve sizes can be specified without incurring significant performance penalties.

1.2   Triage

It is often desirable to preview a set of possible targets (or a very large target) to judge the relevance of the data to an investigation. Such an assessment, which can be performed in a forensic laboratory or in the field, helps an investigator prioritize and filter targets. In the case of file carving, only an in-place approach will deliver the necessary short turnaround time.

Going a step further, it is possible to perform in-place file carving on live machines that cannot be taken down for practical or legal reasons. Live carving has the potential to increase voluntary cooperation by equipment owners because critical machines can run uninterrupted. While it would be more challenging to present the results of live file carving operations in court, the results may be useful in justifying a search warrant for seizure of the equipment and a more stable "dead" investigation. In a less restrictive environment, such as an internal corporate inquiry, where the goal is not to go to court, live carving has even more applications. The primary benefit of live in-place carving is that large amounts of additional storage are not required. In fact, if network block device [5] connectivity is used between the target and an investigator's machine, only additional storage for metadata for carved files is required (this can be stored on a small USB device).

Another important aspect of in-place carving is that it preserves privacy because no copies of the file data are made. Furthermore, it should be easy to gain owner cooperation as the investigator is unlikely to need anything more than a USB device to initiate and store the carving results.

The forensic triage – whether in the lab or in the field – could be performed in parallel on a group of machines controlled by a single investigator over a local network. The idea of an on-the-spot investigation has been explored in a more general setting by the Bluepipe Project [3], where file carving is just a special function that could be performed and controlled in parallel.

So far, we have argued that traditional file carving approaches, which create new files for each candidate, are wasteful and carry significant and unavoidable performance overhead. The main contribution of this work is to present an architecture for in-place carving and to demonstrate that the benefits of file-based access to the candidates can be realized by recreating file metadata without copying file contents.

2.   Related Work

This section describes representative work on file carving and the technologies used to develop in-place carving tools.

2.1   File Carving

File carvers (e.g., [6, 7]) read databases of file headers and footers, and rules defining specific file types, and then search target disk images for occurrences of files of these types. The headers and footers are typically binary character strings. The rules help reduce false positives. For example, a rule may associate the footer closest to a discovered header; another rule may indicate that files should be no larger than a specified size. The goal is to identify the starting and ending locations of files in disk images and "carve" (copy) sequences of bytes into regular files.

File carving is a powerful technique because files can be retrieved from raw disk images regardless of the type of filesystem. File retrieval is possible even when the filesystem metadata has been completely destroyed. For example, a file deposited on a FAT partition often can be recovered even if the partition is reformatted as NTFS, then ext2, then FAT again, even if bad block checks (which are generally read-only operations) are applied. While filesystem metadata is quite fragile, file data is much more resilient. The problem with current file carvers is that they require considerable additional storage as large numbers of false positives are generated. Good rules for guiding carving operations can reduce the number of false positives (and the storage needed). However, our in-place carving scheme requires virtually no additional storage. Moreover, the amount of time that an investigator has to wait to preview the results is substantially reduced.

2.2   User-Space Filesystems

FUSE [8] is a system for the rapid development of novel filesystems. The FUSE architecture is presented in Figure 2. A FUSE kernel component, which implements a Virtual File System (VFS), traps system calls and redirects them to a user-space filesystem implementation, which is compiled against the FUSE library. This allows new filesystems to be quickly designed and built without the complexity of in-kernel hacking. The FUSE kernel module acts as a bridge to the VFS kernel interfaces.

To instrument system calls in FUSE, the new filesystem supplies a table of functions that redefine standard system calls (e.g., open, read, write and close). Each of the functions can completely redefine the system call or augment its functionality.

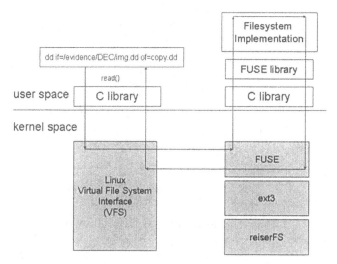

Figure 2. FUSE architecture.

FUSE currently has ports for Linux and FreeBSD and a number of language bindings, including C, C++, Python and Perl. FUSE is being actively developed and is in widespread use; one of the most important uses of FUSE is NTFS support in Linux [10]. FUSE (kernel version 2.6.14) is integrated into the Linux kernel. Our in-place carving system uses FUSE to present a standard filesystem interface for files carved in-place.

2.3   Networked Access to Physical Block Devices

A network block device [5, 11] provides a traditional local interface to a remote (or distributed) block device, enhancing performance [4, 11] and/or accessibility [5]. We use the Linux network block device (NBD) [5] to facilitate in-place carving of live remote targets. The NBD simulates a block device (e.g., hard disk or hard disk partition) using a Linux kernel module and a user-space application on the client side and a user-space application on the server side. Server-side application ports are available for virtually all Unix platforms and for Microsoft Windows.

2.4   CarvFs

In parallel with our in-place file carving efforts related to the ScalpelFS tool, the Dutch National Police Agency (DNPA) has been developing a similar tool called CarvFs [9]. Unlike ScalpelFS, CarvFs does not use a database to store metadata, but instead relies on designation and file

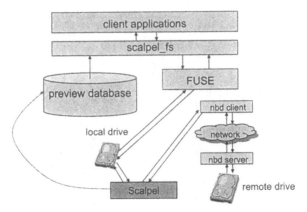

Figure 3.   In-place file carving architecture.

path properties. The DNPA refers to this technique as "zero-storage" rather than "in-place" carving. Furthermore, whereas ScalpelFS focuses on accessing disks either directly or using smb, CarvFs focuses on accessing disk images (primarily ewf). The current release of CarvFs provides patched versions of some Sleuth Kit [1] tools, and a post-processing script to work with Scalpel's preview mode. Currently the viability of integrating the ScalpelFS and CarvFs efforts is being investigated.

3.   In-Place File Carving

This section discusses the architecture and performance of ScalpelFS.

3.1   Architecture

A multi-level architecture is employed to achieve the time and space savings characteristic of our in-place carving approach. The ScalpelFS architecture has three main components: Scalpel v1.60, which provides a new "preview" mode, a custom FUSE filesystem for providing a standard filesystem view of carved files, and a Linux network block device, which allows carving of remote disk targets (Figure 3). The architecture supports live and dead investigative targets, and local and NBD disks. Carving operations may be performed on the same machine that hosts the target disk device (or image) or on a separate investigative machine.

Operating above a remote disk target is the network block device server, which provides live, remote access to the disk. Local disks are accessed directly by the Scalpel file carver that operates in the preview mode. When operating in this mode, Scalpel executes file carving rules specified in its configuration file to identify candidate files for carving on the disk devices. These files are only potentially interesting, as current carving strategies may generate copious amounts of false positives, depending on the carver configuration. Normally, Scalpel would then carve the disk blocks associated with candidate files and write them out to new files. In the preview mode, however, Scalpel produces entries in a database detailing the starting positions of files on a device, whether or not the files are truncated, their length, and the devices on which they reside. These entries have the following format:

filename	start	truncated	length	image
...				
htm/00000076.htm	19628032	NO	239	/tmp/linux-image
jpg/00000069.jpg	36021248	NO	359022	/tmp/linux-image
htm/00000078.htm	59897292	NO	40	/tmp/linux-image
jpg/00000074.jpg	56271872	NO	16069	/tmp/linux-image
...				

The original names of files are typically not available when file carving is used for data recovery, so Scalpel assigns a unique pathname to each carved file. The pathname indicates where the files would be created if Scalpel were not operating in preview mode.

Our custom FUSE filesystem, scalpel_fs, accesses the Scalpel preview database and the targeted disk devices. The scalpel_fs application is implemented in C against the FUSE API and provides the standard Linux filesystem interface to files described in the Scalpel preview database, without carving the files from the target device.

Executing scalpel_fs with arguments detailing a directory to be used as a mount point, a Scalpel preview database and the device that the database was generated from causes the following actions to be taken. First, a directory named scalpel_fs is created under the mount point. Then, using the carved file specifications in the preview database, a tree of filesystem objects is created in a structure determined by the filenames of the entries in the database. Files and directories are modeled as fs_object structs:

```
struct fs_object {
    int type;                   // file or directory
    char *name;                 // this object's fully qualified pathname
    int start;                  // starting index in source image of file
    int length;                 // size in bytes
    char clipped;               // true if the file was truncated
    char *source;               // the source image file name
    struct fs_object *children; // empty for files
    struct fs_object *next;     // peer nodes
}
```

This tree structure provides the information necessary to present the user with a filesystem appearing to contain the carved files from the target devices. For efficiency, a pointer to each fs_object is also entered into a hash table for fast lookups. Listing the contents of the mounted directory shows one directory named scalpel_fs. Inside the scalpel_fs directory are files and directories that mirror those in the filesystem tree created from the Scalpel preview database.

All file-oriented system calls targeting the mount point are intercepted. Preceding most filesystem operations is a call to getattr for the filesystem object in question; this returns a stat structure containing information such as object type (file, directory, etc.), size, creation, access and modification times, and permissions. On receiving the getattr call, scalpel_fs dynamically constructs and returns a new stat structure with type and size taken from the fs_object for the object and creation/modification/access times and permissions duplicating those in the scalpel_fs directory. Directory listings are created on the fly using the "children" structures of the fs_object for the directory being listed. Opening a file returns a file handle after first checking that the fs_object is in the hash table.

Attempts to read a file are handled as follows: the target device is opened and reading begins at the offset given by the start member of the fs_object struct for the file (plus any offset passed to the read operation itself). This is all transparent to the client application and to the user. Other non-write filesystem operations also work transparently (e.g., access, getattr and readdir). Operations that create content (e.g., write, mkdir and link) are disallowed to maintain the forensic soundness of the target. An exception is the delete (unlink) operation, which is allowed, but only in a shallow manner: the fs_object for the deleted file is removed but the target disk device is left untouched. This removes the file from the view provided by scalpel_fs without destroying any data.

At the top level of the system are other user-level applications. They can freely and transparently operate on the files under the mount point as if they were regular files (aside from the disallowed write operations). A user can obtain cryptographic hashes of the files with hashing programs, view the files in text editors or image viewers, or use specialized forensic software on the files. This is particularly useful in an investigation involving image files (e.g., JPG or GIF images) as the images can be previewed as thumbnails by most filesystem browsers. Note that all of this occurs without the need to use large amounts of storage space as in the case of a normal carving operation.

Table 1. Experimental results for an 8 GB target.

Carving Description	Execution Time	Total # of files carved	Total disk space required
regular, all file types, 8GB local disk image	Out of disk space	---	>> 250GB
preview, all file types, 8GB local disk image	80m56s	1,125,627	62MB (for metadata)
regular, constrained set of file types, 8GB local disk image	222m11s	724,544	212GB
preview, constrained set of file types, 8GB local disk image	63m22s	724,544	39MB (for metadata)
regular, image file formats only (JPG, GIF, PNG, BMP), 8GB local disk image	60m35s	9,068	5.9GB
preview, image file formats only (JPG, GIF, PNG, BMP), 8GB local disk image	26m28s	9,068	500K (for metadata)

3.2 Performance Study

We conducted several experiments to test the advantages of in-place carving. This section reports the results of experiments conducted with 8 GB and 100 GB targets.

Table 1 presents the experimental results for an 8 GB target; an empty 250 GB IDE drive was used to store the carving results. The machine performing the carving operations was a 933 MHz Pentium III with 512 MB RAM running CentOS Linux v4.3. An "unrestricted" full carve of the drive, using all the file types supported in the standard Scalpel v1.60 configuration file, crashed with an out of disk space error 7% during Scalpel's second carving pass (after almost 1,000,000 files were carved). Clearly, the disk space required to complete this carving operation would be very much more than 250 GB. In contrast, using Scalpel's "preview" mode, the same carving operation completed within 1 hour and 20 minutes, yielding an index for 1,125,627 files.

For a more concrete comparison, the number of carved file types was reduced substantially and the test was repeated. This time, the full carve took about 3 hours and 42 minutes, carving 724,544 files that consumed 212 GB of disk space. In contrast, the preview carve took only 1 hour and 3 minutes, and consumed only 39 MB (for the in-place carving metadata).

Reducing the number of file types further and carving only image file formats (JPG, GIF, PNG, BMP), resulted in 9,068 carved files in

Table 2.   Experimental results for a 100 GB target.

Carving Description	Execution Time	Total # of files carved	Total disk space required
preview, restricted file types, 100GB, local	103m30s	1,338,766	71MB (for metadata)
preview, restricted file types, 100GB, NBD	131m27s	1,338,766	71MB (for metadata)
regular, restricted file types, 100GB, local	---	1,338,766	5.9TB
preview, image file formats (JPG, GIF, PNG, BMP), 100GB, local	77m15s	470,181	25MB (for metadata)
preview, image file formats (JPG, GIF, PNG, BMP), 100GB, NBD	106m27s	470,181	25MB (for metadata)
regular, image file formats (JPG, GIF, PNG, BMP), 100GB, local	---	470,181	313GB

approximately 60 minutes, requiring 5.9 GB of storage for a normal carving operation. A preview carve with the same parameters finished in 26 minutes and required 500 K of storage for metadata. The results in this case are obviously much closer, but in-place carving is still more efficient. Also, in-place carving has advantages over traditional carving in situations where it is important that no copies of the files are created until the investigation progresses (e.g., child pornography cases).

We were also interested in measuring the performance of carving operations over Linux's network block device (NBD), since we support carving of live remote disk targets over NBD. We ran a simple experiment using the Pentium III machine described above as the NBD server, providing access over a quiet gigabit network to the 8 GB disk image. A Thinkpad T40p with a 1.6 GHz Pentium 4M processor and 2 GB of RAM, also running CentOS Linux, was used to perform carving operations over NBD. Carving only JPG images (in preview mode) required 16 minutes and 10 seconds. Performing the same carve over a 100 megabit LAN increased the time to 31 minutes and 10 seconds. A local preview carve, using a copy of the 8 GB image loaded on the T40p, took 7 minutes and 40 seconds.

Table 2 presents the results of experiments conducted on a 100 GB target. The machine performing the carving operations was a 3 GHz Pentium 4 with 2 GB RAM running Centos 4.3. Using Scalpel in preview mode to carve a heavily restricted set of files types resulted in 1,338,766 files which, if carved by traditional methods, would have required 4.9 TB of space. Our system used approximately 70 MB of space and took 1 hour and 43 minutes.

Carving the 100 GB target for only the image file formats listed above resulted in 470,181 files, requiring approximately 25 MB of space and taking 1 hour and 17 minutes. These files would have required 313 GB if they were copied out of the image.

We also performed experiments over NBD with the 100 GB target. Here we used 2 Pentium 4 machines as described above working over an unloaded gigabit network. Preview carving for the set of image file types listed above took 1 hour and 46 minutes. Preview carving for the heavily restricted set of file types took 2 hours and 11 minutes.

4.   Conclusions

Traditional file carving applications often require large amounts of disk space to execute because they make copies of carved files. Since many of these "recovered" files are false positives, the amount of data carved can exceed the size of the target by an order of magnitude. For larger targets, even more typical over-carving factors of two or three can require too much disk space and have an unacceptable impact on execution time.

The in-place carving approach proposed in this paper recreates file metadata outside the target and uses the original forensic image for retrieving file contents on-demand. This strategy allows carving to be performed faster and with significantly reduced disk storage requirements, without losing any functionality. In-place file carving also facilitates large-scale carving and on-the-spot carving. The architecture uses a custom filesystem, the preview mode of the Scalpel file carver, and a Linux network block device. Both "live" and "dead" forensic targets are supported and carving operations can be executed on the machine hosting the target disk or on a separate investigative machine.

Several enhancements to the in-place carving architecture are being undertaken. Currently, ScalpelFS does not support Scalpel's options for carving fragmented files. We are also working to reduce an investigator's "wait time" by presenting a dynamically updated view of the filesystem as file carving proceeds, allowing the investigator to process files as they become available. This will require modifications to the Scalpel file carver and some minimal changes to ScalpelFS. Finally, we are investigating feedback mechanisms that perform file validation during carving operations, disabling or prioritizing carving rules depending on how many false positives are generated by particular carving rules.

The goal is to provide the investigator with "good" evidence as quickly as possible, and to delay the processing of files that are unlikely to be useful.

Acknowledgements

This work was supported in part by NSF Grant CNS 0627226. The authors are grateful to Daryl Pfeif of Digital Forensics Solutions for suggestions that improved the organization of the paper.

References

[1] B. Carrier, The Sleuth Kit (www.sleuthkit.org).

[2] Digital Forensics Research Workshop (DFRWS), File Carving Challenge – DFRWS 2006 (www.dfrws.org/2006/challenge).

[3] Y. Gao, G. Richard III and V. Roussev, Bluepipe: An architecture for on-the-spot digital forensics, *International Journal of Digital Evidence*, vol. 3(1), 2004.

[4] S. Liang, R. Noronha and D. Panda, Swapping to remote memory over InfiniBand: An approach using a high performance network block device, *Proceedings of IEEE International Conference on Cluster Computing*, 2005.

[5] P. Machek, Network Block Device (nbd.sourceforge.net).

[6] G. Richard III and V. Roussev, Scalpel: A frugal, high performance file carver, *Proceedings of the Fifth Annual Digital Forensics Research Workshop* (www.dfrws.org/2005/proceedings/index.html), 2005.

[7] SourceForge.net, Foremost 1.4 (foremost.sourceforge.net), February 4, 2007.

[8] SourceForge.net, FUSE: Filesystem in Userspace (fuse.sourceforge .net).

[9] SourceForge.net, The Carve Path Zero-Storage Library and Filesystem (ocfa.sourceforge.net/libcarvpath).

[10] The Linux NTFS Project (www.linux-ntfs.org).

[11] D. Tingstrom, V. Roussev and G. Richard III, dRamDisk: Efficient RAM sharing on a commodity cluster, *Proceedings of the Twenty-Fifth IEEE International Performance, Computing and Communications Conference*, 2006.

Chapter 16

FILE SYSTEM JOURNAL FORENSICS

Christopher Swenson, Raquel Phillips and Sujeet Shenoi

Abstract   Journaling is a relatively new feature of modern file systems that is not yet exploited by most digital forensic tools. A file system journal caches data to be written to the file system to ensure that it is not lost in the event of a power loss or system malfunction. Analysis of journal data can identify which files were overwritten recently. Indeed, under the right circumstances, analyzing a file system journal can reveal deleted files and previous versions of files without having to review the hex dump of a drive. This paper discusses data recovery from ReiserFS and ext3, two popular journaled file systems. It also describes a Java-based tool for analyzing ext3 file system journals and recovering data pertaining to overwritten and deleted files.

Keywords: File system forensics, journaling, ReiserFS, ext3

1.   Introduction

Traditional computer forensics involves acquiring and analyzing file system images. Most forensic tools exploit file system features to obtain evidence. For example, the tools may find hidden or deleted data in FAT, ext2 and NTFS file systems by examining the slack space and free space, or by searching through the file system tree itself [3, 8].

Journaling is an advanced file system integrity feature [6, 10, 13] that is not exploited by most digital forensic tools. This feature is employed in virtually all modern file systems, including NTFS (Windows NT/2000/XP), HFSJ (Mac OS X), ext3 (Linux) and ReiserFS (Linux).

A file system journal works by caching some or all of the data writes in a reserved portion of the disk before they are committed to the file system. In the event of an unexpected power loss, malfunction or other anomaly, the journal could be replayed to complete any unfinished writes, preventing file system corruption due to incomplete write operations. This also means that previous file writes are stored for lim-

---

Please use the following format when citing this chapter:

Swenson, C., Phillips, R., Shenoi, S., 2007, in IFIP International Federation for Information Processing, Volume 242, Advances in Digital Forensics III; eds. P. Craiger and S Shenoi;(Boston: Springer), pp. 231-244.

ited periods of time in the journal, i.e., outside the normal file system. Therefore, even if a file is overwritten or securely deleted, it may be possible to recover the old contents by analyzing the journal. Indeed, under the right circumstances, analyzing a file system journal can reveal deleted files and previous versions of files without having to review the hex dump of the entire drive.

This paper focuses on file system journal forensics, with particular attention to the Reiser [9] and ext3 [12] journaled file systems. The next two sections describe the structure and organization of the Reiser (v. 3) and ext3 file systems, including their journaling features. Section 4 discusses how file system journals may be analyzed to recover data about overwritten and deleted files; it also describes a Java-based tool for ext3 journal data recovery and analysis. Section 5 highlights the experimental results obtained when searching ReiserFS and ext3 journals for information about overwritten and deleted files. The final section presents some concluding remarks.

Reserved (64K)	Super Block	Bitmap Block	Data Blocks	. . .	Journal
. . .	Data Blocks	. . .	Bitmap Block	Data Blocks	. . .

Figure 1. ReiserFS block structure.

2.   Reiser File System

This section describes the structure of the Reiser File System (ReiserFS), including its journaling feature [1, 9].

2.1   ReiserFS Structure

ReiserFS has a block structure with fixed-size blocks (usually 4,096 bytes). The ReiserFS block structure is shown in Figure 1.

The superblock is the first block of the ReiserFS structure. The structure of a superblock is presented in Table 1. Unlike some other file systems (e.g., ext2), ReiserFS has only one copy of the superblock.

ReiserFS bitmap blocks are special blocks that identify used and unused blocks. Each bit in a bitmap block acts as a "used bit" for a single block in the file system.

Table 1. Superblock structure 3.6.

Name	Bytes	Description
Block Count	4	Number of blocks in file system
Free Blocks	4	Number of unallocated blocks
Root Block	4	Location of the root block
Journal Information	28	Various aspects of the journal
Block Size	2	File system block size
Object ID Max. Size	2	Maximum size of the OIDs
Object ID Current Size	2	Current size of the OIDs
State	2	Whether the partition is clean
Magic String	12	ReIsEr2Fs
Hash Function	4	File name hash function
Tree Height	2	Height of file system B-tree
Bitmap Number	2	Number of bitmap blocks
Version	2	Version of the superblock
Reserved	2	Reserved
Inode Generation	4	Rebalancing count

Block Header	Key 0	...	Key n	Pointer 0	...	Pointer n

Figure 2. ReiserFS internal block contents.

ReiserFS has three types of data blocks: (i) unformatted data blocks, (ii) internal blocks, and (iii) leaf blocks. An unformatted data block contains raw data that corresponds to the contents of indirect files. An internal block contains pointers to data in the file system B-tree [4]. Figure 2 shows the contents of an internal block (internal B-tree node). A leaf block corresponds to the end node of the file system tree. It contains statistics, information about directories and possibly data itself.

2.2 ReiserFS Journal

ReiserFS in Linux has a fixed-size journal consisting of 8,192 4,096-byte blocks, plus a 4,096-byte header block, corresponding to a total size of approximately 32 MB. Note that the journal is only supported for 4,096-byte blocks. However, this is not a problem, as other block sizes are never used.

The header block uses the first 12 bytes to keep track of which block was last flushed and where to begin the next flush, as well as to mount information. The remaining 4,084 bytes are reserved.

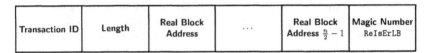

Figure 3. Transaction description block for ReiserFS.

The remainder of the journal comprises a series of transactions in a circular queue. Each transaction begins with a description block, identifying the transaction and providing half of a map that identifies where to put the data blocks (Figure 3). This is followed by the actual data blocks to be written.

A transaction is terminated by a final commit block that contains the remaining portion of the block map and a digest of the transaction. The structure is identical to the description block, except that the magic number is replaced by a 16-byte digest.

3.   Ext3 File System

The ext3 file system extends the earlier ext2 file system [2] by adding a journaling feature [11, 12]. Ext3 has rapidly become the most popular journaled file system in Linux, and is usually the default choice for new installations [5]. This section describes the structure and journaling features of the ext3 file system.

3.1   Ext3 Structure

Ext3, like ReiserFS, is based on a block structure. The block size is the same throughout a single file system; depending on the file system size, however, the default value is either 1,024 or 4,096 bytes. The first 1,024 bytes of an ext3 file system are always reserved. If the file system contains the boot kernel, these bytes will hold boot information.

The ext3 superblock stores general file system information, e.g., name, block size and the last time it was mounted. An ext3 file system has one primary superblock, although backup copies may also be stored throughout the file system. The primary copy begins at the $1,024^{th}$ byte. Table 2 provides details about the ext3 superblock structure.

An ext3 file system maintains file metadata in data structures called inodes. Inodes are stored in special blocks called inode tables. The inodes are 256 bytes long by default.

Table 2. Ext3 superblock structure.

Name	Bytes	Description
Inode Count	4	Total number of inodes in file system
Block Count	4	Total number of blocks in file system
Blocks Reserved	4	Reserved block count to prevent overfill
Free Block Count	4	Number of unallocated blocks
Free Inode Count	4	Number of unallocated inodes
Group 0	4	Block where first block group starts
Block Size	4	Left shifts of 1024 to obtain block size
Fragment Size	4	Left shifts of 1024 to obtain fragment size
Blocks per Block Grp.	4	Blocks in a typical block group
Fragments per Block Grp.	4	Fragment count in a typical block group
Inodes per Block Grp.	4	Inodes in a typical block group
Last Mount Time	4	Seconds from epoch to last mount time
Last Written Time	4	Seconds from epoch to last write time
Mount Information	4	Total and max. mounts of file system
Signature	2	0xEF53
File System State	2	Clean, error, recovering orphan inodes
Error Handling Method	2	Continue, remount as read only, or panic
Minor Version	2	Original or dynamic
Consistency Check	8	Last performed, interval
Creator OS	4	Linux, FreeBSD, etc.
Major Version	4	Original or dynamic
Reserved Block UID/GID	4	UID/GID that can use reserved blocks
First Inode	4	First non-reserved inode in file system
Inode Size	2	Size of inode in bytes
Block Grp. Loc. of Copy	2	If backup copy, group of copy
Feature Flags	12	Features of the file system
File System ID	16	UUID of file system
Volume Name	16	OS's name for the volume
Other Misc. Information	72	Misc.
Journal Information	24	UUID, metadata inode, device
Orphan Inodes	4	Head of orphan inode list
Unused	788	Unused bytes

Each inode structure can hold up to twelve direct pointers, corresponding to the addresses of the file system blocks where the first twelve blocks of the file are located. If the file is too large to fit into twelve blocks (usually 12 KB or 48 KB), pointers are maintained to single, double and triple indirect pointer blocks. A single indirect pointer is the address of a file system block composed of all direct pointers. By extension, double and triple indirect pointers point to file system blocks containing single and double indirect pointers, respectively. Table 3 provides details about the structure of an ext3 inode.

Table 3. Ext3 inode structure.

Name	Bytes	Description
File Mode	2	Permission flags and file type
User ID	2	Lower 16 bits of user ID
File Size	4	Lower 32 bits of size in bytes
ACMD Times	16	Most recent access, creation, mod., del. times
Group ID	2	Lower 16 bits of group ID
Link Count	2	Number of existing links to the file
Sector Count	4	Sector occupied by the file
Flags	4	Assorted flags
Unused	4	Unused bytes
Direct Pointers	48	12 direct pointers
Single Indirect Pointer	4	1 single indirect pointer
Double Indirect Pointer	4	1 double indirect pointer
Triple Indirect Pointer	4	1 triple indirect pointer
Misc. Information	8	NFS gen. number, extended attribute block
File Size	4	Upper 32 bits of size in bytes
Fragment Information	9	Address, count and size
Unused	2	Unused bytes
User ID	2	Upper 16 bits of user ID
Group ID	2	Upper 16 bits of group ID
Unused	2	Unused bytes

Ext3 blocks are clustered into block groups. Block groups are described in a block or set of blocks called the group descriptor table, which always follows the superblock or a copy of the superblock. By default, an ext3 file system invokes a feature called a "sparse superblock," in which not every block group contains a copy of the superblock and group descriptor table; however, if these are present, they are stored in the first several blocks of the group. The number of block groups in a file system depends on the size of a block and the total size of the file system. The number of blocks in a block group is always eight times the number of bytes in a block, and the inodes are distributed evenly among the block groups.

Each block group contains two bitmap blocks, one for blocks and the other for inodes. Each bit in a bitmap reflects the status of one of the blocks or inodes in the group as allocated or unallocated. Blocks and inodes corresponding to older versions of file content or of deleted files, and those that have never been allocated are represented with a 0. Blocks and inodes that hold current file contents or metadata, and those that are reserved by the file system are represented with a 1.

Table 4. Default journal sizes for ext3 file systems (up to 2 GB).

File System Size	Block Size	Journal Blocks	Journal Size
< 2 MB	1,024 B	0	0 MB
2 MB	1,024 B	1,024	1 MB
32 MB	1,024 B	4,096	4 MB
256 MB	1,024 B	8,192	8 MB
512 MB	1,024 B	16,384	16 MB
513 MB	4,096 B	4,096	16 MB
1 GB	4,096 B	8,192	32 MB
2 GB	4,096 B	16,384	64 MB

3.2   Ext3 Journal

The size of the journal in an ext3 file system depends on the size of the file system (Table 4). By default, only metadata is stored in the journal.

Table 5. Ext3 journal superblock structure.

Name	Bytes	Description
Header	12	Signature (0xC03B3998), block type
Block Size	4	Size of journal block in bytes
Block Count	4	Number of blocks in journal
Start Block	4	Block where journal starts
First Transaction Sequence	4	Sequence number of the first transaction
First Transaction Block	4	Journal block of first transaction
Error Number	4	Information on errors
Features	12	Features of the journal
Journal UUID	4	Universally unique identifier of the journal
File System Count	4	Number of file systems using journal
Superblock Copy	4	Location of superblock copy
Journal Blocks per Trans.	4	Max. journal blocks per transaction
FS Blocks per Trans.	4	Max. FS blocks per transaction
Unused	176	Unused bytes
FS IDs	768	IDs of file systems using the journal

The first block in the journal always contains a special journal superblock that has information specific to the journal (Table 5). Journal entries are stored in a circular queue and each entry has one commit block and at least one descriptor block (Table 6). The descriptor block provides the sequence number of the transaction and the file system blocks being stored. If the transaction involves more blocks than can be

Table 6. Ext3 journal transaction descriptor block.

Name	Bytes	Description
Header	12	Sig. (0xC03B3998), seq. num., block type
File System Block	4	File system block where content will be written
Entry Flags	4	Same UUID, last entry in descriptor block, etc.
UUID	16	Only exists if the SAME_UUID flag is not set

described in one descriptor block, another descriptor block is created to accommodate the remaining blocks. The commit block appears only at the end of the transaction.

When a file system is in the data journaling mode, new versions of data are written to the journal before being written to disk. As with a ReiserFS journal, an ext3 journal can provide a wealth of information about the contents of old, deleted or modified files.

4.   Recovering Data from Journals

A journal typically contains raw blocks that are to be written to the hard disk. These blocks may be unformatted user data or possibly blocks in the internal structure of the file system tree. Whenever a file is modified on the drive, the blocks containing raw data, either separately or in the metadata itself, are rewritten along with the metadata. Using the block map at the beginning of the journal can help determine which blocks are associated with which files.

It is important to note that a journal contains more than just deleted files. Previous versions of files can also be found as well as the nature of their recent modifications. While MAC times convey only when a file was modified, created or accessed, a journal tracks which parts of the file were modified most recently.

The following subsections discuss data recovery from journals in the Reiser and ext3 file systems, and a Java-based data recovery tool implemented for the ext3 file system.

4.1   ReiserFS Data Recovery

ReiserFS has a standard journal size of 32 MB, enough for enormous amounts of data, including documents, images and other items. Deleting a file in ReiserFS, even with a secure deletion utility likely would not purge the journal (this, of course, depends on how the utility operates).

Transactions in ReiserFS contain entire blocks of data to be written to the hard drive, serving as a cache for the computer. Furthermore, transactions held in the cache are not deleted until it is overloaded, upon which time the oldest items in the circular queue structure are overwritten. Thus, transactions may be present for quite a while, and will likely contain copies of the most recent data.

A ReiserFS journal may also contain evidence that a file was deleted and overwritten. This evidence usually manifests itself as large blocks of data (used for overwriting) that have suspicious patterns, e.g., all 0s or 1s.

4.2   Ext3 Data Recovery

In an ext3 file system with default journal settings, only changes to metadata are logged in the journal. For example, when a file is edited, the blocks logged in the journal are the primary group descriptor table, the inode of the directory entry and the directory entry of the directory that contains the file, the inode of the file, and the inode and data bitmaps of the file's block group.

In the data journaling mode, all non-journal blocks are logged when modified. Therefore, when a file is edited, all the metadata are logged along with the new file content. While this metadata can be very useful from the point of view of data recovery, only the data blocks stored in the journal are considered for our purposes. To enable the journaling of all the data, it is necessary to mount the file system with the option data=journal (in Linux).

We have implemented a Java-based tool that analyzes ext3 journals for information about modified, deleted and overwritten files, as well as earlier versions of files. The data recovery tool uses a FileInputStream object to open a file system that is passed as a command line argument and it reads the file byte by byte. Upon opening the file, information is extracted from the superblock (number of inodes, number of blocks, block size, and address of the journal inode) and stored for future use.

Based on the information stored in the journal inode, an array of JournalBlock objects is used to hold information about each journal block. The journal superblock is then searched to determine if each block is a descriptor, commit or data block; information about the data blocks is filled in from the data in the descriptor blocks. After this step, with the exception of entries that have had their descriptor entries overwritten, the tool discerns the type of entry of each journal block, its file system address, the sequence of which it was a part, if it was a data entry, and the file system block of which it was a copy.

Next, the tool determines whether or not each block might contain deleted content. This is accomplished by checking to see if each block was

```
mount -o loop -t reiserfs image /mnt/image
echo -e "I am writing this to tell you of secret, evil plans.\n\n\
Dr. Villain\n" >> /mnt/image/home/secret.txt

umount /mnt/image
mount -o loop -t reiserfs image /mnt/image
dd if=/dev/zero of=/mnt/image/home/secret.txt bs=1 count=128
rm -rf /mnt/image/home/secret.txt
umount /mnt/image
```

Figure 4. Script for creating, overwriting and deleting files.

a non-empty data block that was no longer in use according to the data
bitmap or if the content held in the journal version of the block differed
from the current version. If a block satisfies one of these conditions, the
tool uses a FileOuputStream to write a string of header information
about the block, including its file system address, the block of which it
was an older version and which condition it met, along with the contents
of the block.

5.   Data Recovery Experiments

Experiments were performed on the Reiser and ext3 file systems to
evaluate the feasibility of searching file system journals.

5.1   ReiserFS Data Recovery

A sample file system of 384 MB was created and seeded with approximately 71 MB of data using a blank file system and adding in a base
Gentoo Linux 2005.1-r1 Stage 1 x86 install file set. Next the script in
Figure 4 was run to create a file, overwrite it and delete it. The test
system was a Gentoo Linux box running a patched 2.6.12 (with the
gentoo-r9 patch set) kernel using ReiserFS version 3.6.

Existing forensic tools are unable to recover file data without reviewing the hex dump of the entire drive. However, by examining the hex
dump of the file system journal in blocks 18–8211, our data recovery tool
is able to discern that the contents of the file are present in block 1407
– even though the data was overwritten with zeros (Figure 5).

Note that the block containing the directory entry is stored in the
nearby journal block 1409 (Figure 6). Our data recovery tool uses this
type of information to dissect journal blocks when searching for deleted
or modified files.

```
0057f7f0   7f 26 e1 43 00 00 00 00   00 00 00 00 49 20 61 6d   |.&.C........I am|
0057f800   20 77 72 69 74 69 6e 67   20 74 68 69 73 20 74 6f   | writing this to|
0057f810   20 74 65 6c 6c 20 79 6f   75 20 6f 66 20 73 65 63   | tell you of sec|
0057f820   72 65 74 2c 20 65 76 69   6c 20 70 6c 61 6e 73 2e   |ret, evil plans.|
0057f830   0a 0a 44 72 20 56 69 6c   6c 61 69 6e 0a 0a 00 00   |..Dr Villain....|
0057f840   00 00 00 00 a4 81 00 00   01 00 00 00 42 00 00 00   |............B...|
0057f850   00 00 00 00 00 00 00 00   00 00 00 00 7d 00 ed 43   |............}..C|
```

Figure 5. Hex dump of ReiserFS journal block 1407.

```
005816d0   50 00 04 00 80 a9 8a 78   be 29 00 00 c2 29 00 00   |P......x.)...)..|
005816e0   40 00 04 00 73 65 63 72   65 74 2e 74 78 74 00 00   |@...secret.txt..|
005816f0   00 00 00 00 2e 6b 65 65   70 00 00 00 2e 2e 00 00   |.....keep.......|
00581700   00 00 00 00 2e 00 00 00   00 00 00 00 ed 41 00 00   |.............A..|
```

Figure 6. Hex dump of ReiserFS journal block 1409.

We wrote a tool to display the contents of a ReiserFS partition and verify deletes. Figure 7(a) shows a file (`secret.txt`) in the `/home` directory before deletion. Figure 7(b) shows the directory after the file is deleted.

The size of the journal (32 MB) precludes the ability to look too far back in the past. Specifically, when more than 32 MB of data is written to a ReiserFS Linux file system, all previously-written data is not recoverable.

Several types of file deletions have the side effect of flushing the journal. For example, using a standard technique (e.g., issuing the command `dd if=/dev/zero`) to zero a file before deleting it will push a number of blocks containing only zeros into the journal. If a file of size greater than 32 MB is deleted in such a manner, the journal would contain practically nothing else.

Most secure deletion programs bypass an operating system's journaling constructs and directly read from or write to the hard disk. Curiously, the act of bypassing the operating system has the effect of leaving more evidence in the journal.

5.2   Ext3 Data Recovery

Data recovery in an ext3 file system was tested using a 400 MB file system created with an 8 MB journal. The test set used for ext3 was identical to the one use for ReiserFS, except that the mount command was changed to:

```
mount -o loop,data=journal -t ext3 image /mnt/image
```

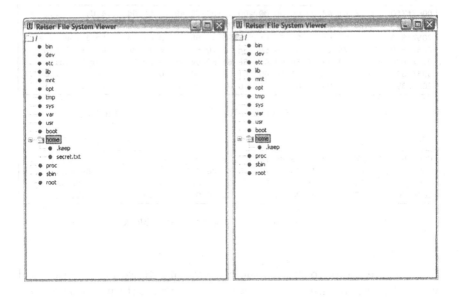

(a) Before deletion   (b) After deletion

Figure 7.   Contents of /home directory.

The data recovery tool searched through the ext3 journal looking for possibly deleted file content. First, it determined which file system block the journal block had originally been a part of by examining the descriptor blocks and whether or not that block was a data block. The tool then dumped the contents of the block into an output file if the data allocation bit of the associated file system block was 0 or if the content was different from the current content of the file system block.

The tool was able to recover data even when files were overwritten and deleted. In the experiments, note that that the old file content is stored in journal block 7903 and the old directory entry is stored in journal block 7901. Figure 8 shows that the overwritten data is recoverable from the journal.

6.   Conclusions

Because a file system journal caches data about file writes, analyzing the journal can provide valuable information about earlier versions of files. Under the right circumstances, a journal reveals information about deleted files and previous versions of files without having to review the hex dump of the drive. A journal may also yield evidence about files that are overwritten or removed by a secure deletion utility.

```
08c6000  49 20 61 6d 20 77 72 69  74 69 6e 67 20 74 68 69  |I am writing thi|
08c6010  73 20 74 6f 20 74 65 6c  6c 20 79 6f 75 20 6f 66  |s to tell you of|
08c6020  20 73 65 63 72 65 74 2c  20 65 76 69 6c 20 70 6c  | secret, evil pl|
08c6030  61 6e 73 2e 0a 0a 44 72  2e 20 56 69 6c 6c 61 69  |ans...Dr. Villai|
08c6040  6e 0a 00 00 00 00 00 00  00 00 00 00 00 00 00 00  |n...............|
...
08c58d0  68 6f 6d 65 01 88 01 00  0c 00 03 02 73 79 73 00  |home........sys.|
08c58e0  01 10 00 00 20 03 0a 01  73 65 63 72 65 74 2e 74  |.... ...secret.t|
08c58f0  78 74 00 00 00 00 00 00  00 00 00 00 00 00 00 00  |xt..............|
```

Figure 8.   Hex dump of ext3 journal.

Despite the importance of a journal as an evidence container, few, if any, digital forensic tools consider journaled data during evidence recovery. Our Java-based tool demonstrates the feasibility of recovering data from ext3 journals, and the experimental results obtained for the Reiser and ext3 file systems are very promising.

Future work should focus on analyzing journals in NTFS and HFSJ, the default file systems for newer versions of Windows and Mac OS X, respectively. NTFS is similar to ReiserFS; moreover, NTFS's variable-sized journal feature removes certain limitations to data recovery imposed by ReiserFS [7]. However, neither NTFS nor HFSJ is as well documented as ReiserFS and ext3. Consequently, the tasks of developing forensically-sound journal data recovery and analysis tools for these file systems would be much more difficult.

File system journals contain valuable evidence pertaining to cases ranging from child pornography and software piracy to financial fraud and network intrusions. Digital forensic investigators should be aware of the data cached in file system journals and its use in digital investigations. Meanwhile, the digital forensics research community should focus its efforts on file system journal forensics and develop novel journal data extraction and analysis techniques that could be implemented in the next generation of computer forensic tools.

References

[1] F. Buchholz, The structure of the Reiser file system (homes.cerias .purdue.edu/~florian/reiser/reiserfs.php).

[2] R. Card, T. Ts'o and S. Tweedie, Design and implementation of the Second Extended File System, *Proceedings of the First Dutch International Symposium on Linux* (web.mit.edu/tytso/www/linux /ext2intro.html), 1994.

[3] B. Carrier, *File System Forensic Analysis*, Addison-Wesley, Craw-fordsville, Indiana, 2005.

[4] T. Cormen, C. Leiserson, R. Rivest and C. Stein, *Introduction to Algorithms*, MIT Press, Cambridge, Massachusetts, 2001.

[5] Fedora Project Board, Fedora Core (fedoraproject.org).

[6] G. Ganger and Y. Patt, Soft Updates: A Solution to the Metadata Update Problem in File Systems, Technical Report CSE-TR-254-95, Computer Science and Engineering Division, University of Michigan, Ann Arbor, Michigan, 1995.

[7] NTFS.com, Data integrity and recoverability with NTFS (www.ntfs.com/data-integrity.htm).

[8] S. Piper, M. Davis, G. Manes and S. Shenoi, Detecting misuse in reserved portions of ext2/3 file systems, in *Advances in Digital Forensics*, M. Pollitt and S. Shenoi (Eds.), Springer, New York, pp. 245–256, 2005.

[9] H. Reiser, ReiserFS v3 whitepaper (www.namesys.com/X0reiserfs .html), 2002.

[10] M. Rosenblum and J. Ousterhout, The design and implementation of a log-structured file system, *ACM Transactions on Computer Systems*, vol. 10(1), pp. 26–52, 1992.

[11] S. Tweedie, Journaling the Linux ext2fs filesystem, presented at the *Fourth Annual Linux Expo* (jamesthornton.com/hotlist/linux-filesystems/ext3-journal-design.pdf), 1998.

[12] S. Tweedie, Ext3: Journaling filesystem (olstrans.sourceforge.net /release/OLS2000-ext3/OLS 2000-ext3.html), July 20, 2000.

[13] U. Vahalia, C. Gray and D. Ting, Metadata logging in an NFS server, *Proceedings of the USENIX Technical Conference on Unix and Advanced Computing Systems*, pp. 265–276, 1995.

VII

NETWORK FORENSICS

Chapter 17

USING SEARCH ENGINES TO ACQUIRE NETWORK FORENSIC EVIDENCE

Robert McGrew and Rayford Vaughn

Abstract   Search engine APIs can be used very effectively to automate the surreptitious gathering of information about network assets. This paper
describes GooSweep, a tool that uses the Google API to automate the
search for references to individual IP addresses in a target network.
GooSweep is a promising investigative tool. It can assist network forensic investigators in gathering information about individual computers
such as referral logs, guest books, spam blacklists, and instructions for
logging into servers. GooSweep also provides valuable intelligence about
a suspect's Internet activities, including browsing habits and communications in web-based forums.

Keywords: Network forensics, search engines, evidence gathering

1. Introduction

Individuals and groups involved in penetration testing of network assets often use search engines to locate target websites. The search results
may reveal information about unsecured administrative interfaces to the
websites, vulnerable versions of web applications and the locations of
these applications. Similarly, attackers seeking to deface websites or host
phishing websites often attempt to identify targets with older versions of
web applications with known vulnerabilities. Large numbers of potentially vulnerable hosts can be enumerated quickly using search engines.
The Google Hacking Database [5] posts the results of such searches and
provides applications that run the searches on target websites [5].

Information about computing assets collected by search engines can
also be used in network forensic investigations. This paper describes
the design and implementation of GooSweep, a tool for gathering network forensic information by performing searches using specific ranges

Please use the following format when citing this chapter:

McGrew, R., Vaughn, R., 2007, in IFIP International Federation for Information Processing, Volume 242, Advances in
Digital Forensics III; eds. P. Craiger and S Shenoi;(Boston: Springer), pp. 247-253.

of IP addresses and their corresponding host names. Written in Python, GooSweep uses the Google Search Engine API to gather information about target networks without requiring direct communication with the networks [6]. In particular, GooSweep can provide useful network forensic information related to server compromise and web use policy violations. While the quality and quantity of information obtained by GooSweep may vary dramatically from one case to another, its ability to gather potentially valuable forensic information quickly and efficiently makes it a powerful tool for network forensic investigations.

The next section discusses how search engines can be used to obtain information pertaining to hosts and applications. Section 2 describes the GooSweep tool and its application to network forensics. The final section, Section 3, presents our conclusions.

2.   Searching for Hosts

An Internet search for references to a specific IP address often returns instructions that inform users how to log into the host. For example, if an organization has a database server, there may be instructions on the organization's web server for employees, informing users about client software for connecting to the server, as well as the IP address and/or host name of the server. If an email server is among the hosts searched, its presence and purpose will often be apparent in the results, especially if users of the server post information to publicly-archived mailing lists. If these mailing list archives are accessible to the public via the web and indexed by search engines, emails to the list from users will often include detailed header information. The header information may contain the host name and IP address of the originating email server (allowing it to be indexed and discovered using the technique described in this paper), along with detailed version information about the email server software, client software and time stamps. Email message content provides useful information as well—one of our searches returned a post by a systems administrator seeking help with a specific software package.

Client workstations also provide varying amounts of information that may be indexed by search engines. Some web servers, including many government and academic systems, maintain access logs that are publicly accessible. This information can be used by a forensic investigator to identify the sites visited by users. In some cases, these log files include time stamps, operating system and web browser version information, and the referring URLs (the websites that led users to the destination) [1]. The referrals may also cite other websites that the users visited or reveal the search terms they used to arrive at the site that logged them.

Communications channels such as Internet Relay Chat (IRC), web-based forums and website guest books also record and display IP and host name information that may be indexed by search engines. When a user joins an IRC channel (analogous to a chat room) on most IRC networks, a line similar to the following is displayed to other users:

```
11:41 -!- handle [n=username@c-xx-xx-xx-xx.hsd1.mi.example.net]
          has joined \#channelname
```

In this example, `handle` is the name adopted by the user in the channel, `username` is the user name on the single-user workstation or multi-user system, and text following the @ symbol is the host name of the computer that connected to the IRC server [7]. Often, users who frequent IRC channels will post logs of interesting chat sessions on the web. In the case of many open source projects, where meetings are held over IRC, all chat sessions on project channels are automatically logged and are publicly accessible. Search engines index all this information, enabling it to be found by tools like GooSweep. Web-based forums and guest books work in a similar way, logging and, sometimes, displaying the IP address or host name of the user who made the post in an effort to discourage spam and abuse.

Security-related information can also be found regarding hosts in a subnet. Spam blacklists, which contain lists of hosts known to relay spam email, are used by system administrators to track and block unwanted email; by design they contain host names and IP addresses [3]. If a system was once compromised and used as a platform for attacks or to host phishing sites, often there will be discussion on public mailing lists about blocking the machine or shutting down the host. This information is valuable to a forensic investigator as historical information about hosts or networks, or as intelligence about hosts and networks that were involved in an attack.

Querying Internet search engines for information about individual hosts in a range of IP addresses is promising because of the type of results it can return. In addition to facilitating network intelligence and penetration testing activities, the information gathered can be very valuable in incident response and forensic investigations.

3.   GooSweep

GooSweep is a Python script that automates web searches of IP address ranges and their corresponding host names. Like many other search engines, Google does not permit automated scripts to use its normal web interface—these scripts increase the load on the interface and ignore advertisements. However, Google provides an API for programmers to develop applications that utilize its search engine [2]. This enables Google to provide a separate interface for scripted search requests and also to limit the rate at which automated searches are conducted.

GooSweep uses the Google Search Engine API to perform searches. The API currently limits each script user to 1,000 requests in a 24-hour period. GooSweep uses a single API request for each IP address and each host name. With reverse-DNS resolution of host names enabled, an investigator can use GooSweep to search a class C subnet in a 24-hour period (256 hosts, each with an IP address and host name search, requires a total of 512 API requests). Fortunately, many networks do not have host names assigned to every IP address in their address ranges; this reduces the number of API requests required to scan a network. Consequently, an investigator can typically run GooSweep on two class C subnets in a 24-hour period. The "burst mode" can be employed for larger IP address ranges. This mode causes a script to idle after its API requests are expended; the script is activated when more requests can be issued. GooSweep generates an HTML report with the search results, including the number of websites found that match each host in the IP address range.

3.1   Running GooSweep

Executing GooSweep requires a Python interpreter [8] and the Py-Google interface to the Google Search Engine API [4]. PyGoogle requires the SOAPpy web service library to be installed as well [9]. A GooSweep user must register for a Google API key to run scripts that issue queries. This key must be placed in a location specified by the PyGoogle documentation (typically in a file named .googlekey in the user's home directory). The GooSweep script itself is contained in a file named goosweep.py, which does not require any separate installation procedures. GooSweep has been extensively tested on Linux systems. Several users have had success running it on Windows systems without modification.

GooSweep may be executed from the command line using the following syntax:

```
./goosweep.py [-h num] [-r] [-b num] <[-d filename]
  | [-o report ]>  <-s subnet>
```

The required -s argument specifies the subnet to be searched. The argument is specified in "dotted-quad" format, with an asterisk as a wild card to denote the part of the address that is to be changed for each search. For example, -s 192.168.5.* directs GooSweep to scan the IP address range 192.168.5.0 through 192.168.5.255.

Either or both of the -o and -d arguments are required to produce an output. A filename should be supplied to -o to produce an HTML report with horizontal bars indicating the relative number of hits for each host. A filename should be supplied to the -d option to generate a comma-delimited output file for analysis using other programs, e.g., Microsoft Excel,

The -b option, if specified, supports the burst mode. The Google API limits each user to 1,000 API requests in a 24-hour period. The burst mode option enables a user to specify the number of searches that GooSweep should perform in a 24-hour period. After performing the specified number of searches, GooSweep idles for the remainder of the 24-hour period and then continues with another set of searches. This allows GooSweep to automatically perform large scans without violating the limitations imposed by the Google API. Users may also use the -b option to budget the number of GooSweep API requests per day so that other Google API applications can run simultaneously.

The -h option enables the user to specify how often GooSweep should output hash marks (#) to the screen to indicate the progress of its search. The option may be turned off if GooSweep is being run as part of a wrapper script or application, or the option may be set as necessary to determine if GooSweep is running at a normal pace. The default option outputs one hash mark for every eight hosts searched.

The -r option allows the user to specify that a reverse-DNS lookup should be performed for each IP address, and if a host name is returned, that it is to be searched for as well. This option is turned off by default.

GooSweep was originally designed to provide information about a target network in a stealthy manner, without sending any packets to the target. A reverse-DNS lookup submits a DNS request to the target network, assuming that the result is not cached in a local DNS server. Issuing a large number of DNS requests can set off intrusion detection system sensors (these requests are often submitted by attackers performing network enumeration or reconnaissance). The -r option should be turned off during penetration testing in order to "fly under the radar." In general, reverse-DNS lookups should be activated in network forensic scenarios that involve scanning one's own networks.

The following is a sample GooSweep scan and dialog:

```
./goosweep.py -s 192.168.5.* -o report.html -r -h 4
#######...###
Generating report (report.html)
Completed.
```

For privacy reasons, the subnet scanned is in the "private" non-routable range. A report generated by the scan consists of an HTML

GooSweep 0.8 results for ███████████.*

Report generated: Mon Nov 13 12:55:47 2006

IP Address	Hits	Relative Popularity
2	4	
7	2	
10	1	
12	2	
55	1	
112	1	
127	1	
160	1	
163	1	

Figure 1. Sample GooSweep report.

table with each row containing an IP address, a host name (if the -r option is specified and a name is found), the results returned for each host, and a bar chart showing the number of hits for each host relative to other hosts in the scan. To assist digital forensic investigators, the IP addresses and host names are rendered as hyperlinks to the relevant Google search engine results.

3.2   GooSweep Example

Figure 1 illustrates the results of executing GooSweep, targeting a network typically used by students. The results have been censored to obscure the actual IP addresses scanned. IP addresses in the range that resulted in no search engine hits are omitted for brevity.

For each result with one or more hits, the IP address can be selected to view the corresponding Google search results. For most of the IP addresses in the example, web server logs were found at other academic institutions that had logged visits by these hosts. The visits were to web pages related to topics such as programming assistance and upcoming conferences. One IP address resulted in finding a security-related paper published at an academic conference that used a host in the address range in an example. The results dated as far back as 2004 and as recent as the current year (2006). Note that while this example was executed without reverse-DNS lookups, some of the web server logs contained the results of their own reverse-DNS lookups, allowing the naming scheme for this IP address range to be determined without having to issue queries using GooSweep.

4. Conclusions

GooSweep leverages the latest Internet search engine technology to provide valuable information gathering capabilities for network forensic investigators. There is no guarantee that GooSweep will be fruitful in any given situation, but few, if any, forensic techniques or tools can make this claim. Nevertheless, given its ease of execution and the richness of the information it can gather, GooSweep is an attractive tool for network forensic investigations. GooSweep and its source code [6] are available free-of-charge to members of the information assurance and digital forensics community.

References

[1] Apache Software Foundation, Apache Common Log Format (httpd .apache.org/docs/1.3/logs.html#common), 2006.

[2] Google, Google APIs (code.google.com/apis.html).

[3] N. Krawetz, Anti-spam solutions and security (www.securityfocus .com/infocus/1763), 2004.

[4] B. Landers, PyGoogle: A Python interface to the Google API (py-google.sourceforge.net).

[5] J. Long, The Google Hacking Database (johnny.ihackstuff.com/gh db.php).

[6] R. McGrew, GooSweep, McGrew Security Services and Research (www.mcgrewsecurity.com/projects/goosweep), 2006.

[7] J. Oikarinen and D. Reed, RFC 1459: Internet Relay Chat Protocol, IETF Network Working Group (www.ietf.org/rfc/rfc1459.txt? number=1459), 1993.

[8] Python Software Foundation, Python programming language (py thon.org).

[9] G. Warnes and C. Blunck, Python web services (pywebsvcs.source forge.net).

Chapter 18

A FRAMEWORK FOR INVESTIGATING RAILROAD ACCIDENTS

Mark Hartong, Rajni Goel and Duminda Wijeskera

Abstract   Positive train control (PTC) or communication-based control systems (CBTC) control trains using wireless network infrastructures. Consequently, investigations of accidents involving PTC- or CBTC-controlled trains require network forensic analysis. This paper describes a forensic analysis framework that leverages the communications capabilities of PTC systems. The framework incorporates a centralized database architecture that securely stores PTC-related and other digital data, and provides for efficient and flexible querying of the data during accident analysis.

Keywords: Positive train control, accident investigations, centralized logging

1.   Introduction

The North American freight and passenger railroads are currently introducing wireless-network-based control systems collectively known as positive train control (PTC) or communications-based train control (CBTC) systems to enhance railroad safety and security [7]. PTC systems control the authority of trains to occupy specific track segments, enforce speed limits and other restrictions, maintain safe inter-train distances and provide protection for railroad maintenance employees. PTC commands run at the application layer of a wireless communications network. Accordingly, they have the same advantages and disadvantages as other applications based on wireless protocol stacks. A major disadvantage is the susceptibility to mal-actions at all layers, potentially resulting in undesirable incidents or railroad accidents.

When PTC systems are employed, investigations of railroad accidents and recreations of potential accident scenarios require forensic analysis of wireless-based communications networks in addition to the usual

Please use the following format when citing this chapter:

Hartong, M., Goel, R., Wijeskera, D., 2007, in IFIP International Federation for Information Processing, Volume 242, Advances in Digital Forensics III; eds. P. Craiger and S Shenoi;(Boston: Springer), pp. 255-265.

examination of physical equipment, human factors and environmental conditions. Unfortunately, current railway networks do not have mechanisms for the comprehensive, secure and centralized collection of forensic data. This hinders the resolution of accident investigations as well as the prompt implementation of corrective actions. For example, the investigation of the 2005 Graniteville (South Carolina) train collision [12] by the Federal Railroad Administration (FRA) and National Transportation Safety Board (NTSB) took eleven months.

Digital control and state data exchanged over wireless communications networks required for operating PTC systems can be augmented with additional digital forensic data to support accident investigations. This paper describes a forensic analysis framework that leverages the communications capabilities of PTC systems. The framework incorporates a centralized database architecture that securely stores PTC-related and other digital data, and provides for efficient and flexible querying of the data during accident analysis.

The next section describes related work in railroad accident investigations and network forensics. Section 3 introduces PTC systems, and describes the proposed forensic architecture and data items used for incident/accident analysis of PTC-controlled trains. Sections 4 and 5 show how data in the forensic repository can be used for accident recreation and post-accident analysis, respectively. The final section, Section 6, presents our conclusions.

2. Related Work

Safe railroad operation is considered to be a national priority by the United States Government, which invests significant resources for this effort through the FRA and NTSB. These organizations have regulatory mandates to investigate accidents and major railroad incidents [16, 18]. In doing so, they ask questions similar to those asked by forensic examiners: What happened? How did it happen? Why did it happen? How could it be prevented from happening again?

Network forensics involves the acquisition, presentation and analysis of network traffic and other digital evidence for legal proceedings [13]. Current forensic practices involve passive or active monitoring [6, 11], and techniques for evidence presentation and automated reasoning [19].

In contrast, accident investigations do not determine guilt and liability; rather, their goal is to quickly and efficiently improve system safety. The FRA has recognized that the immediate access and evaluation of accident data assists in implementing operational improvements, ideally before the track is put back into service [17]. Thus, the automated gath-

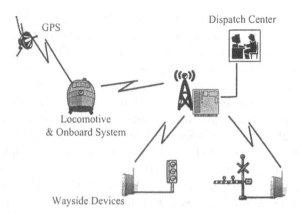

Figure 1. Generic PTC architecture.

ering of auditable evidence is very desirable for the purpose of railroad investigations.

3. Positive Train Control Systems

Locomotive crews in North America have traditionally communicated with office dispatchers and wayside devices using two-way radios, wayside signals or instructions written on paper that are handed over at various stations. The process did not require nor did it facilitate forensic data gathering capabilities. However, this began to change in the 1980's when Class I railroads in the United States and Canada developed the Advanced Railroad Electronic System (ARES) for integrating communications, command and control for railroad operations and business applications, and for enforcing positive train separation (PTS). The FRA subsequently expanded ARES to include the enforcement of speed restrictions and the protection of roadway workers within their authorities in addition to PTS. These three functions are now referred to as Level 1 Positive Train Control (PTC) [1, 2].

The generic PTC architecture presented in Figure 1 has three major functional subsystems:

- Wayside units, i.e., highway grade crossing signals, switches, interlocks, and maintenance of way workers.

- Mobile units, i.e., locomotives and other on-rail equipment with their onboard computers and location systems.

- Central office dispatch/control units.

In the PTC architecture, the dispatch office grants access requests for trains to occupy track segments. Trains enter and exit track segments when permitted by the track owner's dispatch office. Wayside devices monitor the track conditions and passing trains, and actively participate in communicating data between trains and dispatch offices.

For analysis purposes, we assume that PTC systems interoperate using trust management [8], where each railroad company maintains a certificate authority that issues and verifies the authenticity and validity of certificates presented by recognizable entities. Dispatch offices, trains and wayside devices on their own tracks are issued certificates and public/private key pairs to communicate with each other directly. To enable one railroad company's train that may be driven by a crew belonging to a second company to use a track segment belonging to a third company, the trust roots of all three railroad companies must cross certify each other. This helps ensure the authenticity and integrity of the collected data for accident investigations and reconstructions.

4.   Network Forensics for Railway Accidents

The outcome of accident analysis is usually a description of one or more chains of interactions that produce multiple accident scenarios. The scenarios may occur due to human error, unexpected environmental conditions, unanticipated faults (e.g., equipment failure), and various communications-related issues (e.g., delayed or dropped packets carrying PTC information or deliberate attacks on network assets). Proper collection and analysis of accident data can be used to compute accident frequency and patterns. These can pinpoint locations needing special operational attention and safety improvements.

A preliminary logical design for collecting data from dispatch offices, trains and wayside devices, and maintaining it at a centralized repository is shown in Figure 2. Although NTSB and FRA investigators gather operational, environmental, human factors and maintenance data [3], due to space constraints, this paper considers only data related to operations and the environment.

A large amount of operational data is provided by mandatory locomotive event recorders [17]. Other data, such as track classifications are inferred from specific technical parameters that railroad companies are required to maintain to achieve specific levels of safe railroad operation. Track classifications are important because they regulate the maximum allowable speed of trains.

Environmental factors can significantly impact railroad operations. Precipitation and fog often reduce signal visibility, flash floods can wash

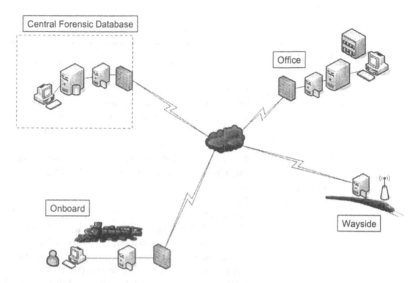

Figure 2. Centralized forensic data collection framework.

out tracks, excessive heat may warp tracks, crosswinds reduce stability and may even blow railcars off the tracks. Ice and snow may cause regional delays or shutdowns, and pre-existing accumulations of rain, ice and snow not associated with current weather conditions may also cause serious problems. Environmental and operational data collection and monitoring systems include EMD's Functionally Integrated Railroad Electronics (FIRE) and GE Transportation Systems' Expert On-Alert [10]. However, due to the absence of regulatory requirements, economic considerations mainly determine whether or not railroad companies deploy automated data collection and monitoring systems.

Tables 1–3 summarize the three types of operational and environmental data that may be obtained from central offices, onboard systems and wayside systems, respectively.

4.1 Forensic Database Architecture

We propose a centralized database to store, manage and query data items used for incident/accident analysis of PTC-controlled trains. Currently, this data is widely scattered, requiring significant efforts to collect and organize it before any analysis can be performed. For example, regulations mandate only a 48-hour retention period for locomotive event recorder data. Furthermore, while the recorders are tamper resistant, they are neither tamper proof nor crash hardened.

Table 1. Office data.

Data Class	Data Type	Attribute
Operational	Static	- Date
		- Time
		- Communication System Status
		- Track Characteristics: (i) Track Name & Number, (ii) Track Type, (iii) Track Class & Geometry, (iv) Track Database
		- Train Information: (i) Train ID, (ii) Train Type, (iii) Crew, (iv) Consist Data, (v) Location
	Command	- Date
		- Time
		- Office ID
		- Message Information: (i) Office Authorities & Special Instructions Issued, (ii) Onboard ID, (iii) Onboard Authorities & Special Instructions Acknowledged, (iv) Wayside ID, (v) Wayside Authorities & Special Instructions Acknowledged
Environment		- Date
		- Time
		- Location
		- Temperature
		- Dew Point
		- Wind Speed
		- Precipitation

The proposed centralized forensic database overcomes these limitations by logically storing data collected from locomotives and other devices. The centralized database must implement strict access controls to ensure that the integrity of the forensic data is maintained.

The forensic database comprises several relational tables shown in Figure 3. Tables are created for each PTC system entity that submits or receives operational and environmental data (mostly in the form of network packets). The schema and database design depend on the types of data collected by each entity, while the frequency of transmission and the communications bandwidth determine the data collection rates. Queries issued to the forensic database can reveal the accuracy and integrity of PTC commands sent or received by the various entities.

5. Post Accident Analysis

A promising method to identify the causal factors and the resulting accident scenarios with their evidence is to pre-analyze possible misuse

Table 2. Onboard data.

Data Class	Data Type	Attribute
Operational	Static	- Date
		- Time
		- Communication System Status
		- Train Information: (i) Train ID, (ii) Train Type, (iii) Consist Data, (iv) Crew Data, (v) Track Database, (vi) Location, (vii) Train Control System Status, (viii) Trailing Tons, (ix) Brake Pressure, (x) Throttle Position, (xi) Alerter Status, (xii) Horn & Bell Status, (xiii) Generator, (xiv) Light, (xv) Distance Traveled
	Command	- Date
		- Time
		- Onboard ID
		- Message Information: (i) Onboard Authorities & Special Instructions Issued, (ii) Office ID, (iii) Office Authorities & Special Instructions Acknowledged, (iv) Wayside ID, (v) Wayside Authorities & Special Instructions Acknowledged
Environment		- Date
		- Time
		- Horizontal Visibility Range

Table 3. Wayside data.

Data Class	Data Type	Attribute
Operational	Static	- Device Type
		- Date
		- Time
		- Communication System Status
		- Device Status & Health
		- Device Information: (i) Device ID, (ii) Location
	Command	- Date
		- Time
		- Message Information: (i) Device ID, (ii) Wayside Device Authorities & Special Instructions Issued, (iii) Office Authorities & Special Instructions Acknowledged, (iv) Onboard Authorities & Special Instructions Acknowledged
Environment		- Date
		- Time
		- Device Measured Variable

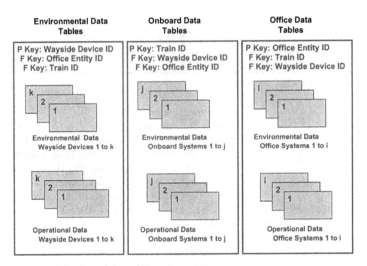

Figure 3.   Forensic database tables and keys.

cases for PTC systems [9]. Use cases specify functional requirements
provided by the system to its actors [14]. On the other hand, misuse
cases [15] specify the foreseeable interactions between potential mal-
actors and the system. Database queries can be crafted to search for
evidence of misuse. For example, the following SQL query against the
database defines an overspeed accident that results in a derailment (if
the query evaluates to TRUE).

```
(SELECT Train Information.Throttle Position
    FROM Onboard Data.Operational.Static Train Information
    WHERE Train Information.Throttle Position = 8)
  AND
(SELECT Train Information.Location
    FROM Onboard Data.Operational:Static
    WHERE Train Information.Location = Curve 1)
  AND
(SELECT Track Characteristics.Track Type
    FROM Office Data.Operation.Static.Track Characteristics
    WHERE Track Characteristics.Track Type = Class 3)
```

6.   Conclusions

The main objective of an accident investigation is to formulate recommendations that prevent future accidents. Ideally, the investigation is
conducted by individuals who are experienced in accident causation and
investigative techniques, and are very knowledgeable about the opera-

tional environment. However, collecting evidence is arduous and time-consuming; data may be minimal, missing or difficult to access. The evidence is also subject to omission, contamination or obliteration; therefore, it should be recorded immediately and preserved carefully, and its chain of custody should be maintained. The proposed methodology for application layer network forensics provides a basis for all these tasks.

There are, however, several implementation issues that must be addressed. In a operational environment where rail traffic is heavy and closely spaced, the volume of operational and environmental data that must be transmitted may exceed the communications bandwidth. Even if the communications infrastructure can handle the network traffic, the database transaction processing capability may be exceeded. The required capabilities can only be determined in the context of railroad operating environments and specific implementations.

Human factors issues are extremely important in accident investigations. FRA studies have revealed that certain kinds of human errors (e.g., improperly lining switches, failing to latch and lock switches, improperly conducting shoving movements) account for an inordinate number of accidents. FRA's 2003 study [4] reports that 133 (91%) of the 146 head-on, rear-end and side collisions were attributed to human causes. Likewise, 2004 accident data [5] reveals that 184 (91%) of the 202 collisions (56 more than in 2003) were due to human factors.

For the database solution to be viable, it is important that queries be created that accurately model accidents. Because safety flaws that are identified by accident investigations are quickly rectified, it is difficult to discern the complex interactions of the safety problems that remain. This factor along with the rarity of accidents makes the task of accurately modeling accidents a challenging endeavor.

Note that the views and opinions expressed in this paper are those of the authors. They do not reflect any official policy or position of the Federal Railroad Administration, U.S. Department of Transportation or the U.S. Government, and shall not be used for advertising or product endorsement purposes.

References

[1] Federal Railroad Administration, Railroad Communications and Train Control, Technical Report, Department of Transportation, Washington, DC, 1994.

[2] Federal Railroad Administration, Implementation of Positive Train Control Systems, Technical Report, Department of Transportation, Washington, DC, 1999.

[3] Federal Railroad Administration, *FRA Guide for Preparing Accident/Incident Reports*, Department of Transportation, Washington, DC, 2003.

[4] Federal Railroad Administration, *Railroad Safety Statistics – 2003 Annual Report*, Department of Transportation, Washington, DC, 2003.

[5] Federal Railroad Administration, *Railroad Safety Statistics – 2004 Annual Report*, Department of Transportation, Washington, DC, 2004.

[6] S. Garfinkel and E. Spafford, *Web Security, Privacy & Commerce*, O'Reilly, Sebastopol, California, 2002.

[7] M. Hartong, R. Goel and D. Wijesekera, Communications-based positive train control systems architecture in the USA, *Proceedings of the Sixty-Third IEEE Vehicular Technology Conference*, vol. 6, pp. 2987–2991, 2006.

[8] M. Hartong, R. Goel and D. Wijesekera, Key management requirements for positive train control communications security, *Proceedings of the IEEE/ASME Joint Rail Conference*, pp. 253–262, 2006.

[9] M. Hartong, R. Goel and D. Wijesekera, Use-misuse case driven analysis of positive train control, in *Advances in Digital Forensics II*, M. Olivier and S. Shenoi (Eds.), Springer, New York, pp. 141–155, 2006.

[10] T. Judge, How healthy are your locomotives? *Railway Age*, April 2001.

[11] S. Mukkamala and A. Sung, Identifying significant features for network forensic analysis using artificial intelligence techniques, *International Journal of Digital Evidence*, vol. 1(4), pp. 1–17, 2003.

[12] National Transportation Safety Board, Collision of Norfolk Southern Freight Train 192 with Standing Norfolk Southern Local Train P22 with Subsequent Hazardous Materials Release at Graniteville, South Carolina, January 6, 2005, Railroad Accident Report NTSB/RAR-05/04, Washington, DC, 2005.

[13] M. Ranum, K. Landfield, M. Stolarchuk, M. Sienkiewicz, A. Lambeth and E. Wal, Implementing a generalized tool for network monitoring, *Proceedings of the Eleventh USENIX Systems Administration Conference*, 1997.

[14] J. Rumbaugh, Getting started: Using use cases to capture requirements, *Journal of Object-Oriented Programming*, vol. 7(5), pp. 8–12, 1994.

[15] G. Sindre and A. Opdahl, Templates for misuse case description, *Proceedings of the Seventh International Workshop on Requirements Engineering: Foundations of Software Quality* (www.nik.no/2001/21-sindre.pdf), 2001.

[16] U.S. Government, Investigations, Section 225.31, Federal Railroad Administration, *Title 49, Code of Federal Regulations*, Washington, DC, pp. 367–368, 2006.

[17] U.S. Government, Event Recorders, Section 229.135, Federal Railroad Administration, *Title 49, Code of Federal Regulations*, Washington, DC, pp. 409–413, 2006.

[18] U.S. Government, Functions, Section 800.3, National Transportation Safety Board, *Title 49, Code of Federal Regulations*, Washington, DC, p. 121, 2006.

[19] W. Wang and T. Daniels, Network forensic analysis with evidence graphs, *Proceedings of the Digital Forensics Research Workshop*, 2005.

VIII

PORTABLE ELECTRONIC DEVICE FORENSICS

Chapter 19

FORENSIC ANALYSIS OF XBOX CONSOLES

Paul Burke and Philip Craiger

Abstract   Microsoft's Xbox game console can be modified to run additional operating systems, enabling it to store gigabytes of non-game related files
and run various computer services. Little has been published, however,
on procedures for determining whether or not an Xbox console has been
modified, for creating a forensic duplicate, and for conducting a forensic investigation. Given the growing popularity of Xbox systems, it is
important to understand how to identify, image and examine these devices while reducing the potential of corrupting the media. This paper
discusses Xbox forensics and provides a set of forensically-sound procedures for analyzing Xbox consoles.

Keywords: Xbox consoles, forensic analysis

1.   Introduction

The fine line between personal computers and video game consoles was
blurred with the November 15, 2001 release of Microsoft's Xbox gaming system. Hobbyists have expanded the uses of the Xbox by loading
the Linux operating system, functionally transforming it into a low-end
personal computer. With this modification the Xbox can function as a
file server, a Web server, or a multimedia hub for television and stereo
systems.

A "modded" Xbox can provide significant challenges in a computer
crime investigation. It is difficult to determine visually if an Xbox has
been modified to run additional operating systems or if it stores non
game-related files, which may be of probative value in a criminal or civil
case. Unfortunately, no established procedures exist for: (i) identifying
whether or not an Xbox has been modified; (ii) creating a forensic duplicate of the storage media; and (iii) differentiating known-good files from

Please use the following format when citing this chapter:

Burke, P., Craiger, P., 2007, in IFIP International Federation for Information Processing, Volume 242, Advances in
Digital Forensics III; eds. P. Craiger and S Shenoi;(Boston: Springer), pp. 269-280.

other files that may reside in Xbox memory. This paper focuses on the forensic analysis of Xbox consoles. It describes the internal workings of the Xbox, and provides procedures for investigators to use in determining if an Xbox contains evidence and for extracting the evidence in a forensically-sound manner. The limitations of these procedures are also discussed.

2.   Background

Since Microsoft launched the Xbox gaming console on November 15, 2001, cumulative sales of the system have reached 24 million units worldwide [7]. Unlike its console competitors, the PlayStation 2 and the GameCube, the Xbox largely relies on stock PC hardware modified for use as a game console. Every Xbox contains equipment similar to that in a PC: hard drive, DVD drive, dedicated graphics hardware with TV-out, Ethernet and USB (albeit via a custom connector).

As with many popular electronic devices, computer hobbyists have modified the original Xbox for uses not intended by the developers. One of the most significant is to modify an Xbox to run an operating system other than the default operating system, enabling the Xbox to become functionally identical to a low-end personal computer.

Microsoft has implemented several security measures within the Xbox to thwart would-be hackers from running foreign software. These measures work together to create a chain of trust between each step of software execution [14]. From the point of view of forensic investigations, the two most important security elements are hard drive password protection and the file system used in the Xbox.

The Xbox employs an obscure option, the Security Feature Set [1], offered within the ATA specification. The Security Feature Set allows a computer to lock the hard drive using two 32-byte passwords. Once locked, the hard drive will not respond to requests to access its data and will cause Windows and Linux to generate errors if an attempt is made to access data on the disk. In the case of the Xbox, the drive is locked so that only one password is required to unlock the disk. This password is cryptographically generated from a unique string located in the Xbox ROM coupled with the serial and model numbers of the hard drive [12]. There are several ways around the locking mechanism, some of which will be described later. It is important to note that, in most cases, the Xbox will not boot with an unlocked drive and that a locked drive from one Xbox will not function on another.

The data on an unmodified Xbox hard drive consists of operating system files, game cache files and saved game files. The disk does not have a partition map *per se*; it is believed that the offsets are preprogrammed into the Xbox itself [6]. Microsoft designed a derivative of the FAT file system, called FATX, for the Xbox. FATX bears a strong resemblance to FAT32, containing only minor changes to the file system layout [13]. However, these changes are significant enough to prevent FAT32 forensic utilities from reading FATX.

Vaughan [16] was the first to examine Xbox security issues and forensic recovery. He discusses Xbox modification and provides several methods for bypassing the ATA password protection on the Xbox hard drive. He also describes the procedures necessary for building a FATX-enabled kernel and performing Linux-based forensics on a FATX image. Dementiev [5] largely mirrors Vaughan's coverage, but additionally describes methods for data extraction from within Windows.

This paper complements and extends the work of Vaughan and Dementiev. Specifically, it focuses on issues regarding the forensic validity of imaging methods, and attempts to provide a straightforward, forensically-sound method for data extraction. While other approaches modify the hard drive by permanently unlocking it or install hardware to access the contents of the drive, the approach described in this paper is much less intrusive, requiring no low-level physical interaction with the Xbox unit.

3. Forensic Procedures

A forensically-sound procedure for analyzing an Xbox must ensure that the digital evidence is not tainted or modified in any way. Such a procedure has three primary steps: initial assessment, creating a forensic duplicate of the Xbox storage media, and analysis of the storage media. Initial assessment covers the beginning stages of the investigation, including the determination of whether or not the Xbox has been modified. After the Xbox is confirmed as being modified, the next step is to build an analysis and acquisition workstation and image the Xbox in a forensically-sound manner. The final step involves both logical and physical analyses of the storage media.

Linux is an ideal operating system for analyzing the Xbox as a kernel-level file system driver is available from the Xbox Linux Project [11]. This means that images of the Xbox disk partitions can be mounted and interacted with using Linux in a native manner (i.e., without using external programs). Several alternatives exist for reading FATX volumes in Windows. However, our tests have demonstrated that they generally do not support logical analysis at a level necessary for forensics; for example, they do not support file times or provide a file listing interface.

These tools may also prevent forensic suites like EnCase and FTK from properly representing the media at a logical level as they do not present the volumes as Windows drives. Furthermore, they require the disk to be removed from the Xbox, unlocked and connected to the analysis machine. As noted above, our interest is in procedures that are non-intrusive and forensically sound.

Our procedures are based on the assumption that the forensic examiner has an understanding of the Linux operating system environment. The acquisition process involves booting the Xbox from a Linux-based CD and extracting the partition data over a local network to the analysis machine. The analysis machine is then modified to enable it to process the Xbox FATX file system.

Tests were performed on a version 1.6 Xbox, which was "soft modded" via the Ndure exploit (described below). Linux was loaded on the primary partition of the Xbox as test data. Despite the limited number of tests performed, we believe that the proposed methods should function on most modified Xbox units as the modifications are not expected to impact our methods.

3.1   Initial Assessment

The first step is to determine whether or not the Xbox being investigated has been modified to run foreign code. There are two primary modification methods. The first, called "hard modding," involves physically modifying the Xbox to override the built-in protections against executing foreign code. The second method, "soft modding," breaks the software protection using code exploits. For the purposes of this paper, the two methods have the same functional effect – a modified Xbox will execute foreign programs, including Linux. Therefore, we do not differentiate between hard modded and soft modded Xboxes as far as forensic analysis procedures are concerned.

Hardware modification usually leaves obvious traces of tampering. This method of modification requires that the Xbox console be physically opened to install circuitry, often a replacement BIOS chip. The six screws that hold the console case together are located under the case and are concealed by a combination of stickers and rubber pads (Figure 1). Attempts to open the case generally result in the removal or destruction of the stickers and rubber pads.

An Xbox's connections and peripherals are good indicators that it has been modified. For example, if the Xbox is connected to a network and is running without a connection to a TV, it is likely that it is being used as a Linux-based server. USB-to-Xbox controller adapters with tradi-

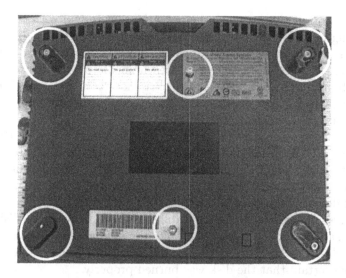

Figure 1. Xbox screw locations.

tional USB keyboards and mice are also suspect as these could allow the machine to be used like a traditional PC. The presence of a network cable does not necessarily imply modification, as a legitimate Microsoft service called Xbox Live utilizes the Internet for gaming. Other modifications, such as custom cases, do not necessarily indicate lower-level hardware modification, although those with the expertise to make such customizations are more likely to attempt modifications.

A general method for determining if an Xbox has been modded is to attempt to boot a Linux-based boot CD from the unit. Our tests have shown that the hash of the hard drive does not change during this process, provided Linux is executed immediately. In fact, although portions of the Xbox software are loaded before Linux, e.g., the routine to temporarily unlock the hard drive, they do not appear to modify the disk contents in any way. Our tests also indicated that only read operations are performed at that point of the boot process. That said, we did note that the Xbox would reformat any memory units attached to the controllers at startup if nonstandard data is found on them. Therefore, we recommend removing all memory units before booting the Xbox.

It should be noted that the internal clock of the Xbox is reset when the unit loses power even for a short amount of time; this is because the Xbox uses a capacitor instead of a battery to power its clock. The capacitor charge lasts for about one hour. Therefore, if an Xbox has to be removed from its environment during a seizure, it should be plugged into an outlet as soon as possible. An internal clock reset does not modify the hard drive, but the reset has the potential to interfere with certain soft modding exploits [17], including preventing Linux from being loaded. A dialog box appears at boot before any Xbox or Linux software is loaded. However, if the dialog box is dismissed immediately (by depressing the A button on the controller) the clock is not reset and the dialog box reappears at the next boot. This is the recommended course of action if the capacitor is accidentally drained.

In developing and testing our procedures we used a Xebian [19] boot CD specially designed for the Xbox. According to the Xbox Linux project, Xbox CD/DVD drives are frequently of inferior quality and have difficulty reading CD-Rs [18]. When burning a boot CD, it is recommended that the examiner burn the CD ISO to a DVD-R instead, as this forces the Xbox to rely on a different laser to read the disk. The boot CD will function normally despite the difference in media. We recommend testing the burned DVD-R on a modified Xbox before analysis to make certain that the disk was burned properly.

Any attempt to boot an unmodified Xbox with Xebian or any other non-Microsoft disk will display an error message:

> Your Xbox can't recognize this disk. Make sure it is an Xbox game, DVD movie or audio CD. Also check to see if the disk is dirty or damaged. Remove the disk to continue.

If the Xbox successfully boots into Linux it can be surmised that the unit has been modified in some manner and may contain Linux. The error message listed above is also displayed if the boot CD/DVD cannot be read; therefore, it is recommended to try multiple types of media (CD–RW, DVD+/–R, DVD+/–RW). Once the Xbox has booted into the Xebian environment, its hard drive and associated media are ready for acquisition and analysis.

3.2   Preparing an Analysis Machine

Preparing a workstation for FATX analysis is relatively simple. We recommend using a dedicated forensic computer. However, a machine with the latest hardware may not be appropriate as it must be compatible with the 2.4 Linux kernel. We chose to use Debian, but any other Linux distribution should work. The only requirements are adequate hard drive space to hold the acquired images along with the availability of basic compilation tools and an SSH client.

It is necessary to apply a patch from the Xbox Linux Project [11] to build a Linux kernel that can process the FATX file system. At the time of this writing, the Xbox Linux patch for kernel 2.6 was still in an experimental stage and not suitable for use in analysis. However, the patch for kernel 2.4 is still available and works well. After downloading the source for the latest 2.4 kernel from `kernel.org` one can apply the patch available from the Xbox Linux Project. When building the kernel, it is important to ensure that `CONFIG_FATX_FS` and `CONFIG_BLK_DEV_LOOP` are either built into the kernel or are modularized.

3.3 Creating a Forensic Duplicate

Having determined that an Xbox has been modified, the next step is to create a forensic duplicate of the hard drive. After the Xbox has successfully booted into Xebian and the analysis workstation is prepared, the two systems should be connected using a crossover Ethernet cable. The default IP address of Xebian is 192.168.0.10/24; the IP address of the analysis workstation should be set to an address within this subnet. Next, SSH is used to connect to the Xbox as root using the aforementioned IP address. Note that the password for root is "xebian." At the prompt, information about the individual Xbox may be extracted by running the command `xbox_info -a`.

Table 1. Sample Xbox partition layout.

Device Name	Size	Size
/dev/hda50	4882 MB	5120024576 B
/dev/hda51	500 MB	524288000 B
/dev/hda52	750 MB	786432000 B
/dev/hda53	750 MB	786432000 B
/dev/hda54	750 MB	786432000 B

The Xbox partition structure is slightly different from that of a normal PC when viewed in Linux. Partitions are enumerated from minor node 50 up. Table 1 presents the partition layout of a factory-default Xbox.

A forensic duplicate of the individual partitions from the analysis machine may be created over SSH using the commands:

```
# ssh root@192.168.0.10 "dd if=/dev/hda50" > xbox-50.dd
```

We recommend imaging individual partitions instead of the entire disk to simplify the task of mounting the partitions; this is because Linux does not have native support for mounting partitions embedded within an image. After the acquisition is complete, hashing can be performed using the `md5sum` utility on the analysis machine and the Linux CD running on the Xbox.

The command `ls -l /dev/hda*` can be used to determine if any other (user-added) partitions exist on the hard drive. Some Xbox hard drives are shipped with 10 GB – as opposed to the original 8 GB – drives; many users partition the extra 2 GB for use with Linux. Multiple extra partitions may also show if a new, larger hard drive was installed (this requires a hardware modification of the Xbox).

3.4 Xbox Memory Units

Xbox memory units that provide portable storage for saved games can provide a challenge to investigators. These memory units are small (typically 8 MB) flash storage devices designed to plug into the Xbox controller. Our tests have revealed that the Xbox will format memory units at bootup that contain non saved-game data (e.g., personal documents or pictures). This formatting appears to be what is commonly referred to as a "quick format," where not all data is zeroed out. Regardless, the operation is destructive. Theoretically, this allows a booby trap to be set: data can be placed on the memory unit and left plugged in; if another party attempts to access it, the saved information is destroyed before it can be recovered. Formatting the memory unit appears to completely wipe out the file allocation tables and directory entries of the previous FATX file system; however, at least some of the data area is left intact. In a scenario where such formatting has occurred, a tool such as `foremost` [10] can be used to successfully extract the remaining file data. It appears that this formatting behavior is only present in Xboxes that have not been hardware modified to load a replacement Dashboard at bootup, but this has not been tested.

As noted by Dementiev [5], if a memory unit is placed in an attached controller before bootup, Xebian Linux will acknowledge the device and present it as a USB storage device. The devices are enumerated through SCSI emulation so they will appear as `/dev/sda`, `/dev/sdb`, etc., and can be imaged in the same manner as a partition. However, as noted above, an Xbox is booted in this way renders the memory units subject to possible formatting. Furthermore, we have observed that attempts to hot plug Microsoft memory units after booting into Linux have always failed.

Despite our best efforts, we were unable to devise a forensically-sound procedure for imaging memory units. Due to the formatting issues mentioned above, we attempted to image memory units using a USB adapter included with Datel's Action Replay for the Xbox. But this approach revealed several problems. One problem stems from the fact that Microsoft-branded memory units do not present themselves as proper USB storage devices. Most USB mass storage devices transmit a `bInterfaceSubClass` field of `0x06`, which denotes that a SCSI-transparent command set should be used to interface with the device [15]. Instead, Microsoft memory units transmit a code of 0x66. This confuses most operating systems that attempt to interface with the unit, as no transport protocol is officially assigned to the transmitted code.

Attempts to bypass this behavior revealed that the memory units also do not respect the established storage protocols. Forcing Linux to interact with a unit using the SCSI-transparent command set also failed; our subsequent discussions with a Linux kernel developer revealed that Microsoft memory units are not standard mass storage devices. Some research has already focused on the problem, as the Xbox-Linux 2.4 kernel patch includes certain basic modifications to the USB stack to enable these memory units to register. However, our attempts to use the patch on a device other than the Xbox resulted in the device not registering properly.

Some memory units (such as the one included with Datel's Action Replay) will act as proper devices and can be imaged through the Action Replay USB adapter or by hot plugging the memory unit into a controller after boot. All Xbox memory units formatted by the Xbox have no partition layout.

3.5   Logical Analysis

Xbox partitions can be mounted for analysis after they have been acquired and transferred to the analysis machine. Each partition can be mounted through the loopback device read-only as follows:

```
# mount -t fatx -o ro,loop xbox-50.dd /mnt/xbox-50
```

At this point, traditional Linux forensics tools can be employed to examine the images for content [4]. For example, one can generate a timeline of file access events using Sleuth Kit and macrobber [3]. Both these tools create a linear timeline based on MAC times extracted from the file system. If individual files are identified as being of interest, they can be copied from the mounted file system.

It is also possible to use the Samba daemon [9] to share the contents of a mounted partition's directory over a network. The analysis computer may then be attached to a Windows computer, which will see the partition as a network drive. Tools such as EnCase and FTK running on the Windows computer can then be used to import and analyze the information on the partitions. It should be noted that this is a logical analysis so operations such as string searches will not locate any content in unallocated space on a partition.

We have collected a set of file hashes that have been found to be consistent between Xbox units (version 1.6); the hash set is posted at [2].

The hash values should help eliminate some of the files from consideration in a logical analysis; these known-good files can be ignored when processing the set of files found on the partitions.

3.6   Physical Analysis

A logical analysis cannot detect evidence in the form of deleted files, stray data and information in slack space. Therefore, it is necessary to analyze each partition image physically as well. Linux utilities such as xxd, strings, grep and foremost may be used to identify case-related information.

Some information about the file system can be extracted using a hex editor (e.g., the Linux xxd hex viewer, which is usually included with the ubiquitous UNIX editor vim [8]). For example, searching for deleted file markings (0xE5) in the directory should make deleted entries apparent. Steil's analysis of the FATX file system [13] describes the binary structure of these entries.

The strings utility is included in the GNU binutils package and should be installed by default on all Linux systems. When run on the Xbox partition image, it will return printable character content that may be in English. This can provide a good starting point to determine if any evidence exists on the partition in ASCII form.

GNU grep allows the user to search for strings located in a file based on regular expressions. When coupled with xxd, it can be used to locate the area of the file where the string occurs:

```
# xxd xbox-50.dd | grep -i 'credit cards'
```

Note that this example will not identify words or phrases that span two lines.

Finally, foremost may be employed to extract specific file types from the image based on their file signatures. The utility relies on scanning an image for file information unique to that type of file and then extracting the data following that information. Since this is independent of any file system, the utility will recover any deleted files that are present. While it is not perfect, foremost can recover data that would otherwise only be retrievable using a hex editor.

4.   Conclusions

Since an Xbox contains hardware and software approaching that of a personal computer, it should be considered to be an evidentiary item at a crime scene. Nevertheless, Xbox forensic analysis is still in its infancy. As of early 2007, no major forensic tool suite supports the

Xbox's FATX file system and partition layout, and no standard methods exist for extracting electronic evidence from an Xbox hard drive.

The Xbox forensic analysis procedures presented in this paper are by no means exhaustive. Due to the myriad Xbox models and the abundance of modification methods, there is a strong possibility that the procedures may not work as intended. Still, they should be useful to examiners. We also hope that they will stimulate the digital forensics research community to develop more sophisticated methods for Xbox forensics.

Acknowledgements

We wish to thank Ron Jewell of the Forensic Science Center at Marshall University, Huntington, West Virginia for donating the Xbox consoles used in our research. We also wish to thank Jonathan Medefind for his assistance in modifying Xbox consoles.

References

[1] H. Bögeholz, At your disservice: How ATA security functions jeopardize your data (www.heise.de/ct/english/05/08/172/), 2005.

[2] P. Burke and P. Craiger, Xbox media MD5 hash list, National Center for Forensic Science, Orlando, Florida (www.ncfs.org/burke .craiger-xbox-media-hashlist.md5), 2006.

[3] B. Carrier, The Sleuth Kit (www.sleuthkit.org).

[4] P. Craiger, Recovering evidence from Linux systems, in *Advances in Digital Forensics*, M. Pollitt and S. Shenoi (Eds.), Springer, New York, pp. 233–244, 2005.

[5] D. Dementiev, Defeating Xbox (utilizing DOS and Windows tools), unpublished manuscript (personal communication), 2006.

[6] A. de Quincey and L. Murray-Pitts, Xbox partitioning and file system details (www.xbox-linux.org/wiki/Xbox_Partitioning_and_File system_Details), 2006.

[7] Microsoft Corporation, Gamers catch their breath as Xbox 360 and Xbox Live reinvent next-generation gaming (www.xbox.com/zh-SG /community/news/2006/20060510.htm), May 10, 2006.

[8] B. Moolenaar, Vim (www.vim.org).

[9] Samba.org, The Samba Project (www.samba.org).

[10] SourceForge.net, Foremost version 1.4 (foremost.sourceforge.net).

[11] SourceForge.net, The Xbox Linux Project (sourceforge.net/projects /xbox-linux).

[12] SpeedBump, Xbox hard drive locking mechanism (www.xbox-linux
.org/wiki/Xbox_Hard_Drive_Locking_Mechanism), 2002.

[13] M. Steil, Differences between Xbox FATX and MS-DOS FAT (www.
xbox-linux.org/wiki/Differences_between_Xbox_FATX_and_MS-DO
S_FAT), 2003.

[14] M. Steil, 17 mistakes Microsoft made in the Xbox security system
(www.xbox-linux.org/wiki/17_Mistakes_Microsoft_Made_in_the_Xb
ox_Security_System), 2005.

[15] USB Implementers Forum, Universal Serial Bus Mass Storage Class
Specification Overview (Revision 1.2) (www.usb.org/developers
/devclass_docs/usb_msc_overview_1.2.pdf), 2003.

[16] C. Vaughan, Xbox security issues and forensic recovery methodology (utilizing Linux), *Digital Investigation*, vol. 1(3), pp. 165–172,
2004.

[17] Xbox Linux Project, Clock loop problem HOWTO (www.xbox-
linux.org/wiki/Clock_Loop_Problem_HOWTO), 2006.

[18] Xbox Linux Project, Xbox Linux boot CD/DVD burning HOWTO
(www.xbox-linux.org/wiki/Xbox_Linux_Boot_CD/DVD_Burning_
HOWTO), 2006.

[19] Xbox Linux Project, Xebian (www.xbox-linux.org/wiki/Xebian),
2006.

Chapter 20

SUPER-RESOLUTION VIDEO ANALYSIS FOR FORENSIC INVESTIGATIONS

Ashish Gehani and John Reif

Abstract   Super-resolution algorithms typically improve the resolution of a video frame by mapping and performing signal processing operations on data from frames immediately preceding and immediately following the frame of interest. However, these algorithms ignore forensic considerations. In particular, the high-resolution video evidence they produce could be challenged on the grounds that it incorporates data or artifacts that were not present in the original recording.

This paper presents a super-resolution algorithm that differs from its counterparts in two important respects. First, it is explicitly parameterized, enabling forensic video analysts to tune it to yield higher quality in regions of interest at the cost of degraded quality in other regions. Second, the higher resolution output is only constructed in the final visualization step. This allows the intermediate refinement step to be repeatedly composed without tainting the original data.

Keywords: Video recordings, super-resolution analysis, parameterization

1.   Introduction

Surveillance cameras are ubiquitous – monitoring potential interlopers, vehicular traffic and pedestrians, ATM users, and shoppers at stores. When a crime occurs, the recorded footage is often used to identify the perpetrator, the location of the incident and the sequence of events that transpired. Meanwhile, video cameras are commonly embedded in mobile devices such as cell phones and PDAs, enabling users to opportunistically produce recordings of incidents that may subsequently serve as evidence in legal proceedings.

Obviously, the better the quality of a video recording, the greater its value to an investigation and subsequent legal proceedings. However, for a variety of reasons, including lighting, camera features, distance,

Please use the following format when citing this chapter:

Gehani, A., Reif, J., 2007, in IFIP International Federation for Information Processing, Volume 242, Advances in Digital Forensics III; eds. P. Craiger and S Shenoi; (Boston: Springer), pp. 281-299.

angle and recording speed, a video recording may be of lesser quality, requiring it to be enhanced to provide adequate detail (resolution).

This paper describes a super-resolution algorithm that extracts data from video frames immediately preceding and following a given frame (temporal context) to improve its resolution. Super-resolution algorithms typically map the contextual data to a higher resolution representation, and then perform signal processing operations to improve the frame's quality. As a result, the high resolution version can be challenged on the grounds that it introduces elements not present in the original data. The algorithm presented in this paper is novel in that it maintains the additional data in an intermediate representation where every point is from an input frame; this effectively eliminates legal challenges based on the introduction of data to the original video evidence.

2. Background

A digital video recording "projects" points from three-dimensional continuous surfaces (objects in a scene) to two-dimensional finite regions (pixel elements on a sensor grid). In the process, a point in $\mathbf{R}^3$ (triple of real values that uniquely identify a location in the scene) is first mapped to a point in $\mathbf{R}^2$ (pair of real values that identify the registration location on the sensor grid); the set of these points constitutes the "image space." All the points that fall on a pixel in the sensor then map to a single point in $\mathbf{N}^2$ (pair of values that uniquely identifies the pixel's location on the sensor). The set of locations form the "representation grid." Since a collection of points in $\mathbf{R}^2$ combine to yield a single discrete value (pixel intensity), the set of sensor output values is called the "approximated image space."

A video sequence is formed by repeating the spatial registration process at discrete points in time. The instant in time when a frame was captured is represented with a temporal index. The temporal index is usually an integer counter. However, in the case of motion-activated recordings, the temporal index is an arbitrary strictly monotonically increasing sequence.

The set of points that undergoes spatial projection varies from frame to frame (Figure 1). Since points close to each other on an object are likely to have the same visual character, the human eye is unable to discern that different points are being registered. Video compression algorithms exploit this feature by replacing sets of points with single representatives. For example, quantization algorithms map a range of intensity levels to a single intensity level because it can be represented more succinctly. On the other hand, super-resolution algorithms extract

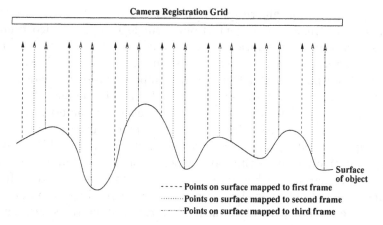

Figure 1. Object sampling.

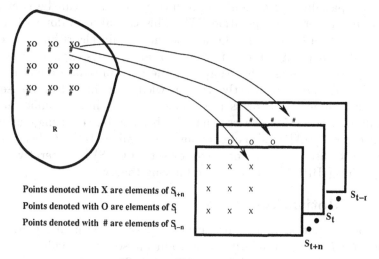

Figure 2. Object mapping.

and utilize variations in the intensity levels to increase the detail in each video frame.

Frame resolution can be increased using spatial domain signal processing, e.g., linear or spline interpolation. However, these algorithms cannot recover subpixel features lost during the subsampling process. Consecutive frames, $f_t, \ldots, f_{t+n}$, of a video sequence register different sets of points, $S_t, \ldots, S_{t+n}$, on the object, as illustrated in Figure 2. Therefore, super-resolution algorithms can outperform spatial domain techniques by enhancing each frame using data from temporally proximal frames.

Super-resolution algorithms have been studied for almost a decade. These algorithms use elements from a single image or video frame to construct a higher resolution version via spline interpolation [16]. However, this technique cannot recover lost subpixel features. Consequently, newer algorithms use data from several temporally proximal video frames or multiple images of the same scene. While the details differ, these algorithms employ similar observation models to characterize the degradation of high resolution frames to lower quality frames. As a result, the super-resolution algorithms have a similar structure [10]. The first step is coarse motion estimation, which typically estimates the motion between frames at block granularity. Next, data from contextual frames is interpolated onto a grid representing the desired high resolution output. The final step involves image restoration operations such as blur and noise removal.

If the motion between frames is known *a priori*, low resolution frames can be spatially shifted and the resulting collection can be combined using nonuniform interpolation [17]. This can also be done when the camera aperture varies [8]. Other spatial domain algorithms use color [13] and wavelets [9]. Frequency domain approaches exploit aliasing in low resolution frames [15]. Moreover, the blur and noise removal steps may be incorporated directly [7]. Knowledge of the optics and sensor can be included to address the problem of not having sufficient low resolution frames [5]. The issue has also been addressed using maximum *a posteriori* (MAP) estimates of unknown values [11]. Other general approaches use projection onto convex sets (POCS) [14], iterative back-projection (IBP) [6], and adaptive filtering theory [4].

3.   Motivation

Super-resolution algorithms have been designed without regard to the *Frye* and *Daubert* standards for introducing scientific evidence in U.S. courts. The *Frye* standard derives from a 1923 case where systolic blood pressure was used to ascertain deception by an individual. The method was disallowed because it was not widely accepted by scientists. The *Frye* standard was superseded in 1975 by the Federal Rules of Evidence, which require the evidence to be based in "scientific knowledge" and to "assist the trier of fact." In 1993, the Daubert family sued Merrell Dow Pharmaceuticals claiming that its anti-nausea drug Bendectin caused birth defects. The case reached the U.S. Supreme Court where the *Daubert* standard for relevancy and reliability of scientific evidence was articulated.

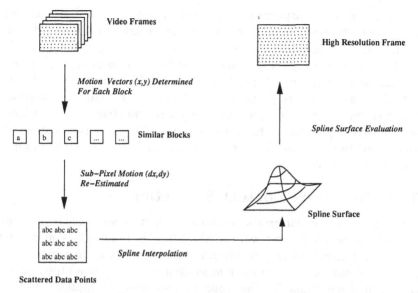

Figure 3. Super-resolution algorithm.

Super-resolution algorithms typically map the contextual data to a higher resolution representation, and then perform signal processing operations to improve the frame's quality. As a result, the high resolution version frame can be challenged on the grounds that it introduces elements not present in the original data. This is a side-effect of algorithm design, which is to use an observation model that results in an ill-posed inverse problem with many possible solutions. The algorithm introduced in this paper uses a different analytical technique that maintains the additional data in an intermediate representation where every point is from an input frame. This technique eliminates legal challenges based on the introduction of data to the original video evidence.

4. Algorithm Overview

The proposed super-resolution algorithm is illustrated in Figure 3. Each frame of a video sequence is enhanced independently in serial order. To process a given frame, a set of frames is formed by choosing several frames that are immediately previous to and immediately after the frame under consideration.

The frame being improved is then broken up into rectangular blocks. Extra data about each block in the frame is then extracted. For a given block, this is done by performing a search for one block from each of the frames in the set of frames (defined above) that best matches the frame. A sub-pixel displacement that minimizes the error between each of the contextual blocks and the block under consideration is analytically calculated for each of the blocks in the frame.

The data thus obtained is a set of points of the form (x, y, z), where z is the image intensity at point (x, y) in the XY plane. The set thus obtained corresponds to points scattered in the XY plane. To map this back to a grid, a bivariate spline surface, comprising tensor product basis splines that approximate this data, is computed. Since this is done for each frame in the sequence, a sequence similar in length to the input is produced as output.

5.   Temporal Context Extraction

Our algorithm enhances the resolution of a video sequence by increasing the size of the data set associated with each frame. Considering the "reference frame," whose resolution is being improved, we examine the problem of extracting relevant information from only one other frame, the "contextual frame." The same process may be applied to other frames immediately before and after the reference frame in the video sequence to obtain the larger data set representing the region in object space that was mapped to the reference frame.

Ideally, whenever an object in the reference frame appears in the contextual frame, it is necessary to identify the exact set of pixels that correspond to the object, extract the set, and incorporate it into the representation of the object in the reference frame. We use a technique from video compression called "motion estimation" for this purpose.

5.1   Initial Motion Estimation

The reference frame is broken into blocks of fixed size (the block dimensions are an algorithm parameter). The size of the block must be determined as a function of several factors that necessitate a tradeoff. Smaller blocks provide finer granularity, allowing for local movements to be better represented. The uniform motion field is forced on a smaller number of pixels, but this increases the computational requirements. Depending on the matching criterion, smaller blocks result in more incorrect matches. This is because larger blocks provide more context, which increases the probability of correctly determining an object's motion vector.

For each block, a search for a block of identical dimensions is performed in the contextual frame. A metric that associates costs inversely with the closeness of matches is used to identify the block with the lowest cost. The vector, which connects a point on the reference block to the corresponding point of the best match block in the contextual frame, is denoted as the initial motion estimate for the block.

Matching Criteria If a given video frame has width F_w and height F_h, and the sequence is T frames long, then a pixel at position (m, n) in the fth frame, is specified by $VS(m, n, f)$, where $m \in \{1, \ldots, F_w\}$, $n \in \{1, \ldots, F_h\}$, and $f \in \{1, \ldots, T\}$. If a given block has width B_w and height B_h, then a block in the reference frame with its top left pixel at (x, y) is denoted $RB(x, y, t)$, where $x \in \{1, \ldots, (F_w - B_w + 1)\}$, $y \in \{1, \ldots, (F_h - B_h + 1)\}$, and t is the temporal index. For a fixed reference frame block denoted by $RB(x, y, t)$, the block in the contextual frame that has its top left pixel located at the position $(x + a, y + b)$ is denoted by $CB(a, b, u)$, where $(x + a) \in \{1, \ldots, (F_w - B_w + 1)\}$, $(y + b) \in \{1, \ldots, (F_h - B_h + 1)\}$, and where the contextual frame has temporal index $(t + u)$. The determination that the object, represented in the block with its top left corner at (x, y) at time t, has been translated in exactly u frames by the vector (a, b), is associated with a cost given by the function $C(RB(x, y, t), CB(a, b, u))$.

We use the mean absolute difference (MAD) as the cost function. Empirical studies related to MPEG standards show that it works just as effectively as more computationally intensive criteria [1]. The corresponding cost function is given by:

$$MAD(RB(x, y, t), CB(a, b, u)) = \qquad (1)$$
$$\frac{1}{B_w B_h} \sum_{i=0}^{(B_w - 1)} \sum_{j=0}^{(B_h - 1)} |VS(x + i, y + j, t) - VS(x + a + i, y + b + j, t + u)|$$

Motion Vector Identification Given a reference block $RB(x, y, t)$, we wish to determine the block $CB(a, b, u)$ that is the best match in the $(t + u)^{th}$ frame, with the motion vector (a, b) constrained to a fixed rectangular search space centered at (x, y). This is illustrated in Figure 4. If the dimensions of this space are specified as algorithm parameters p and q, then $a \in \{(x - p), \ldots, (x + p)\}$, and $b \in \{(y - q), \ldots, (y + q)\}$ must hold. These values can be made small for sequences with little motion to enhance computational efficiency. If the motion characteristics of the sequence are unknown, p and q may be set so that the entire frame is searched.

The "full search method" is the only method that can determine the best choice $CB(a_{min}, b_{min}, u)$ without error, such that:

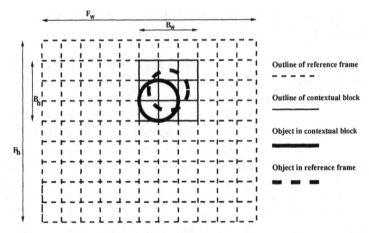

Figure 4. Contextual block determined with integral pixel accuracy.

$$\forall a \in \{(-x+1), \ldots, (F_w - B_w - x + 1)\}, \tag{2}$$
$$\forall b \in \{(-y+1), \ldots, (F_h - B_h - y + 1)\},$$
$$\mathcal{C}(RB(x,y,t), CB(a_{min}, b_{min}, u)) \le \mathcal{C}(RB(x,y,t), CB(a,b,u))$$

The method computes $\mathcal{C}(RB(x,y,t), CB(a,b,u))$ for all values of a and b in the above mentioned ranges and keeps track of the pair (a,b) that results in the lowest cost. The complexity of the algorithm is $\mathcal{O}(pqB_wB_h)$ when p and q are specified, and $\mathcal{O}(F_wF_hB_wB_h)$ when the most general form is used.

5.2   Re-Estimation with Subpixel Accuracy

Objects do not move in integral pixel displacements. It is, therefore, necessary to estimate the motion vector at a finer resolution. This is the second step in our hierarchical search.

Our analytical technique for estimating the motion of a block with sub-pixel accuracy is illustrated in Figure 5. By modeling the cost function as a separable function, we develop a measure for the real-valued displacements along each orthogonal axis that reduce the MAD value.

Let the function $\mathcal{F}(x,y)$ contain a representation of the reference frame with temporal index t, i.e.,

$$\forall x \in \{1, \ldots, F_w\}, \forall y \in \{1, \ldots, F_h\} \tag{3}$$
$$\mathcal{F}(x,y) = VS(x,y,t)$$

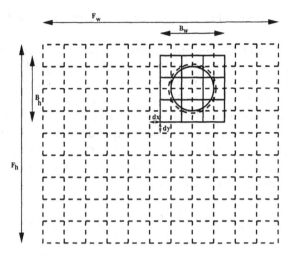

Figure 5. Sub-pixel displacement to improve reference area match.

Furthermore, let the function $\mathcal{G}(x, y)$ contain a representation of the contextual block for which the motion vector is being determined with sub-pixel accuracy. If $RB(x_0, y_0, t)$ is the reference block for which the previous stage of the algorithm found $CB(a_{min}, b_{min}, u)$ to be the contextual block with the closest match in frame $(t + u)$, then define:

$$x_{min} = x_0 + a_{min}, \; x_{max} = x_0 + a_{min} + B_w - 1 \tag{4}$$
$$y_{min} = y_0 + b_{min}, \; y_{max} = y_0 + b_{min} + B_h - 1$$

Note that the required definition of $\mathcal{G}(x, y)$ is given by:

$$\forall x \in \{x_{min}, \ldots, x_{max}\}, \forall y \in \{y_{min}, \ldots, y_{max}\} \tag{5}$$
$$\mathcal{G}(x, y) = VS(x, y, u)$$

Instead of (a_{min}, b_{min}), which is the estimate that results from the first stage of the search, we seek to determine the actual motion of the object that can be represented by $(a_{min} + \delta a_{min}, b_{min} + \delta b_{min})$. Therefore, at this stage the vector $(\delta a_{min}, \delta b_{min})$, which we call the "sub-pixel motion displacement," must be found.

LEMMA 1 δx *can be calculated in* $\mathcal{O}(\log{(Y B_w B_h)})$ *space and* $\mathcal{O}(B_w B_h)$ *time.*

Proof: This statement holds when the intensity values between two adjacent pixels are assumed to vary linearly. Note that Y is the range of possible values of the function (or the range of possible values of a pixel's color).

If the sub-pixel motion displacement is estimated as $(\delta x, \delta y)$, then the cost function is $C(RB(x, y, t), CB(a + \delta x, b + \delta y, u))$. We can use mean square error (MSE) as the matching criterion and treat it as an independent function of δx and δy. We apply linear interpolation to calculate $\mathcal{F}$ and $\mathcal{G}$ with non-integral parameters. To perform the estimation, the function must be known at the closest integral-valued parameters. Since the pixels adjacent to the reference block are easily available, and since this is not true for the contextual block, we reformulate the above equation without loss of generality as:

$$MSE(\delta x) = \sum_{x=x_{min}}^{x_{max}} \sum_{y=y_{min}}^{y_{max}} [\mathcal{F}(x + \delta x, y) - \mathcal{G}(x, y)]^2 \tag{6}$$

This is equivalent to using a fixed grid (contextual block) and variably displacing the entire reference frame to find the best sub-pixel displacement (instead of intuitively fixing the video frame and movement of the block whose motion is being determined).

Assuming that the optimal sub-pixel displacement along the x axis of the contextual block under consideration is the δx that minimizes the function $MSE(\delta x)$, we solve for δx using the constraint:

$$\frac{d}{d(\delta x)} MSE(\delta x) = 0 \tag{7}$$

$$= \sum_{x=x_{min}}^{x_{max}} \sum_{y=y_{min}}^{y_{max}} \left[[\mathcal{F}(x + \delta x, y) - \mathcal{G}(x, y)] \frac{d}{d(\delta x)} \mathcal{F}(x + \delta x, y) \right]$$

Since $\mathcal{F}(x, y)$ is a discrete function, we use linear interpolation to approximate it as a continuous function for representing $\mathcal{F}(x + \delta x, y)$ and computing $\frac{d}{d(\delta x)} \mathcal{F}(x + \delta x, y)$. We now consider the case of a positive δx.

$$\forall \delta x, \ 0 \leq \delta x \leq 1,$$

$$\mathcal{F}(x + \delta x, y) = \mathcal{F}(x, y) + \delta x \left[\mathcal{F}(x + 1, y) - \mathcal{F}(x, y) \right] \tag{8}$$

$$\frac{d}{d(\delta x)} \mathcal{F}(x + \delta x, y) = \mathcal{F}(x + 1, y) - \mathcal{F}(x, y) \tag{9}$$

By rearranging terms, we obtain the closed form solution:

$$\delta x = \tag{10}$$

$$\frac{\sum_{x=x_{min}}^{x_{max}} \sum_{y=y_{min}}^{y_{max}} \left[\left[\mathcal{F}(x + 1, y) - \mathcal{F}(x, y) \right] \left[\mathcal{F}(x, y) - \mathcal{G}(x, y) \right] \right]}{\sum_{x=x_{min}}^{x_{max}} \sum_{y=y_{min}}^{y_{max}} \left[\mathcal{F}(x + 1, y) - \mathcal{F}(x, y) \right]^2}$$

Similarly, an independent calculation can be performed to ascertain the negative value of δx that is optimal. The solution for the case of a negative δx is a minor variation of the technique described above. Finally, the MSE between the reference and contextual block is computed for each of the two δx's. The δx that results in the lower MSE is determined to be the correct one.

The closed form solution for each δx adds $B_w B_h$ terms to the numerator and the denominator. Each term requires two subtractions and one multiplication. This is followed by computing the final quotient of the numerator and denominator summations. Therefore, the time complexity is $\mathcal{O}(B_w B_h)$. Note that computing the MSE is possible within this bound as well. Since the function values range up to Y and only the running sum of the numerator and denominator must be stored, the space needed is $\mathcal{O}(\log Y B_w B_h)$. □

We now show that it is possible to obtain a better representation of a block in the reference frame by completing the analysis of sub-pixel displacements along the orthogonal axis.

LEMMA 2 *The cardinality of the set of points that represents the block under consideration from the reference frame is non-decreasing.*

Proof: After a δx has been determined, the block must be translated by a quantity δy along the orthogonal axis. It is important to perform this calculation after the δx translation has been applied because this guarantees that the MSE after both translations is no more than the MSE after the first translation; this ensures algorithm correctness. The δy can be determined in a manner analogous to δx, using the representation of the MSE below with the definition $x' = x + \delta x$. The closed form for a positive δy is defined below. The case when δy is negative is a minor variation.

$$\forall \delta y,\ 0 \leq \delta y \leq 1,\ \delta y = \tag{11}$$
$$\frac{\sum_{x=x_{min}}^{x_{max}} \sum_{y=y_{min}}^{y_{max}} [\, [\mathcal{F}(x', y+1) - \mathcal{F}(x', y)]\,[\mathcal{F}(x', y) - \mathcal{G}(x', y)]\,]}{\sum_{x=x_{min}}^{x_{max}} \sum_{y=y_{min}}^{y_{max}} [\mathcal{F}(x', y+1) - \mathcal{F}(x', y)]^2}$$

If the sub-pixel displacement $(\delta x, \delta y)$ results in an MSE between the contextual and reference blocks exceeding a given threshold, then the extra information is not incorporated into the current set representing the reference block. This prevents the contamination of the set with spurious information. It also completes the proof that either a set of points that enhances the current set is added, or none are – since this yields a non-decreasing cardinality for the set representing the block being processed.   □

By performing this analysis independently for each of the contextual blocks that corresponds to a reference block, we obtain a scattered data set representing the frame whose resolution is being enhanced. If the sampling grid were to have infinite resolution, an inspection of the values registered on it at the points determined to be in the image space would find the data points to be a good approximation. By repeating this process with a number of contextual frames for each reference frame, we can extract a large set of extra data points in the image space of the reference frame. At this stage, the resolution of the video frame has been analytically enhanced. However, the format of scattered data is not acceptable for most display media (e.g., video monitors). Therefore, the data must be processed further to make it usable.

6.   Coherent Frame Creation

We define a "uniform grid" to be the set $H_{P,k} \cup V_{Q,l}$ of lines in $\mathbf{R}^2$, where $H_{P,k} = \{x = k\alpha \mid k \in \{0, 1, 2, \ldots, P\}, \ \alpha \in \mathbf{R}, \ P \in \mathbf{N}\}$ specifies a set of vertical lines and $V_{Q,l} = \{y = l\beta \mid l \in \{0, 1, 2, \ldots, Q\}, \ \beta \in \mathbf{R}, \ Q \in \mathbf{N}\}$ specifies a set of horizontal lines. Specifying the values of P, Q, α, and β determines the uniform grid uniquely. Given a set S of points of the form (x, y, z), where z represents the intensity of point (x, y) in image space, if there exist M, N, α, and β such that all the (x, y) of the points in the set S lie on the associated uniform grid, and if every data point (x, y) on the uniform grid has an intensity (that is a z component) associated with it, then we call the set S a "coherent frame." Each of the frames in the original video sequence was a coherent frame. We seek to create a coherent frame from the data set D, with the constraint that the coherent frame should have the same number of points as the data set D.

The general principle used to effect the transformation from scattered data to a coherent frame is to construct a surface in $\mathbf{R}^3$ that passes through the input data. By representing this surface in a functional form with the x and y coordinates as parameters, it can then be evaluated at uniformly-spaced points in the XY plane to produce a coherent frame.

Numerous methods are available for this purpose, the tradeoff being the increased computational complexity needed to guarantee greater mapping accuracy. While the efficiency of the procedure is important, we would like to make our approximation as close a fit as possible. Note that although we will be forced to use interpolation techniques at this stage, we are doing so with a data set that has been increased in size, so this is not equivalent to performing interpolation at the outset and is certainly an improvement over it. We use B-spline interpolation with degree k, which can be set as a parameter to our algorithm.

7.   Implementation Issues

Given an arbitrary scattered data set, we can construct a coherent frame that provides a very good approximation of the surface specified by the original data set. However, if we were to work with the entire data set at hand, our algorithm would not be scalable due to the memory requirements.

Noting that splines use only a fixed number of neighboring points, we employ the technique of decomposing the data set into spatially related sets of fixed size. Each set contains all the points within a block in image space. The disadvantage of working with such subsets is that visible artifacts develop at the boundaries in the image space of these blocks.

To avoid this we "compose" the blocks using data from adjacent blocks to create a border of data points around the block in question, so that the spline surface constructed for a block is continuous with the surfaces of the adjacent blocks. Working with one block at a time in this manner, we construct surfaces for each region in the image space, and evaluate the surface on a uniform grid, to obtain the desired representation. A coherent frame is obtained when this is done for the entire set.

LEMMA 3 *Creating a block in a coherent frame requires* $\mathcal{O}(B_w B_h \sigma(k) T)$ *operations using data extracted from temporal context.*

Proof: T frames are incorporated and degree k polynomial-based B-spline tensor products are used to perform the transformation from scattered to gridded data. Lemma 2 guarantees that the input set does not degenerate. The complexity of splining depends on the number of points, which is $B_w B_h$, the product of the block width and height. $\sigma(k)$ is the cost to perform splining operations per point in the data set.

Since B-splines have the property of "local support," i.e., only a fixed number of adjacent B-splines are required for evaluating any given point in the space spanned by them (such as the surface being represented), and each B-spline can be represented as a fixed length vector of coefficients, the approximation of a surface specified by a set of points has time complexity that is only bound by the degree of the polynomials used and the multiplicity of the knots [2, 12]. This proves the lemma. □

LEMMA 4 *The resolution of a video sequence can be enhanced in $O(n)$ time, where n is the size (in bits) of the raw video data, if:*
(a) the degree of splines used in interpolation is fixed,
(b) a constant number of frames of temporal context is used, and
(c) motion estimation range is limited to a fixed multiple of block size.

Proof: We assume that there are L frames to process, each of which has $\frac{F_w F_h}{B_w B_h}$ blocks. For each block, it takes $\mu(B_w, B_h)$ time to perform motion estimation (assuming fixed range exhaustive search) and re-estimation of the motion with sub-pixel accuracy, by Lemma 1. Transforming the data set obtained for a block takes $\mathcal{O}(B_w B_h \sigma(k) T)$ time, by Lemma 3.

Therefore, processing an L frame video sequence using T frames of temporal context to enhance the resolution of each frame, yields the higher resolution version in $\mathcal{O}(F_w F_h L [\frac{\mu(B_w, B_h)}{B_w B_h} + \sigma(k) T])$ time.

On limiting the range of motion estimation to a fixed multiple of block size, $\mu(B_w, B_h) = O(1)$, using a constant number of frames of temporal context results in $T = O(1)$. Finally, while in theory B-spline interpolation has complexity $\mathcal{O}(k \log^2 k)$, constructing a B-spline and evaluating it along with all its derivatives can be done in $\mathcal{O}(k^2)$ operations in practice. However, if k is fixed, then $\sigma(k) = O(1)$.

Since $n = F_w F_h L$ and if the above specified constraints hold, then enhancing the resolution of the video sequence has a time complexity bound of $O(n)$. $\qquad\qquad\qquad\qquad\qquad\qquad\qquad\qquad\qquad\square$

8.   Experimental Results

We developed the GROW program as a proof of concept. GROW provides a flexible command line interface that allows the individual specification of parameters. These include the horizontal and vertical dimensions of the blocks used for motion estimation, the blocks used for spline interpolation, the extra border used for composing blocks for spline interpolation, the degrees of the splines used, the factors by which the output frame is scaled up from the original, the maximum range in which to perform motion estimation, the number of previous and later frames used to enhance a frame, the error threshold that is acceptable during motion estimation and that for spline interpolation.

The parameters serve to guide but not enforce the algorithm. For example, splining starts with the degree entered by the user but automatically drops to lower degrees (as less context is used) when the surface returned is not close enough to the points it is approximating. The error threshold specified for splining is used to scale up the bounds that are calculated using heuristics from the literature [3]. Intermediate results, such as sub-pixel displacements, are calculated and kept in high precision floating point format. When error thresholds are crossed, the data in question is not used. Thus, occlusion and peripheral loss of objects are dealt with effectively using only reference image data for the relevant region.

To evaluate the performance of GROW, we use the signal-to-noise ratio (SNR) to measure distortion:

$$SNR = 10 \log \frac{\sqrt{\frac{1}{B_w B_h} \sum_{x=x_{min}}^{x_{max}} \sum_{y=y_{min}}^{y_{max}} \mathcal{F}(x, y)}}{\frac{1}{(B_w B_h)^2} \sum_{x=x_{min}}^{x_{max}} \sum_{y=y_{min}}^{y_{max}} [\mathcal{F}(x, y) - \mathcal{G}(x, y)]^2} \tag{12}$$

In the definition, $\mathcal{G}$ represents the high resolution video sequence, and $\mathcal{F}$ represents the high resolution sequence obtained by running GROW on the low resolution version associated with $\mathcal{G}$. The low resolution version is obtained through the sub-sampling of $\mathcal{G}$.

Table 1. Effect of parameter variations on output frame SNR.

Super-Resolution Technique	s	t	p	l	SNR
Spline Interpolation (w/o Temporal Context)	16	16	0	0	28.39
Spline Interpolation (w Temporal Context)	8	8	2	2	30.40
Spline Interpolation (w Temporal Context)	4	4	2	2	30.59

Table 1 compares the signal strengths of the sequence produced by GROW for various parameters: the range for initial motion estimation on each axis (s, t) and the number of previous and later frames used (p, l). The first row represents the use of spline interpolation with 16×16 motion estimation blocks (s, $t = 16$) and no proximal frames (p, $l = 0$). The second row, corresponding to the use of 8×8 motion estimation blocks and two previous ($p = 2$) and two later ($l = 2$) frames (five frames total), results in a noticeably higher SNR. The third row, with 4×4 motion estimation blocks and five total frames, shows further improvement in the SNR, but at the cost of increased computation.

Figure 6 shows five frames of a video sequence. The higher resolution output corresponding to the third frame in Figure 6 is generated using all five frames as input to GROW.

Figure 7(a) shows the original frame whose resolution is being increased. Figure 7(b) shows the result of spline interpolation. Figure 7(c) shows the frame obtained by applying GROW. Artifacts that arise in the final images are due to errors in initial block matching and splining. Forensic video analysts can tolerate these artifacts in portions of the

Figure 6.   Original frames.

Figure 7.   (a) Original frame; (b) Higher resolution version using spline interpolation; (c) Higher resolution version using GROW.

frame that are of no consequence; in exchange they get greater detail in regions of interest.

Certain aspects, such as spline degree selection, have been automated in GROW. Others, such as splining error bounds, are semi-automatically calculated using heuristics and minimal user input. To obtain an optimal image sequence, it is necessary for the user to manually adjust the values fed into the algorithm. Significantly better results can be obtained by hand tuning GROW than by applying spline interpolation without temporal context. This is clear from the results in Table 1, where spline

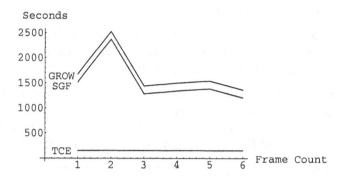

Figure 8. Time requirements (Splining (SGF); Temporal context extraction (TCE).

interpolation without proximal frames (first row) does not yield as strong a signal as the best case output of GROW (third row).

Note that the improvement in spline interpolation by adding temporal context is accomplished at little cost. This is verified in the graphs in Figure 8, where the time requirement for temporal context extraction is minimal compared with that for spline construction and evaluation.

9.   Conclusions

This paper describes how temporally proximal frames of a video sequence can be utilized to aid forensic video analysts by enhancing the resolution of individual frames. The super-resolution technique enables video analysts to vary several parameters to achieve a tradeoff between the quality of the reconstructed regions and the computational time. Another benefit is that analysts can further enhance regions of interest at the cost of degrading other areas of a video frame. Moreover, temporal extraction is performed first, with the mapping to a regular grid only occurring for visualization at the end. This is important for maintaining the integrity of evidence as video frames may be processed repeatedly without tainting the intermediate data.

References

[1] V. Bhaskaran and K. Konstantinides, *Image and Video Compression Standards: Algorithms and Architectures*, Kluwer, Boston, Massachusetts, 1996.

[2] C. de Boor, *A Practical Guide to Splines*, Springer-Verlag, New York, 1978.

[3] P. Dierckx, *Curve and Surface Fitting with Splines*, Oxford University Press, New York, 1993.

[4] M. Elad and A. Feuer, Super-resolution restoration of an image sequence: Adaptive filtering approach, *IEEE Transactions on Image Processing*, vol. 8(3), pp. 387–395, 1999.

[5] R. Hardie, K. Barnard, J. Bognar, E. Armstrong and E. Watson, High-resolution image reconstruction from a sequence of rotated and translated frames and its application to an infrared imaging system, *Optical Engineering*, vol. 37(1), pp. 247–260, 1998.

[6] M. Irani and S. Peleg, Improving resolution by image registration, *Computer Vision, Graphics and Image Processing: Graphical Models and Image Processing*, vol. 53(3), pp. 231–239, 1991.

[7] S. Kim, N. Bose and H. Valenzuela, Recursive reconstruction of high resolution image from noisy undersampled multiframes, *IEEE Transactions on Acoustics, Speech and Signal Processing*, vol. 38(6), pp. 1013–1027, 1990.

[8] T. Komatsu, T. Igarashi, K. Aizawa and T. Saito, Very high resolution imaging scheme with multiple different-aperture cameras, *Signal Processing: Image Communication*, vol. 5(5-6), pp. 511–526, 1993.

[9] N. Nguyen and P. Milanfar, An efficient wavelet-based algorithm for image super-resolution, *Proceedings of the International Conference on Image Processing*, vol. 2, pp. 351–354, 2000.

[10] S. Park, M. Park and M. Kang, Super-resolution image reconstruction: A technical overview, *IEEE Signal Processing*, vol. 20(3), pp. 21–36, 2003.

[11] R. Schulz and R. Stevenson, Extraction of high-resolution frames from video sequences, *IEEE Transactions on Image Processing*, vol. 5(6), pp. 996–1011, 1996.

[12] L. Schumaker, *Spline Functions: Basic Theory*, Wiley, New York, 1981.

[13] N. Shah and A. Zakhor, Resolution enhancement of color video sequences, *IEEE Transactions on Image Processing*, vol. 8(6), pp. 879–885, 1999.

[14] H. Stark and P. Oskoui, High resolution image recovery from image-plane arrays using convex projections, *Journal of the Optical Society of America*, vol. 6(11), pp. 1715–1726, 1989.

[15] R. Tsai and T. Huang, Multiple frame image restoration and registration, in *Advances in Computer Vision and Image Processing*, T. Huang (Ed.), JAI Press, Greenwich, Connecticut, pp. 317–399, 1984.

[16] M. Unser, A. Aldroubi and M. Eden, Enlargement or reduction of digital images with minimum loss of information, *IEEE Transactions on Image Processing*, vol. 4(3), pp. 247–258, 1995.

[17] H. Ur and D. Gross, Improved resolution from sub-pixel shifted pictures, *Computer Vision, Graphics and Image Processing: Graphical Models and Image Processing*, vol. 54(2), pp. 181–186, 1992.

IX

EVIDENCE ANALYSIS AND MANAGEMENT

Chapter 21

SPECIALIZING CRISP-DM FOR EVIDENCE MINING

Jacobus Venter, Alta de Waal and Cornelius Willers

Abstract   Forensic analysis requires a keen detective mind, but the human mind has neither the ability nor the time to process the millions of bytes on a typical computer hard disk. Digital forensic investigators need powerful tools that can automate many of the analysis tasks that are currently being performed manually.

This paper argues that forensic analysis can greatly benefit from research in knowledge discovery and data mining, which has developed powerful automated techniques for analyzing massive quantities of data to discern novel, potentially useful patterns. We use the term "evidence mining" to refer to the application of these techniques in the analysis phase of digital forensic investigations. This paper presents a novel approach involving the specialization of CRISP-DM, a cross-industry standard process for data mining, to CRISP-EM, an evidence mining methodology designed specifically for digital forensics. In addition to supporting forensic analysis, the CRISP-EM methodology offers a structured approach for defining the research gaps in evidence mining.

Keywords: Data mining, evidence mining, CRISP-DM, CRISP-EM

1. Introduction

Edmond Locard, a pioneer in forensic science, formulated the Exchange Principle: Every Contact Leaves a Trace [5]:

> "Searching for traces is not, as much as one could believe it, an innovation of modern criminal jurists. It is an occupation probably as old as humanity. The principle is this one. Any action of an individual, and obviously, the violent action constituting a crime, cannot occur without leaving a mark. What is admirable is the variety of these marks. Sometimes they will be prints, sometimes simple traces, and sometimes stains."

Please use the following format when citing this chapter:

Venter, J., de Waal, A., Willers, C., 2007, in IFIP International Federation for Information Processing, Volume 242, Advances in Digital Forensics III; eds. P. Craiger and S Shenoi; (Boston: Springer), pp. 303-315.

Electronic traces of actions and activities are continually being left behind in the Age of the Internet [16, 21], enabling Locard's Exchange Principle to be extended to include electronic "marks." This situation creates new opportunities for criminal investigators to uncover evidence. However, the electronic evidentiary discovery process is severely limited by the growing volume of data and the linking of unstructured pieces of data to create evidence trails [17].

Digital forensic investigations involve four major phases: evidence acquisition, examination, analysis and presentation [17]. A variety of commercial tools are available for supporting investigations. However, most existing software tools for forensic analysis are based on keyword searches; unless very specific knowledge regarding the information to be retrieved is available, the process of retrieving information is complex, manual and time consuming. Some progress has been made in providing automated support for forensic analysis [9]. However, the tools do not cover the full spectrum of analysis activities, and they do not possess the functionality to adequately reduce the volume of data, let alone find information that investigators did not know existed [17].

Despite its importance, the area of forensic analysis has received relatively limited research attention. For example, our analysis of all 77 research articles published from 1994 through 2006 in the journal *Digital Investigation* revealed that only 26% (20 articles) focused on the examination or analysis of digital evidence. Eighteen of the twenty articles dealt with processing digital evidence to support manual interpretation. In all, only two articles [10, 18] focused on the important task of automating the search for electronic evidence. As Garfinkel [9] indicates, digital forensic examiners have become victims of their own success despite the fact that cannot analyze all the data provided to them by the previous phases of the forensic process.

Forensic analysis requires a keen detective mind, but the human mind does not have the capability (or time) to process the millions of bytes on a computer hard disk. Most analysis methods do not scale very well and, therefore, are unable to cope with large data sets [17]. A new generation of forensic tools is required to support human analysts, at the same time, automating many of the tasks that are currently being performed manually.

This paper argues that digital forensic analysis can greatly benefit from research in knowledge discovery and data mining, which has developed powerful automated techniques for analyzing massive quantities of data to discern novel, potentially useful patterns. The research is multi-disciplinary in nature, drawing from several fields including expert systems, machine learning, intelligent databases, knowledge acquisition, case-based reasoning, pattern recognition and statistics [2].

Previous research in knowledge discovery and data mining related to criminal investigations has focused on mining data from case databases to support crime prevention efforts [4, 16]. However, what investigators really need is support during the analysis phase: automated assistance to find specific data elements in specific cases. This point is underscored by Pollitt and Whitledge [17] who emphasize that research should focus on forensic applications of data mining tools and on developing knowledge management strategies specific to the context of criminal investigations. We use the term "evidence mining" to refer to the application of data mining and knowledge discovery techniques to support the analysis phase of digital forensic investigations.

This paper focuses on the application of evidence mining to support digital forensic investigations. It discusses a novel approach involving the specialization of CRISP-DM, a cross-industry standard process for data mining, to CRISP-EM, an evidence mining methodology designed specifically for digital forensics. In addition to supporting forensic analysis, the CRISP-EM methodology offers a structured approach for defining the research gaps in evidence mining.

2.   Evidence Mining

Evidence validates facts and it may be used as testimony in courtroom proceedings or a formal hearing. In this context, the interest is not in general trends that assist in crime prevention. Instead, the focus is on the finding of proof in order to testify about the facts.

Mena [16] observes that criminal analysis uses historical observations to come up with solutions – unlike criminology, which re-enacts a crime in order to solve it. In this sense, "evidence mining" is more like criminology. Evidence mining aims to "re-enact" the crime by analyzing the electronic evidence left behind by the subjects' actions. Evidence mining aims to uncover, through the application of knowledge discovery principles and techniques, electronic artifacts that can form part of the evidence set to assist in the development of crime scenarios.

Evidence mining is a new term or, at least, a scarcely used term. A search of the ACM [1], IEEE [11] and SCOPUS [19] digital libraries returned no relevant results for "evidence mining."

3.   Evidence Mining Using CRISP-DM

The CRISP-DM consortium developed the Cross-Industry Standard Process for Data Mining (CRISP-DM) [3]. Clifton and Thuraising-

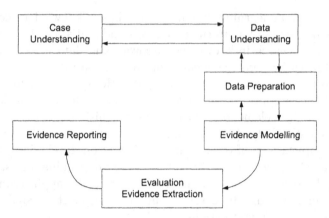

Figure 1.   Main phases of CRISP-EM.

ham [7] identified CRISP-DM as a notable effort in process standardization. Moreover, the KDNuggets poll of April 2004 indicated that CRISP-DM was the most popular methodology among the respondents [12].

CRISP-DM has several characteristics that render it useful for evidence mining. It provides a generic process model that holds the overarching structure and dimensions of the methodology. The methodology then provides for specialization according to a pre-defined context (in the CRISP-DM terminology this is indicated as a specialized process). We have used such a specialization to create CRISP-EM (Cross-Industry Standard Process for Evidence Mining). Mena [16] proposed using CRISP-DM to detect crimes without providing much detail or establishing a specialization of CRISP-DM. We propose CRISP-EM as an approach for meeting the requirements of a process that supports evidence mining. Our goal is not to create a new digital forensic process but to support the analysis phases of existing forensic processes.

4.   CRISP-DM Specialization

The main phases of CRISP-EM are shown in Figure 1. Although CRISP-EM follows the basic structure of CRISP-DM, some of the major phases are renamed to fit the context of digital investigations.

4.1   Specialization Strategy

CRISP-DM [3] proposes the following specialization strategy:

- Analyze the specific context.

- Remove details not applicable to the context.

- Add details specific to the context.

- Specialize (or instantiate) generic content according to concrete characteristics of the context.

- Possibly rename generic content to provide more explicit meanings in the context for the sake of clarity.

The next four subsections discuss the application of this specialization strategy.

4.2   Analyzing the Context

The first phase of the specialization strategy is to analyze the context. When CRISP-EM is placed within the context of a specific criminal case, it should be used to provide support to an investigator or prosecutor, not to mine for trends in case databases. Such a project is close enough to normal data mining that CRISP-DM in its original format would suffice.

Digital forensic investigations have four principal phases: evidence acquisition, examination, analysis and reporting. The acquisition phase collects evidence in a manner that preserves its integrity. Normally, a copy of the original evidence (image) is made and all further processing is done using the image (or a copy of the image). The second phase is evidence examination, which involves rudimentary processing of the evidence using keyword searches or examining locations specific to the operating system (e.g. for a user name). The third phase is evidence analysis. During this phase, the information obtained during the evidence examination phase is evaluated in the context of the case and the evidence is further processed to uncover facts about events, actions, etc. that are relevant to the case. The information provided by the examination phase is placed in context with the case and is further processed to uncover facts that stipulate to events, actions, etc. relevant to the case. The fourth and final phase is to present the evidence to the concerned parties in and out of court.

The context for evidence mining is phases three (evidence analysis) and four (evidence presentation). It is important to note that the data gathering aspects of the CRISP-DM methodology (part of the Data Preparation phase) and the digital forensic acquisition phase are not within the same context. Because of this context difference, it is more appropriate to use the term "data collation" instead of "data collection" in CRISP-EM.

Table 1. Original and renamed phases.

Original CRISP-DM Phase	Renamed CRISP-EM Phase
Business Understanding	Case Understanding
Data Understanding	Data Understanding
Data Preparation	Data Preparation
Modeling	Event Modeling
Evaluation	Evaluation and Evidence Extraction
Deployment	Evidence Reporting

4.3   Renaming Generic Content

The original CRISP-DM phases and the renamed CRISP-EM phases are shown in Table 1. The first phase is renamed to Case Understanding because each evidence mining project is associated with a specific case. The names of the next two phases (Data Understanding and Data Preparation) remain the same as the intent of these phases for evidence mining is the same as for data mining. The principal differences, however, pertain to the last three phases. A specific evidence mining project is likely to span only one case. Therefore, the intent is to produce specific evidence for the case at hand rather than to build a model that can be used for future cases.

Consequently, the Modeling phase is replaced by the Event Modeling or Scenario Development phase. This phase creates plausible scenarios from the electronic evidence available in the data set. In the next phase, the evidence is presented to the investigator and/or prosecutor who evaluate the scenarios presented, select the relevant scenarios and extract the relevant evidence (hence the phase is renamed to Evaluation and Evidence Extraction). The final phase is Evidence Reporting, where the evidence is reported to an investigator, prosecutor or in court.

The renaming of terms continues within the details of the methodology. A notable example is Generic Task 1.2 in CRISP-DM "Collect Initial Data," which is renamed to "Collate Initial Data" in CRISP-EM. This is done to distinguish between acquiring forensic evidence (data collection) and putting together evidence for analysis (data collation).

4.4   Specializing Generic Content

To maintain the context of an investigation, it is necessary to not only develop specialized tasks but also to specialize the phases and the generic tasks. In particular, the original CRISP-DM descriptions for the generic process phases must be adapted to fit within the evidence mining context. The adapted descriptions are shown below. The major changes from the original descriptions are shown in italics. It is important to note that these process phases fit within the analysis phase of the larger digital forensic process and are not meant to replace the overall process.

- **Case Understanding:** This initial phase focuses on understanding the *investigation* objectives and requirements from a case perspective, and converting this knowledge to an *evidence* mining problem definition and a preliminary plan designed to achieve the objectives.

- **Data Understanding:** This phase starts with an initial data collation and proceeds with data familiarization, the identification of data quality problems, the discovery of patterns in the data and the detection of interesting subsets that create hypotheses for hidden information.

- **Data Preparation:** This phase covers all the activities involved in converting the initial raw data to the final data set, which is input to *event modeling* tool(s). Data preparation tasks are likely to be performed multiple times and not in any prescribed order. The tasks include table, record and attribute selection, *entity recognition and co-reference resolution*, and the transformation and cleaning of data for *event modeling* tools.

- **Event Modeling:** In this phase, various *evidence modeling and event reconstruction* techniques are selected and applied and their parameters are calibrated to optimal values. Typically, several techniques can be applied to an *evidence* mining problem. Many of these techniques have specific requirements on the form of data. Therefore, it may be necessary to return to the Data Preparation phase.

- **Evaluation and Evidence Extraction:** At this stage in the project, a *set of scenarios or event lines have been built* that are of high quality from a data analysis perspective. Before proceeding to the final reporting of the evidence, it is important to thoroughly evaluate the *scenarios/event lines* and review the steps executed in order to construct and extract *the relevant scenarios/event lines* that achieve the *case* objectives. A key objective is to determine if important *case* aspects have not been considered adequately. A decision on the use of *evidence* mining results should be reached at the end of this phase.

- **Evidence Reporting:** A project generally does not conclude
  with the creation of event lines and the extraction of evidence.
  Even if the purpose of evidence mining is to increase knowledge
  about the data, the knowledge gained should be organized and
  presented appropriately to enable the *investigator* to use it for *evidentiary purposes*. This *may* involve *augmenting chosen event lines
  with other data pertinent to the investigation*. In many cases it is
  the investigator, not the data analyst, who performs the *reporting*
  steps. However, even if the data analyst is not involved in the
  reporting effort, it is important for the *investigator* to understand
  the actions that must be carried out to make use of the *extracted
  event lines and evidence*.

4.5   Adding/Removing Content

New content has to be added to address evidence mining requirements
whereas other content that does not make sense in the evidence mining
context has to be removed. Some of the key changes are discussed below.

- **Initial Data Mining:** The development of event lines is a complex task that requires more advanced data pre-processing and
  preparation than "traditional" data mining. The initial data mining task was added to the Data Preparation phase to facilitate
  the additional inputs to the Event Modeling phase. The output
  of this task is a richer data set that includes classified and categorized data. Understanding the crime triangle of "willing offender,"
  "enabling environment" and "vulnerable target" [6] will help in
  developing the pre-processed data as all three of these aspects are
  present in every crime instance and, as such, will also be present
  in the storyboarding. Therefore, identifying entities and classifying them as potential offender, environment or victim indicators
  would be very useful in the next phase.

- **Develop Event Scenarios:** The primary purpose of the Event
  Modeling phase is to support the investigator through the development of hypotheses regarding a crime and how it occurred based
  on electronic artifacts found in the evidence set. In this context,
  a hypotheses is an answer to a question about what crime took
  place and what can be right or wrong (adapted from [6]). The
  set of hypotheses (scenarios) constitute a roadmap that enables
  the investigator to conduct an effective and efficient investigation.
  The original CRISP-DM Build Model task is replaced by the Develop Event Scenarios task. The replacement is necessary because

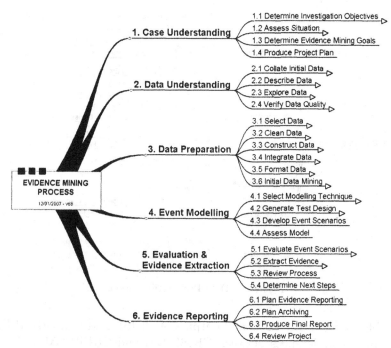

Figure 2. CRISP-EM second level.

the model built by the evidence mining process is in actuality the scenarios.

5. CRISP-EM Summary

The previous section discussed the development of a specialized process for evidence mining. This section summarizes the CRISP-EM process and provides details of the Data Preparation phase.

The major phases of the evidence mining process are shown in Figure 1. Figure 2 presents the next level of the CRISP-EM process in "mind map" format. Details of the Data Preparation phase are shown in Figure 3. Substantial further research is required to complete all the aspects of the process and to implement it completely.

6. Research Gaps

The CRISP-EM framework supports a structured approach for defining research gaps. CRISP-EM provides a level of granularity that makes it easier to identify where existing knowledge discovery and data mining techniques suffice and where new techniques would be required due to

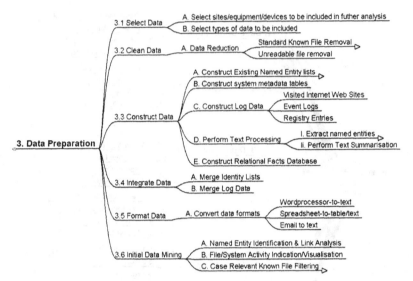

Figure 3. Data Preparation phase.

the differences in the tasks and outputs of CRISP-DM and CRISP-EM. The biggest differences between CRISP-DM and CRISP-EM lie in the Event Modeling, and Evaluation and Evidence Extraction phases. It is, therefore, obvious that the largest research gaps would also be in these areas. Three examples of identified research gaps are described below.

- **Example Case Files:** Sample data sets are required for the new evidence mining techniques. These data sets, called "example case files" in this context, must contain known event lines in various forms in order to test the effectiveness of the techniques. Sufficiently large data sets that contain mixed data must also be developed to test the efficiency of the algorithms. No such example case files currently exist. Research efforts should focus on developing plausible crime "stories" and ways for mixing them within other data sets. Furthermore, the example case files would have to be created automatically as creating them manually would be extremely time consuming.

- **Coping with Uncertainty:** Uncertainty is a major challenge when developing event lines. The available data is often incomplete, leading to beliefs that fall short of evidence and produce fallible conclusions. Probabilistic reasoning models [14] may be used to build scenarios; they also address problems such as co-reference resolution, record linkage and theme extraction. The association of probability values to event lines would also facilitate prioritization during the Evaluation and Evidence Extraction phase.

- **Automating Investigative Processes:** Human investigators have special skills and experience that enable them to extract evidence from unstructured information. However, the number of human investigators is limited, manual investigative processes are slow and laborious, and human concentration diminishes with fatigue. Automated knowledge discovery techniques can be parallelized to handle large volumes of data efficiently. Unfortunately, these techniques do not exhibit the skill of human investigators. Knowledge discovery techniques involving intelligent agents [8, 20, 22] can be used to automate certain aspects of the investigative process, reducing the burden on human investigators.

7. Conclusions

Forensic investigators are being inundated with massive volumes of electronic evidence, and the situation is only expected to become worse. A new generation of forensic tools are needed to automate analysis tasks that are now being performed manually. Research in knowledge discovery and data mining has developed powerful automated techniques for discovering useful patterns in massive quantities of data. Evidence mining is the application of these techniques in the analysis phase of digital forensic investigations. The CRISP-EM process described in this paper specializes the well-known CRISP-DM data mining methodology to provide sophisticated knowledge discovery and data mining support for digital forensic investigations. CRISP-EM is not yet a proven process; nevertheless, it offers a powerful framework for the initial, mostly manual, application of evidence mining. Also, it provides a basis for researching new methods and techniques for enhancing evidence mining and implementing the underlying processes.

References

[1] Association for Computing Machinery (ACM), (www.acm.org).

[2] S. Bandyopadhyay, U. Maulik, L. Holder and D. Cook, *Advanced Methods for Knowledge Discovery from Complex Data*, Springer-Verlag, Secaucus, New Jersey, 2005.

[3] P. Chapman, J. Clinton, R. Kerber, T. Khabaza, T. Reinartzrysler, C. Shearer and R. Wirth, CRISP-DM 1.0: Step-by-Step Data Mining Guide, The CRISP-DM Consortium, SPSS (www.crisp-dm.org /CRISPWP-0800.pdf), 1999.

[4] H. Chen, W. Chung, J. Xu, G. Wang, Y. Qin and M. Chau, Crime data mining: A general framework and some examples, *IEEE Computer*, vol. 37(4), pp. 50–56, 2004.

[5] W. Chisum and B. Turvey, *Crime Reconstruction*, Elsevier, Burlington, Massachusetts, 2007.

[6] R. Clarke and J. Eck, Become a Problem-Solving Crime Analyst, Jill Dando Institute of Crime Science, University College London, London, United Kingdom (www.jdi.ucl.ac.uk/publications/other _publications/55steps), 2003.

[7] C. Clifton and B. Thuraisingham, Emerging standards for data mining, *Computer Standards & Interfaces*, vol. 23(3), pp. 187–193, 2001.

[8] I. Dickinson and M. Wooldridge, Towards practical reasoning agents for the semantic web, *Proceedings of the Second International Joint Conference on Autonomous Agents and Multiagent Systems*, pp. 827–834, 2003.

[9] S. Garfinkel, Forensic feature extraction and cross-drive analysis, *Digital Investigation*, vol. 3(S1), pp. 71–81, 2006.

[10] P. Gladyshev and A. Patel, Finite state machine approach to digital event reconstruction, *Digital Investigation*, vol. 1(2), pp. 130–149, 2004.

[11] Institute for Electrical and Electronics Engineers (IEEE), (www .ieee.org).

[12] KDNuggets, Data mining methodology poll (www.kdnuggets.com /polls/2004/data_mining_methodology.htm), 2004.

[13] J. Keppens and B. Schafer, Knowledge based crime scenario modeling, *Expert Systems with Applications*, vol. 30(2), pp. 203–222, 2006.

[14] K. Korb and A. Nicholson, *Bayesian Artificial Intelligence*, Chapman and Hall/CRC Press, Boca Raton, Florida, 2004.

[15] A. Louis, A. de Waal and J. Venter, Named entity recognition in a South African context, *Proceedings of the Annual Research Conference of the South African Institute of Computer Scientists and Information Technologists*, pp. 170–179, 2006.

[16] J. Mena, *Investigative Data Mining for Security and Criminal Detection*, Elsevier, Burlington, Massachusetts, 2003.

[17] M. Pollitt and A. Whitledge, Exploring big haystacks: Data mining and knowledge management, in *Advances in Digital Forensics II*, M. Olivier and S. Shenoi (Eds.), Springer, New York, pp. 67–76, 2006.

[18] M. Rogers, K. Seigfried and K. Tidke, Self-reported computer criminal behavior: A psychological analysis, *Digital Investigation*, vol. 3(S1), pp. 116–120, 2006.

[19] Scopus, (www.scopus.com).

[20] W. van der Hoek, W. Jamroga and M. Wooldridge, A logic for strategic reasoning, *Proceedings of the Fourth International Joint Conference on Autonomous Agents and Multiagent Systems*, pp. 157–164, 2005.

[21] I. Witten and E. Frank, *Data Mining: Practical Machine Learning Tools and Techniques*, Morgan Kaufmann, San Francisco, California, 2005.

[22] M. Wooldridge, *An Introduction to Multiagent Systems*, John Wiley, Chichester, United Kingdom, 2002.

Chapter 22

APPLYING THE BIBA INTEGRITY MODEL TO EVIDENCE MANAGEMENT

Kweku Arthur, Martin Olivier and Hein Venter

Abstract   This paper describes the design of an integrity-aware Forensic Evidence Management System (FEMS). The well-known Biba integrity model is employed to preserve and reason about the integrity of stored evidence. Casey's certainty scale provides the integrity classification scheme needed to apply the Biba model. The paper also discusses the benefits of using an integrity-aware system for managing digital evidence.

Keywords: Evidence management, Biba integrity model, Casey's certainty scale

1.   Introduction

The Internet has enabled the sharing of resources between millions of computer systems around the world. Applications such as email, retail banking and general information interchange (through file transfer and peer-to-peer networks) have positively influenced the lives of Internet users. However, vulnerabilities in applications, operating systems and networks connected to the Internet are constantly emerging—with cyber criminals making it their mission to identify and exploit these vulnerabilities. Their exploits can be categorized as "true cyber crime" and "e-enabled cyber crime" [3]. True cyber crime is a dishonest or malicious act that would not exist outside an online environment, e.g., virus attacks, suspicious probes (hacking) and denial-of-service attacks. E-enabled crime is a criminal act that was encountered before the advent of the Internet, but which is increasingly perpetrated using the Internet, e.g., fraud and identity theft [3].

Investigative methodologies, forensic tools, and host- and network-based forensic techniques have rapidly evolved to combat the unrelenting increase in cyber crime. However, a major challenge is the reliability and

Please use the following format when citing this chapter:

Arthur, K., Olivier, M., Venter, H., 2007, in IFIP International Federation for Information Processing, Volume 242, Advances in Digital Forensics III; eds. P. Craiger and S Shenoi; (Boston: Springer), pp. 317-327.

integrity associated with digital evidence from disparate sources. Given the nature of forensic investigations and the ease with which digital evidence (especially metadata) can be created, altered and destroyed [10], it is extremely important to protect evidence and preserve its integrity.

This paper describes the design of a Forensic Evidence Management System (FEMS) that determines and protects the integrity of digital evidence stored in the system, regardless of whether the evidence was entered as a basic fact or was inferred from pre-existing evidence by the system. The well-known Biba integrity model [14] is employed. The Biba model labels data within integrity classes. In the model, an application may only read data with an integrity classification equal to or higher than its own integrity classification. Also, the application may only write data to containers with integrity classifications that are equal to or lower than its own classification. Since data can only flow from higher to lower integrity classes, low integrity data cannot contaminate high integrity data.

An integrity classification scheme is required to apply the Biba model in the context of digital evidence. Casey's certainty scale [5] is useful for expressing the certainty of facts and inferences in a networked environment. Since certainty equates to integrity, Casey's scale is an ideal starting point for expressing the integrity of digital evidence in FEMS. In fact, we use the terms certainty and integrity interchangeably in this paper.

The remainder of this paper is organized as follows. Section 2 provides background information about data classification, information flow, the Biba integrity model and Casey's certainty scale. Section 3 describes the FEMS architecture. Section 4 discusses information flow within FEMS and illustrates the benefits of using an integrity-aware system. The final section, Section 5, presents our conclusions.

2.   Background

Information has great value, and practically every enterprise gathers and uses information to gain a competitive advantage. At the same time, malicious agents actively attempt to exploit this information for financial gain. The recent CSI/FBI Computer Crime and Security Survey [8] reveals the massive costs associated with the loss or disclosure of private or proprietary information. As a result, enterprises must implement security mechanisms aimed at mitigating the risks of information loss and disclosure.

2.1 Data Classification and Information Flow

The risk of financial loss is one of the principal motivations for implementing data classification and access control and, in general, controlling information flow in an organization. Data classification involves the assignment of sensitivity levels to specific data assets [18]. A data classification exercise has to performed within the organization before an appropriate access control model can be implemented. Consequently, a risk analysis is undertaken, all organization critical assets are identified, the impact of the loss of these assets is determined, and appropriate controls are adopted to protect the assets [6]. A technical access control implementation incorporates preventative, detective and/or corrective controls, e.g., access control lists, intrusion detection systems and patch management. The access control model ultimately controls information flow, often implementing security principles such as least privilege and need-to-know [9].

2.2 Biba Integrity Model

The Biba integrity model was the first to address integrity in computer systems [17]. It is based on a hierarchical lattice of integrity levels (similar to the Bell-LaPadula confidentiality model). The Biba model orders subjects (s) and objects (o) using an integrity classification scheme, denoted by $I(s)$ and $I(o)$, respectively. The integrity classification scheme controls object modification. The Biba model is based on two properties [14]:

- **Simple Integrity Property:** Subject s can read object o only if $I(s) \geq I(o)$.

- *** Integrity Property:** If subject s can read object o, then s can write to object p only if $I(o) \geq I(p)$.

These rules address the integrity of information in a natural way. Suppose a person A is known to be untruthful. If A creates or modifies documents, then others who access this document should distrust the truth of the statements in the document. Furthermore, if people are skeptical about a report based on flawed evidence, the low integrity of the source evidence (object) should imply low integrity for any evidence (object or inference) based on the source evidence (object).

2.3 Casey's Certainty Scale

If properly programmed and configured, all information technology and network objects are capable of producing log data reflecting their

Table 1. Proposed scale for classifying integrity levels (adapted from [5]).

Level	Description/Indicator	Qualification
C0	Evidence contradicts known facts	Erroneous/Incorrect
C1	Evidence is highly questionable	Highly Uncertain
C2	Only one source of evidence exists and it is not protected from tampering	Somewhat Uncertain
C3	The source(s) of evidence are more difficult to tamper with but there is not enough evidence to support a firm conclusion or there are unexplained inconsistencies in the evidence	Possible
C4	Evidence is protected from tampering or multiple, independent sources of evidence agree but the evidence is not protected from tampering	Probable
C5	Agreement of evidence from multiple, independent sources that are protected from tampering but uncertainties exist (e.g., temporal errors, data loss)	Almost Certain
C6	Evidence is tamper proof and unquestionable	Certain

activity [7, 15]. In the event of an incident, these audit logs could assist with reconstructing and understanding the activities that led to the incident [12]. Therefore, event auditing capabilities are typically enabled with respect to the classification of data, applications and systems to be protected. From this, one can understand why it is necessary for web servers, FTP servers, mail servers and access control mechanisms to generate logs. However, the logs are prone to data corruption, loss, tampering, incorrect interpretation and lead time in transmission that could render the evidence useless. Time-based differences such as timezone bias and differing system clock speeds and settings also contribute to errors. Therefore, it stands to reason that levels of certainty must be associated with digital evidence as well as with evidence sources.

Casey's certainty scale [5] was developed to address the inherent uncertainties related to digital evidence in networked environments. In particular, it enables certainty (integrity) assessments to be associated with digital data. Casey's proposal is illustrated in Table 1. The first column of the table lists the seven certainty (integrity) levels. The second column indicates the preconditions that lead to the integrity conclusions in the third column. Note that the higher the certainty (integrity) level, the greater the integrity associated with the evidence source and, hence, the inferences based on the evidence.

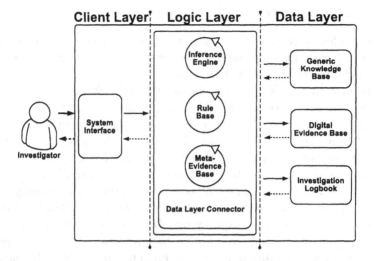

Figure 1. Forensic Evidence Management System (FEMS) architecture.

3. Forensic Evidence Management System

Digital forensic techniques are employed when crimes are commissioned through the use of computers and the evidence is electronic in nature. Digital evidence sources include digital cameras, log files, network traffic, local and removable storage devices, and metadata such as MAC times [16]. If a cyber crime is suspected, a digital forensics specialist is tasked to investigate the electronic crime scene to reveal the root cause or perpetrator. Proprietary tools (e.g., FTK [1]) are often used during the investigative process. Unix-based and open source tools such as grep and dd may also be used in digital forensic investigations [11].

The multitude of digital evidence sources presents a major challenge to investigators. An aggregated forensic evidence store could greatly assist investigators by providing them with holistic views of the forensic evidence pertaining to cases and insights into the quality of their inferences.

Our integrity-aware Forensic Evidence Management System (FEMS) was designed with these issues in mind (Figure 1). The FEMS architecture distributes its components within a client layer, logic layer and data layer. The client layer serves as the investigator's interface to the system. The logic layer houses the processing rules. The data layer stores the data used in an investigation and provides the necessary abstraction layer between the investigator and the raw evidence stored in the system.

3.1   System Components

FEMS has several components: system interface, rule base, meta-evidence base, inference engine, investigation logbook, digital evidence base and generic knowledge base (Figure 1).

The system interface is the channel through which a forensic investigator accesses facts within FEMS. The investigator uses queries to interrogate the system for evidence; these queries include hypotheses that the investigator tests against facts within the system. The system interface also enables the investigator to update data.

The rule base is a store for the action(s) to be taken given any particular fact in the system. The rule base also represents knowledge about facts that can be inferred by the system [4]. We assume that the rules do not necessarily exist *a priori*; they may be entered *a posteriori* based on the specific case at hand. In addition to supporting inferences, the rule base is incorporated due to its ease of implementation and the intuitive nature of rule generation [2]. For example, a rule may specify integrity labels to be associated with facts from a specific evidence source or facts derived from an evidence source.

The meta-evidence base, which is directly interfaced with the rule base, only houses inferred evidence. Queries to the system that have been confirmed or refuted by the system are routed to and noted in the meta-evidence base.

The inference engine implements Casey's certainty scale. It draws its inputs from the rule base and the meta-evidence base in ascribing certainty labels to evidence and inferences.

The investigation logbook records all investigative actions. The automated documentation of actions is certainly not new. Several forensic tool suites (e.g., Encase, FTK and ProDiscover) offer this feature; FTK, for example, even provides for customizable reports. In the FEMS context, system queries, hypotheses, rules, data and inferences are recorded. The logbook thus traces the inputs and the reasoning used to reach the investigative conclusions.

The digital evidence base interfaces to forensic tools, e.g., EnCase and FTK. The evidence base also incorporates inputs from log correlation sources, logical access records (including access control matrices), and physical access records such as work attendance registers.

The generic knowledge base houses static information such as software names, versions and descriptions. It also includes a database of known files: standard operating system files and hashes for generic file signatures such as GIF or JPG compressed files. The generic knowledge base has the same function and is referenced in the same way as

FTK's "Known File Filter" [1] and NIST's National Software Reference Library [13].

3.2   Evidence

Digital evidence in FEMS is often stored in the form of facts:

- Fact 1: web proxy 223.1.3.27 return code 200 = OK: Request succeeded

- Fact 2: web proxy 223.1.3.27 return code 400 = Bad request: Request could not be understood by the server

Fact 1 above is interpreted as "client request successful," while Fact 2 is interpreted as "client request not understood by the proxy server." Facts may be represented as predicates.

For a murder case in the physical world, the fact that gunshot residue was found on suspect S could be expressed by the predicate $GSR(S)$. Similarly, if S was placed at the scene of the crime, the corresponding predicate is $AtScene(S)$. Other predicates may be used to represent various facts about S, about the crime itself, and about other agents.

The physical world is a realm where intangible properties such as time, space and physical location cannot be controlled or amended by agents (humans). It is also characterized by its deterministic and finite nature, where an action has a definitive source and destination. On the other hand, actions in a digital environment may be virtually independent of time and physical location and, more often than not, the source of an action is obfuscated. Also, in the digital world, properties such as time and location can be amended by agents. Consequently, something that may be easy to prove in the physical world could be difficult, if not impossible, to prove in the digital world.

The differences between the two worlds are important because it is possible to automatically derive facts in the digital world from augmented forensic tools. Suppose, for example, that it is relevant whether or not a certain picture or email messages were on a suspect's computer. These facts could be added automatically to an evidence knowledge base when the hard drive of the suspect's computer is imaged and analyzed using a digital forensic tool. Note, however, that not all facts in the digital world can be derived automatically. Due to the subjective nature of pornography, the question of whether or not a picture found on a suspect's computer is a pornographic image may only be answered by a human investigator.

The integrity of evidence can expressed by associating integrity levels from Casey's certainty scale with facts. For example, if image I was found on a disk, the fact may be represented as $OnDisk(I, C6)$. Certain deduction rules are applicable regardless of the integrity of the facts on which they operate. Suppose that an image containing data that was hidden using steganography is found on a computer. An investigator would want to know whether or not there is evidence of the presence of a tool for decoding the hidden message. This rule would apply regardless of the certainty of the preconditions. Alternatively, a rule that categorizes the image based on an applied compression algorithm would also be applicable regardless of the image integrity label.

In line with the Biba model, the certainty of a fact derived by such a rule will depend on the certainty of its preconditions. In actuality, the new fact will, in general, have the lowest certainty of its preconditions. For example, suppose an image came from a removable disk that had been corrupted by a virus. Clearly the evidence source cannot be trusted completely. The Casey scale states that the certainty of a fact can increase if it is supported by independent sources. Consider the requirement for the C5 level in Table 1: "Agreement of evidence from multiple, independent sources that are protected from tampering but uncertainties exist (e.g., temporal errors, data loss)." Therefore, the converse to our earlier example is that, if the image was retrieved from a secure FTP application, which is subsequently corroborated by FTP session logs in the evidence management system, then the integrity of the image and other evidence based on the image is improved. In other cases, some facts that have been well established may lead one to form a rather tentative hypothesis about other facts, in which case the certainty of the new fact will be lower than its preconditions. Consequently, there is a need for trusted upgraders and downgraders. This issue is discussed in the next section.

4.　Information Flow

The flow of information within FEMS is described using a computer intrusion scenario. Such an incident usually warrants a thorough forensic investigation.

Consider an intrusion that exploits a web browser vulnerability to compromise a computer. Assume that the intruder subsequently accesses a financial system by harvesting authentication information from the compromised computer. In this context, the forensic investigator would interrogate FEMS for configuration files, source code, executable programs (e.g., rootkits), Internet activity logs and password-protected text files. These queries would be submitted using the FEMS system interface and then brokered by the data layer connector, which parses information returned by the data layer.

Table 2. Upgrader matrix.

	C0	C1	C2	C3	C4	C5	C6
C0	C0	C0	C0	C0	C0	C1	C1
C1		C1	C1	C1	C1	C2	C2
C2			C2	C2	C2	C3	C3
C3				C3	C3	C4	C4
C4					C4	C5	C5
C5						C5	C6
C6							C6

Suppose that the intruder has modified event logs during the attack. Therefore, the Internet activity logs may have been tampered with. However if these logs had been generated and sent directly to a secure log correlation server, then the rule base might infer: *LCorrelation(Internet log, C6)*, i.e., the log-related information is tamper proof and unquestionable.

At this point, the intruder's access must be verified in the audit logs of the financial system. However, assume that the audit logs are deemed to be unreliable because they are not explicitly protected from tampering. This situation could be expressed by the fact: *FinSyst(log, C2)*. Using this fact and the inference rule: *for (LCorrelation(log, C6) ≥ FinSyst(log, C2)) update_meta-evidence*, it would be deduced by the inference engine (and sent to the meta-evidence base) that, although the financial system logs verified that the victim's credentials were used at a specific time, conclusions based on this information should not be trusted.

We are now in a position to discuss the concepts of upgraders and downgraders. An upgrader is any evidence or evidence source with an integrity label ≥ C5 (and corroborated by two or more trusted evidence sources), which is used to improve the certainty associated with facts or inferences in FEMS. In contrast, a downgrader is any evidence or evidence source with an integrity label ≤ C1. Upgraders and downgraders are influential because they cause the inference engine to modify evidence integrity labels.

The log correlation evidence source in our example is considered to be an upgrader. This is because, all else being equal, the implementation of a correlation solution is typically fortified. Therefore, as a direct consequence of the Biba model, the log correlation evidence source is allowed to upgrade the integrity label of the financial system log. Table 2 presents a sample upgrader matrix. Using the available information, the inference engine upgrades the integrity label of the financial system log to C3.

Although the financial system logs may be included within the log correlation system, they may not positively influence the integrity of other evidence in the system until their own integrity is enhanced. The investigation logbook is programmatically instructed to record all logical steps and inferences throughout this process.

5.   Conclusions

The Forensic Evidence Management System (FEMS) is an attractive solution to the problem of assessing, maintaining and reasoning about the integrity of digital evidence in networked environments. The solution uses Casey's certainty scale in conjunction with the well-known Biba integrity model. The FEMS architecture incorporates a rule base, meta-evidence base, inference engine, digital evidence base and generic knowledge base for reasoning about the integrity of evidence. It also offers a system interface for evidence input and queries, and an investigation logbook that records all investigative actions. The principal benefit of FEMS is that it provides investigators with holistic views of the forensic evidence pertaining to their cases and insights into the quality of their inferences.

References

[1] AccessData, Forensic Toolkit (FTK) (www.accessdata.com).

[2] Aprisma, Event correlation in Spectrum and other commercial products (www.aprisma.com/literature/white-papers/wp0551 .pdf), 2000.

[3] K. Burden and C. Palmer, Cyber crime – A new breed of criminal? *Computer Law and Security Report*, vol. 19(3), pp. 222–227, 2003.

[4] L. Burns, J. Hellerstein, S. Ma, C. Perng, D. Rabenhorst and D. Taylor, Towards discovery of event correlation rules, *Proceedings of the IEEE/IFIP International Symposium on Integrated Network Management*, pp. 345–359, 2001.

[5] E. Casey, Error, uncertainty and loss in digital evidence, *International Journal of Digital Evidence*, vol. 1(2), 2002.

[6] H. Doernemann, Tool-based risk management made practical, *Proceedings of the IEEE Joint Conference on Requirements Engineering*, p. 192, 2002.

[7] D. Forte, The art of log correlation: Tools and techniques for correlating events and log files, *Computer Fraud and Security*, pp. 7–11, June 2004.

[8] L. Gordon, M. Loeb, W. Lucyshyn and R. Richardson, *2006 CSI/FBI Computer Crime and Security Survey*, Computer Security Institute (i.cmpnet.com/gocsi/db_area/pdfs/fbi/FBI2006.pdf), 2006.

[9] S. Harris, *CISSP Certification*, McGraw-Hill Osborne, Emeryville, California, 2005.

[10] C. Hosmer, Proving the integrity of digital evidence with time, *International Journal of Digital Evidence*, vol. 1(1), pp. 1–7, 2002.

[11] R. Morris, Options in computer forensic tools, *Computer Fraud and Security*, pp. 8–11, November 2002.

[12] A. Muscat, A log-analysis-based intrusion detection system for the creation of a specification-based intrusion prevention system, *Proceedings of the University of Malta Annual Computer Science Research Workshop*, 2003.

[13] National Institute of Standards and Technology (NIST), National Software Reference Library (www.nsrl.nist.gov).

[14] C. Pfleeger and S. Lawrence-Pfleeger, *Security in Computing*, Prentice Hall, Upper Saddle River, New Jersey, 2003.

[15] B. Smith, Thinking about security monitoring and event correlation (www.lurhq.com/confarticle.htm).

[16] P. Stephenson, The right tools for the job, *Digital Investigation*, vol. 1(1), pp. 24–27, 2004.

[17] H. Tipton, Integrity models (www.ccert.edu.cn/education/cissp/his m/023-026.html).

[18] J. Tudor, *Information Security Architecture: An Integrated Approach to Security in the Organization*, Auerbach/CRC Press, Boca Raton, Florida, 2001.

X

FORMAL METHODS

Chapter 23

INVESTIGATING COMPUTER ATTACKS USING ATTACK TREES

Nayot Poolsapassit and Indrajit Ray

Abstract   System log files contain valuable evidence pertaining to computer attacks. However, the log files are often massive, and much of the information they contain is not relevant to the investigation. Furthermore, the files almost always have a flat structure, which limits the ability to query them. Thus, digital forensic investigators find it extremely difficult and time consuming to extract and analyze evidence of attacks from log files. This paper describes an automated attack-tree-based approach for filtering irrelevant information from system log files and conducting systematic investigations of computer attacks.

Keywords: Forensic investigation, computer attacks, attack tree, log file filtering

1.   Introduction

Following a large-scale computer attack an investigator (system administrator or law enforcement official) must make a reasoned determination of who launched the attack, when the attack occurred, and what the exact sequence of events was that led to the attack. The system log file, which contains records of all system events, is often the starting point of the investigation. However, extracting and analyzing relevant information from log files is almost always performed manually; these tasks are prone to error and often produce inconclusive results.

There are three major contributing factors. First, a standard model does not exist for log file organization. Log files are usually flat text files (Figure 1), which limits the ability to query them. Second, there is no minimum requirement for information that needs to be stored in a log file; log files are invariably massive, and most of the information they contain is not relevant to the investigation. Finally, there are no established procedures for filtering and retrieving information from log

Please use the following format when citing this chapter:

Poolsapassit, N., Ray, I., 2007, in IFIP International Federation for Information Processing, Volume 242, Advances in Digital Forensics III; eds. P. Craiger and S Shenoi; (Boston: Springer), pp. 331-343.

```
1697 05/04/1998 08:51:19 00:00:06 172.016.113.084 172.016.113.064/28  cp
2525 05/04/1998 09:12:42 00:00:01 172.016.114.158 172.016.114.128/28  nessus
2538 05/04/1998 09:13:21 00:00:07 172.016.114.159 172.016.114.128/28  nessus
2701 05/04/1998 09:16:02 02:42:20 135.013.216.191 135.013.216.10/24   mv
2731 05/04/1998 09:17:09 00:05:00 135.013.216.182 135.013.216.10/24   telnet
3014 05/04/1998 09:23:44 00:00:07 172.016.114.158 172.016.114.128/28  ftp
3028 05/04/1998 09:24:54 00:00:07 172.016.114.159 172.016.114.128/28  cp
3461 05/04/1998 09:37:14 00:00:13 172.016.114.159 172.016.114.128/28  telnet
4598 05/04/1998 10:01:51 00:00:01 196.037.075.158 196.037.075.10/24   finger
4612 05/04/1998 10:02:37 00:00:01 196.037.075.050 196.037.075.10/24   xterm
4834 05/04/1998 10:09:39 00:00:01 172.016.114.158 172.016.114.128/28  rlogin
4489 05/04/1998 10:10:22 00:00:01 195.073.151.050 195.073.151.10/24   smtp
4859 05/04/1998 10:10:33 00:00:01 195.073.151.150 195.073.151.10/24   smtp
4930 05/04/1998 10:11:36 00:00:06 172.016.114.158 172.016.114.128/28  telnet
5014 05/04/1998 10:13:55 00:00:06 172.016.114.148 172.016.114.128/28  bind
5092 05/04/1998 10:14:59 00:00:10 172.016.114.159 172.016.114.128/28  suid
5308 05/04/1998 10:21:38 00:00:01 194.027.251.021 194.027.251.021/24  smtp
5323 05/04/1998 10:23:11 00:00:01 196.037.075.158 196.037.075.5/24    ssh
5456 05/04/1998 10:28:50 00:00:01 194.027.251.021 194.027.251.021/24  ftp
5467 05/04/1998 10:29:26 00:00:01 196.037.075.158 196.037.075.10/24   sftp
5730 05/04/1998 10:36:58 00:00:03 135.008.060.182 135.008.060.10/24   ssh
7270 05/04/1998 11:09:08 00:00:02 135.008.060.182 135.008.060.10/24   mv
8098 05/04/1998 11:33:26 00:00:13 172.016.114.158 172.016.114.128/28  telnet
9057 05/04/1998 11:57:00 00:00:01 172.016.112.207 172.016.112.10/24   smtp
9113 05/04/1998 11:58:26 00:00:08 172.016.114.148 172.016.114.128/28  telnet
9352 05/04/1998 12:48:01 00:00:01 172.016.113.078 172.016.113.64/28   cp
```

Figure 1. Sample system log file.

files other than sequential backward scans starting from the most recent entry. Therefore, investigators typically rely on their experience and intuition to conduct *ad hoc* manual searches of log file entries.

To address this problem, we propose an attack-tree-based approach for filtering log files. The attack tree model captures the different ways a particular system can be attacked based on knowledge about system vulnerabilities and exploits. The filtering approach then selects the records from the log file that are relevant to the attack by matching against the attack tree. Subsequently, SQL queries may be used to extract evidence from the filtered records in an automated manner.

The next two sections present the basic attack tree model, and an augmented model that associates malicious operations with attack trees. Section 4 describes our attack-tree-based approach for filtering log files. The final section, Section 5, presents our concluding remarks.

2.   Attack Trees

Attack trees have been proposed [2, 5, 8] as a systematic method for specifying system security based on vulnerabilities. They help organize intrusion and/or misuse scenarios by (i) identifying vulnerabilities and/or weak points in a system, and (ii) analyzing the weak points and dependencies among the vulnerabilities and representing these dependencies in the form of an AND-OR tree.

An attack tree is developed for each system to be defended. The nodes of the tree represent different stages (milestones) of an attack. The root node represents the attacker's ultimate goal, which is usually to cause damage to the system. The interior nodes, including leaf nodes, represent possible system states during the execution of an attack. System states may include the level of compromise (e.g., access to a web page or acquisition of root privileges), alterations to the system configuration (e.g., modification of trust or access control, or escalation of privileges), state changes to specific system components (e.g., placement of a Trojan horse), or other subgoals that lead to the final goal (e.g., the sequence of exploited vulnerabilities). The branches of an attack tree represent change of states caused by one or more actions taken by the attacker.

Changes in state are represented as AND-branches or OR-branches in an attack tree. Each node in an attack tree may be decomposed as:

- A set of events (exploits), all of which must be achieved for the subgoal represented by the node to succeed. These events are combined by an AND branch at the node. An example is a root account compromise, which involves changing the file mode of /proc/self/ files and executing the suid command (CVE-2006-3626).

- A set of events (exploits), any one of which will cause the subgoal represented by the node to succeed. These events are combined by an OR branch at the node. An example is a root compromise resulting from a stack buffer overflow that exploits the libtiff library in SUSE v10.0 (CVE-2006-3459) or the SQL injection in Bugzilla v2.16.3 (CVE-2003-1043).

Attack trees are closely related to attack graphs used for vulnerability analysis [1, 3, 4, 6, 9, 10]. The difference lies in the representation of states and actions. Attack graphs model system vulnerabilities in terms of all possible sequences of attack operations. Ritchey and Ammann [7] have observed that scalability is a major shortcoming of this approach. In contrast, attack trees model system vulnerabilities in terms of cause and effect, and the sequential ordering of events does not have to be captured in an attack tree. Therefore, it is much simpler to construct an attack tree than an attack graph. One criticism of attack trees (vis-a-vis attack graphs) is that they cannot model cycles. However, we believe that this criticism is valid only when attack trees are used to represent sequences of operations leading to attacks, not when they are used to represent the dependencies of states that are reached. Another criticism is that attack trees tend to get unwieldy when modeling complex attack scenarios, but the same is true for attack graphs.

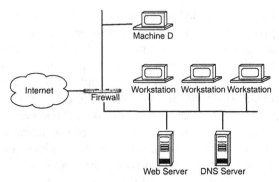

Figure 2.   Corporate network configuration.

Figure 2 presents the network configuration of a hypothetical company. We use this network configuration to demonstrate how an attack tree is used to represent system vulnerabilities.

The company has installed a firewall to protect its network from the Internet. The company's web server is located in the de-militarized zone (DMZ). Other machines are on the local area network behind the firewall. The company's system administrator has configured the firewall to block port scans and flooding attacks. The firewall allows incoming connections only via port 25 (smtp) and port 80 (http).

Assume that a disgruntled employee, John Doe, plans to attack the company's network. He performs a vulnerability scan of network and determines that he needs to obtain root privileges on the web server to achieve his objective.

John Doe discovers that there are two alternative ways for gaining root privileges – his ultimate goal. One is by launching the FTP/.rhost attack. In this attack, the .rhost file on the web server is overwritten by a .rhost file of John Doe's choosing (say the .rhost file on his own machine) by exploiting a known vulnerability. This exploit causes the web server to trust John Doe's machine, enabling John Doe to remotely login on the server from his machine without providing a password. Having gained access to the web server, John Doe conducts the well-known setuid buffer overflow attack and obtains root privileges.

The second way to attack the web server is via a buffer overflow attack on the local DNS server. John Doe knows that the system administrator uses an old unpatched version of the BIND DNS application program. This enables him to perform the BIND buffer overflow attack on the local DNS server to take control of the machine. Next, he installs a network sniffer on the DNS server to observe sessions across the network.

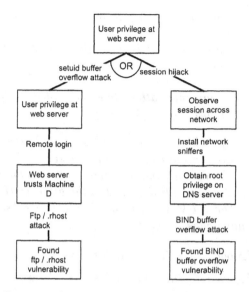

Figure 3. Attack tree for the corporate network.

Eventually, he hijacks the system administrator's `telnet` session to the web server and gains root privileges.

The two attacks are concisely represented in the simple attack tree in Figure 3. In general, an attack tree can be created to capture all the ways a system can be breached (clearly, it would not represent unknown or zero-day attacks). Such an attack tree can greatly simplify log file analysis: it is necessary to search the log file only for those operations that lie in the paths leading to the attack. For example, with reference to the attack tree in Figure 3, if an investigator knows that the root account at the web server was compromised, he needs to examine the log file only for the sequences of operations in the left and right branches of the attack tree. These operations must be in the same temporal order as the nodes going down the tree; any other order is not relevant to the attack. In fact, if the attack-tree-based log file analysis approach does not manifest a sequence of events leading to a specific attack, the attack in question is an unknown or zero-day attack.

3.   Augmented Attack Trees

To facilitate the use of attack trees in forensic investigations, we define an "augmented attack tree," which extends the basic attack tree by associating each branch of the tree with a sequence of malicious operations that could have contributed to the attack.

DEFINITION 1 *An atomic event is an ordered pair* ⟨*operation, target*⟩.

DEFINITION 2 *An atomic event is an incident if its execution contributes to a system compromise.*

DEFINITION 3 *An augmented attack tree is a rooted labeled tree given by* $AAT = (V, E, \epsilon, Label, SIG_{u,v})$, *where*

1. *V is the set of nodes in the tree representing different states of partial compromise or subgoals that an attacker needs to move through in order to fully compromise a system.* $\mathcal{V} \in V$ *is the root node of the tree representing the ultimate goal of the attacker (full system compromise). The set V is partitioned into two subsets, leaf_nodes and internal_nodes, such that*

   (i) *leaf_nodes* $\cup$ *internal_nodes* $= V$,

   (ii) *leaf_nodes* $\cap$ *internal_nodes* $= \phi$, *and*

   (iii) $\mathcal{V} \in$ *internal_nodes*

2. $E \subseteq V \times V$ *constitutes the set of edges in the attack tree. An edge* $(u, v) \in E$ *defines an "atomic attack" and represents the state transition from a child node v to a parent node u* $(u, v \in V)$. *An atomic attack is a sequence of incidents. The edge* (u, v) *is said to be "emergent from" v and "incident to" u.*

3. ϵ *is a set of tuples of the form* ⟨*v, decomposition*⟩ *such that*

   (i) $v \in$ *internal_nodes and*

   (ii) *decomposition* $\in$ [*AND-decomposition, OR-decomposition*]

4. *Label is the name of the exploit associated with each edge*

5. $SIG_{u,v}$ *is an attack signature (defined below).*

DEFINITION 4 *An incident-choice is a group of related incidents, the occurrence of any one of which can contribute to a state transition in the attack tree.*

DEFINITION 5 *An attack signature* $SIG_{u,v}$ *is a sequence of incident-choices* ⟨*incident-choice$_1$, incident-choice$_2$, ..., incident-choice$_n$*⟩ *for which the sequence* (*incident$_{i,1}$, incident$_{j,2}$, ..., incident$_{m,n}$*) *constitutes an atomic attack.*

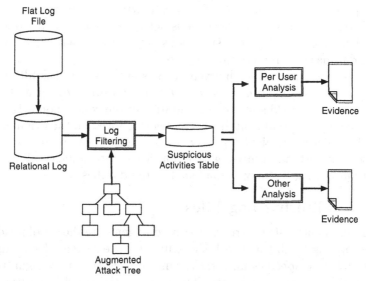

Figure 4. Log file investigation process.

The attack signature corresponding to the attack discussed in Bugtraq:3446 (CVE-1999-1562) – involving the execution of wuftp on a target machine (say A) and resulting in a cleartext password disclosure – is represented by:

```
((ftp, A),(debug, A),(open localhost, A), ("user name root", A),
    ("password xxx", A), (quote user root, A),(quote pass root, A))
```

DEFINITION 6 *A node* $v \in$ *internal_nodes is an* AND-decomposition *if all the edges incident to the node are connected by the AND operation, or there is exactly one edge incident to the node.*

DEFINITION 7 *A node* $v \in$ *internal_nodes is an* OR-decomposition *if all the edges incident to the node are connected by the OR operation.*

For an AND-decomposition node v, every subgoal of v represented by a child of v must be reached in order to reach v. For an OR-decomposition, the goal v is reached if any one of the subgoals is reached. Note that reaching a child goal is a necessary, but not sufficient, condition for reaching the parent goal.

4. Conducting a Forensic Investigation

Figure 4 shows how an augmented attack tree may be used to support a forensic investigation. First, the augmented attack tree is used to prepare the set of incidents for all the attack signatures. Next, the attack tree is used to filter suspicious activities (operations) from non-suspicious ones. Finally, the suspicious activities are written to a relational database for further investigation.

A database structure with seven fields is used to store the filtered log file: *id, time stamp, source, source-group, operation, target* and *duration*. The *source* field stores the IP address of the connection originator. The *source-group* field contains the network address of the originator, if available. The *target* field similarly stores the destination address of the network connection. If investigative policies dictate, additional information from the log file may be included in the database.

4.1   Filtering Log Files

The augmented attack tree is first used to generate the set of incidents corresponding to all the attack signatures for the system. Each edge in the attack tree specifies an attack signature. Each attack signature is a collection of several incidents. The union of these incidents covers all the activities that can result in system compromise. The attack being investigated must have resulted from some incidents from this set of incidents. The set of incidents is then used to filter suspicious activities from normal activities.

The log file filtering algorithm (Algorithm 1) sequentially executes SQL queries to extract suspicious activities from the original log file. The results are written to a separate table called the Suspicious-Activities-Table for further investigation. This table has the same schema as the log file, but is significantly smaller.

The algorithm starts at the root node of the attack tree. It traverses every edge incident to the root node. For each edge, the algorithm extracts the attack signature $SIG_{u,v}$ given by the label of the edge. As mentioned earlier, the attack signature is the sequence of steps where an attacker may or may not have a choice of incidents (operation on a particular machine/target) to execute. For each step in the attack signature, the algorithm searches the log file for matching operations. An incident in the table matches the signature if the operation is executed on the particular machine or against the particular target as indicated in the attack signature. Note that only matched incidents that were executed prior to the time that the root node was compromised are suspected. Next, the suspected incidents are recorded into the Suspicious-Activities-Table by the selection procedure.

After the algorithm finishes exploring a particular edge e[u,v], it sets a time threshold for node v by selecting from the earliest incidents in e[u,v].

Algorithm 1 (Log File Filtering)

{**Description:** This algorithm traverses an augmented attack tree in a depth-first manner starting at the root. It examines all the edges under the current node u for suspicious incidents. If any suspicious activity is seen in the log file, it extracts the activity record and stores it in a separate file. When all the nodes have been visited, the algorithm returns the suspicious activity records as potential evidence.}

{**Input:** node u (initial from root), database table System-Log-File-Table}

{**Output:** database table Suspicious-Activities-Table}

BEGIN

if u is a leaf node **then**

    return

else

  for all $v \in Adj[u]$ **do**

    $SIG_{u,v} \leftarrow get\_SIGNATURE(e[u,v])$

    for all $\{incidents\}_i \in SIG_{u,v}$ **do**

      $Record_i \leftarrow SQL\{SELECT$ *id, timestamp, source, source-group,*

                    operation, target, duration $FROM$ System-Log-File-Table

                          $WHERE$ *operation, target* $Like$ $\{incidents\}_i$

                                AND $timestamp < u.timestamp;\}$

      if $Record_i \neq \{ \}$ **then**

        Insert $Record_i$ into Suspicious-Activities-Table

      end if

    end for

    Set $v.timestamp$ = earliest timestamp of all $Record_i$ from the previous loop

    Recursively call Investigate(v, System-Log-File-Table)

    Mark e[u,v] if all $Record_i$ are not empty AND node v is previously compromised in Investigate(v)

  end for

  if node u has an AND-Decomposition AND all edges e[u,v] incident to u are fully marked **then**

    Mark node u as "Compromised"

  end if

  if node u has an OR-Decomposition AND there exists an e[u,v] incident to u already marked **then**

    Mark node u as "Compromised"

  end if

end if

END

This threshold is assumed to be the time when node v was compromised. Therefore, there is no need to suspect any incident in the subtree(s) under v that executed after this time. Next, the algorithm recursively calls itself to investigate the subtree under v from which the edge e[u,v] emerged. All the subtrees under the node are explored recursively. After all the subtrees under the root node or any intermediate node u have been explored, the algorithm marks an edge e[u,v] if it finds evidence that shows that all the steps in the attack signature $SIG_{u,v}$ have been executed. If node u has an AND-decomposition, node u is considered compromised when all exploits (represented by edge e[u,v]) incident to u together with the state v from where the exploit emerged are marked. If node u has an OR-decomposition, node u is compromised when any one of its branches together with the state v are marked. Upon completion, the algorithm returns the augmented attack tree (with certain nodes marked as compromised) and the Suspicious-Activities-Table.

4.2   Identifying Likely Attack Sources

The next step is to process the Suspicious-Activities-Table produced by the log file filtering algorithm for candidate sources of the attack. This is accomplished by sorting the table entries by source aggregated by source-group to produce the list of candidate sources. Further investigation of this list can be performed on a per source basis either to reinforce or discard specific sources.

Algorithm 2 implements this task. The output of the algorithm is a table named Evidence-Log(source) where "source" is the identity of the source being investigated. This table has almost the same schema as the Suspicious-Activities-Table; the only difference is that it has an extra column called *exploit*. This field holds the exploit label corresponding to a relevant edge of the attack tree. If the algorithm returns a non-empty table, it supports the suspicion of the suspected source. On the other hand, if the algorithm returns an empty table, no decision can be made about the involvement of the suspected source. This is because of the possibility of zero-day attacks. Therefore, the algorithm should be used very carefully – it only provides evidence of activities that were possibly involved in an attack.

Algorithm 2 is similar to the log file filtering algorithm. The difference is that SQL queries are executed on a per source basis for sources in the Suspicious-Activities-Table. The algorithm marks the suspected records with the corresponding exploit labels. An investigator may use these labels to map the evidence back to exploits in the attack tree.

The Evidence-Log(source) Table holds the activities that are believed to be responsible for an attack on the system. The records are stored in chronological order. Typically, if an internal node is marked by the algorithm, it is almost certain that the suspected activity is responsible for the attack.

5.   Conclusions

This paper has two main contributions. The first is an attack-tree-based filtering algorithm that eliminates information from a log file that

Algorithm 2 (Likely Attack Source Identification)

{**Description:** This algorithm takes an augmented attack tree and the Suspicious-Activities-Table generated by Algorithm 1 and filters the table based on a suspected source of attack. The algorithm traverses the augmented attack tree in a depth-first manner starting at the root. It examines all the edges under the current node u for suspicious incidents corresponding to the specific source. If any suspicious activity is seen in the log file, it extracts the activity record and stores it in a separate file. When all the nodes have been visited, the algorithm returns the set of suspicious activities for a specific source.}

{**Input:** node u (initial from root), specific-source, database table Suspicious-Activities-Table}

{**Output:** database table Evidence-Log(specific-source)}

BEGIN

if u is a leaf node **then**

    return

else

  for all $v \in Adj[u]$ **do**

    Sequence $SIG_{u,v} \leftarrow get\_SIGNATURE(e[u,v])$

    for all $\{incidents\}_i \in SIG_{u,v}$ **do**

      $Record_i \leftarrow SQL\{SELECT\ id,\ timestamp,\ source,\ source\text{-}group,$
               $operation,\ target,\ duration\ FROM\ \text{Suspicious-Activities-Table}$
                     $WHERE\ source = specific - source\ AND$
                     $operation, target\ Like\ \{incidents\}_i$
                     $AND\ timestamp < u.timestamp; \}$

      if $Record_i \neq \{\ \}$ **then**

        Insert $Record_i$ in Evidence-Log(specific-source)

        Mark $Record_i$ in Evidence-Log(specific-source) with the exploit label from the edge e[u,v]

      end if

    end for

    Set $v.timestamp =$ the earliest timestamp of all $Record_i$ from the previous loop

    Recursively call Investigate(v, specific-source, Suspicious-Activities-Table)

    Mark e[u,v] if all $Record_i$ are not empty AND node v is previously compromised in Investigate(v)

  end for

  if node u has an AND-Decomposition AND all edges e[u,v] incident to u are fully marked **then**

    Mark node u as "Compromised"

  end if

  if node u has an OR-Decomposition AND there exists edge e[u,v] incident to u already marked **then**

    Mark node u as "Compromised"

  end if

end if

END

is not related to the attack being investigated. The second is an additional filtering algorithm that extracts evidence corresponding to a particular source's role in an attack. Both the algorithms produce relational tables that are significantly smaller than the original log file and are, therefore, more manageable from an investigator's point of view. Furthermore, since the tables are relational in nature, they can be used as input to a database engine for rapid processing of evidence.

The approach is limited by its inability to handle unknown or zero-day attacks. This is because it assumes that knowledge exists about how system vulnerabilities can be exploited; this knowledge is, of course, not available for unknown or zero-day attacks. If such attacks are suspected, it is important not to discard the original log file as it may be needed for a future investigation. Another limitation arises from the assumption that the log file records all network events, whereas in reality individual machines maintain their own logs. The approach also assumes that the log file contains accurate information, i.e., the attacker has not tampered with the entries. Our research is currently investigating these issues with the goal of improving the attack-tree-based log file filtering algorithms.

References

[1] P. Ammann, D. Wijesekera and S. Kaushik, Scalable, graph-based network vulnerability analysis, *Proceedings of the Ninth ACM Conference on Computer and Communications Security*, pp. 217–224, 2002.

[2] J. Dawkins, C. Campbell and J. Hale, Modeling network attacks: Extending the attack tree paradigm, *Proceedings of the Workshop on Statistical Machine Learning Techniques in Computer Intrusion Detection*, 2002.

[3] S. Jha, O. Sheyner and J. Wing, Minimization and reliability analysis of attack graphs, Technical Report CMU-CS-02-109, School of Computer Science, Carnegie Mellon University, Pittsburgh, Pennsylvania, 2002.

[4] S. Jha, O. Sheyner and J. Wing, Two formal analyses of attack graphs, *Proceedings of the Computer Security Foundations Workshop*, pp. 45–59, 2002.

[5] A. Moore, R. Ellison and R. Linger, Attack modeling for information survivability, Technical Note CMU/SEI-2001-TN-001, Software Engineering Institute, Carnegie Mellon University, Pittsburgh, Pennsylvania, 2001.

[6] C. Phillips and L. Swiler, A graph-based system for network vulnerability analysis, *Proceedings of the New Security Paradigms Workshop*, pp. 71–79, 1998.

[7] R. Ritchey and P. Ammann, Using model checking to analyze network vulnerabilities, *Proceedings of the IEEE Symposium on Security and Privacy*, pp. 156–165, 2000.

[8] B. Schneier, Attack trees: Modeling security threats, *Dr. Dobb's Journal*, December 1999.

[9] O. Sheyner, J. Haines, S. Jha, R. Lippmann and J. Wing, Automated generation and analysis of attack graphs, *Proceedings of the IEEE Symposium on Security and Privacy*, pp. 273–284, 2002.

[10] L. Swiler, C. Phillips, D. Ellis and S. Chakerian, Computer-attack graph generation tool, *Proceedings of the DARPA Information Survivability Conference and Exposition*, vol. 2, pp. 307–321, 2001.

Chapter 24

ATTACK PATTERNS: A NEW FORENSIC AND DESIGN TOOL

Eduardo Fernandez, Juan Pelaez and Maria Larrondo-Petrie

Abstract   A pattern is an encapsulated solution to a problem in a given context that can be used to guide system design and evaluation. Analysis, design and architectural patterns are established formalisms for designing high quality software. Security patterns guide the secure design of systems by providing generic solutions that prevent a variety of attacks. This paper presents an attack pattern, a new type of pattern that is specified from the point of view of an attacker. The pattern describes how an attack is performed, enumerates the security patterns that can be applied to defeat the attack, and describes how to trace the attack once it has occurred. An example involving DoS attacks on VoIP networks is used to demonstrate the value of the formalism to security designers and forensic investigators.

Keywords: Attack patterns, forensics, secure systems design, VoIP networks

1.   Introduction

Many problems occur in similar ways in different contexts or environments. Generic solutions to these problems can be expressed as patterns. A pattern is an encapsulated solution to a problem in a given context that can be used to guide system design and evaluation [10]. Analysis, design and architectural patterns are established formalisms for designing high quality software. Another type of pattern, the antipattern, focuses on design pitfalls [13]. Security patterns, on the other hand, guide the secure design of systems by providing generic solutions that prevent a variety of attacks [9, 18]. However, it is not clear to an inexperienced designer which pattern should be applied to stop a specific attack. Likewise, the patterns have limited forensic applications because they do not emphasize the *modus operandi* of attacks.

Please use the following format when citing this chapter:

Fernandez, E., Pelaez, J., Larrondo-Petrie, M., 2007, in IFIP International Federation for Information Processing, Volume 242, Advances in Digital Forensics III; eds. P. Craiger and S Shenoi; (Boston: Springer), pp. 345-357.

In order to design a secure system or investigate a security breach it is important to understand the possible threats to the system. We have proposed a systematic approach to threat identification involving the analysis of the use cases of a system [9]. This method identifies high-level threats such as "the customer can be an impostor," but once a system is designed, it is necessary to analyze how the various system components could be exploited in an attack.

This paper presents an attack pattern, a new type of pattern, which draws on our previous research on security patterns and threat identification. An attack pattern is specified from the point of view of an attacker. It describes how an attack is performed, enumerates the security patterns that can be applied to defeat the attack, and describes how to trace the attack once it has occurred (including specifying the types of evidence and the locations where the evidence may be found). An example involving DoS attacks on VoIP networks is used to demonstrate the value of the formalism to security designers and forensic investigators.

2.   Attack Patterns

An attack pattern is presented from the point of view of an attacker. It specifies a generic way of performing an attack that takes advantage of specific vulnerabilities in a certain environment. The pattern also presents a way to counteract the development of the attack in the form of security patterns and to analyze the information collected at each stage of the attack.

This section presents a template for an attack pattern [2], which has been used for architectural patterns (design) and security patterns (defense) [18]. However, certain sections of the template have been modified to fit the new attacker's viewpoint. The sections of the attack pattern template are described below.

- **Name:** Specifies the generic name given to the attack in a standard attack repository (e.g., CERT [4] or Symantec [21]).

- **Intent:** A short description of the intended purpose of the attack.

- **Context:** A description of the general environment, including the conditions under which the attack occurs. This may include system defenses as well as system vulnerabilities.

- **Problem:** Defines the goal of the attack pattern, which (from the attacker's point of view) is the "problem" of attacking the system. An additional problem occurs when a system is protected by certain defensive mechanisms and these mechanisms have to be overcome. The forces (a term used in pattern writing) are the factors that may be required to accomplish the attack, the vulnerabilities to be exploited, and the factors that may obstruct or delay the attack.

- **Solution:** Describes the solution to the attacker's problem: How the attack is performed and its expected results. UML class diagrams may be used to describe the system before and during the attack. Sequence diagrams could be used to display the messages exchanged during the attack. State or activity diagrams may be used to provide additional detail.

- **Known Uses:** Specific incidents that are involved in the attack. Details of previous attacks are useful in deciding how to stop the attack and where to look for evidence.

- **Consequences:** Describes the benefits and drawbacks of the attack from the attacker's viewpoint. In particular, whether the effort and cost of the attack are commensurate with the results obtained, and the possible sources of failure.

- **Countermeasures and Forensics:** This new section of the template is required for attack patterns. It describes the measures taken to stop, mitigate and trace the attack. This implies an enumeration of the security patterns that are effective against the attack. From a forensic viewpoint, this section of the template describes the information can be obtained at each stage when tracing the attack and the information that can be deduced to identify the specific attack. Also, it may indicate the additional information that should be collected to support a forensic investigation.

- **Evidence Locations:** This section may include a diagram with selected UML classes and associations relevant to a forensic investigation. UML class diagrams are useful because of their abstraction properties. The attack pattern is not a comprehensive representation of all the classes (network components) and associations involved in an attack. Rather, the pattern should represent the classes that are relevant to the investigation. When primary sources (e.g., firewalls and IDSs) do not contain enough evidence, investigators must examine secondary sources such as terminal devices (including wireless devices), servers and network storage devices.

- **Related Patterns:** This section of the template includes patterns of other attacks with different objectives that are performed in a similar way or attacks with similar objectives that are performed in a different way.

3.   VoIP Denial-of-Service Attack

This section presents an attack pattern that describes a denial-of-service (DoS) attack against a VoIP network.

- **Intent:** The VoIP DoS attack is intended to overwhelm the client's and/or server's resources and disrupt VoIP operations by producing a flood of messages or by degrading the quality of messages, preventing subscribers from using the service effectively.

- **Context:** VoIP services should be available to subscribers trying to establish voice conversations over VoIP channels. The VoIP network should have adequate capabilities (routing, bandwidth and QoS) to meet peak communication loads. Some VoIP systems use control protocols (e.g., MGCP and Megaco/H.248) and security mechanisms (e.g., access control and firewalls) to manage the media gateways deployed across the infrastructure. More secure VoIP implementations may employ intrusion detection systems, firewalls on phones and authentication facilities.

- **Problem:** The problem from the point of view of an attacker is to conduct a DoS attack against VoIP services. The attack can be carried out by exploiting the following vulnerabilities:

    - VoIP security is in a relatively immature state; security expertise and standards are lacking. Users might inadvertently expose the system. While basic countermeasures such as IDSs and firewalls are available, administrators may not configure them correctly.

    - VoIP networks have been designed and deployed with an emphasis on functionality rather than security [23]. Advanced defenses (e.g., strong authentication mechanisms) are rarely employed.

    - VoIP is vulnerable to DoS attacks that are not an issue in the circuit-switched public telephone system.

    - With the rush to implement new VoIP systems, features and standards, implementation flaws are common. Moreover, IP-PBXs include many layers of software that may contain vulnerabilities. Programming errors (e.g., not checking the size of the parameters in a protocol request) can be exploited in several ways:

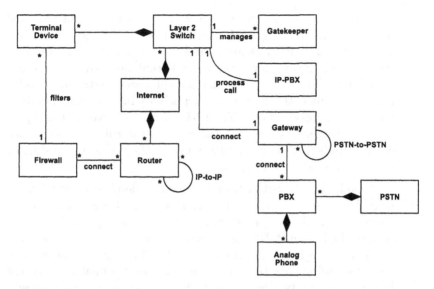

Figure 1. Class diagram for the H.323 architecture.

* Remote Access: An attacker can obtain remote (possibly administrator level) access.

* Malformed Request DoS: A carefully-crafted protocol request (packet) could result in a partial or complete loss of functionality.

* Load-Based DoS: A flood of legitimate requests could overwhelm the system [5].

- As with any network-based service, enterprise VoIP must communicate with other components on a LAN and possibly over an untrusted network such as the Internet, where packets are easy to intercept.

- Because RTP carries media, which must be delivered in real-time for acceptable conversations, VoIP is vulnerable to DoS attacks that impact voice quality (e.g., jitter and delay).

- VoIP tools offer good cover traffic for DoS attacks because VoIP networks run continuous media over IP packets [22].

■ **Solution:** H.322 and SIP are the primary protocols used in VoIP systems. In this paper, we consider an attack on the H.323 protocol. A SIP attack (see, e.g., [1]) can be considered to be a variant of the H.323 attack pattern or a separate pattern.

Figure 1 shows the class diagram of the structure of an H.323 system. The Layer 2 switch provides connectivity between H.323 components. The gateway takes a voice call from the circuit-switched public telephone network (PSTN) and places it on the IP network. The PSTN uses PBX switches and analog phones. The Internet (IP network) has routers and firewalls that filter traffic to terminal devices. The gateway queries the gatekeeper with caller/callee numbers, which the gatekeeper translates into routing numbers based on the service logic. The IP-PBX server serves as a call processing manager, setting up and routing the calls to other voice devices. Softphones are applications installed in terminal devices (e.g., PCs or wireless devices).

One method to launch a DoS attack is to flood a server with repeated requests for service. This causes severe degradation or complete unavailability of the voice service. A flooding attack can also be launched against IP phones and gateways by sending a large number of "register" or "invite" events. The target system is so busy processing packets from the attack that it is unable to process legitimate requests, which are either ignored or processed so slowly that the VoIP service is unusable. The TCP SYN flood attack (or resource starvation attack) can be used to obtain similar results. This attack floods the port with synchronization packets that are normally used to create new connections.

A distributed DoS (DDoS) attack uses multiple systems to produce a flood of packets. Typically, the attacker installs malicious software (Trojans) on compromised terminal devices known as "zombies," which are directed to send fake traffic to targeted VoIP components. Targeted DoS attacks are also possible when the attacker disrupts specific connections.

Figure 2 shows the class diagram for DoS attacks in an H.323 network, in which any VoIP component can be a target. Note that the classes "Attack Control Mechanism" and "Zombie" denote the malicious software introduced by the attacker.

Figure 3 shows the sequence of steps necessary to launch a server flood attack. An attacker (internal or remote) generates call requests using a valid user name on a VoIP system to overwhelm the IP-PBX. The attacker may disrupt a subscriber's call attempt by sending specially crafted messages to the ISP server or IP-PBX, causing the device to over allocate resources so that the caller receives a "service not available" (busy tone) message. This is an example of a targeted attack.

Out-of-sequence voice packets (e.g., media packets received before a session is accepted) or a very large phone number could open the

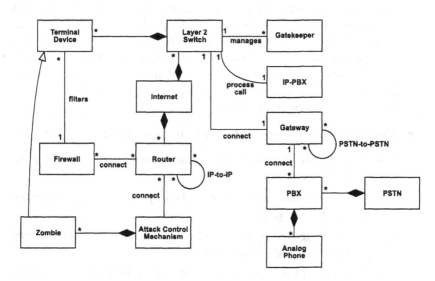

Figure 2. Class diagram for DoS attacks in a H.323 network.

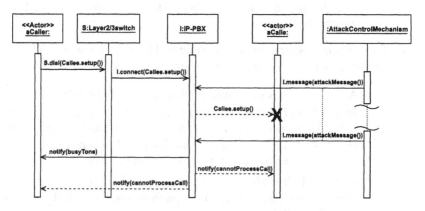

Figure 3. Sequence diagram for a DoS attack in a H.323 network.

way to application layer attacks (a.k.a. attacks against network services). Buffer overflow attacks can paralyze a VoIP number using repeated calling. For example, an attacker could intermittently send garbage (e.g., the header and the payload are filled with random bytes that corrupt the callee's jitter buffer voice packets) to the callee's phone in between those of the caller's voice packets. This causes the callee's phone to so busy trying to process the increased packet flow that the jitter (delay variation) causes the conversation to be incomprehensible [1].

- **Consequences:** The consequences of a successful attack include:

  - A DoS attack renders key voice resources (e.g., media gateways) inoperable.

  - Flooding a firewall prevents it from properly managing ports for legitimate calls.

  - QoS is degraded by jitter and delay, causing the VoIP network to become totally unusable.

  - Zombies in the targeted network launch DoS attacks on other networks.

  Attacks may fail for several reasons:

  - Attacks can be defined in theory, but are difficult to carry out in practice. The main reasons are lack of knowledge, testing opportunities and entry points for attackers.

  - Countermeasures may be able to defeat the attack or mitigate its effects.

- **Countermeasures and Forensics:** The attack can be defeated or mitigated by the following countermeasures:

  - A DoS attack is mitigated by disabling and removing unnecessary network services, reinforcing the operating system, and using host-based intrusion detection systems (see [6] for an IDS pattern). This makes it harder for attackers to introduce Trojan horses to compromise terminal devices.

  - IDSs and firewalls ensure that packets with very large sequence numbers and garbage packets are discarded (see [18] for a firewall pattern).

  - Stateful firewalls (see [18] for a pattern) with deep packet inspection technology can be used to analyze voice packet headers and contents to ensure that they are safe.

- The authenticated call feature (see [8] for a pattern), which performs device and user authentication prior to permitting access to VoIP services, can be used to protect against targeted attacks.

Several network forensic mechanisms may be employed:

- Terminal device logs not only provide call details (e.g., start and end times of calls), but also reveal the presence of Trojans.

- Router logs and firewall logs provide information on how the attacker entered the network and how the exploits were performed.

- Certain attacks selectively send events to the ISP or IP-PBX; these attacks can be traced by examining logs on these devices.

- Network forensic analysis techniques such as IP traceback and packet marking can be used for attack attribution. During a DoS attack, the target system receives enough traceback packets to reconstruct the attack path [19]. Locating attackers with the IP traceback technology is also a potential security mechanism to counter DoS attacks. Effective traceback requires the cooperation of all network operators along the attack path.

- Comparing traffic patterns against predefined thresholds (as is done by some IDSs) is an effective method for detecting DDoS attacks. It also helps detect malicious traffic (e.g., observing congestion in a router's buffer) before it enters or leaves a network.

- Event logging enables network administrators to collect important information (e.g., date, time and result of each action) during the setup and execution of an attack. For example, logs may identify the type of DDoS attack used against a target.

- Positioning honeypots and other network forensic appliances on selected VoIP components can help in the event of a successful attack.

- In a VoIP network, the attack pattern technique may be complemented with a network forensics analysis tool to offer a better view (interpretation) of the collected voice packets.

- **Evidence Locations:** Based on Figure 2, secondary sources of forensic information in VoIP networks include terminal devices (softphones, hardphones and wireless VoIP phones), gatekeepers, gateways and IP-PBXs.

- **Related Patterns:** Security patterns for defending against these and related attacks are presented in [1, 8, 17]. Some general security patterns such as firewalls [18], IDSs [6] and authentication [18] can be used to control attacks. An attack pattern can be developed to describe similar attacks on SIP networks.

4.   Discussion

Attack patterns can guide forensic investigators in the search for evidence. They also serve as a structured method for obtaining and representing relevant network forensic information. Investigators often find it difficult to determine which data should be collected. Data collection often involves identifying all the components involved in the investigation, deciding which are most likely to be of interest, finding the location of the components, and collecting data from each component [12].

Attack patterns are useful when attackers break into VoIP network segments that are not monitored by security devices. Therefore, investigators should look for evidence in secondary data sources such as terminal devices. Attack patterns also enable investigators to ensure that they have considered all possible contexts and evidence sources by referring to the appropriate attack templates.

Much of the value of the attack pattern formalism comes from the fact that an attack, which is described dynamically in a sequence diagram, makes direct reference to the system components, which are described by a class diagram. The sequence diagram uses objects from classes in the class diagram; thus, messages can be related to the components where they are sent (classes represent the system components). The parameters of the messages are data that can be found in the corresponding components. In other words, the combination of sequence and class diagrams provide guidance to forensic investigators on what evidence can be found after an attack and where to look for the evidence.

Other approaches for describing attacks and their effects include fault trees and attack trees [14]. A fault tree uses combinations of AND and OR nodes to specify the conditions under which a system will fail. An attack tree specializes the notion of a fault tree by specifying the conditions for an attack to succeed. Probabilities of occurrence may be assigned to conditions or events in a fault tree or attack tree. However, these probabilities are difficult to estimate and require detailed system descriptions, which renders the approach impractical for generic analyses and for systems that have not yet been constructed. Consequently, attack trees are mostly used to determine the risk of attacks and the associated costs.

Another tool is an attack net, which is a Petri net whose places represent attack steps and transitions represent events that activate steps [15]. Attack nets have been used in a web-based system to collect expert knowledge about attacks [20]. An attack net can represent the dynamics of an attack very effectively, but it does not take system components into account, which limits its forensic applications. The Analyst's Notebook, a product based on attack nets, is useful for tracing the propagation of attacks in computer networks [3]. However, it works at the hardware component level and cannot abstract similar types of components, which leads to a proliferation of units that must be considered.

Hoglund and McGraw [11] also use the term "attack pattern." Their attack pattern is simply a description of a step in a generic attack, e.g., string format overflow in `syslog()`. Moreover, they do not provide a systematic discussion of patterns and do not consider any forensic aspects. Moore and colleagues [16] also use the term; their attack pattern describes the goal of an attack, attack steps, preconditions and postconditions. In fact, their attack pattern is essentially one step in our attack pattern. Anwar and co-workers [1] use the term "design patterns," which are really security patterns, but they do not consider system components and forensic aspects.

5. Conclusions

An attack pattern provides a systematic description of the attack objectives and attack steps along with strategies for defending against and tracing the attack. The attack pattern template presented in this paper is intended to document and organize generic attack patterns. The example involving DoS attacks on VoIP networks demonstrates the value of the formalism to security designers and forensic investigators. We are currently constructing a catalog of attack patterns for VoIP networks, including wireless implementations. We are also using the formalism as the basis for an integrated methodology for building secure systems.

Acknowledgements

This research was supported by a grant from the U.S. Department of Defense administered by Pragmatics, Inc., McLean, Virginia.

References

[1] Z. Anwar, W. Yurcik, R. Johnson, M. Hafiz and R. Campbell, Multiple design patterns for VoIP security, *Proceedings of the Twenty-Fifth IEEE Conference on Performance, Computing and Communications*, 2006.

[2] F. Buschmann, R. Meunier, H. Rohnert, P. Sommerlad and M. Stal, *Pattern-Oriented Software Architecture: A System of Patterns, Volume 1*, Wiley, Chichester, United Kingdom, 1996.

[3] E. Casey, Investigating sophisticated security breaches, *Communications of the ACM*, vol. 43(2), 48–54, 2006.

[4] CERT Coordination Center, Carnegie Mellon University, Pittsburgh, Pennsylvania (www.cert.org).

[5] M. Collier, The value of VoIP security (www.cconvergence.com /showArticle.jhtml?articleID=22103933), 2004.

[6] E. Fernandez and A. Kumar, A security pattern for rule-based intrusion detection, *Proceedings of the Nordic Conference on Pattern Languages of Programs*, 2005.

[7] E. Fernandez, M. Larrondo-Petrie, T. Sorgente and M. VanHilst, A methodology to develop secure systems using patterns, in *Integrating Security and Software Engineering: Advances and Future Vision*, H. Mouratidis and P. Giorgini (Eds.), IGI Publishing, Hershey, Pennsylvania, pp. 107–126, 2006.

[8] E. Fernandez and J. Pelaez, Security patterns for voice over IP networks, *Proceedings of the International Multiconference on Computing in the Global Information Technology*, p. 33, 2007.

[9] E. Fernandez, M. VanHilst, M. Larrondo-Petrie and S. Huang, Defining security requirements through misuse actions, in *Advanced Software Engineering: Expanding the Frontiers of Software Technology*, S. Ochoa and G. Roman (Eds.), Springer, New York, 123–137, 2006.

[10] E. Gamma, R. Helm, R. Johnson and J. Vlissides, *Design Patterns: Elements of Reusable Object-Oriented Software*, Addison-Wesley/Pearson, Boston, Massachusetts, 1994.

[11] G. Hoglund and G. McGraw, *Exploiting Software: How to Break Code*, Addison-Wesley/Pearson, Boston, Massachusetts, 2004.

[12] K. Kent, S. Chevalier, T. Grance and H. Dang, *Guide to Integrating Forensic Techniques into Incident Response*, NIST Special Publication 800-86, National Institute of Standards and Technology, Gaithersburg, Maryland, 2006.

[13] P. Laplante and C. Neill, *AntiPatterns: Identification, Refactoring and Management*, CRC Press, Boca Raton, Florida, 2006.

[14] N. Leveson, M. Heimdahl, H. Hildreth and J. Reese, Requirements specification for process-control systems, *IEEE Transactions on Software Engineering*, vol. 20(9), pp. 684–707, 1994.

[15] J. McDermott, Attack net penetration testing, *Proceedings of the New Security Paradigms Workshop*, pp. 15–22, 2000.

[16] A. Moore, R. Ellison and R. Linger, Attack modeling for information security and survability, Technical Note CMU/SEI-2001-TN-001, Software Engineering Institute, Carnegie Mellon University, Pittsburgh, Pennsylvania, 2001.

[17] J. Pelaez, Security in VoIP networks, Master's Thesis, Department of Computer Science and Engineering, Florida Atlantic University, Boca Raton, Florida, 2004.

[18] M. Schumacher, E. Fernandez, D. Hybertson, F. Buschmann and P. Sommerlad, *Security Patterns: Integrating Security and Systems Engineering*, Wiley, Chichester, United Kingdom, 2006.

[19] K. Shanmugasundaram, N. Memon, A. Savant and H. Bronnimann, ForNet: A distributed forensics network, *Proceedings of the Second International Workshop on Mathematical Methods, Models and Architectures for Computer Network Security*, pp. 1–16, 2003.

[20] J. Steffan and M. Schumacher, Collaborative attack modeling, *Proceedings of the ACM Symposium on Applied Computing*, pp. 253–259, 2002.

[21] Symantec, Antivirus Research Center (www.symantec.com).

[22] TMCnet.com, CRN finds security risk in VoIP applications (www.tmcnet.com/usubmit/2006/01/27/1320122.htm), January 27 2006.

[23] C. Wieser, J. Roning and A. Takanen, Security analysis and experiments for VoIP RTP media streams, *Proceedings of the Eighth International Symposium on Systems and Information Security*, 2006.